ON GLOBAL WIZARDRY

ON GLOBAL WIZARDRY

TECHNIQUES OF PAGAN SPIRITUALITY AND A CHRISTIAN RESPONSE

PETER JONES
General Editor

Main Entry Editions, Escondido, CA

ON GLOBAL WIZARDRY

First printing, 2010
Published in the United States of America
Printed in Guadalupe, Costa Rica por la CLIR

Cover design: Sarah Sisco

ISBN13: 978-0-9746895-1-7
ISBN10: 0-9746895-1-3

Editor's Note: Authors have used a variety of Bible translations, including their own from the original. Translation inquires should be addressed to individual authors. All chapters used by permission. Authors retain use of their own material. The following authors have made specific copyright statements:

James Herrick: This chapter is adapted from materials originally appearing in *The Making of the New Spirituality: The Eclipse of the Western Religious Tradition* (InterVarsity Press, 2004).

TABLE OF CONTENTS

1. FOREWORD
JOHN FRAME 9

2. PREFACE
PETER JONES 12

3. MODERN SHAMANISM
JAMES HERRICK 16

4. ASTROLOGY & THE AGE OF AQUARIUS
MARCIA MONTENEGRO 31

5. THE GLOBAL MAINSTREAMING OF WITCHCRAFT
LINDA HARVEY 44

6. KABBALAH
FRED KLETT 59

7. GNOSTICISM
DAVE DOVETON 71

8. THE BROAD RED ROAD TO DESPAIR
MARCUS TOOLE 87

9. SYNCRETISM IN THE JUNGLE
DAVI CHARLES GOMES 98

10. TECHNIQUES OF AFRICAN PAGAN SPIRITUALITY
YUSUFU TURAKI 115

11. CHINESE SPIRITUALITY
SAMUEL LING 131

12. JUNG & THE NEW SPIRITUALITIES
RANDALL VERARDE 143

13. The Spirituality of Quantum Mechanics
Frank Stootman 157

14. Ecology, Neopaganism & Global Warming
E. Calvin Beisner 171

15. Pagan Contemplative Techniques
Pamela Frost 186

16. Hollywood, Entertainment & NeoPaganism
Joel Pelsue 203

17. Christian Spirituality
Andrew Young 219

18. Old Testament Pagan Divination
Michael Heiser 232

19. The Prototokos Paradigm
Ted Hamilton 245

20. The Antithesis
Peter Jones 258

21. Endnotes 272

22. Subject & Name Index 301

23. Scripture Index 314

Acknowledgments

I wish to thank all who have so generously given of their creativity, time, energy and financial resources to sponsor, attend, plan and execute the 2008 and other think tank gatherings. These include:

- the Reverend Ted Hamilton, senior pastor of New Life Presbyterian Church in Escondido, California, with the church's staff, session and members, many of whom opened their homes to receive out-of-town attendees;
- speakers from all over the world who came and lectured at their own expense;
- our local steering committee, especially Alicia, Janice, Mike and Pam;
- the truthXchange Board and supporters;
- volunteer editorial assistants: Brian Mattson, Lana Berck, Art Bergquist and my beloved and faithful wife, Rebecca, without whose long-term vision, dogged determination and hard work this volume containing the individual work of eighteen authors would never have seen the inside of a cover.

May the wisdom, passion and collective efforts of God's saints that are represented here be of great service to many who are puzzled by and distraught about the present spiritual climate, which so blithely opens its arms, its home and its churches to the old gods of paganism.

FOREWORD

JOHN FRAME

The occult usually occupies a tiny corner of our attention: we glance at a horoscope in the morning paper, note in the movie section that a new Harry Potter will open soon. People decorate their homes for Halloween, and the stores are full of costumes of ghosts, monsters and witches. We note that there are even junior witches' kits on the shelves, wherewith little boys and girls can learn to recite incantations and pronounce spells and curses on one another. But for most of us, all of this is a curious scene on the periphery of our consciousness. Amid all the large philosophical, religious, political, artistic and other cultural movements, the mystical paranormal seems to deserve only a bemused glance or a quick laugh.

Few of us, therefore, imagine that this kind of spirituality is a historical and worldwide movement of enormous cultural power, one that has sought for centuries, and still seeks, to dominate our world. The essays in Global Wizardry, however, greatly expand our viewpoint. This book takes our momentary experiences of popular pagan practices and connects them to broad, deep and sinister forces that are making a totalitarian claim on contemporary civilization. As Peter Jones says in his Preface, secular humanism, once the movement most feared by Christians, has been replaced by the rise of religious paganism. The hope of some that secularism would bring an end to religion has proved forlorn: this is the most religious age ever. But the religion of this age is as much opposed to biblical Christianity as secular humanism ever was, and as determined to destroy faith in the God of Scripture. And, as an ancient and widespread movement, it has far deeper roots in our cultural consciousness than secular humanism could ever hope to achieve. Indeed, one may look at secular humanism as a form of religious paganism, which has, after a fleeting prominence, yielded to forms of a more profound kind.

So we need to get beyond glancing at these movements of alternate spirituality and start taking seriously what is happening in our midst. *Global Wizardry* gives you the meat of it, with careful analysis and Christian theological discernment. The authors are scholars and understand the various forms of paganism in depth. And, as Christian believers, they understand the intellectual, religious and practical import of these movements.

Here you will find a serious treatment of astrology that goes beyond and beneath the newspaper horoscope: a worldview that enthralls many of our neighbors and friends. You will learn about paganism in its Native American, South American, Chinese and African forms, including Shamanism, and how opinion makers in Western civilization gain sustenance and reinforcement from these traditions. And the book doesn't stop there. Paganism also finds support where many do not expect to find it, for example, in Judaism (Kabbalah). Witchcraft, too, turns out to be a serious option for many people today, and it lurks in the background, to say the least, of much feminist activism. Much of this goes back to ancient Gnosticism, newly appreciated today by modern scholars and even by professing Christian theologians.

This paganism reaches out to those venues that we regard as more typical of life in the contemporary West. Many have sought to apply pagan worldviews to Jungian psychology, quantum physics and environmental studies. We can find them expressed in modern techniques of contemplation (Thomas Merton, Thomas Keating) and in Hollywood films.

These movements are parallel to one another, indeed congruent. So they form a single movement, in effect. They work together, drawing on one another for support and inspiration, affirming one another, while they unite in opposing biblical Christianity. The resulting movement is, then, a work of Satan, seeking to confront Christianity head-on. Christians need to respond with the same understanding of the dimensions of the battle, and with the same militancy. In the end, only spiritual weapons will suffice for this battle (Eph 6:10–20). But God expects us to bear witness, and we do that best when we have an in-depth knowledge of these movements.

Of course, what we need most is biblical wisdom, which this book also provides. Paganism was also a major issue, *the* major issue, in both

Old Testament and New Testament times. (Another name for paganism is *idolatry,* worship of anything other than the true God.) So the present volume also contains essays showing how God himself dealt with these movements in Bible times, and how he calls us to deal with them today. It turns out that paganism is a vast and powerful worldview, opposing biblical theism at every point. We can never respond to it adequately until we recognize, theoretically and practically, the comprehensive lordship of Jesus Christ over all the world, and over every aspect of our lives and our culture. The issue is nothing less than whether God is God.

PREFACE

PETER JONES

Global wizardry is already on our doorstep. Leaders in modern "transpersonal psychology" now believe that the healing of the planet from violence and greed can only come through rediscovering the experience of the shaman. In his book Future of Psychology (2000) Professor Stanislav Grof, describes "technologies of the sacred," now employed, that introduce people into transpersonal or paranormal states, what he calls "essential shamanism." These methods are the worldwide techniques of pagan spirituality described in the following chapters. Jungian psychology is now an open purveyor of the occult.

For many Christians, spiritual experience is all the rage. For some on the Left in the contemporary Evangelical movement, the Reformation principle of *sola scriptura* has rightly been repealed. Convinced that Postmodern deconstruction renders suspect all rational judgments, and considers as hopelessly subjective all intelligent conclusions drawn from Scripture, we are now told by some leaders in the Emergent Church movement that "the more irreconcilable various theological positions appear to be, the closer we are to experiencing truth."[1] Notice: truth is "experienced," not processed by the mind. Indeed, our God-given minds no longer have any decisive role in determining truth. What we now need are evangelical "intuitive mystics" who establish "truth" in irrational moments of spiritual transport and "spirit-led" religious communities who progress via group "conversations" in close contact with the surrounding culture. Doctrine and preaching based on Scripture have become as dubious for the good of the church as the Spanish Inquisition. With this new "hermeneutic," Scripture is effectively muzzled while subjectivity is given free rein. Forty-one years ago, Francis Schaeffer had something to say about this:

> ...if the Scriptures are not discussed as open to verification where

> they touch the cosmos and history, why should one accept the evangelical upstairs [irrational experience] any more than...an encounter under the name of Vishnu [the supreme god of Hinduism]?[2]

That is precisely the subject of this present volume. If *experience* is the Christian's source of truth, how do we distinguish it from pagan religious versions, especially when many in the church are now toying with all kinds of spiritual techniques practiced in all the pagan religions from time immemorial? "Interspirituality" is now a common practice in many mainline churches, where the radical Emergents are finding a receptive home. Do not worry, say some. We can "Christianize" yoga and the labyrinth. But Marshal McLuhan in 1964, at the first blush of Eastern spirituality in the West, reminded us (without any occultic connotation!) that "the medium *is* the message."

Is it harmless to use any kind spiritual technique that seems to work? Well, first we must understand that, in contradistinction to Christianity, paganism *majors* in spiritual techniques, all of them designed to produce a sense of mystical *identification* with the divine. These techniques are surprisingly universal. I began to realize this as I sat utterly transfixed by a lecture by Dr. Yusufu Turaki on African ancestor-worship at an international conference in South Africa. (See chapter 8.) To my amazement, the neo-Jungian transpersonal psychology I had just been studying, which proposes healing through induced experiences of occultic shamanism, was virtually identical to the "primitive" techniques of traditional African spirituality. For them, the medium really *has* the message. At that moment was born the subject for our 2008 think tank.

The book's essential thesis is this: if, as contemporary religious thought contends, all religions are the same, then the spirituality of all those religions is also essentially the same, whether in its Eastern or "primitive" versions or in its Western "interfaith" version. Here is an example of "interspirituality" that could be multiplied thousands of times. *The Chaplaincy Institute for Arts and Interfaith Ministries* of Berkeley, CA, declares:

> This is what makes the Chaplaincy Institute, and the Interfaith movement we are proud to be a part of, so important. Our students are prophetically proclaiming that one divine, sublime truth that all know but have such a hard time embracing: there are no outsiders. There is

> no "them," and there is no "us."[3]

Students are taught about the world's major religions and faith traditions, including the meaning of prayer. A student at the Institute states:

> The moving experience of "prayer" included Native American drumming and chanting (used to open and bless the occasion), the Whirling Dervishes of Sufism (flowing like water yet opening like flowers), and blessings extended by Buddhist and Hindu priests to the participants, who went home "singing"![4]

This exemplifies what we noted above, that many in our "interfaith" world now believe that truth is about good intentions, not doctrine; that religion is about love, not sharp intellectual or theological distinctions; that the essence of religion is a universal spiritual experience, not religious doctrines. This is why those who dismiss organized religion and doctrine no longer define themselves as secular humanists or atheists. Instead they say, "I'm not religious—but I *am* spiritual." Though it was once thought that the twenty-first century would end all religion, nothing could be further from the truth.[5] When the "stars" come out at night in Hollywood, they often go to a Hindu or Buddhist temple, a Scientology meeting, a yoga session or a Kabbalistic séance. We live in a very spiritual time.

A heightened search for human fulfillment beyond the purely material is a hallmark of our culture. People seek non-material powers by which they hope to gain "salvation," which now often means psychological therapy and holistic healing, rather than a place in heaven. The ideal spirituality is "integral," comprehensive and inclusive, insisting on unity and balance, which provides calm in the midst of challenging circumstances, as well as meaning, value, spiritual insight, wise discernment and compassion.

If all religions are ultimately the same, then such a smorgasbord approach to spiritual techniques is valid. But what if all religions are not the same? What if Christianity is radically different from all forms of spiritual paganism? Then, of course, using the spiritual techniques of religious systems that are antithetically opposed to the Gospel would produce confusion and, ultimately, apostasy. Alas, naïveté about spirituality is found in much of Evangelicalism. Well-intentioned Christians are slowly drawn into spiritual techniques that are rooted in paganism. The invasion will, like unseen termites, eat the heart out of the structural beams of biblical orthodoxy, leaving churches and denominations looking good on the surface, but ready to crumble under the least pressure.

This compendium of essays on spiritual techniques has two goals:

1. to demonstrate that the techniques common to pagan religions are really one in their basic beliefs about God, the world and spirituality. As Paul says, they "worship the creature rather than the Creator" (Rom 1:25), not only in their doctrines but also in their religious practices;
2. to warn Christians who, for various reasons and under the influence of certain leaders, are employing "spiritual" methods and "disciplines" that eventually deny the Lord they desire to know and worship.

Dear reader, one key question defines the battle for the soul of the church in our very "spiritual" time: Will we worship Nature or the God who created Nature? This question defines a conflict as old as history itself. The conflict began in the Garden of Eden, where Adam and Eve faced the Serpent's invitation to worship themselves instead of their Creator. It continued as Israel was tempted to worship the Nature gods of Baal and Asherah and all the others of the nations around her. The conflict was evident as Paul considered the pantheon of gods in whom the Athenians trusted, and it was still present as the early Church Fathers denounced Gnosticism. Now, Christians around the globe must recognize and combat the worship of Nature in all its ancient or modern forms, whether African animism or interfaith Neopaganism.

When Christ returns, will he find faith on the earth? Only if Christians are courageously faithful in their belief and practice, whatever the cost. And it is worth the cost, for Christ is everything God wanted us to understand about himself—and ourselves. He is a person, not a fuzzy, mystical experience. He is the objective revelation of the Father in Word and deed. By his life, death and resurrection he brings us to God by a historic act of atonement, liberating us from sin and guilt. We appropriate this truth by faith in hearing and believing the preached Word. We do not need pagan techniques and irrational experiences to draw near to him. He has drawn near to us. Thus we, in our turn, draw near to God.

1

MODERN SHAMANISM
SPIRIT CONTACT & SPIRITUAL PROGRESS

JAMES HERRICK

It was absolutely astonishing. I saw the form of a very tall, overpoweringly confident, almost androgynous human being. A graceful, cream-colored garment flowed over a figure seven feet tall, with long arms resting calmly at its side.[1]

—Shirley MacLaine

This experiment seemed to show that scientists can learn a good deal by working with Amazonian shamans. Some observers have suggested that shamanism, as classically defined, is reaching its end. But bringing scientists and shamans together seems more like a beginning.[2]

—Jeremy Narby

INTRODUCTION

In the 1997 science fiction film, *Contact,* actress Jodie Foster undertakes a painful journey through a wormhole in space to another realm that can only be described as heavenly. There she meets an alien, appearing as her deceased father, who reveals celestial secrets unknown to other human beings. Foster is transported back home, where others can scarcely believe the newly revealed truths she bears. This captivating movie scene draws from the genre of science fiction to picture the journey of a shaman into the spiritual realm and back to the world of mortals.

The term *shaman* originated among the Tungus-speaking people of Siberia, and described an individual who professed to have healing powers, the ability to see the future, and to summon demons.[3] Sixteenth and seventeenth century European explorers in South America also observed local healers who claimed to communicate with spirits, often with the aid of tobacco, hallucinogenic drugs and self-inflicted wounds. Exorcised by Catholic monks and debunked by Enlightenment philosophers, shamans became a curiosity associated by Westerners with new worlds and exotic lands.

However, if the essence of shamanism is to gain hidden knowledge through contact with spirits, demons, the dead or beings from other worlds, then its practice has a long and vigorous tradition in the Western world. For centuries, magicians, witches, mediums and alchemists have claimed to receive information or direction from spirits. Shamanism has recently attracted great public interest, complementing the "new" spiritual outlook with roots in ancient pagan and occult practices. How, in an allegedly scientific and rationally enlightened age, has shamanism managed to reassert itself? As with other components in the New Spirituality, persuasive public texts have played a crucial role.

Philip Jenkins underlines the importance of the 1932 publication, *Black Elk Speaks*, which "introduced a White audience to the riches of Native American spirituality and shamanism," adding that "Black Elk's words proved a major inspiration to many hopeful White imitators in the 1960s and beyond."[4] Jeremy Narby and Francis Huxley write that in the 1950s "Western observers began participating in shamanistic sessions involving hallucinogenic plants, [and] found, to their astonishment, that they could have experiences similar to those described by shamans." *Life* magazine popularized shamanism in a 1957 story: "In Mexico, American banker Gordon Wasson ate psilocybin mushrooms in a session conducted by Mazatec shaman Maria Sabina." Wasson described to *Life*'s readers his experience of "flying out of his body." Narby and Huxley report that "hundreds of thousands of people read Wasson's account, and many followed his example."[5]

In the 1960s Carlos Castenada described his apprenticeship with a Yaqui Indian shaman named Don Juan in a series of books read by hundreds of thousands of university students. *The Teachings of Don Juan: A Yaqui Way of Knowledge* and its sequels "became worldwide bestsellers."[6] Castenada's training involved in part the use of the hallucinogen peyote and techniques for conjuring spirits. "In the wake of Castenada's books, millions of people became interested in shamans in a hands-on way," write Narby and Huxley. "There was a great flowering of neoshamanism in the New Age movement, concentrated in the United States, but increasingly spreading around the world."[7] The 1980s and 90s saw the publication of dozens of New Age accounts of messages channeled from spirit beings and direct contact with a host of otherworldly entities.

This chapter explores the reemergence of shamanism in the modern Western world. The notion that a spiritually-gifted elite can garner information directly from beings in the spiritual realm, or perhaps on another planet, is now a widely accepted component of religious thought. Spirit contact, once limited to occult works and practices, surfaces today in popular fiction, the personal accounts of New Age gurus, the UFO movement, spiritual biographies, the literature of angelic visitation, countless movies, video and online games, and in other popular cultural sources.

SWEDENBORG: MODERN WESTERN SHAMANISM

The presentation of an updated shamanism in works written for the general public is not new. The famous religious writer Emanuel Swedenborg (1688–1772) claimed to have been instructed by beings on other planets as well as by angels. A scientist, engineer, artisan and mystic, Swedenborg influenced a variety of nineteenth-century writers and thinkers, including Ralph Waldo Emerson and Joseph Smith.

Swedenborg insisted that virtually everything he wrote on spiritual matters after 1744 was revealed to him directly by spirits in almost daily episodes of spirit contact. In *The Worlds in Space,*[8] he claims to have traveled among various planets and learned from their inhabitants a variety of spiritual secrets. The book has maintained a readership for more than two hundred years, and is still published by the Swedenborg Society. "I have been enabled to talk with spirits and angels, not only those in the vicinity of our earth, but also those near other worlds," he writes.[9] These other worlds include Mars, Venus, Saturn, Mercury and Jupiter, planets well known to eighteenth-century astronomers. Swedenborg's "space" travel is a strictly interior, spiritual journey in which he encounters beings he terms "spirits" who belong to the planets of our solar system. "As I have said several times before, a spirit is taken from place to place by nothing but changes in his inner state."[10] Swedenborg entered an altered mental state in order to achieve the spirit contact that was a daily experience for him for over twelve years.

In his quest for alien contact, Swedenborg seeks spiritual knowledge. *The Worlds in Space* is filled with passages in which planetary spirits correct the false teachings of Christian orthodoxy on such issues as the Trinity, and the incarnation and resurrection of Christ. One of the principal lessons conveyed in this unusual book is that literal readings of the Bible are misleading; Swedenborg is at pains to instruct his readers that planetary spirits have conveyed to him undiluted spiritual truth which often contradicts biblical teaching.

For Swedenborg, to understand the spirits and planets, and their place in the cosmic scheme of things is to achieve great spiritual power. But, as he admits, there are risks associated with acquiring cosmic knowledge through direct spirit contact. Swedenborg as shaman is a conduit of secret spiritual knowledge, but he is also at the mercy of alien beings who themselves exact knowledge *from* him. In keeping with contemporary alien contact literature, Swedenborg frequently mentions the physical abuse these planetary spirits are more than ready to inflict on uncooperative hosts. For instance, when he failed to comply with an alien request for information, "[s]o as to show their annoyance they brought a kind of painful contraction of the right side of my head as far as the ear."[11] Similar incidents are frequently reported in *The Worlds in Space*. Some of his alien acquaintances from Jupiter reveal to Swedenborg how they "draw out from a person's memory all he has done and thought." If they "find fault with his actions or thoughts," their response is to "chastise him by means of pains in the joints, the feet or the hands, or around the epigastric region."[12] Another punishment for bad thinking was "spells of choking until the victim was very distressed ... and finally a death sentence."[13] It is an unavoidable feature of Swedenborg's account that alien entities are inclined toward violence, a characteristic that attends shamanistic practices both ancient and modern.

When informed about the earthly and historical life of Jesus Christ, the spirits reply that this is "of no interest to them," though Jesus' spiritual nature and authority were deemed important.[14] Other historical details of Jesus' life such as "that he was born as a baby, lived as a man, looked like any other man, was crucified and so forth" were considered among enlightened spirits to be "scandalous ideas."[15]

To communicate with spirits, one must possess special shamanic qualities. "Only those whose interiors are open," writes Swedenborg, "can hear those speaking from heaven." Special faith and a great capacity for love are important to this capacity for contact. "No one is allowed to talk with spirits and angels ... unless he is, as regards faith and love, capable of associating with angels." Because so few meet these criteria "there are few today allowed to talk and converse with angels." Of course, crucial to this process is "belief in spirits and angels" as well as the belief that "these put a person in touch with heaven."[16] Being in touch with heaven means "traveling ... in spirit" as one is "guided through varying states of inner life, which appear ... like travels through space." Both "the outward and return journeys" require "continuous guidance" from spirits.[17] This is the essence of shamanism—to be found qualified to speak with spirits, and to be guided by them on an inner journey that involves risks, pain, ecstatic experience, and vast personal knowledge. Swedenborg helped to reintroduce this ancient spiritual practice to the Western world. Through his influence and that of a host of other public advocates, the notion of spirit contact has made its way into the new spiritualities of our own day.

BULWER-LYTTON'S LITERARY SHAMANISM

A century after Swedenborg, the Anglo-American occult movement placed a version of shamanism at the center of public attention. In the 1830s and 40s a series of popular novels by authors such as the Rosicrucian and occultist George Edward Bulwer-Lytton popularized occult practices and familiarized the European and American reading public with the idea of contacting spirits, demons and ascended masters using secret techniques. Bulwer-Lytton, a nineteenth century Stephen King, churned out spine-tingling page-turners for an enthusiastic audience. His novels incorporating occult themes include *Godolphin* (1833), *Asmodeus at Large* (1833), *Pilgrims of the Rhine* (1834), and *The Last Days of Pompeii* (1834).[18]

Bulwer-Lytton's most influential occult novel was the 1842 bestseller, *Zanoni*, the story of a five thousand-year-old alchemist and his student, set during the French Revolution. Such was the demand for *Zanoni* in America that "readers could buy pirated editions for as little as six cents."[19] Philip Jenkins writes that "characters like Zanoni ... exercised a powerful spell on the esoteric subculture on both sides of the Atlantic."[20] Reading *Zanoni* amounted to taking an introductory course in magic and spiritism. The most riveting element in the novel, however, was the young hero's encounter with spirits from another realm who imparted to him esoteric knowledge. The book popularized the traditional practices of shamanism, a fact that did not escape the notice of occultists such as Madame H. P. Blavatsky and later, Aleister Crowley.[21]

Aleister Crowley: Popularizing Shamanic Magic

Crowley, more than any other figure, revived ritual magic and shamanic practices for the modern West. He was instrumental in developing the highly influential occult organization known as the Order of the Golden Dawn. Crowley authored dozens of books and pamphlets between 1911 and 1940, and managed to keep himself almost continuously before the public eye. Seeing himself as "the prophet of a New Aeon that would supplant the Christian Era," he sought a religion to replace Christianity. By following this new faith, adherents would "become the gods" we had previously "merely worshiped."[22] A self-professed Satanist, Crowley created intense pubic interest in the occult with books such as *Magick* (1911), *The Book of Lies* (1913), *Confessions of a Drug Fiend* (1922) and *The Confessions of Aleister Crowley* (1929). Biographer Lawrence Sutin writes that Crowley "anticipated the spread of Eastern spirituality in the West."[23] The shamanistic elements in Crowley's novels—instruction in conjuring spirits, seeking secret knowledge from departed individuals, or lashing out at enemies with demonic assistance—provided their greatest intrigue. Public thirst for stories of the occult knew no bounds well into the twentieth century.[24]

Nineteenth- and twentieth-century shamanism combined several elements currently reflected in new spiritual systems: the rejection of biblical theology, the elevation of reason and science, a pantheistic belief in a divine energy permeating the cosmos, and the elevation of spiritually gifted individuals who make direct contact with the spirit world. Particularly prominent was the notion of spiritual evolution, for "great mystics or prophets might represent souls in a very advanced state of spiritual progress, who should be regarded as the rightful teachers of humanity, Masters or Secret Chiefs."[25] Among the most influential of these "advanced souls" was the great Victorian occult leader, Madame Blavatsky (1831–1891), founder of Theosophy.

MADAME BLAVATSKY AND VICTORIAN SHAMANISM

Blavatsky's spiritual system is eclectic in its sources, but fundamentally occult and shamanistic in orientation. She, like Swedenborg and Mormonism's Joseph Smith, saw herself as a human conduit of secret spiritual truths from another realm. In several lengthy books Blavatsky argued strenuously that mystical, astrological, Gnostic, Hermetic and magical teachers of old understood the cosmos correctly. She rejected the biblical tradition out of hand. No less a student of spiritual culture than Carl Jung noted in the 1930s that Madame Blavatsky and Theosophy were the harbingers of a completely new spiritual orientation for the Western world.[26] Blavatsky traveled extensively in search of spiritual secrets, claiming that much of her knowledge had been obtained in the lamaseries of Tibet. During her many travels she studied firsthand the religious, spiritualist and magical traditions of Europe and the East.

Along with Colonel Olcott (1832–1907) and William Q. Judge, Blavatsky founded the Theosophical Society in New York in 1875. In 1878, Olcott and Blavatsky traveled to India, where they settled. Eventually the headquarters of the Theosophical Society was established in Madras where local Christian missionaries feverishly opposed its work. In December of 1878, Blavatsky visited England, where she was welcomed by a number of spiritual explorers. From 1879 through 1888, Blavatsky edited *The Theosophist*. She wrote incessantly on magic, the occult and spiritualism, and her collected works run to fourteen volumes. Blavatsky was involved in an extensive and widely publicized scandal in 1884 when the British press accused her of faking dramatic spiritual phenomena. She was forced to go into seclusion, and wrote her most famous work, *The Secret Doctrine* (1888), shortly before her death.

Blavatsky built Theosophy out of elements including occultism, spiritism, mysticism, shamanism, and her peculiar understanding of world religions. A committed spiritualist, Blavatsky "chose the name *theosophy* ('knowledge of God' or 'divine wisdom') for her doctrine, which was based on the idea that all of the world's religions and spiritual traditions down through history were derived from a long-lost 'secret doctrine' that had been revealed to her by ... divine beings." [27] Blavatsky referred to these divine beings as the brothers, The Mahatmas, or The Masters, and alleged that they resided in Tibet and communicated with her both telepathically and in visions.

Blavatsky claimed that the knowledge she received by shamanic means was of ancient origin, and had been carefully preserved in order to be revealed at the appropriate time to carefully selected individuals. She allegedly received secret information from a host of spirits, masters and departed spiritual leaders. Philip Jenkins writes that she "relied on material channeled from great spiritual Masters, members of the Great White Brotherhood, a select club that included Jesus, the Buddha, Confucius, Mesmer and Cagliostro, as well as real-life occultists she had consulted over the years." [28] Blavatsky labeled Christianity and the biblical tradition a spiritual aberration that deviated from its ancient mystical and pantheistic sources. Though Blavatsky claimed direction from spirit beings and ascended masters, Theosophical thought draws heavily on standard Gnostic sources, the Medieval mystic Meister Eckhart, Renaissance writers in the school of Bruno, the German mystic Jacob Bohme, some Romantic philosophers, and Indian cosmology as reflected in the Hindu Vedas, Upanishads and *Bhagavad Gita*.

Blavatsky augmented her spiritual system with messages from two "Mahatmas"—Koot Hoomi and Morya—who conveyed their views by means of "spiritual communication from beyond." [29] This communication was sometimes despicably racist. Like many Victorian intellectual figures, Blavatsky believed that the evolutionary juggernaut would leave behind the "lower and degraded" human races, while a homogenous, perfected race would inexorably emerge. The perfected humans' "mental constitution may continue to advance and improve, till the world is again inhabited by a single, *nearly homogenous race, no individual of which will be inferior to the noblest specimens of existing humanity*."[30] Blavatsky, the notorious spiritual charlatan of Victorian London, apparently included herself among these "noblest specimens." Blavatsky noted that such a racist and evolutionary view was fully consistent with the magical tradition. What scientists were saying about evolution "clashes in no way with our kabalistic assertions."[31]

JOHN MACK: UFO ABDUCTEES AS SHAMANS

Shamanic ideas continue to permeate the strange frontier that barely separates science and spirituality. For instance, the late John Mack, once a professor of psychiatry at Harvard Medical School, was a self-styled expert on the experiences of individuals who claim to have been abducted by aliens. Mack's bestselling book, *Abduction: Human Encounters with Aliens*, reports his interviews with several persons who allege that beings from another dimension or another planet have contacted and even kidnapped them.[32] Mack's unusual clinical work finds a place in this chapter because of his suggestion that abductees are themselves modern shamans with important spiritual messages from beyond.

Mack writes from the perspective of a medical expert in search of the facts behind his clients' curious reports and explanations for their bizarre experiences. As a trained psychiatrist and member of the Harvard faculty, he inspires unusual credibility. Mack's book recounts clinical sessions in which clients are encouraged to remember the details of their abductions, often after being placed into a hypnotic trance to assist their recall. But, he is quick to point out that he may be dealing with something other than actual memory in his interviews with the abducted. To think of memory "as 'true' or 'false,'" he writes, "may restrict what we can learn about human consciousness" from abductees.[33] Mack's curious qualification—that thinking of memory as true or false is restricting—makes sense if one considers his clients to be, not victims of abductions, but mouthpieces for guiding spirits, that is, shamans.

Mack's extensive experience with UFO abductees has convinced him that the cosmos, like Swedenborg's planets and Houston's realm of the psyche, is filled with "intelligences." He writes, "what the abduction phenomenon has led me (I would now say inevitably) to see is that we participate in a universe or universes that are filled with intelligences from which we have cut ourselves off, having lost the senses by which we might know them."[34] Surrounded by intelligences with whom we no longer know how to communicate, the need for shamanic intermediaries between humanity and these higher minds is clear. The alien intelligences can guide us into truths we know not of, Mack contends, teaching us to stop war, ecological disaster and racial conflict.[35]

Mack writes of the "long story of humankind's relationship to vehicles and creatures appearing from the heavens that goes back to antiquity."[36] Moreover, mythology traditionally has provided language for communicating the essence of these encounters. This "connection between humans and beings from other dimensions has been illustrated in myths and stories from various cultures for millennia."[37] Myth is as central to Mack's explanation of the alien abduction phenomenon as it is to Houston's understanding of the encounters of inner journeying.

But, Western understanding of consciousness has stifled perception of the true nature of contacts with the other side. "Throughout history, many societies have acknowledged consciousness as something more potent than we have in the West—as a sieve or receiver and transmitter of communication with forces, not always visible, other than ourselves."[38] Thus, Mack concludes, "it would seem that today's UFO abductees are continuing an amply documented tradition of ascent and extraterrestrial communication." The meaning of "extraterrestrial communication" is relatively clear, but what does Mack mean by "ascent"? Apparently there is a spiritual issue at stake here, with abductees taking a step up spiritually through their experiences with alien beings.

As support for the view that abductees are on a spiritual journey, Mack cites folklorist Peter Rojcewicz who "has compared the experience of today's abductees" with "aerial and abduction phenomena" in earlier times and other cultures. Rojcewicz finds "the possibility of the existence of an intelligence, a spirit, an energy, a consciousness behind UFO experiences and extraordinary encounters of all types, that adapts its form and appearance to fit the environment of the times."[39] Thus, Mack believes that, in addition to UFO abductees, "contemporary examples of such entities in the West might be the spirit guides that are reported by many individuals."[40]

In *Abduction,* Mack entertains the idea that consciousnesses from another dimension are actively seeking to contact and influence the human race. In order to receive the benefits of such contact, one's worldview must allow openness to these cosmic conversations. Religions and worldviews that allow for such a possibility are to be commended. Those that limit the view of consciousness or that demonize contact with spirits are to be censured, for we are on the verge of a new, shamanic religious consciousness.

"What function," he asks, "do events like UFO abductions and various mystical experiences play in our psyches and in the rest of the cosmos?"[41] His answer to this question appears to be a religious one. "The UFO abduction experience, while unique in many respects, bears resemblance to other dramatic, transformative experiences undergone by shamans, mystics, and ordinary citizens who have had encounters with the paranormal."[42] The abductee takes on the crucial role of providing a bridge between mundane experience and the spirit world beyond, in much the same way as the mystic or shaman of lore. "The mystic or shaman, like the abductee, makes a pilgrimage, usually with ardor, to receive a new dimension of experience or knowledge."[43]

Mack even finds that abductees often perceive their alien visitors as animals—"owls, eagles, raccoons and deer"—which he quickly points out is remarkably similar to the reports of tribal shamans regarding their encounters with beings from the spirit world. "The connection with animal spirits is very powerful for many abductees." Mack believes that "this shamanistic dimension needs further study" because such events "cannot be understood within the framework of the laws of Western science" even though "they are fully consistent with beliefs developed thousands of years ago by other non-Western cultures."[44] Joseph Campbell also noted that the Hindu term marga "means 'path or track, trail of an animal, to be followed,' and this is precisely what is implied by C. G. Jung's term 'the archetypes of the unconscious.'" Following these animal guides "we are led—if we can follow—beyond maps, according to the Indian view, to the seat from which all the gods have sprung, which is the revelation of the deepest source and being of ourselves."[45]

Mack notes that abductees, like all shamans, possess a peculiar openness to diverse spiritual experiences. "I have the impression that the abductees as a group are unusually open and intuitive individuals, less tolerant than usual of societal authoritarianism, and more flexible in accepting diversity and the unusual experiences of other people."[46] Abductees may, in fact, be of an entirely different species than the rest of us. Mack writes of some abductees "being told by an alien female that she was their true mother." The abductees felt that "in some vague but deep way that this is actually true, i.e., that they are not 'from here' and that the Earth mother and father are not their true parents."[47] Mack suggests in *Abduction* that such accounts of alien parentage, as well as of strange sexual experiments conducted on some abductees, are related to alien efforts to prepare the human race for the next stage in its physical and spiritual evolution.

The abductee is for Mack, then, a uniquely spiritual being, a religious seer, a shaman bearing messages from another realm, and the harbinger of a new human race. Many other modern-day shamans have claimed that beings from other planets were trying to contact and educate the human race, usually implying that our spiritual and social progress would thus be enhanced. Sometimes the initial contact is more spiritual than physical. Thus, Wilfred Kellogg claimed that his massive tome, *The Urantia Book*, a "history of the galaxy and the solar system," came to him through channeling messages from aliens.[48]

Mack's work with UFO abduction claimants is remarkable, both in the fact that his own status lends credence to the reports of abductees, and in his tendency to view the abductees as contemporary shamans. In a fashion typical of modern efforts to appropriate science to spirituality, Mack argues that Western science is currently undergoing "spectacular advances in physics, biology, neuroscience, and psychology" which may "shed light on" abduction experiences and other mystical or shamanistic phenomena.[49]

In a similar vein, Whitley Streiber has written about his experiences with aliens in enormously popular books such as *Communion*[50] and *Transformation: The Breakthrough*.[51] He has also collected various evidences for alien contact in *Confirmation: The Hard Evidence for Aliens among Us*.[52] As the titles of these books imply, Streiber finds a virtually religious significance in human encounters with aliens, which he terms the "visitor experience." He writes, "the 'visitor experience' is old. Two hundred years ago a farmer might have come in from plowing and said, 'I just saw fairies dancing in the glen.' A thousand years ago he might have seen angels flying." Though the experience is ancient, it now has a new dimension. "That we could ever conceive of being in relationship with this force is what is new about the visitor experience in modern times." This is possible because, "thankfully, the very way we think and perceive our universe may be changing."[53]

MASS MEDIA SHAMANISM: SELLING THE NEW SPIRITUALITY

Shamanism continues to assert itself in popular books, movies, television programs, and in the spiritually saturated plots of the online gaming world. In his best-selling book, *The Seat of the Soul* (1989), physicist and frequent Oprah Winfrey Show guest, Gary Zukav, takes for granted the existence of "nonphysical Teachers" who come to us from "levels of Light" that are beyond our immediate perception.[54] These "impersonal consciousnesses" are often involved in instructing human beings in the higher spiritual truths, such as the evolutive nature of the cosmos and the fundamental unity of all things. In other words, these spirit beings accept some of the basic tenets of the new spiritualities, and are here to teach them to us. "This is not their home, so to speak. They are teachers to our plane. They are free to teach in our plane without being of our plane." That these Teachers can come to us in our plane without becoming one with our plane is a result of their having transcended duality altogether. They live in the plane of the ultimate unity of all things, and this "is simply the natural dynamic of evolution." Zukav assures his readers that "as you evolve beyond [duality], and also when you leave your physical body and journey home to your nonphysical plane of reality, you will not exist in dualism."[55]

Zukav takes for granted several foundational elements of the new spiritualities—the fundamentally evolutive nature of the universe, the spiritual evolution of human beings, and the essential unity and divinity of all things. Compatible with these is the presence of spirit teachers to guide us in our evolutionary progress. Moreover, these entities and "advanced human souls" go on to inhabit "millions, indeed, billions of life-filled planets."[56] In fact he asserts that "there is not one planet that lacks a level of active consciousness, some of it akin to our human form, and some of which does not come close to our form." These members of "the Angelic kingdom" are here to "guide and interact with us" in order to assist our evolution. Moreover, they have assisted with "the evolution of other galaxies and Life forms there."[57]

Zukav's fundamental thesis is compatible with the position outlined by Emanuel Swedenborg more than two hundred years ago, and has been reiterated in innumerable popular religious texts in the modern period. It is present in Madame Blavatsky's treatises, but also in John Mack's alien abductee accounts. Other examples are present in contemporary popular spiritual writing. For example, Neale Donald Walsch affirms in his *Conversations with God* that there is life on other planets, that human beings have been visited by aliens, and that we currently are being observed.[58]

In the cosmos of the new spiritualities there is no sovereign deity, though minor deities abound—spirits or aliens, inner guides or higher selves, ascended masters or highly evolved intelligences. By whatever name, they have something of profound spiritual significance to tell humanity as they seek to instruct us in proper theology through their human mouthpieces.

The theological perspective articulated by spirit guides consistently contradicts that of the biblical tradition. Swedenborg's planetary spirits repudiate the historical details of the Christian Gospel, Blavatsky's ascended masters reveal ancient spiritual secrets that prove Christianity to be a spiritual aberration, and contemporary shamans proclaim a distinctly un-Christian religious pluralism derived from a highly subjective mystical experience that is seldom subjected to scrutiny.

Lacking a sovereign deity, the new spirituality's evolving universe yields up its secrets by alleged direct spirit contact. There seem no limits to what the spirits know, and wish us to know. Author Jeremy Narby reports experiments in which shamans help research scientists resolve difficult experimental issues. Of one such collaborative effort he writes, "this experiment seemed to show that scientists can learn a good deal by working with Amazonian shamans." Thus, he concludes, "bringing scientists and shamans together seems more like a beginning."[59] In the New Spirituality, shamanism and science are beginning a long embrace that will shape our spiritual future. Is the Church ready to respond?

2

Astrology & the Age of Aquarius

Marcia Montenegro

Sarah, twenty-three, sips a cappuccino at her favorite coffeehouse. She checks her watch, then reaches for the discarded newspaper lying on the next table. She has just enough time before meeting her friend at the movies. Turning to the Comics page, she finds the horoscope column for Taurus. Sarah reads her horoscope most days. Sometimes it offers helpful advice. As a Christian, she feels slightly uneasy, but her friend Emily, from church, says, "It's okay as long as you don't believe in it. It's just for fun." Sarah reassures herself and heads off to the movies.

Jennifer, thirty-four, finds the horoscope too vague. Desiring more personalized information, she has made an appointment with an astrologer to get her birth chart read. Somewhat apprehensively, she steps into the office. She is pleasantly surprised to find it contemporary and bright, and to see that the astrologer is a fashionably dressed woman also in her thirties. Jennifer enjoys the session, amazed at the accuracy of the astrologer. Before leaving, she eagerly makes an appointment to get an update in six months.

Today's astrologers believe that the Age of Aquarius has already dawned. Apparently, so do the millions of Jennifers and Sarahs who read their daily horoscope in the newspaper or online. Astrology has plenty of followers and is here to stay as a challenge to the Christian faith. Astrology's scientific veneer lends it credibility for some people. Others point to Bible passages about the heavens, interpreting them as encouragement to read patterns in the sky. Many Christians read newspaper horoscopes as harmless entertainment.

However, according to God's Word, astrology is a deadly serious topic. It is a form of occult divination that reads hidden meanings from the natural world, and opens the astrologer to spirit guidance. This chapter seeks to expose astrology's true nature and its appeal by answering these questions: Where does astrology come from? What is astrology? What happens in an astrology session? What is the Age of Aquarius? Does astrology "work"? What does the Bible say about astrology? How should Christians respond?

WHERE DOES ASTROLOGY COME FROM?

Pagan Gods in the Sky

Astrology was a part of early astronomy when man first observed the skies. Astronomy, the scientific study of space and heavenly bodies, was intertwined with the astrological interpretation of the movements of these bodies, making astrology and astronomy the same discipline. Chaldean sky watchers noticed that some stars, along with the sun and moon, moved in regular patterns. The ancients thought such patterns must have meaning, and began to link these movements to events on earth. Many ancient cultures believed that the planets (which they viewed as stars) were gods or the homes of gods. Early astrologers initially interpreted these heavenly movements only for kings and rulers.

Astrology made its way into Greek society, in which charts were first made for people other than rulers, and later migrated to Rome, where the planets were given the names of Roman gods. These are the planet names as we currently know them (Jupiter, Mars, etc.). The constellations (the zodiac) were named after animals, except for Libra and Aquarius, and linked to a "ruling planet." Venus ruled Taurus and Libra, Mercury ruled Gemini, the sun ruled Leo, the moon ruled Cancer, and so forth. Most of these rulerships are still respected in Astrology today, though the discovery of the three outer planets (Uranus, Neptune, and Pluto) has shifted the rulerships for a few signs.[1]

Through medieval times, men believed that heavenly bodies influenced earthly events and foretold the destiny of men. The positions of the sun, moon and planets were plotted at birth in a circle, known as a horoscope. During the Age of Enlightenment, astronomy and astrology became separate disciplines.

Western astrology was significantly altered in the twentieth century when it absorbed psychological terms and concepts, especially from Carl Jung, an admirer of astrology. It became less fatalistic and offered the client more options for interpretation, and more ways to harness the forces of the birth chart. Astrology absorbed Jung's teaching that man shared a collective unconscious, as well as his idea of synchronicity (the belief that seemingly unrelated events are connected). The planets came to be viewed as universal archetypes—symbols with meaning and influence for everyone. This Jungian legacy continues in astrology today.

The outer planets, Uranus, Neptune and Pluto (discovered in 1781, 1846 and 1930 respectively), which move more slowly, developed into generational and social indicators, not just personal ones. The meaning attached to these planets was tied to the time of their discoveries. Uranus, discovered during the Industrial Revolution, came to signify technology and vast upheaval. Neptune, discovered around the time of the new fields of psychology and film, was associated with both fields as well as with dreams, imagination, the unconscious and creativity. Discovered at the time of the atom bomb, Pluto was linked to power, death and rebirth.

Other influences, such as belief in reincarnation, karma and spiritual guides came from the occult Theosophical Society and from Eastern spirituality. The birth chart came to be seen as an esoteric blueprint of a person's character, talent, spirituality, weakness and potential. Real life outcomes depended on how a person tapped into these resources.

What Is Astrology?

The Astrologer as Priest

The medieval concept, "as above, so below," is threaded through many areas of the occult, including astrology. The occult views the apparent world as a mask hiding a deeper level of reality. Thus, the planetary patterns in the heavens are cloaked by an astrological code that must be deciphered by the astrologer. The astrologer becomes the priest-interpreter of the chart, the prophet who unveils the message of the heavens for the client.

The birth chart is the astrologer's most common tool, but there is also electional astrology, which determines the most propitious time for a certain event, such as a wedding or vacation. Charts can be compared to each other or combined to assess relationships. Mundane astrology interprets charts cast for a city, country, building, or an event such as an earthquake or political election. Horary astrology answers a question. Some astrologers specialize in medical or financial astrology. The birth chart displays the planetary positions at the time and place of birth in a circle divided into twelve areas, called houses. The outer circle of the chart represents the rotation of the earth in twenty-four hours.

After the chart is cast and the houses are set up according to the birth time, the zodiac signs fall sequentially into the houses, and the planets are then placed into the chart according to their positions along the fixed zodiac belt used by most Western astrologers. The astrologer also measures distances between the planets to detect any adverse or favorable relationships between the planets. These relationships, called aspects, indicate pressure points or areas of ease.

The houses represent areas of one's life; the planets represent the archetypal personality traits; and the zodiac signs indicate how these energies are limited or expanded. The planetary relationships, or aspects, give further information on how these energies combine or clash. One might say that the planets are the "what," the houses are the "where," and the zodiac signs are the "how." The astrologer then assesses the chart and synthesizes the information in order to read the chart. The very complexity of this procedure adds to the appeal of astrology and seems to verify its accuracy.

As do most occult arts, astrology incorporates the elements of earth, air, water and fire, dividing the zodiac signs into these four categories. Additionally, astrology ties the zodiac into what are called the "qualities" of cardinal, fixed and mutable. These qualities correspond respectively to the beginning, middle and end of each season, signifying the drive, strength or flexibility of the particular sign they describe. Circling the zodiac, one finds that each zodiac sign represents an element and a quality. For example, Aries, the first fire sign and the one that comes at the beginning of spring, is cardinal. Leo is the fixed fire sign at full strength in midsummer. The mutable sign is Sagittarius, its heat dissolving and fading at the end of autumn, right before Capricorn (a cardinal earth sign) is ushered in at the winter solstice. This pattern recurs with the other three elements of earth, air and water, revealing astrology's deep relationship to the cycles of nature.

Astrology's pattern also reflects a cyclical view of time rather than a linear one. Aries, the first zodiac sign, is cardinal fire, while Pisces, the last sign, is mutable water. Aries is the initiating spark of spirit and life, while Pisces is a dissolution into the all, a yielding to the elements required before rebirth takes place again with Aries. This cycle reflects the dying of the leaves, grass and flowers that rot into the earth, giving seed for new life. Such a progression mirrors the pagan view of life that takes nature as its model. This pagan cyclical outlook infuses the interpretation of the chart, minimizing death and promoting both a fatalistic acceptance of recurring life patterns and a complementary belief in reincarnation. It is ironic that many astrologers promote a transcendent New Age view of spiritual evolution, while at the same time accepting the cyclical patterns found in astrology. Spiritual evolution through reincarnation, as posited in the New Age, theoretically marks advancement, but patterns in nature are merely repetitive.

The horoscope columns in newspapers and magazines simply show the sun sign, which is the zodiac position of the sun within a given time period. Nevertheless, though these horoscopes are rather generic, the advice given is based on the positions of the sun, moon and planets relative to each zodiac sign, and proffers an astrological worldview.

What Happens in an Astrology Session?

Guidance from False Gods

The astrologer views the birth chart as a master guide to a person's physical, mental, emotional and spiritual components. Since most astrologers believe in reincarnation—the belief that a person dies and comes back over and over again as another person for perhaps thousands of years—the chart also reveals a person's lessons from past lives (karmic lessons), and his or her karmic purpose in this life. Because many astrologers believe that the time and place of birth is chosen either by the client or by someone else, they assume that the birth chart has a deliberate correlation to the client's life.

Each astrologer has a style, but may start with the most prominent feature in the chart. The reading begins by describing influences from childhood or issues concerning relationships, money or career and then announces "trends" or a "forecast." The forecast is the interpretation of how the client will be affected by the slower-moving planets (from Saturn and farther out) as they approach significant areas of the birth chart. There are other technical forecasting methods, such as a progressed chart (each day representing a year). The forecast is to prepare the client for issues and areas triggered in this future time period.

Some typical things said during a session might be:

- "Your father was distant when you were young, so you now choose cold, distant men."
- "Your attraction to charming but unstable partners reflects insecurities about your worth."
- "Imagination and creativity are your strong point, but you are easily misled or deceived."
- "In the next three to eighteen months, you will be challenged with limitations in your marriage."

Astrology is a pure form of occult divination. Divination is the practice of getting information beyond the normal means of the five senses, and was originally the way to seek the guidance of pagan gods. This is done by reading hidden meanings in the natural world or in patterns, through paranormal abilities (such as psychic abilities), by using an occult tool that purportedly channels information supernaturally, or through contact with spirit beings.

Most astrologers believe one or more of the following:

- God is an energy from which we all come and to which we will all return.
- Jesus was only one of many advanced spiritual teachers.
- Jesus was the Avatar of the Age of Pisces.
- People evolve spiritually by learning lessons through many lives.
- A sacred energy connects all humanity.
- People must realize their divine essence.
- People are masters of their lives and futures.
- All faiths are true and lead to the same place.
- The only sin is not loving yourself, not realizing your own divin-

ity, or not seeing that this world is illusory.

- People do not need redemption or a Savior; they need awakening to their true divine Self.
- The answers lie within you.
- There is no absolute truth or morality.

As the astrologer reads the chart, the above beliefs color the astrologer's interpretations and advice. Clients are therefore assimilating the astrologer's beliefs while listening to information on their own lives.

What Is the Age of Aquarius?

Visualize World Peace

Imagine a world where we have universal peace and brotherhood; we use developed powers of the mind; there is a marriage of technology, science and spirituality; total equality reigns; gender has been transcended; people act for the good of the group but tolerate individuality; and the "outer teacher" has been replaced by the "inner teacher." This is the Age of Aquarius as astrologers and others envision it. Aquarius is ruled by Uranus, the planet that represents technology, revolution, nonconformity, communal harmony, advanced mind abilities and freedom from old forms. Trends in society toward Eastern styles of inward meditation and contemplation fit hand in glove with astrological beliefs about the Aquarius concept of turning to the "inner teacher." Postmodern rejection of absolute truth harmonizes perfectly with the Aquarian concept that there are many truths.

Although astrologers do not agree exactly when the Age of Aquarius began, most believe it began in the late twentieth century, and that we are entering the final transition now. The Age of Aquarius is an "earth age." These earth ages, lasting about two thousand years, are based on the orientation of the earth's North Pole towards the constellations. Due to the earth's orbit, these ages move through the zodiac in reverse order—from Gemini to Taurus to Aries to Pisces to Aquarius and so forth. The Age of Pisces began around the time of Christ's birth, and Jesus is perceived as the Avatar of the Age of Pisces. An Avatar in Hinduism is an incarnation of the god Vishnu, but the term migrated into the

New Age to express the earthly materialization of any advanced spiritual teacher. The Age of Pisces was a time of outer teachers who would enable mankind to one day find wisdom within.

Jesus exemplifies the Piscean qualities of suffering, sacrifice, compassion and universal love. Pisces is the fish, and so is the Christian symbol, but Christianity was a passing manifestation that will fade with the Age of Pisces and be transformed by an Aquarian world. Scandals in the church, such as the Roman Catholic pedophile outrage and the moral fall of various evangelical ministers and leaders, as well as radical theological departures from tradition (such as acceptance of homosexual ministers and same-sex unions), seem to confirm the belief that established Christianity is dying or being transformed.

There is an expectant excitement among astrologers and others in related spiritualities that society will undergo marked changes, including earth shifts such as floods, earthquakes and structural alterations. Some believe that those unprepared for the Age of Aquarius will die in these physical catastrophes.

Whereas Christianity sees the sinful nature of man and the fallen world under the sway of the evil one, astrologers and New Agers see the spirit of man purged of the old and renewed.

DOES ASTROLOGY "WORK"?

Seven Ways Astrology Persuades

Serious astrologers are not con artists, but devout followers of an occult practice. If astrology did not seem to offer anything of value, astrologers would be out of business. Here are seven reasons why astrology seems to work for the astrologer and the client:

1. Both astrologer and client desire to believe.
2. The planets and the zodiac reflect human traits we all share.
3. Countless combinations in the chart result in countless options.
4. Inaccurate information is forgotten.
5. Coincidence seems to affirm astrological predictions.
6. Broad statements made by astrologers are applied specifically.
7. Demonic guidance may intervene.

Astrologers assert authority and power over their clients, who defer to them or try to please them by agreeing with what is said.

The zodiac signs and planets reflect common human characteristics because in ancient times those studying the heavenly bodies ascribed human characteristics to their gods. Each god embodied a trait or traits and related behaviors: Aries (ruled by Mars) was warlike and fierce; Sagittarius (ruled by the largest planet Jupiter) was expansive and generous; and Gemini (ruled by fast-moving Mercury the messenger) was linked to communication and travel. Psychological principles blended with astrology expanded on these themes.

As an example of both the second and sixth points above, the astrologer makes a statement such as, "You are attracted to unstable or uncommitted romantic partners." This could be true in many ways for people who have been divorced or have had many ups and downs in relationships. It is also a normal experience for younger people who, due to immature judgment about relationships, choose partners who do not want commitments.

An astrologer, seeing the planet Uranus approaching the tenth house of career, might declare: "In the next six months to a year, you will see radical changes at your workplace, or you will make a sudden career change." In this case, the client will interpret as fulfillment specific events, such as getting a new boss or coworker, having new duties on the job or experiencing unexpected changes at work.

When I practiced astrology, I focused less on the person than on the chart, often feeling guided by a flow of energy from the chart to my mind. At times, I believed I was being aided by my spirit guide (a supposedly benevolent spirit who assists those on a spiritual path). I also recorded many charts for people whom I knew only by their place and time of birth. Therefore, I was not getting clues from body language, or even any information from the person, as would be the case in a reading with the client physically present.

Furthermore, many astrologers practice Eastern-style meditation, though they may use an expression such as "centering." Such meditation often brings the meditator into an altered state of mind, a condition similar to a light trance or hypnotic state. In this state, one's critical thinking and judgment are suspended and one's mind is open to whatever influences are present.

This sort of meditation is often recommended for those who practice the divinatory arts. A book by astrologer Jane Evans advises astrologers to meditate on the chart and to "enter" it. She writes:

> The astrologer can be taken . . . inward to realization. Like a lightning flash that reveals a whole landscape formerly in darkness, insight suddenly illuminates the horoscope giving pattern and meaning to what was hitherto just a collection of symbols...A door opens to communication with the Inner Self, whether your own or that of the person whose horoscope is being studied.[2]

Although there is a technical element in assessing a chart, once the reading begins the astrologer consciously or unconsciously opens a door to paranormal experience with spirits. It is not surprising that most astrologers, psychics and mediums routinely acknowledge having spirit guides.

It is crucial to realize this spiritual element of astrology. Astrology is not just a false belief or a pseudo-science, but a door to demonic contact. The Bible tells us that Satan can disguise himself as an angel of light (2 Cor 11:13–15), and we know he is the great deceiver. It is not unreasonable to conclude that the fallen angels (demons) who rebelled with him might also disguise themselves as "guiding spirits." Dismissing astrology as nonsense leads to underestimating its impact, deception, and danger as a practice contrary to God's Word and as a worldview that opposes the gospel of Jesus Christ.

WHAT DOES THE BIBLE SAY ABOUT ASTROLOGY?

Astrology Is Divination

Occult divination, termed "soothsaying" in some Bible translations, is clearly forbidden in many passages, such as Deuteronomy 18:10–12:

> There shall not be found among you anyone who ...practices divination or tells fortunes or interprets omens, or a sorcerer or a charmer or a medium or a wizard or a necromancer, for whoever does these things is an abomination to the Lord.

Astrology is ridiculed as powerless in Isaiah 47:12–15, and explicitly or implicitly condemned in other passages, like Deuteronomy 4:19

(ESV): "And beware lest you raise your eyes to heaven, and when you see the sun and the moon and the stars, all the host of heaven, you be drawn away and bow down to them and serve them." Many other passages forbid consulting or worship of the heavens, or the host of heaven.[3] Astrology is denounced in Daniel 2 as a replacement for seeking God for wisdom and counsel. Contrary to the claims of some, astrology is not a gift from God. God does not give gifts that he forbids. God gives only "good" and "perfect" gifts, according to James 1:17, and God defines what is good.

Many wonder about the story of the Magi in Matthew's Gospel. The Magi were "wise men," most likely Persians who counseled rulers and were learned in the sciences, dream interpretation and medicine. At the time, astronomy and astrology were one and the same, and this area would also be included as part of their knowledge. Matthew is unclear about the exact nature of the Star of Bethlehem, and no one knows why the wise men believed it to signify the birth of the King of the Jews. Matthew indicates that the star stood over the place where Jesus was; it is impossible for a heavenly body to do this. Many scholars believe this star was the Shekinah, the glory of God, hovering over the dwelling of Jesus.[4]

That God used the wise men, even though they probably practiced a form of astrology, does not mean that God endorses astrology. God used the false prophet Balaam and the pagan rulers Pharaoh and Cyrus for his purposes. Examining biblical texts referring to the wisdom of man reveals that such wisdom is nothing compared to God's wisdom (Is 29:14; Jer 8:9; Rom 11:33–34; 1 Cor 1:19ff). The wise men being guided this way to Jesus and bowing down to him as King illustrates man's wisdom subjecting itself to God's wisdom, as well as demonstrating that the first worshipers of Jesus were Gentiles, foreshadowing the Gospel going to the Gentiles. God's use of certain people does not denote his approval of their beliefs or practices, especially when such practices are denounced in his Word.

Astrology seeks answers in the natural world rather than in God's Word, thus honoring creation over the Creator. Astrology practices occult divination, which is forbidden by God. Finally, astrology opens the door for guidance from demons.

How Should Christians Respond?

Speaking in Truth and Love

Although there are many scientific arguments against astrology, Christians would do well to realize that such arguments may not be terribly effective in discussing the issue with non-Christians. Four problems arise in using this approach. First, such arguments are rather technical, and the astrologer will be able to respond with more technicalities that will only confuse the issue. Second, most astrologers are aware of the scientific arguments against astrology and dismiss them because those who believe in it are convinced that it "works." Third, astrologers and astrology fans become defensive when criticisms are leveled against astrology. Fourth, astrologers believe that astrology functions according to spiritual laws that go beyond the understanding of science. According to them, humanity is evolving to a point where these spiritual laws will eventually validate astrology.

The Christian should keep in mind that astrology is a spiritual deception, more than an intellectual one. The battle is spiritual, not intellectual, and prayer is essential. Beyond this crucial understanding, let me also offer a few practical suggestions.

What to Avoid

- Avoid consulting your horoscope! Christians who consult a horoscope will have zero credibility with an astrologer or a believer in astrology. Only Christians who do not consult their horoscopes and know why they do not consult them should engage in this dialogue.
- Avoid the "twins" issue. To disprove astrological predictions, some Christians try to use the fact that twins do not follow the same life path or share the same personality traits. This is not a very fruitful line of argument, since astrologers believe that even slight variations can be significant. The charts for twins, though similar, will vary, since they are born several minutes apart, and each twin actualizes the potential of the chart differently. Bringing up the twins issue will only reveal the challenger's lack of knowledge about astrology.

- Avoid asking why a chart is done for the birth time rather than the time of conception. Most astrologers believe that a person is not fully human until the baby takes its first breath, an event that marks a person's official entrance into the world. Prior to birth, the soul may not have entered the body. Debating this will be pointless.
- Avoid ridicule. Do not characterize astrology as silly or wonder how anyone can believe it. This approach is condescending and will prevent fruitful discussion, triggering hostility. Astrology is highly complex and astrologers are usually intelligent. Speak with gentleness and respect (1 Pt 3:15–16; Col 4:5–6).

Ways to Speak

- Ask open-ended questions. Try questions such as, "Why are there twelve signs?" "Who decided that?" "What or who determines the time of birth and why?" "Where is God in the chart?"
- Get to know the person. Enter into a genuine dialogue, asking about the person's spiritual background, what they think Christianity is, or why they rejected it. Ask why the person likes astrology and what the benefits are. By listening to the answers, the Christian will understand the issues that tie the person to astrology and gain a better understanding of the person.
- Use the information given as a springboard for discussion.[5] Dialogue and discussion offer more opportunities to share biblical truth than does lecturing.
- Care about the person. Perhaps there are ways of helping your friend with specific aspects of his or her life.
- Invite him into your home. He may never have seen or felt the peace and joy of a Christian home, where trust in a loving Father offers deep peace and joy.
- Pray, focus on the nature and attributes of God and Jesus, and avoid rabbit trails and arguments. The goal of the Christian in this discussion should be to witness about redemption through Jesus Christ rather than to debunk astrology.

3

The Global Mainstreaming of Witchcraft

Linda Harvey

On New Year's Eve in Rio de Janeiro, two million people gather at midnight on Copacabana beach to honor the goddess Yemanja (a blend of Afro-Brazilian *orishas* and the Virgin Mary), who is said to bring good fortune to her worshipers. Spiritists pepper the beach with sacred shrines, while drums and dancing "raise the energy." Foreign tourists flock to the hottest New Year's party on earth, enthusiastically join the pagan event, and don the traditional white apparel.

Brazil is not alone in its embrace of pagan ritual. Sorcery is now a respected phenomenon, thanks to the cultural influence of ecology, feminism, and a general disdain for the Judeo-Christian heritage. What will be the effects on those who bow before a pantheon of fickle deities and believe that ritual and superstition are doorways to oneness with the divine?

The Roots of Witchcraft

Witchcraft, usually practiced in covens, seeks to control circumstances: getting out of debt, winning a lover's heart, or healing an illness. Its rituals are directed toward nature-based divinities.[1] The primary deity of witches and wiccans is the goddess, accompanied by a "horned" god as consort. Sometimes she is revered as Maiden, Mother and Crone, terms that correspond to the life cycle of a woman. Witches treasure the duality of male-female, which produces sexual energy to raise the spiritual power needed for spells, cleansing and healing.

The practice of witchcraft is inconsistent. Ultimately, however, the practitioner worships the self, whose instincts and desires are empowered by occult spiritual forces. The focus of witchcraft is to take control of one's own (or another's) life. The enlightened witch invokes the goddess of choice (Diana, Isis, Hecate, Oshun, etc.), who infuses the coven with the power to accomplish its own desires. At the height of the ritual, there is an intense feeling of spiritual power, when the priestess believes she becomes one with the goddess and nature/earth, both of which conveniently want exactly what the coven wants. No wonder discontented women and adolescents are reviving this belief system. For those who squirm under the constraints of Christian living, witchcraft beckons with untold enticements.

The godhood of self is a stated pillar of witchcraft, as expressed in the 1974 Principles of Wiccan Belief, adopted by the Council of American Witches. The introduction states: "We are not bound by traditions from other times and other cultures, and owe no allegiance to any person or power greater than the Divinity manifest through our own being."[2]

Sensual instincts are welcomed, embraced and renamed. Sex itself is a central focus, both symbolically and physically. The lust of the eyes and the pride of life are celebrated, and beauty in humans and nature is seen as a manifestation of the divine. Environmental and political concerns fit nicely with the adorations witches offer the natural world.

Asserting the self by obeying impulses is a treasured ethic. "Go for it!" would be an appropriate advertising slogan. Humility and patience are seen as pathetic remnants of Judeo-Christian domination and patriarchy. There is no need for missionary work, since witches worry only about themselves. The self-indulgent, affluent West is a perfect spawning ground for Neopaganism.

Myth in Practice: The Emergence of Modern Witchcraft

Never in history has a society enjoyed the prosperity, peace and longevity of current Western culture. How ironic that America is setting another new standard: the return to primitive superstition and spiritism. Neopaganism is exploding in the West, particularly among youth.

Modern interest in witchcraft revived in the early twentieth century. Dr. Margaret Murray's *The Witch Cult in Western Europe* (1921) outlined medieval witch practices and Church persecution, claiming that witchcraft remained a surviving underground religion.[3] In 1951, witchcraft laws in England were repealed, clearing the way for public discussion and review. In 1954, Gerald Gardner's *Witchcraft Today* was published in England and became a guidebook for those attracted to the "ancient ways." Gardner, like Murray, believed witchcraft was an ancient practice suppressed by Christian authorities who feared it as a "dangerous rival."[4]

The claim that Christianity suppresses paganism through power politics provides some women a rationale for witchcraft both outside and inside Christian churches. (We will discuss this later.) Witchcraft has flourished mostly outside traditional religious circles, and in Western countries is wholly tied to the feminist movement's rebellion against patriarchy. Driven by anger and neurosis, it often resembles a metaphysical self-help program. At the highest levels of academia, leaders in feminist spirituality glory in reinventing history. An aversion to fact is a celebrated aspect of pagan mutiny.

In the 1970s and 80s, the work of Marija Gimbutas of UCLA contributed to interest in witchcraft. Her archaeological research of ancient Europe showed evidence, she claimed, of pre-Christian matriarchies centered on goddess worship. The highly subjective findings of Gimbutas found that ancient structures, markings and objects were adorned with symbols of the primary goddess deity. She saw amplified roles for females and minimal status of males, despite the widespread recovery of phallic objects and markings. She also hypothesized that prehistoric cultures distributed goods through female lines of inheritance.[5] Many of Gimbutas' findings are now disputed.

In *Goddess Unmasked: The Rise of Neopagan Feminist Spirituality*, Philip G. Davis notes the absence of "a single translated text from any of the most important goddess cultures to tell us what these ancient people actually believed."[6] After reviewing excavations in Malta, Catal Huyuk (Turkey), the Balkans, ancient Britain, the Indus Valley and Crete,[7] Davis concludes:

> The findings of our investigation . . . indicate that none of the societies most often cited as authentic ancient Goddess cultures actually conforms to our expectations. Not a single one provides clear evidence of a single, supreme female deity; not a single one exhibits the signs of matriarchal rule. . . . In each of these cases, the story of the Goddess is a fabrication in defiance of the facts.[8]

Yet these ideas prevail as dogma in university social science classes. Practitioners of witchcraft are well-established in the university setting and within Christian denominations. By 1986, three wiccan priestesses held faculty positions at Harvard Divinity School,[9] which was founded in the seventeenth century to prepare men for Gospel ministry. More recently, the school sponsored a women's spirituality conference, where "Protestant, Catholic, Evangelical, Mormon, Jewish, Muslim and Wiccan feminists contributed to the effort to recover the history of religion in American feminism."[10]

The Structure of Witchcraft Practice

In the book of Deuteronomy, we find one of many biblical passages that forbid witchcraft:

> There shall not be found among you anyone who makes his son or his daughter pass through the fire, or one who practices witchcraft, or a soothsayer, or one who interprets omens, or a sorcerer, or one who conjures spells, or a medium, or a spiritist, or one who calls up the dead. For all who do these things are an abomination to the Lord. (Dt 18:10–12, NKJV)

Exodus 22:18, 1 Samuel 15:23, Acts 19:19, Galatians 5:20 and other passages carry stern prohibitions against sorcery as incompatible with allegiance to Yahweh/Christ. Despite the gracious provision of the Almighty in creation, his gift of the law through the prophets, and his provision of a Savior, humans have always been tempted to flirt with, date and marry other gods. To preserve us from the eternal consequences of such unfaithfulness, our Lord warns us repeatedly about Satan's deceptive strategy. Satan can appear as "an angel of light" (2 Cor 11:14) and so can his followers. Some people claim to have seen a goddess or god, a beatific vision, a spirit guide or even a dead person. Is it really the spirit of Uncle Charlie or Eleanor Roosevelt? Probably not. Seekers approach the occult realm using a wide variation of ceremonial forms. Demons care little what ritual calls them, as long as the name of Christ is absent.

Today's witchcraft has an inconsistent structure, as do other types of spiritism. Ritual is the focus of witchcraft worship. Witches gather for coven ceremonies or other activities on dates that correspond to ancient pagan holidays. These are called "Sabbats." The most significant day, Samhain (pronounced sow-in or sow-een) falls on October 31 (Hallow-een) and is the witch "new year." Imbolc, or Candlemas (Festival of Light) is on February 2. The ancient fertility holiday of Beltane occurs on May 1 (May Day). Lammas (Lughnasa) is August 1 and celebrates the initial ingathering of the harvest. There are four lesser "sabbats"—the two solstices (winter/Yule, December 21; and midsummer/Litha, June 21) and the two equinoxes (spring/Ostara, March 21 and autumn/ Mabon, September 21). Non-holiday gatherings are called "esbats."[11]

Ceremonies can involve rites of passage, divination, initiation, worship of certain divinities, or the practice of magic and spells. Many rituals begin with cleansing—both of the self (by bathing or donning special cloth-ing) and of the "sacred space." Witches often attend the ritual "skyclad" (nude), symbolizing purification. The high priestess determines a ritual area and purifies it. An altar is set up and the "quarters" (four corners) of the working circle are designated, corresponding to north, south, east and west. Then the priestess marks out the circle in a clockwise direction with an implement, usually a dagger-like object called an "athame." A circle can be "cast" using a wand, fingers or a coven holding hands. Any ritual items, such as water, salt, candles, herbs or oil are "blessed."

Invocations are pronounced, sometimes in the four directions, to the chosen deity or deities, to animal spirits or to the great universal spirit. The formal ritual then begins with the sound of a bell or some other signal denoting the start of the central activity. If spell-working is on the agenda, the priestess and others become one with the invoked gods in a ritual called "drawing down the moon." In Christian terminology, the coven is inviting demonic possession of the high priestess and others.

There is much room for falsification at this point. The priestess (or others), speaking for the goddess or another spirit, speaks to the coven via the spirits, channeling an out-of-body experience not remembered later. This "drawing down" may be accompanied by chanting, music, drumming or dance to "raise energy" contained within the cast circle. Initiations, dramas and the specific steps of a spell usually occur at this point. There may also be discussion. A food element, "cakes and wine," usually follows.

The "Great Rite," sexual intercourse between the high priestess and the high priest, is done symbolically in most covens by plunging the athame (dagger) into a cup of wine, but sometimes it is actually performed. When the ritual is completed, the circle is closed by the priestess or others moving around the space in a counterclockwise motion.[12]

"Magick," as it is called, includes symbols, procedures and words that supposedly carry great power. Nothing must be said in the ritual, or elsewhere in a witch's life, that is not carefully phrased, and tact is not the objective. A controlled framing of reality is the goal. Witch Laurie Cabot states, "Wording your spell correctly is important. Words are powerful instruments in and of themselves."[13] *Teen Witch* author Silver Ravenwolf says, "We believe that to give evil a name is to give evil power."[14]

At the high point of the ritual, the spell is "cast." The invoked power peaks and is sent to its destination to achieve the desired goal. Thousands of spells, varying in structure, purpose and props, are available in books and web sites. The "magickal" mind calls intentionally on non-Christian powers, taking steps in a specific sequence to achieve an objective. Christians rely instead on God's will, timing and methods. He does not require a ritual for his worshipers to communicate with him. Witches maintain that their rituals resemble Christian prayer, but Almighty God needs neither a specific sequence of actions, nor a circle to focus his supreme and omnipresent power. He is always available to his children by the indwelling of his Spirit and the intimacy of prayer.

Like the pagans of ancient times, witches believe that manipulation of the metaphysical requires a drama on earth. Activities such as dancing for rain, meditating using poppets, or sticking pins in voodoo dolls exemplify this performance approach. The witch also believes that intensely focused desire, directed at a goal, will produce a magical outcome.[15]

The witchcraft mindset trusts in symbols and patterns and seeks meaning through process. The labyrinth, now a tool for prayer and meditative walking (even in nominally Christian churches, such as the National Cathedral in Washington, DC), carries its own power, the Neopagan believes, and is, like the cast circle, a "sacred pattern." Lauren Artress is a female minister who sensed the labyrinth's power at a cathedral in France, then worked to bring one to Grace Cathedral in San Francisco. She describes the experience of walking the labyrinth:

> To walk a sacred path is to discover our inner sacred space: that core of feeling that is waiting to have life breathed back into it through symbols, archetypal forms like the labyrinth, rituals, stories and myth.[16]

God is not separate or transcendent, Artress believes, but is within each person. Certain symbols, actions and patterns aid the pagan mind to discover that self-divinity. Witch Isaac Bonewits concurs: "Neopagans believe that divinity is both immanent (internal) and transcendent (external)." Like most witches, Bonewits has no fear of "possession," which is a part of the internal manifestation of divinity.[17]

Alone or in smaller groups, witches also engage in clairvoyance; in healing rituals (through herbs and potions); and in fortune-telling (divination) through astrology, Tarot cards and crystals. Charms or amulets bring good fortune. Some witches seek contact with "familiars" (animals and the spirits believed to inhabit them).

Covens are common, but the internet has led to an increase in solitary witchcraft, especially among youth. Adherents gravitate toward a particular witch tradition, such as the Celtic, Druid, Egyptian/Isis, Shamanic, Gardnerian, Dianic, Faerie, Stregherian or Eclectic.

The Origin and Nature of Witch Power

The origin of their power is only vaguely understood by most witches to be the goddess and her god consort or a universal god figure. The cauldron accommodates many models of spiritual power, similar to the Eastern notion of a universal force that connects the entire web of polytheism. Spiritual progress leads to ever-higher spiritual enlightenment. Belief in reincarnation fuels the politics of radical environmentalism, since all species deserve the same respect. After all, one might become a mongoose, zebra or raven in a next life. The earth itself often becomes the goddess, as in "Gaia" worship.

This universal power is concentrated in the individual. Thus another model of power emerges: power from within. Jung's "collective unconscious" and concept of inner divinity[18] hold significant influence among witches. The coven's sense that "all are one" can be used to justify metaphysical mischief. Expulsion from Eden for delusions of godlike grandeur was the original punishment of mankind; nevertheless, modern witches turn defiantly away from the revealed God.

The "power within" justifies an array of ancillary notions. To obey the goddess, one must obey one's impulses.[19] The brain is considered a vast, untapped energy source, thus occult practices are described as "higher order thinking" (bright and progressive as opposed to the dimness of Christianity). Witch Starhawk describes the energy of "chi," which "flows in certain patterns throughout the human body, and can be raised, stored, shaped, and sent."[20] Hinduism calls such energy "chakras." Belief in this supernatural force-field forms the basis for alternative healing therapies.[21]

Witches believe in "good" and "evil" spiritual power—"white" magic and "black" magic. Their ethic espouses the "threefold law": whatever one does returns to the person in triple strength. This reinforces the caution against doing harm. The Wiccan Rede was probably developed by Gerald Gardner in the 1950s,[22] even though it sounds medieval: "An ye harm none, do what ye will." But what are the parameters of "harm"?

Despite the threefold law, spiritual power is often abused. Revenge and jealousy can inflame witch emotions and produce hexing or cursing, and the "goddess" accommodates this through one's own "divine" impulse. After learning about the "craft," whether in novels, in cyberspace or through older friends, middle school wiccans now routinely try to put curses on their rivals through gossip, spells or the Internet.

Feminist spirituality historian Cynthia Eller describes the potential of "magick":

> ...the power of magic is naked, unbridled power: it is the capability to kill or to heal, to curse or to bless. Magic is morally neutral, a simple cause and effect process...in the wrong hands, magic could be like a thermonuclear device in the trunk of a terrorist's car.[23]

While we disagree that magic is "morally neutral," it does offer true power. However, self-appropriated authority does not lead to good judgment, whereas the indwelling Holy Spirit softens the human conscience and prompts self-restraint.

In 1 Peter 5:8, the apostle describes Satan as a roaring lion, looking for someone to devour. As pagan practices increase, spiritual darkness will become a potent, though invisible, reality.

MUTINY FROM WITHIN: WITCHCRAFT AND CHRISTIANITY

Many pagans and witches reject traditional faith, but Margot Adler's classic book from the 1980s, *Drawing Down the Moon: Witches, Druids, Goddess-Worshipers and other Pagans in America Today* discusses the predominance of ex-Catholics and ex-Jews in the "craft."[24] An astonishing recent trend is the number of people who openly practice witchcraft *within* Christian churches, often encountering little resistance.

In 1993, ordained Lutheran feminist Chung Hyun Kyung stepped to the podium at a Christian feminist conference in Minneapolis, entitled "Re-Imagining God." Taking a bite out of an apple, Kyung ridiculed the Genesis account of Eve's transgression, then distributed apples to the audience of several thousand.[25] This ground-breaking conference was attended by ministers and representatives from the Presbyterian Church USA, the United Methodist Church, the Evangelical Lutheran Church in America, the United Church of Christ, the Roman Catholic Church and the Episcopal Church, among others. Speakers denied Christ's incarnation and atonement, openly celebrated lesbianism, and invited the audience to invoke the goddess "Sophia," said to be the divine "wisdom" referenced in the book of Proverbs. A mock communion of milk and honey was offered to her.[26] This conference was followed by other "Re-Imagining" events in subsequent years.

Reactionary anger to priestly or ministerial dismissal of women is at the root of much of the interior corruption of mainline denominations. Elizabeth A. Johnson writes in *She Who Is*:

> In the Christian community... for most of its history women have been subordinated in theological theory and ecclesial practice at every turn...They are called to honor a male savior sent by a male god whose legitimate representatives can only be male....This process is strongly aided and abetted by male-centered language and symbol systems....[27]

The first priority is to alter *language*. Once meanings change, a new framework for ideology exists. Truth is flipped on its head, and deep heresy abounds. "Christ" no longer means the Christ of Scripture; "sin" is determined by humans; and "love" becomes an embrace of sin and idolatry. The authority of Scripture is undermined, yet these folks remain *inside* Christian seminaries, congregations and communities. Why?

Miriam Therese Winter, a PhD from Princeton Theological Seminary, wrote *The Chronicles of Noah: Genesis and Exodus according to Women*. She explains that:

> ...we need to be able to *bypass* the complex layers of application and interpretation within the canon. This is essential for women who for countless generations have absorbed and internalized the message of *female degradation* encoded in patriarchal texts [emphasis added].[28]

Winter feels justified in producing a new canon, where Asherah is another aspect of "Godde," to be "understood differently" by women.[29] To Winter, Rachel's *teraphim* (household idols) are sacred objects justifiably important to her. Winter believes that creation is sacred. She rejects "unequivocally" the dominion of humans over the earth:

> The temptation to subjugate and subdue violates the integrity of the web of life. Ancient civilizations understood this, for Gaia was once the name for both the deity and planet earth.[30]

Winter writes substitute scripture with these new insights. Eve did circle dances in the Garden. Drawn to the fruit-bearing tree, she fell asleep in its branches. Eve named the animals, while Adam was frightened by Eve's rituals. Eve bore two daughters, with whom she danced by the apple tree, making ritual and talking to the serpents. Lonely Adam "knew his world was slipping away, for he could no longer control it." So he and Eve *voluntarily* left Eden.[31]

With two other women, Winter wrote *Defecting in Place: Women Claiming Responsibility for their Own Spiritual Lives*, a survey of over seven thousand women in United States churches. One chapter on "alternate liturgy" lists names of grass roots groups. Among them are Sacred Space, Earth Cycle Group, Lilith, Sophia's Group, Cakes for the Queen of Heaven, Moonwomen, the Moon Ritual Gathering Group and Dianic

Moon Worship Group. Also mentioned were lesbian groups: Lesbian Catholics Together and SLUTS (Seminary Lesbians under Theological Stress).[32]

SEX: THE DRIVER OF REVOLUTION

An examination of pagan feminism reveals the priority of sex. After the satiation of resentment and pride, sexual desire becomes the chief measuring rod for esoteric experience. The spirit that does not affirm sexual impulses must be discarded for a new deity.

In her book about feminist spirituality, Eller explains why a woman named Suzanne has rejected fundamentalist Christianity in favor of witchcraft: "Suzanne credits feminist spirituality with restoring to women the right to be sexual."[33] Eller describes the feminist spirituality movement at the time her book was published (1995):

> The sociological profile of the feminist spirituality movement can be summed up like this: white, of middle-class origins, fairly well educated (beyond high school), of Jewish or Christian background.... in their thirties or forties, and disproportionately lesbian.[34]

Though the age profile is shifting downward, sex is still a common theme. Sex of all types becomes a permissible, key element in the magical process. Male/female attraction of the divine couple gives the ritual its intensity, yet this dynamism easily shifts to other forms of sexuality, such as bisexuality or pansexuality.

The witch Starhawk describes with nostalgia ancient temple rites, including prostitution. Referring to the Babylonian tales of Enuma Elish and the Epic of Gilgamesh, Starhawk embellishes the Sumerian fertility myths of goddess Inanna and her consort Dumuzi. Notes Starhawk, Inanna is "sexually aggressive and eager for satisfaction." Yet it is not a totally heterosexual scene. She believes that:

> The texts again and again show us women's erotic celebration of each other. Inanna's girlfriends praise her sexual parts as if they have intimate knowledge of them. In a society in which the erotic was seen as sacred, sexual identity may have been much more fluid than it is today.[35]

Oh, for the good old days! And another benefit Starhawk sees is that "Inanna never gets pregnant. Her sexuality is celebrated for its power to give pleasure, and renew all the life of the earth, not for reproduction."[36]

This empty sexuality is also celebrated by Riane Eisler. She tells us Jehovah forced Eve to give up her sacred groves and goddess worship. Because Eve "clung to the old faith more tenaciously than did Adam, her punishment was to be more dreadful," Eisler claims. Henceforth, Eve "... would have to submit in all things. Not only her sorrow, but her conception—the number of children she must bear—would be greatly multiplied."[37]

Out-of-wedlock sexuality is not just acceptable in witchcraft, it is a sacred right. Starhawk sums it up: "In Witchcraft, ... sexuality, as a direct expression of the life force, is seen as numinous and sacred.... Marriage is a deep commitment, a magical, spiritual and psychic bond. But it is only one possibility out of many for loving, sexual expression."[38]

Homosexuality and crossgender sexuality are embedded in witchcraft ritual, says Christopher Penczak in *Gay Witchcraft*. He notes that "Magick as a spiritual path is one filled with transgenderism. A magician of any sort must fluidly shift shapes between genders." Knowledge of both masculine and feminine aspects of oneself is the reason "why gays, lesbians, bisexuals and transgendered people were recognized as potentially talented in the mystical arts."[39] While initially put off by the seeming heterosexual nature of the traditional witchcraft ritual, Penczak realizes that witchcraft can easily accommodate flexible sexuality.

Children as Witches

Researchers estimate the total number of pagan practitioners in the United States to be approximately one and a half million.[40] This figure measures only adults, however. The biggest growth in recent years has been among youth. A recent search for "wicca" on the networking site, MySpace, yielded over thirty thousand hits. The term "pagan" was used in the profiles of members some seventy thousand times. MySpace members are predominately under age thirty. On the website Witches' Voices, there are almost four thousand youth listings (mostly teens) from the United States, and many more from other countries. Television shows like *Charmed* and *Buffy the Vampire Slayer* were teen sensations and more such programs are introduced each season. They convey a slick image: the hot teen babe with a Book of Shadows, stimulating the trend of "pop" witchcraft among teens. How-to books on witchcraft beliefs and spells abound. From authors like Silver Ravenwolf, Isobel Bird, and Cate Tiernan, popular novels feature teen girls with ordinary girl concerns—grades, dates, clothes—who solve problems by meeting together for ritual. Boys reach for authors Jonathan Stroud, Tony Abbott, Kathryn Lasky and P. B. Kerr. Nancy Drew and the Hardy Boys have given way to magical beasts, evil warlocks (as opposed to "good" wizards), vampires and animal spirits.

Along with the witch worldview come disturbing ideas for youth. "Empowerment" from pagan spirits is dangerous but tempting. What better way to take revenge on the bully at school, the strict teacher or a romantic rival, than through a curse? The youth who feels slighted, inadequate or unhappy, has only to search for the right occult method.

The desire for higher self-esteem draws youth to a new entertainment theme: special undiscovered powers. Such new Gnosticism figures in many recent titles: from the Harry Potter books and the Philip Pullman trilogy to teen heroes and heroines in *animé* cartoons and comics like PoKeMon and YuGiOh! Kids enjoying a favorite book, game or DVD imagine supernatural contests solved by the hero's special knowledge (*gnosis*), which is discovered through ritual and revelation from helper spirits.

Publishers exploit the lucrative youth market, while gatekeeper parents sleep. In the past, parents' objections would have restrained publishing objectives. But when the influential publisher Scholastic Publishing set the pace for explicitly occult material, HarperCollins, Miramax Books, Little Brown, Hyperion and others followed, churning out youth "fantasy" books full of divination, witchcraft and shamanism.

Much of the recent wave of youth occult literature has sprung from the United Kingdom, with authors including J. K. Rowling, Philip Pullman, Garth Nix, Eoin Colfer, Jonathan Stroud and Marianne Curley. The worldwide market for their work shows no signs of slowing. One might think the Christian Church would step in to save the day. Yet most churches are silent about the need for spiritual discernment. Even worse, some churches are now part of the problem as they use cultural trends to attract youth. One trend is outright mysticism, in the form of "contemplative prayer."

"Emerging" churches appeal to youth tastes in music and worship style, but some of these discard basic Christian doctrine as they practice a form of spiritism. One example is the Youth Ministry and Spirituality Project, a program that operated for several years in San Francisco. While that program has disbanded, its founder, Mark Yaconelli, has been widely influential in bringing "contemplative prayer" and occult practices into Christian youth ministry, often in collaboration with the mammoth youth group supplier, Youth Specialties. Yaconelli advocates meditating, ritual, "silence," and use of labyrinths in youth activities.[41] Originating in San Francisco, the YMSP advocates meditating, ritual and "silence," during which one senses the leading of "the spirit." What spirits will youth with little biblical background summon by such an open-ended invitation?

The world's children are naked and cold with only sorcery as a blanket, while the body of Christ lounges on the sidelines.

The Party Primitive

Some Christian families will probably be on Copacabana Beach in Rio de Janeiro, as goddess worship marks the New Year. Witchcraft and paganism hardly cause a raised eyebrow in the formerly Christian West. That group of laughing revelers on your cruise ship may be Wiccans, not a Methodist tour group.

A record number of (mostly American) witches and pagans attended the Parliament of the World Religions in Barcelona in 2004. One workshop was called Pagan Dialogue Inside and Outside of the Circle.[42] The 2009 Parliament in Melbourne, Australia focused on "indigenous and aboriginal spiritualities to honor these communities and encourage reconciliation."[43] Many indigenous practices fit the witchcraft profile. For example, in the Afro-Brazilian *terrieros*, the priestess becomes ritually possessed by a goddess. Then the action begins—problems solved, secrets revealed, healings accomplished. Most of these priestesses call themselves "witches" (*bruxas*).

As witchcraft gains stature, we will see an increase in its visible presence. Ceremonial worship is the essence of witchcraft, evidenced in the explosion of pagan events, conferences, parades and festivals in the United States. Marian Singer says that pagan festival attendance is going out the roof, contributing to the strong growth of witchcraft. Public festivals are a "safe" place to practice pagan beliefs and to meet other pagans. Singer's guidebook to pagan festival attendance claims that seventy percent of pagans are solitary practitioners who seek networking.[44]

Public events generate an energy that holds sway over us. At political rallies, Millennium events, and the Olympics, one can sense the crowd dynamic. What happens when witchcraft bursts from the closet into mainstream gatherings? When invocation of a dark deity is the featured program, a world under its sway cannot fail to become enchanted.

As two million people gather on New Year's in Rio, they become "one" in their goals. The moon is "drawn down" by priestesses on the sandy shore, and Yemanja receives thousands of sacrifices. Little boats drift into the sea with messages, gifts, jewels, wine and clothing. Flowers float on the waves. The crowds cast one enormous spell to a goddess said to be a favorite of lesbians and crossdressers.[45] Do the beach revelers know Yemanja's nature? Do they care? Satan has persuaded modern Westerners that Christian ways are outmoded. The primitive is progressive. So tourists, like unwary parents, smile indulgently as Yemanja's priestesses offer blessings. How quaint and interesting, these indigenous customs.

The Almighty God, Creator and Redeemer, has given us commandments, the first of which is, "You shall have no other gods before me."

4

Kabbalah
More Than Red String!

FRED KLETT

Kabbalah has become a hot topic lately. Perhaps you know someone studying it. You have probably heard about Hollywood types like Madonna getting involved in it or perhaps you noticed that several Olympic ice skaters were wearing red string bracelets.[1] If you know anything about Judaism you may know that Hasidic Jews have certain mystical teachings. In another context you may be familiar with the diagram of ten emanations known as the *Tree of Life* that occultists and mystics map out. Kabbalah is currently going through a revival and renaissance far beyond the red string silliness. Some Kabbalists believe the time is ripe for the world to be exposed to this esoteric teaching once reserved for those advanced in Judaism. Mainstream Judaism is now re-embracing Jewish mysticism. A recent perusal of a catalog for the Adult School program of a major Jewish institution yielded fourteen courses connected with Kabbalah! One author commented:

> There is effectively no such thing as "non mystical Judaism," and the term "'Judaism's inner teaching" applies across the board. The major Kabbalists were all completely infused with the ways of Rabbinic Judaism. Indeed many played central roles in the development of Jewish law, in addition to helping to shape the Kabbalistic heritage.[2]

What is Kabbalah?

Simply stated, Kabbalah is the system of Jewish mysticism. Emphasized in Hasidic Judaism, it is becoming more influential in Judaism in general and growing in popularity. Kabbalah as a metaphysical system has greatly influenced "Gentile" occultism. In Hollywood and around the world, it is becoming a popular New Age cult movement. The word Kabbalah itself means *reception*. If you walk into a hotel in Israel, and if you read Hebrew, you will see a sign which says "Kabbalah." The sign is not an invitation to have a mystical experience—it just tells you where to find the Reception desk! According to Jewish mysticism, the mystical tradition was *received* along with other oral Rabbinic tradition such as found in the writings of the Mishnah and Talmud. Kabbalah is characteristically studied in small groups, and sometimes in secret, hence the word Cabal derives from the word Kabbalah.

Central Texts and Figures

The earliest work of Kabbalah is the *Sefer Yetzirah* (Book of Creation) which may date as early as the third to fourth century AD. Tradition claims this was written in the time of Abraham, but critical Kabbalah scholars dispute this dogma.[3] The next major work is the *Bahir* (Brightness), which was written in the twelfth century, though, again, tradition claims a much earlier date.[4] The major Kabbalistic work is the multivolume *Zohar* (Radiance), which was written in the 13th century by Moses De Leon, though tradition claims it to be much older.[5] Isaac Luria, Hayim Vital and Moses Cordovero were the leading Kabbalah scholars of the sixteenth century. Hassidic thought is influenced by the *Tanya*, written by Rabbi Shneur Zalman of Liadi in the eighteenth century. Some modern traditional Kabbalists are Yehuda Ashlag, Jacob Immanuel Schochet and Adin Steinsaltz. Representing a more critical tradition are modern academic scholars such as the great Gershom Scholem, Daniel Matt, Joseph Dan, Arthur Green and Isaiah Tishby. Modern writers in the Jewish Renewal[6] vein include Aryeh Kaplan, Zalman Schachter-Shalomi, David A. Cooper, Avram Davis and even a friend of Hillary Clinton, Michael Lerner of *Tikkun Magazine*. Other authors include leaders of their own Kabbalah organizations such as Michael Laitman of B'nei Baruch and the various members of the Berg family, who run the lucrative and ludicrous Kabbalah Centre of pop star fame.

Basic Kabbalah Concepts

Kabbalah can be complex and confusing. Even within traditional Kabbalah there are internal inconsistencies and contradictions. Adding to the complexity are the differing schools of thought within traditional Kabbalah. In addition, Kabbalah exists in many forms. Eminent scholar Joseph Dan lists six different contexts, ranging from historical scholarship to the New Age Movement, in which people might find the word "Kabbalah" used, and he says in each context "the term conveys a different meaning."[7]

It is helpful to understand that Kabbalah is influenced by Gnosticism and Neoplatonism, as well as the Bible. New Age approaches to Kabbalah often incorporate meditation practices from other traditions. In spite of all this diversity, some basics are common to almost all Kabbalistic thinking. First, Kabbalah posits the existence of four levels of reality, called from highest to lowest: Emanation, Creation, Formation and Action.[8] God in essence is completely unknowable and absolutely one. God in his essence is known as *Ayn Sof* (also spelled *Ein Sof*) meaning *nothing beyond* and *Ayn* meaning *nothingness*. Orthodox Jewish Kabbalist Aryeh Kaplan states:

> one must understand how Judaism in general, and the Kabbalists in particular, view God...People often say that "God is spirit" or that "God is power" or that "God is love." But the fact is that none of these sentences is true. Actually, the sentence "God is..." is a statement that cannot be completed. To complete this sentence would be to place God in the same category as something else. If one understands the true nature of God, then this is impossible... There is...no category in my mind in which I can place Him... Hence the closest one can come to think then about God is to depict nothingness and to realize that behind it is God. It is for this reason that nothingness meditation was seen as a means of drawing close to God.[9]

Because God is so wholly other, we cannot say anything positive about God's essence. God must be described *via negativa*. In other words one cannot say "God is loving," one can only say "God is not non-loving!" A similar idea has been expressed in Gnosticism, Aristotelian and Neoplatonic thought. Charles Hodge has described Aristotle's concept of the divine (which has influenced Jewish thought from Maimonides to the Kabbalists) in this way:

> ...this infinite intelligence, which he called God, was pure intelligence, destitute of power and of will; neither the creator nor the framer of

> the world; unconscious, indeed, that the world exists; as it is occupied exclusively in thought of which it is itself the object.[10]

Though the divine is called nothing, because indescribable, it is also in another sense everything, because nothing else really exists. A foundational verse in Kabbalistic thought is Deuteronomy 4:35: "To you it was shown, that you might know that the Lord is God; there is no other besides him." This is understood as saying there is nothing that exists besides God, rather than that he alone is God.

According to Kabbalah, Ayn Sof emanated the *Ten Sephirot (or Sefirot)*, ten emanations which are divine personal subsistencies. The word Sephirot comes from the Hebrew word for number, which reveals Neopythagorean influences. (Neopythagoreanism is a Greek Philosophy which saw numbers as the chief constituent of reality.) Similarly, the Ten Sephirot are the divine pattern upon which all of reality is based. They are the DNA of the universe containing a pattern expressed on every level of reality.[11] Some Sephirot are masculine and some are feminine. Traditional Kabbalist Jacob Immanuel Schochet writes:

> The *Sefirot* are thus Divine emanations, various phases in the manifestation of Divinity. As we speak of them in terms of numerous gradations, extreme care must be taken to avoid any false misconception of dualism or a plurality in the G–dhead. There is no suggestion whatever that the *Sefirot* are to be taken as distinct and separate from the *En Sof*. On the contrary, there is a basic and intrinsic unity between the *En Sof* and the *Sefirot*...All the attributes of the Holy One, blessed is He, His Will, and His Wisdom, are designated by these names only in relation to the creatures.[12]

The Ten Sephirot are best understood as symbolic anthropomorphisms that express a deep mystery unfolded within the Godhead. God is in essence one, but when seen in relationship to the created order, God can only be understood in terms of these ten emanated Sephirot. So Kabbalah postulates both an ontological view of God and an economic one.

The Breaking of the Vessels

According to Isaac Luria, also known as *The Ari*, Ayn Sof contracted to make a space for creation. This is called *tzimzum*. As Luria put it:

> Having formed a vacuum and a space precisely in the middle of the endless light, a place was formed, where the emanated and the created might reside. Then from Endless Light a single line hung down.... And through that line, He emanated, formed, created all the worlds. Before these four worlds came to be there was one infinite, one name, in wondrous, hidden unity, that even for the closest of the angels there is no attainment in the endless, as there is no mind that can perceive it, for He has no place, no boundary, no name.[13]

The universe came to be at the end of a process of emanation into the space the Ayn Sof created. As the Sephirot were emanated, "vessels" were devised of a lesser light to contain these higher lights. The vessels could not contain the Sephirot, and so they shattered. As a result the lower emanations, and especially the tenth Sephira, *Shekinah*, became trapped in matter, which is what the broken vessels became. An analogy is given of a vessel containing oil. If the vessel is shattered, oil clings to pottery shards. So, too divine sparks are trapped in everything.

Cosmic Confusion?

Christians know from the Scriptures that God is both transcendent and immanent, that is, he is above all things and at the same time present everywhere. Kabbalah also teaches divine transcendence and immanence, but it is not the biblical version. It is a pagan version. As John Frame has explained, biblical transcendence means God is the Creator and Ruler of all things as the Covenant Lord. Biblical immanence means that God is actively involved in creation and redemption, however, in such a way as not to confuse the distinction between the Creator and his Creation.[14] The Ayn Sof of Kabbalah is transcendent, but in an unbiblical, Gnostic sense of being so far removed that you cannot say anything about him. On the other hand, in Kabbalah there is a confused distinction between the Creator and his creation, as divine sparks are trapped in the created world.

Kabbalah has long been accused of pantheistic, or at least panentheistic tendencies. We see this cosmic confusion between the Creator and creature expressed clearly in popular Kabbalistic writings. In a section titled "The All–Ness of God," Avram Davis uses a discussion between a rabbi and a student as a literary device: "Tell me, Rebbe," a man demanded during Shabbat evening prayers. "Just what is God?" "Tell me," Reb Yerachmiel replied, "just what is not?" Davis explains:

> Here, in a sentence, is the heart and soul of my theology. God is All. ...God is the Source of all things and their substance. Thus, we've read: "I am God and there is none else" (Is 45:5). Not simply that there is no other God but that there is nothing else but God. "Adonai alone is God in heaven above and on earth below; there is none else" (Dt 4:39). There is nothing else (*ein od*) in heaven or on earth but God.[15]

A book on Kabbalah written in a popular style quotes a classic sixteenth century Kabbalist on the nature of God and reality:

> In his book *Elimah Rabbati*, Cordovero gives the classic explanation of Ein Sof in the following passage: "Before all emanation there was only Ein Sof which is all reality. Even after Ein Sof emanated all that exists, there still is only Ein Sof and nothing outside of It. There is no entity without the power of God within it. If that were not the case, you would be setting limits to God and attributing duality, God forbid. God is everything, but not everything is God."[16]

Pantheism teaches that God is the all. Kabbalah teaches that all is contained within God, but that God extends beyond the universe. Kabbalah is *panentheistic* in stating that God alone really exists, creation is *in* God, God is *in* creation, and creation came about through emanation rather than being spoken into existence, created out of nothing. Christians certainly believe that God is everywhere and that all of creation reflects his creative brilliance, yet God is not actually *in* his creation and creation is in no way part of him.[17] Clearly the god of Kabbalah is a quite different god than we find in the Hebrew Scriptures!

Kabbalah also understands God as having a feminine aspect as well as a masculine one. In the book *Kabbalah Simply Stated* we find this interesting statement:

> Yes, the word Shekhinah is a feminine noun. Maimonides regarded the Shekhinah as an intermediary between God and our World. Rabbi Nachmanides believed the Shekhinah was the dwelling aspect of God. In the Zohar, the Shekhinah is called, "the indwelling Feminine Presence" who was invited back by her Groom (the community

> of Israel) every Sabbath eve to sustain the world for another six days. Sometimes she's referred to as "The God of Moses," because she protected the Hebrews after they escaped from Egypt. This feminine aspect of God is one of the most powerful images in Kabbalah.[18]

Man According to Kabbalah

Man is created in the image of God, and according to Kabbalah, even our physical bodies correspond to divine attributes. The original configuration of the Sephirot is known as *Adam Kadmon* (primordial man). The configuration of the Sephirot forms the pattern for all in the lower worlds. This is similar to the idea of Platonic forms. Man was originally created as a hermaphrodite, containing both male and female and then later divided in two. Aspects of the soul are a spark of the divine. All men were once one soul and regaining oneness is our ultimate destination in redemption. Souls pre-existed.

One can see the progression from traditional Kabbalah to New Age Kabbalah in the way man is viewed. Traditional Hasidic Kabbalah teaches that Jewish people have a special role in redemption and have an additional, higher, more divine aspect of soul called the *neshama*. Hasidic author Chaim Dalfin wrote: "a Jew is not a creation of God, rather a 'part' of God; therefore a Jew is able to go beyond the boundaries imposed by nature. The reason is, a Jew is not a creation of God; rather a Jew is godliness as he expresses himself in creation through a *neshomah*."[19] The great traditional Hasidic scholar Adin Steinsaltz wrote in his classic book, *The Thirteen Petalled Rose*:

> In its profoundest being, the soul of man is a part of the Divine and, in this respect, is a manifestation of God in the world. To be sure, the world as a whole may be viewed as a divine manifestation, but the world remains as something else than God, while the soul of man, in its depths, may be considered to be a part of God. Indeed, only man, by virtue of his divine soul, has the potential, and some of the actual capacity, of God Himself.[20]

More New Age Kabbalists have expanded this notion of the divinity of the Jewish soul to include all people:

> Jewish mysticism opens up the understanding of God to include God as Immanent Being, present in all life. The Holy Sparks exist within vessels as small as a tiny insect or blade of grass...If God exists in all life, then we humans are part of God. The Oneness of God includes us too...Thus the *Sh'ma*[21] can be seen as a call to become aware of that spark of divinity within ourselves. To nourish it. To help it expand... And it is a call to honor the presence of holiness in all living beings, because they too are part of God. And it is a call to see the connection, the Oneness of us all.[22]

The Fall and Redemption

Because of the "breaking of the vessels," mentioned above, and the Fall of Man, divine sparks (our souls) are trapped and need to be released and reunited with their source and with one another. The restoration of the image of God in man occurs through connection with the upper spiritual realms and the influx of divine energy flowing down from above. The goal is unification with God, becoming like God, eventually being reabsorbed into the divine. Traditional Kabbalists strictly observed the Mosaic Law and rabbinic traditions and embraced humility, righteousness, study and spiritual union. Observing the *mitzvot* (commandments) releases the divine sparks in the world and in ourselves. In this way we purify our souls and help mend the broken world. This is *Tikkun Olam*, correcting or rebuilding the universe. In Tikkun Olam the idea is to partner with God in redeeming ourselves, redeeming the world—and arguably ultimately God! A Kabbalist's job is to free divine sparks and his actions help unite the male and female Sephirot above. By realigning them and facilitating the flow of divine energy in the upper world and down to the lower, he participates with God in bringing redemption. According to Kabbalah, our purpose is to learn to receive light from God as his vessels. Traditional Kabbalah teaches a complex form of reincarnation with eventual resurrection when the Messiah comes. When a critical point is reached in the process of releasing divine sparks through Tikkun Olam, Messiah facilitates the removal of all barriers to the flow of divine light. Ultimately all of creation will attain oneness and reunification with its divine essence. New Age-oriented Kabbalah diminishes the messianic expectation and magnifies the aspect of reincarnation.

Other Kabbalistic Beliefs and Practices

Spirituality at its highest level is a direct experience of the divine and is beyond the rational, as God himself is beyond the rational and beyond description. Higher states of consciousness are reached through meditation on the Hebrew alphabet, especially through visualizing the Hebrew name of God, Yahweh. This practice is understood as fulfilling the verse: "I have set the Lord always before me" (Ps 16:8). Other Hebrew meditations involve mentally recombining the Hebrew letter in God's name and other words in order to focus the mind and open up to the upper worlds. Meditations on the attributes of deity are manifested in the Ten Sephirot. A key practice is to investigate "hidden" meanings in Torah, often revealed by *gematria*, a rabbinic practice of finding additional hidden meanings revealed through the manipulation and rearrangement of the letters of Hebrew words and finding significance through words having the same numeric value.

A very disturbing aspect of Kabbalah (found to a minor degree even in the traditional variety), is the idea of a spirit guide known as a *maggid*. "The *maggid* can be an Angel, or supermundane spirit that acts as a spokesman, conveying teachings to worthy scholars through dreams, a manic writing, or, in some fortunate circumstances through direct contact."[23] Kabbalah teaches that we can create angels through our actions and meditations. Jewish Renewal and New Age Kabbalist Rabbi David Cooper advocates meditation exercises invoking angels.[24] The meditator practices calling on spiritual entities, experiencing their presence, and even having them inhabit one's being. This is similar to practices of invocation and evocation that Wiccans consider to be advanced and risky. The real danger is that the spiritual entities evoked may not be who they represent themselves to be, for even Satan can appear as an angel of light.[25]

Varieties of Kabbalah

There are different types of Kabbalah even within Jewish tradition. The least controversial, Theosophical or Philosophical Kabbalah, focuses on study of Kabbalistic texts and the nature of reality as understood in Kabbalah. More controversial is Ecstatic, Prophetic or Meditative Kabbalah, using forms of meditation considered risky and somewhat dangerous, but regaining in popularity. Practical Kabbalah and Folk Kabbalah are the least respected practices, involving the famous red string and healing amulets. Also considered dangerous, and generally discouraged, Folk Kabbalah still exists in some Jewish circles. Traditional Kabbalah functions within a very Orthodox Jewish practice of the Law of Moses (and rabbinic additions).

The kind of Kabbalah we hear about today being practiced by Hollywood types is a sort of "Kabbalah Lite" that de-emphasizes Jewish Law and mixes in even more New Age ideas. Neokabbalah, found within the Jewish Renewal Movement also has a great deal of New Age influence. Hermetic Kabbalah, often spelled Cabala or Qabala, is a non-Jewish adaptation of Kabbalah. The Florentine scholar Pico della Mirandola (AD 1463–1494) mixed Kabbalah (separated from its Jewish context) with Hermetic (Egyptian) Magick.[26] This combination became the foundation of Western Occultism and Theosophy. Wiccan Stewart Farrar describes Kabbalah as "Probably the biggest single influence on the Western occult tradition." He says: "'Cabalistic magic' lays emphasis on the Tree of Life, with rites appropriate to its various Sephiroth. Just as 'the Tree of Life' is the 'ground-plan of Western occultism,' so Cabalistic concepts pervade the whole of Western magic."[27] The Masonic mystic Albert Pike wrote: "All truly dogmatic religions have issued from the Kabbalah and return to it: everything scientific and grand in the religious dreams of all the illuminati, Jacob Bœhme, Swedenborg, Saint-Martin, and others, is borrowed from the Kabbalah; all the Masonic associations owe to it their Secrets and their Symbols."[28]

So, What Do We Make of This?

Kabbalah is syncretistic at best. Even in its purest Orthodox Jewish form, it remains a mixture of Gnosticism and Neoplatonism, far from the worldview of the Bible. Scholars have recognized these pagan, Greek influences. The panentheistic god of Kabbalah, comprised of the "Ayn Sof" and the "Ten Sephirot," is *not* the God of the Bible. Kabbalah is an amalgam of biblical ideas with pagan Greek ideas of God and the universe. If even traditional Kabbalah is so far from the biblical worldview, how much farther away is that of its modern New Age varieties!

In practice, Kabbalah has parallels in occult "white magick." This Jewish variety of "magick" is understood only to be used for the repair of the world in harmony with God's will and through his power. It is not intended for self aggrandizement —quite the contrary:

> From the kabbalistic perspective, the goals of prayer are essentially theurgic. ...[T]he fundamental motive in prayer is...that the structure of the Godhead be rectified through unification and the sefirot be raised to their root in En Sof. Only through this tikkun can we bring about the desired influx backed down the tree of sefirot and into the world.[29]

There are many decent people (humanly speaking) practicing Kabbalah, and they may find our evaluation harsh, but we must conclude that Kabbalah is a false theology, a false gospel, and a counterfeit salvation. Studying Kabbalah is *not* something in which a Christian should seek spiritual benefit.

Can We Learn Anything Positive?

We can appreciate the values of humility, holiness, mercy, prayer and religious devotion emphasized by traditional Jewish Kabbalists and, to some degree even among New Age Kabbalists. Traditional Kabbalah reinvigorated traditional Judaism by giving everyday obedience new spiritual meaning. As Christians, we also believe that serving God in everyday life has cosmic relevance and great spiritual meaning. We work toward the advancement of the Kingdom of God in all that we do in accord with God's will. Obeying God *is* spiritual! But our obedience is found first in our Messiah Jesus, who, in perfectly obeying God's law was able to be our Savior. In him, God saves us from our sins and remakes us in his image.

On a philosophical level, Kabbalah attempted to solve the problem of God being an absolute unity and yet creating a world of diversity. In its approach, however, there is both a confusion between the Creator and the creature and also a disjuncture between God in his ontological essence and in his economic expression in creation and redemption. As Christians we know that God is, on an *eternal* level, *both* unity and diversity. God is eternally one in essence and three in his persons. In *both* creation and redemption all three persons of the Trinity have a role. We need to recapture the excitement in studying the deep mysteries of God. We have a sure and infallible guide in the Scriptures of the Old and New Testaments. By understanding the Scriptures in their grammatical and historical context and interpreting Scripture by Scripture, we find life's ultimate answers, not through mystical interpretations and mystical experiences. Thank God for his truth!

> So then, just as you received Messiah Jesus as Lord, continue to live in him, rooted and built up in him, strengthened in the faith as you were taught, and overflowing with thankfulness. See to it that no one takes you captive through hollow and deceptive philosophy, which depends on human tradition and the basic principles of this world rather than on Messiah. For in Messiah all the fullness of the Deity lives in bodily form, and you have been given fullness in Messiah, who is the head over every power and authority.
>
> —Rabbi Saul (Paul), Colossians 2:6–10

5

GNOSTICISM
ANCIENT & MODERN

DAVE DOVETON

But the conflict between monotheism and paganism is not merely historical; it is a recurrent battle for the soul of man that has never ceased.

—Jeffrey Satinover

THE QUEST FOR THE GREATER TRUTH

It had been a long and tiring day. I flopped into a chair and limply flicked on the television. What I saw held me riveted: standing behind the altar beside the priest in a Roman Catholic church service, were the leaders of several other religions—Hindu, Buddhist and Muslim. I was surprised; I had only previously heard of such multifaith services, but never actually seen one.

I am an Anglican priest, and in 2007 I arrived in Mauritius, an island in the warm turquoise waters of the Indian Ocean, to take on a new pastoral charge. I found a multi-cultural community living in largely peaceful religious coexistence. I was stunned, however, by the television broadcast. Surely "multifaith" worship services only happen at the Parliament of World Religions, or in places like the "wild west" coast of the United States, where the most exotic new cults seem to blossom. Or do they? On January 5, 2008 the new Episcopal bishop of Nevada was blessed at his consecration by a Muslim imam, a Hindu chaplain, a Baha'i leader, a Jewish rabbi, a Baptist minister and a Roman Catholic bishop.[1] In June of the previous year in the Episcopal Diocese of Newark twin boys were baptized in a ceremony which used Jewish and Muslim blessings. The fact is that these things are happening not at the level of fringe groups and maverick bishops, but at local church level and in the lives of ordinary churchgoers. An Episcopal church in New Jersey advertises that every Sunday a liturgical reading will come from a nonbiblical source, probably the scripture of another religion.

In a pastoral message distributed just before the dawn of the new millennium, Canadian Anglican Bishop Michael Ingham predicted:

> The big emerging movement of the future—still young but now unstoppable—will be global interfaith consciousness. Human nature has not ceased to be spiritual, but human beings have become tired of the relentless and destructive competitiveness of religions each claiming to be the only way.... People by the millions are now crossing religious boundaries ... and meeting each other as human beings and as fellow seekers after truth.[2]

The message is clear—we are all fellow seekers after truth, and we need to discover the truth each possesses. Father Bede Griffith says that the time has come "to share in one another's spiritual riches."[3]

Such inclusivity implies that there is nothing final or complete about the revelation of Jesus Christ. It also redefines our spiritual quest—we should be looking for a truth of which our religions are only a part. Matthew Fox, an ex-Roman Catholic priest, asserts that divinity is greater than any religion: "There is one underground river—but there are many wells into that river: an African well, a Taoist well, a Buddhist well, a Jewish well, a Muslim well, a goddess well, a Christian well and aboriginal wells. Many wells, but one river."[4]

Such theories are not new. In the first three centuries of the church a family of unorthodox Christian groups arose known collectively as Gnostic churches. They took Jesus as a savior figure but believed there was deeper truth behind doctrine, to be discovered through myth. A broad and varied philosophy, Gnosticism had Indian, Asian and Mediterranean roots. By opening themselves to pagan belief systems, these groups produced teachings which were ultimately anti-Christian in perspective. Gnostic belief was vigorously opposed by the early Church Fathers, many of whom wrote extensive tracts against the heresy. Though Gnostic influence waned, aspects of it resurfaced during the Middle Ages, mainly in sects such as the Cathars and the Templars.

Thomas Molnar traces universalist tendencies back to humanist thinkers of the Middle Ages, a syncretism of Greek philosophies, Eastern religious belief systems and Hermetism.[5] At the end of the fourteenth century a Catholic philosopher, Giovanni Pico della Mirandola advocated an amalgamation of Christian and pagan beliefs in nine hundred theses. He then attempted unsuccessfully to defend this universal religion before a commission of theologians and churchmen.

Our century has its own syncretizing thinkers. Michael Ingham, a heterodox bishop, attempts to adapt Christian belief to a more profound "cosmic religion" of mankind. John Shelby Spong advances twelve theses to reformulate the Christian faith so that it can be blended into the universal religion.[6]

Enter the Goddess

> Our Mother who is within us, we celebrate your many names. Your wisdom come. Your will be done, unfolding from the depths within us.[7]

Some speak of God as the underground river with many wells; some of a mountain to be reached by many paths. Matthew Fox suggests that though different religions worship the same God, they call him by a variety of names, or as he puts it—divinity has multiple faces,[8] including a feminine face.

In the Greco-Roman world the vast array of pagan religions and philosophical schools included a group of religions known as the Mystery Religions. Many of these worshiped gods and goddesses linked to the cycles of death and rebirth in nature. The "mother goddess" in particular embodied these mysterious forces. She was a cosmic Matriarch and source of life, invoked by many names and described in various ways. Aspects of the mother goddess are found in Isis, the great mother Cybele, Demeter and Kore-Persephone, among others.[9]

In the Gnostic systems this divine female principle reappears under different guises. Valentinian Gnostics taught that Sophia was the Divine Feminine power; both the mother goddess that created the cosmos and the one who brings enlightenment to the Gnostic Christian. This goddess Sophia has many of the attributes of the pagan goddess[10] Ishtar or Astarte. Contemporary feminist theologians like Carter Hayward[11] openly reject the Trinity and advocate devotion to "Sophia" and "Christa," which are nothing more than versions of the Divine Feminine, and display a pagan understanding of the godhead. Gnostic liturgies such as the Eucharistic prayer are found in the Gnostic Acts of Thomas, in which God is addressed as both Mother and Father.[12] Today, the liturgies of many mainline churches reflect the convictions of senior church leaders who are responsible for the spiritual oversight of hundreds of thousands of souls. These leaders deliberately speak of God in terms of a dyad—male and female.[13]

Valentinian Gnosticism was the most influential form and posed the greatest threat to the church. Valentinians could recite orthodox Christian creeds, yet what they believed and understood by those creeds was quite unorthodox. Irenaeus warned, " Such persons are, to outward appearances, sheep, for they seem to be like us, from what they say in public, repeating the same words of confession that we do; but inwardly they are wolves."[14] The Valentinians ostensibly believed in one God; however, they insisted that a distinction be drawn between images of God in Scripture and what those images represent. They maintained that descriptions of God as Lord, King or Judge were only images of God, not the reality. The real God should be understood as the "ultimate source" or what Valentinus called "the depth."[15]

In some Christian denominations today we see features similar to Valentinian Gnosticism. The outward forms are Christian, but underneath lies a Gnostic belief system. Those who abandon Trinitarian terminology for God believe, as did the Gnostics, that since we can only talk about God by analogy,[16] we may substitute other analogies for the orthodox Trinitarian formula of Father, Son and Holy Spirit, such as Compassionate Mother, Beloved Child and Life-giving Womb.[17]

Tertullian denounced the Valentinians for this practice, saying they had divided God into a "dispersed and mutilated deity" and were returning to the pagan myths they had heard as children from their nursemaids.[18] Irenaeus countered the Gnostic teachings that humans can name God, saying that God makes, but humanity is made.[19] Gnostic teachings about the Godhead were little more than human creations, whereas humans are creatures and cannot usurp the place of the Creator, who reveals himself and names himself. The Scriptures name God as the Father, the Son and the Holy Spirit in the New Testament, and as the Lord, or Yahweh in the Old. If humans have the right to name God and thus to identify him, God is no longer the self-revealed God of the Bible. God as Father, Son and Holy Spirit gives way to any and all pagan, nonbiblical names.

Pagan Symbols in the Courts of the Lord

> Today, the occult penetrates the lowered defenses of the Christian tradition .... The entire symbology of Christianity yields to other, sometimes older symbologies with their underlying creeds and doctrines.[20]

Thomas Molnar's observation aptly describes the service that journalist Terry Mattingly attended in 1993 at the Cathedral of St. John the Divine in New York. Mattingly recorded the most meaningful moment of the service:

> Before the bread and wine were brought to the altar, the musicians offered a rhythmic chant that soared into the cathedral vault: "Praises to Obatala, ruler of the heavens; Praises to Yemenja, ruler of the waters of life; Praises to Ausar, ruler of Amenta, the realm of the ancestors; Praises to Ra and Ausar, rulers of the light and the resurrected soul."[21]

The invocation of ancient Egyptian and West African gods in a Christian cathedral beggars belief. Some Christian Protestant denominations are incorporating pagan, Gnostic belief systems into their worship by naming new gods and by including non-Christian symbols. Symbols are nonverbal ways of communicating the truths enshrined in our faith. The apostle Paul uses the "cross" not only to refer to Christ's finished work of redemption, but as a symbol for the entire gospel message.[22] The Bible uses many such symbols: lamb of God, dove, fire, living water, etc. Such symbols have been used in Christian art, literature, theology and worship to help us define our relationship with God and communicate with the Lord in worship.

Grace Cathedral in San Francisco has a side chapel with walls adorned by sacred symbols from Islam, Hinduism, Judaism and Buddhism.[23] This interfaith chapel ostensibly provides a "sacred space" where a person of any faith can pray, but such symbols import a new theology of worship into a Christian church. A "multifaith space" denies the exclusive claim of Jesus to be the only Savior by acknowledging the existence of other gods, creeds and doctrines—all antithetical to Christian belief. It is a short step from here to the practice of the Carpocratian Gnostics who maintained images of Jesus along with pagan images and statues of Greek philosophers and had "modes of honouring those images, after the manner of the Gentiles."[24]

Goddess Worship and the Lady of the Labyrinth

Pagan symbolism in Christian churches sometimes occurs almost unnoticed in architectural features or trendy "spiritualities" such as reciting the goddess rosary in a Lutheran church[25] or in the interdenominational Magdalen Group.[26] The same Grace Cathedral in San Francisco boasts a beautifully paved terrazzo stone area,[27] in which is engraved an ancient labyrinth pattern, which visitors and worshippers at the cathedral are invited to "walk." The labyrinth is copied from the one built into the floor at Chartres Cathedral in France at the beginning of the thirteenth century. The pattern of the Chartres labyrinth has both Gnostic and Sufi symbolism and is based on alchemical and astrological numerology and geometry. According to Hermetic schools,

> Cathedrals such as Chartres are portals to a higher state of consciousness. The Chartres mystery school taught the esoteric knowledge of how we can apprehend representations of sacred reality with our senses and emotions in a special manner. The initiatory training of the Chartres School allowed initiates to experience a Cathedral (or any other sacred place) as a reality on the threshold of the spiritual dimension through which we can gain access to an actual experience of ultimate reality.[28]

Walking the labyrinth does not mean strolling along it to admire its ancient art. The stated purpose of the Grace labyrinth is to help us "hear our wisdom and the wisdom attempting to reach us."[29] By walking the labyrinth, we give up conscious control, becoming receptive to altered states of consciousness. We are exhorted to allow the mystery to live within us and to open ourselves to the "deep knowledge."[30] There are three stages[31] to walking the labyrinth—release or purgation, receiving or illumination, and then the return to the world. Experiencing the sacred, receiving the illumination, and being transformed—but hang on a minute! Doesn't that sound like worship to you? No wonder this labyrinth is called a "church without walls." People with any religion or no religion can take part in this mystical religious ritual. However, what connects the participant with the divine is not Christ. There is no need for a redeemer because we all have the divine within; we just need to realize it and experience it. The labyrinth turns out to be a new model of spiritual cosmology. It describes God's relation to the world in a new way. But this new spiritual understanding of reality turns out to be quite old.

For Lauren Artress, who is the driving force behind the use of labyrinths, walking the labyrinth is a spiritual process that leads us to experience the "god within," the "sacred feminine." To be transformed, we need to understand God in a totally different way. "In the old traditional understanding of God," says Artress, "God is 'He'—the God in the sky, the transcendent God who is out there, who keeps all the rules. What people need to discover is the other side of God. That is the God who is within, and many people experience that as the sacred feminine."[32]

The labyrinth was used in pagan worship of the goddess as far back as Neolithic times. It recurred in Cretan and Minoan mythology, from whence it migrated into Greek religious mythology. Apparently, *labyrus* means a double-headed axe, [33] and the labyrinth was "the house of the double axe," or the temple of the goddess in which mystery rituals were celebrated. It was used to describe a pagan understanding of our relationship with the divine, and as a means of communicating with the goddess.

The Primacy of Experience

"If it feels right it must be right" is the common slogan that makes experience the ultimate authority. Recently, Marcus Borg, a famous biblical scholar, was giving a testimony of how he abandoned orthodox Christian belief. Persuaded that all religions are the product of culture, he concluded that religion's purpose was to serve our psychological and social needs. In his early thirties he had several experiences which he describes as "nature mysticism" (the divine can be found in nature).

> These experiences, besides being ecstatic, were for me "ah-ha" moments. They gave me a new understanding of the meaning of the word "God." I realized that "God" does not refer to a supernatural being "out there".... Rather I began to see the word "God" refers to "the sacred" at the centre of existence, the "holy mystery" which is all around us and within us. God is the non-material ground and source and presence.[34]

Borg describes the abandonment of a theistic worldview (in which God the Creator is distinct from his creation) in favor of a worldview in which nature is divine. This total shift was based purely on mystical experience. Tertullian remarked that the Marcionite Gnostics depended first on their sense experience before arriving at their false view of God: "They ...suppose that another god must be assumed to exist, because they are more able to censure than deny Him whose existence is so evident, deriving all their thoughts about God from the deductions of sense."[35] Irenaeus vehemently attacked the Carpocratians: "So unbridled is their madness, that they declare they have in their power all things which are irreligious and impious, and are at liberty to practice them; for they maintain that things are evil or good, simply in virtue of human opinion."[36]

The current false prophets are merely putting new form to old beliefs. The goal of the Gnostic was to bypass the rational mind to achieve "enlightenment" or *gnosis*. The goal of the new Gnostics is to *pursue the experience* of the divine. Says Matthew Fox:

> It is clear that once we return to the depth or core of religion we find much more than dogmas, concepts, institutions, commands. We find a striving for experience of the divine, however that be spoken of, we find both form and formlessness, male and female, experience and practice. We also find that in their core and depth we do not encounter many different religions so much as one experience that is expressed variously and with great diversity and color flowing in the name of different traditions and cultures.[37]

Embracing a pagan-Gnostic enlightenment experience, and believing that the divine is within all of us goes hand in hand with abandoning doctrinal orthodoxy. Says Borg, "Now I see that it is not a question of belief, and there is much that I do not believe. I do not believe that Christianity is the only way of salvation, or that the Bible is the revealed will of God, or that Jesus is the unique Son of God."[38]

Similar sentiments are expressed by Ann Holmes Redding, an ordained priest in the Episcopal Church, who adheres simultaneously to Islam and Christianity.[39] When she heard a Muslim cleric teaching on Islamic methods of prayer, she was so moved that she was drawn in total surrender to Islam. Redding does not believe in the doctrine of original sin, nor does she have an orthodox understanding of the Trinity. She believes that Jesus is only divine inasmuch as he was a human being, and all humans share in divinity. Walter Melnyk, a former Episcopal priest, believes in two mutually contradictory faiths, "walking between" the worlds of pagan druidry and Christianity,[40] while Rev. Chris Horseman, an English vicar, holds a degree in white witchcraft.[41] This faith is not an assent to a creed or a coherent body of doctrinal formulation.

Christian faith means believing in what God has done for us in Christ, and such belief must be expressed in a rational body of doctrine. The reworked Gnostic faith is without substance, based on the ephemeral ecstatic experiences of the individual.

The Problem: Ignorance and Forgetfulness

The Gnostic idea of salvation is similar to that found in certain forms of Hinduism and Buddhism. Gnostics believe that the cause of sin and suffering in the world is not sin but ignorance. Gnostics look to salvation not from sin, but from spiritual ignorance through the attainment of *gnosis* (or enlightenment). The Gnostic Gospel of Philip states: "Ignorance is the mother of [all evil]. Ignorance will eventuate in [death, because] those that came from [ignorance] neither were nor [are] nor shall be. [But those who are in the truth] will be perfect when all truth is revealed."[42]

Exactly the same beliefs are reappearing in astonishingly similar forms. A statement from the Episcopal Diocese of Northern Michigan asserts: "We do harmful and evil things to ourselves and one another, not because we are bad, but because we are blind to the beauty of creation and ourselves. In other words we are ignorant of who we truly are."[43]

As in most pagan systems, human trauma and pain are the result of a fault *in creation* (or, as for the Marcionites, the *fact of creation*). Valentinian Gnostics said that all materiality was formed from three experiences: terror, pain and confusion. Thus, suffering is part of existence and removed from the sphere of human culpability. Gnostics do not accept the concept of the Fall. Since there was no Fall and hence no sin, there is no need of a Savior who pays the price for sin. Substitutionary atonement is meaningless. Says John Spong,

> Human beings did not fall from perfection into sin as the church had taught for centuries; we were evolving, and indeed are still evolving, into higher levels of consciousness. Thus the basic myth of Christianity that interpreted Jesus as a divine emissary who came to rescue the victims of the fall from the results of their original sin became inoperative. So did the interpretation of the cross of calvary as the moment of divine sacrifice when the ransom for sin was paid.[44]

Several centuries ago, Hippolytus described the Gnostic Jesus as "the messenger (who) wakes the man to his soul's true identity—to know its heavenly origin and consequently its present state—a fall into material existence." Spong is abandoning the orthodox biblical teaching on the Fall and presenting a Gnostic Jesus who accomplished nothing on the cross.

It is no surprise to see the emasculation of the doctrine of atonement from modern theologies and liturgies. Some churches now use the Gnostic gospels in their services and announce that "the theology of this worship is not focused on the sacrificial nature of Jesus but on the relational wisdom of Jesus."[45]

THE PERSON OF JESUS

For the presiding Bishop of the Episcopal Church, Jesus is the route to God for Christians, whereas people of other faiths approach God through their own social contexts, relating to God and experiencing God in human relationships.[46] Thus for her, Jesus is one way, but not the exclusive way to God. The Centre for Progressive Christianity (with many denominational affiliates) echoes this approach to the person of Jesus. It has "found an approach to God through the life and teaching of

Jesus" and "recognize[s] the faithfulness of other people who have other names for the way to God's realm, and acknowledge that their ways are true for them, as our ways are true for us."[47]

Thus Jesus is not the unique revelation and incarnation of God, but merely the exemplar of a relationship with God. If Jesus is the way to God only for Christians, then he is not the universal Savior of humankind. If Jesus is reduced to personal and subjective experience, he becomes merely a savior figure, not the Savior. Orthodox doctrine holds that Jesus reveals God not just in a private, interior or subjective way, but that he reveals God publicly. His death on the cross is a public fact, public truth and Christian truth is public universal truth. Jesus is Savior for all. The gospel affects the transformation not only of the individual soul, but of the world.

For most Gnostics, the task of Jesus is a provisional one; he is their teacher and guide until they reach the level of an enlightened one. He is not the Truth, but the revealer of the truth that God is within us: "[Matthew] said, Lord I want [to see] that place of life.... The Lord said, Everyone who has known himself has seen [it...]."[48]

The aim of the Gnostic was to achieve enlightenment through gnosis and to progress from being merely a Christian to being "a christ." The Gospel of Philip speaks of one who receives the "power of the cross" and who is no longer a Christian, but a christ. The person who achieves spiritual transformation also achieves spiritual insight and becomes what they see: "You saw the spirit, you became spirit; you saw Christ, you became Christ."[49] An official American Episcopal Church statement goes even further. It describes Jesus as the revealer of the truth that "...all persons are the living Christ. Each and every human being, as a human being, is knit together in God's spirit, and thus an anointed one—Christ."

This Jesus is not the only Son of God who became incarnate, entering history as a unique individual at a particular time. He is, rather, consubstantial with creation, thus making all creation part of God's "body." All creation is the incarnation, as in the Gnostic Gospel of Thomas in which Jesus says: "It is I who am the light which is above them all, it is I who am the all. From me did the all come forth, and unto me did the all extend. Split a piece of wood and I am there. Lift up a stone, and you will find me there."[50] One of the Church Fathers called the Valentinians "Dionysian," because their Jesus was closer to the Greek god Dionysius. Dionysius died *as creation*—a sacrifice to redeem the world and to bring it to rebirth. This belief is opposed to orthodox teaching that Jesus died *as sacrifice for sin*, to redeem a fallen humanity and a fallen world. The Gnostic teaching emphasizes the *tragedy of the human condition*; the orthodox teaching emphasizes the *sinfulness of human nature*.

Salvation through Altered Consciousness

The Gnostic Jesus is a teacher of wisdom or gnosis. His purpose was to call people to *metanoia*. This metanoia is not defined as the New Testament defines it—a change of mind when faced with Christ's call, resulting in a reversal of direction in our lives. The Christian metanoia turns to face an external call from God. In contrast, Gnostic metanoia turns inward to face the soul and the god within. Inward examination of the soul is necessary for a person to realize its fragmented state, but also for awareness of the "divine spark within." The next step is to undergo a process of internal transformation through altered states of consciousness. This was variously expressed as a "waking from sleep" or passing from "darkness to light."

Both ancient and modern Gnostics aim at self-knowledge—this is a similar aim to that of modern psychotherapy. Gnostics want to dispel ignorance by internal self-examination. Self-identity then becomes crucial. If I find out who I really am by special insight, I can overcome the evils of doubt, despair and confusion that hinder the progress of my soul. For the Gnostics, "understanding" releases the soul from bondage to the "planetary powers" or cosmic forces that are to blame for the imprisonment of the soul. At St. Andrew's Episcopal Church in Seattle courses are taught in "evolutionary astrology." This amazing "new" spiritual discipline, "begins with the premise that each person is a soul that is in the process of progressive evolution and eventually toward reconnection with the 'Divine.'" Says Dan Keusal, teacher of the course: "Just as the Magi followed a star to find Jesus, we can look to the stars for help in discerning 'Spirit's plan for us.'"[51] One must "be true to oneself." The Gnostic Gospel of Truth held that each person must receive "his own name" (his true identity). The Kingdom of God becomes a state of transformed consciousness and self discovery. All concept of the rule of God is abandoned.

Mysteries that Transform

According to the Gnostic Gospel of Philip, transformation occurs through the acquisition of *gnosis*. Sacramental rituals are the means whereby the Gnostic participates in the mysteries that transform. This gospel is a baptismal catechesis and describes the sacrament of baptism as the "Bridal Chamber," the most important of the sacraments or mysteries. According to this teaching, the ultimate aim is the reintegration or healing of the soul, so that eventually it can be reunited with the "ground of being" or "the depth." The impersonal divinity of Gnostic belief is what might be called in modern terms "the great stream of consciousness, the unseen force that unites everything." As a contemporary writer on the use of the labyrinth writes: "Western culture is beginning to realize that the soul is not only in the body; more accurately the body is in the soul. There is a world soul and our task is to en-soul the world. We have lost connection to that unseen force that unites us."[52]

Through this mystery the Gnostic Christian achieves a transcendence of all the binary opposites of the created world: "Light and darkness, life and death, right and left, are brothers of one another. They are inseparable. Because of this, neither are the good good nor the evil evil, nor is life life, nor death death. For this reason each one will dissolve into its earliest origin. But those who are exalted above the world are indissoluble, eternal."[53] The supreme binary is transcended in the male/female opposition; this occurs in the "bridal chamber," so called because it symbolizes the reuniting of male with female. Ultimately this also symbolizes the fusion of the individual soul with the divine.

Monism is the essence of pagan belief: the creation is part of the Creator, rather like a spider spins his web out of his own bodily substance. It is in reality the worship of nature; it sees the created universe as part of God or, as Sallie McFague puts it, "the body of God."[54] The monist vision of reality has far-reaching consequences. As the famous adage goes, "ideas have consequences." As this vision takes root in the soil of the church and the academy, theology and liturgy gradually adopt the rhythms and cycles of nature. The Church of All Saints Hoboken, NJ proudly states that a new creation season has been included in the liturgical year, and worshipers are welcome to bring up symbols of nature such as grass and rocks to the altar, together with the bread and the wine at the time of the offering.[55] At Grace Episcopal Church, Syracuse, New York, the Reverend James Knowles performed a Native American ceremonial cleansing ritual in which smoke was fanned toward worshipers using a feather. These were then asked to face the four cardinal points of the compass while Knowles said a prayer to the sun, the moon, the turtle and the alligator.

CONCEPTS OF TIME AND HISTORY

Feminist scholar Sallie McFague asks, "What if all life—God's and ours, as well as that of all others on earth—was seen to be on a continuum, more like a circle or a recycle symbol, than like a dualistic hierarchy?"[56] Monism has implicit within it not only a cyclical concept of the unity of all things, but a cyclical concept of time itself. Mircea Eliade speaks of the "time of the eternal returns."[57] The meaning of life is interpreted in terms of the cycles of nature, specifically the cycle of birth, growth to maturity, degradation, death, then rebirth. In pagan religions, the gods, a part of creation, die and rise again in harmony with the rhythms and periods of the seasons.

In Christian understanding, time is linear, with a beginning and an end. History is not reversible or repeatable. The end of history will reveal the meaning and value of people's lives, their actions and behavior, because outside of time stands our Creator God who is also the Judge. The end will reveal the triumph of his saving plan for mankind and the restoration of creation—the new heavens and new earth, brought to even greater heights of glory than they had at the beginning. Because God stands outside time and history, all creation is contingent on him and is accountable to him.

For the Gnostics, history and the world have no meaning—they are only to be escaped: "Once wakened from his mortal sleep, the Gnostic understands that he bears no responsibility for the primordial catastrophe the myth narrates for him, and hence he has no relation with Life, the World, and History."[58] In contrast, genuine Christianity affirms the meaning and importance of history, reason and faith. All three are necessary for a proper understanding of God's relationship with the world.

Consequences for the Church

Many leaders in today's Gnosticizing movements know that they are changing people's beliefs, but naïvely think such change is positive. Christ Church Cathedral in Houston, Texas has a group that meets to study the Gnostic Gospel of Mary (Magdalene). The resident canon theologian at the cathedral, Betty C. Adams, has written a book promoting the acceptance and study of Gnostic teachings about Mary Magdalene. Says Adams: "The public seems to have a limitless appetite for anything to do with Mary Magdalene, and it's changing our beliefs in subtle—and not-so-subtle—ways."[59]

Thomas Molnar calls us to be alert to the penetration of occult doctrines and creeds into our thinking, as occurred within Gnosticism. "These bring to our faltering contemplative and active values not an increased spirituality as it is superficially assumed, but a call to pantheism and nihilism."[60] Once we include pagan symbols and myths into our thinking, we begin to include pagan cosmologies and pagan gods. Scholars who have studied the dynamics of Gnostic belief warn us of the ultimate danger of being inclusive in our approach to faith. The inevitable consequence is a rapid devolution into the embrace of evil. Modern theologies such as "sacred nature" and the "divine feminine" follow the same path. "Their embrace of nature as divine inevitably forces them to include not just matter, but evil as well within the Godhead."[61]

When a resurgent Gnostic paganism, accompanied by a rising occultism, begins to replace the void left by a Christianity in decadence, the foundational elements of reason and history lose their importance in the structure of our belief. Truth is held in mystery, not in the Word of God or in reason. Reason is replaced by irrationalism and the Gnostic division of human beings into two classes—the enlightened beings who transcend the created world, and the profane class that remains in ignorance. Faith, understood as belief in a coherent body of teachings to which a community mutually assents, is replaced by a spirituality that seeks to unite opposites by the integration of all things, beginning with the fusion of the individual soul with the divine.

History loses its meaning and its place as the arena of God's self-revelation. It has no beginning and does not proceed to an ultimate end and goal under the control and direction of a sovereign and transcendent Creator. Linear history is replaced by a cyclical concept of time, with no external transcendent reference to impart meaning. Belief and worship focus on the natural world and its cycles. It should not surprise us if our calendar and dating systems are subsumed one day into a larger pagan frame of time measurement.

Another consequence flows from the fact that paganism is ultimately the divinization of nature, the belief that Creator and creature share the same substance. This divinization applies not only to the rocks and trees, but, as Jeffrey Satinover observes, to inner human nature as well. Our human instincts become divinized and thus we allow instincts to rule us—the instincts of pleasure, desire, and self-gratification are given free reign. "In thus spiritualizing the instincts, pagan worship tends naturally to the violent, the hedonistic and the orgiastic....violent intoxication, temple prostitution, the ritual slaughter of enemies, self-mutilation, even child sacrifice: all these historical phenomena can be understood not as pathological, but as predictable, and points to the unfettering of human nature."[62]

In one sense Michael Ingham is right—human beings have not ceased to be spiritual. However, the "big emerging movement of the future" turns out not to be some wonderful new utopian, multifaith phenomena, but the age-old pagan procession of idolatry. Those Christians who succumb to the temptation to join in will be hitching their caravan to a truly pagan procession.

6

THE BROAD RED ROAD TO DESPAIR

AMERICAN INDIAN ANIMISM

MARCUS TOOLE

ANIMISM

Native religion is broadly classified as Animism. Animism is any religious system in which daily spirituality is primarily focused on interacting with spirits found in the environment. Though they differ in many ways, traditional Cree and Tlingit religions both see the physical world as a shadow of a more real spirit world. Animals, plants, rocks, mountains, the sun and even the earth itself have their conscious, self-aware, living counterpart in the spirit world. These spiritual entities are more real, and in many ways more important, than the physical objects that represent them. To the Cree Traditional elder (medicine man) or the Tlingit Ix (shaman), everything we see is a shadow of a more real spiritual realm. In addition, Native people tend to describe their relationships to these spirit entities using kinship terms. Cree people refer to most of these spirits as grandfathers. Earth is called Mother, or Mother Earth. Tlingit classify this spirit world in terms of their system of totems. Animal spirits represented on the totem of a given clan share kinship with that clan. For example, Raven is Brother to half of the Tlingit clans. These clans are called Raven clans. The other half of Tlingit clans are brethren to Eagle and are called Eagle clans.[1] From the Cree medicine man's perspective, one cannot see reality until one sees the spirit world behind the shadows. Even Cree Christians talk about the importance of seeing spiritual realities behind the physical realities.

The Creator

Animism can be monotheistic (belief in one God), dualistic (belief in two equal but opposite ultimate powers as god), polytheistic (belief in multiple gods) or pantheistic (belief that the universe itself is God). Cree religion, Tlingit religion, Cherokee religion, and Sioux religion (and, as far as I know, most forms of North American animism) are monotheistic. Most Native American Canadians, First Nations Canadians, and Native Alaskans who adhere to Native Medicine believe in a single Creator, High God, High Spirit or Great Spirit to which ultimate honor is due. Apparently, much South American animism is polytheistic, while Asian animism tends to be dualistic or pantheistic. The Tlingit traditional word for "Creator" literally translates into "the over-my-head spirit." Cree people call this ultimate spirit Manato in Cree and "the Creator" in English. The Cree see Manato as a personal, thinking being who communicates through dreams and visions, who shows likes and dislikes, and who dispenses curses and blessings. Though Manato is personal, the Cree medicine men see the Creator as somewhat removed from the physical world. Consequently, the grandfathers (localized spirits in the environment) have a place equal to, or even greater than that of Manato in the daily spiritual life of Cree religion.

Mother Earth

In Cree and most plains cultures, the most important spirit after Manato is Mother Earth, who gave birth to the Cree people. Like other plains people, the Cree believe that humans came out of the womb of Mother Earth, who is thus revered as the source of human life. Cree, Sioux and others understand the sweat lodge to be the womb of mother earth, into which they enter when participating in sweat lodge activities. They see themselves enveloped by a powerful spiritual entity and in some way becoming part of her.[2]

Cree do not understand Mother Earth to be a nonpersonal life force or earth consciousness. Mother Earth is an offendable, personal entity who, like the Creator, communicates through dreams and visions, has likes and dislikes and can bless or curse. Most Cree Christians I know see Mother Earth and other grandfathers as real but demonic entities. I have had enough experience with the Cree spirit world to know that these things have an objective existence, external to human imagination. The grandfathers and other animistic spirits should be understood to be real, wicked, but finite creatures ultimately subject to the Lordship of Christ.

In Cree Religion, Mother Earth gave means for interacting with Manato and with the rest of the grandfathers. She gave tobacco, the pipe, sweet grass and sage to be used in worship, and the sweat lodge so that humans can reenter her womb and be reunited to her in an intimate way.[3] Tobacco was given as a healing agent and as a means for communicating with and honoring the spirit world. Whenever any plant is picked for ceremonial purposes, tobacco is placed where it is taken from the earth. Tobacco is given as an offering to heal Mother Earth and to honor and appease the grandfather behind the medicine taken.

The physical plant, fungus or root is seen as a shadow of a spirit behind it. When the traditionalist uses an object from nature, the spirit behind the object must be respected and thanked. As Cree slaughter a deer, for example, they repeatedly say: "Hai hai, hai hai, hai hai!" which means "Thank you, thank you, thank you!" The deer spirit is thanked for giving its body for food. The deer spirit, if sufficiently appeased, will take on another body and give itself again as food in exchange for honor. Parts of the deer's body will then be used for ceremonial purposes to honor the deer spirit, which often enters the lodge where the ceremony is taking place. When animal spirits enter a lodge they often do so in a physically perceivable form and will receive offerings of tobacco, sweet grass, prayer, physical pain and even the spirit of a child in exchange for their favors.

The Pipe and Sweet Grass

The pipe is understood to be the conduit of spirit power between the medicine man (pipe bearer) and the spirit world. Brother Adolphus Kootenay, a former Sioux medicine man who converted to Christianity, says that the pipe represents a covenant between the medicine man, Mother Earth and the grandfather spirits from which he derives his power.[4] When the pipe is smoked, the tobacco spirit enters the body and imparts spirit power to the body and then sends the prayers of the medicine man through exhaled smoke up to the Creator. The tobacco spirit physically connects the medicine man to the Creator and other spirits worshiped. This is often shown pictorially in plains Native Art. According to Brother Adolphus, the pipe, the drum and other ceremonial objects invoke the spirits and make them locally present.

Brother Adolphus makes a reasonable argument that demonic spirits which are finite are more likely to be locally present in places where ceremonial objects are located. Because of this, he argues that those who frequent ceremonial places or objects will have a harder time fighting off temptations and other spiritual troubles because they are exposed to demons more often.[5] My ministry experience leads me to agree with Brother Adolphus. A good secondary reason to stay away from sweats and other traditional ceremonies is the potential for becoming a special object of attention on the part of a demon.

Because of its role as a conduit of spirit power and its relationship to tobacco, the pipe is perhaps the most sacred object in Cree religion. If worshipers fail to pray to and honor the spirit in the pipe, they risk death. Mishandling or otherwise disrespecting a pipe is one of the most dangerous things a human being can do. Brother Adolphus tells the story in his book of the day he finally decided to burn his pipe. Convinced that he would die the moment he put it in the fire, he stalled. Finally, he dropped it into the flames, closed his eyes, and waited for death. Instead, the stem of the pipe burned and the pipe stone itself broke apart in the fire.

Before entering any ceremony, traditionalists will wash themselves in the smoke of sweet grass or a mixture of sweet grass and another herb. This process of bathing in smoke is called "smudging." Sweet grass, buffalo grass, sage, cedar and other smudges are given by Mother Earth for cleansing people of spiritual impurities and for taking their prayers to the Creator or Manato. Tobacco, sweet grass and other smudges are mediators between humans and God and act as substitutes for the role of the Holy Spirit and Jesus. Traditionalists entering a Christian church will often say, "I pray the sweet grass way." On the other hand, a Christian offered sweet grass for smudging at a traditionalist wake will say, "I pray the Jesus way." When a Cree starts refusing sweet grass, persecution begins. The traditionalist community will accuse the Cree of converting to White Man's religion. Crees may go to church, but a Cree who does not attend ceremonies or participate in smudging at funerals is persecuted by the family and, at times, even by the tribal government. Traditionalists can tell the difference between real Christians who put away Native Spiritual practices and people who go to a Christian church and talk about believing in Jesus but who do not put away the worship of spirits.

Other Spirits and the Sundance

Other important grandfathers are the Eagle Spirit (also known as the Thunderbird Spirit), the Sun Spirit and the White Buffalo Spirit—all specifically associated with the Sundance. "Sundance" carries different meanings in different native cultures. In the Sioux version, male dancers traditionally have pieces of animal bone or metal inserted into the muscle of their chests, while women dancers have the bones inserted into their upper arms. Pregnant women and women in their menses share in the maternal essence of Mother Earth and are so filled with spirit power that if they come in contact with the pipe, they endanger the pipe and themselves. Consequently they must stay away from ceremonies where the pipe is used, such as Sundances and sweats. I heard one medeicine man say that when a woman gives birth she is doing the woman's Sundance. (The participation of women in the Sundance, the sweats and possessing and smoking pipes is a recent innovation according to the older people I know.) In the Sioux Sundance, a bone attached to the believer on one end is attached by a leather strap to a central pole. The dancer pulls against the pole for four days, unless the barbs pull out or the dancer collapses.

The Cree Sundance generally does not involve body piercing. The lodge is set up similarly. The center pole is taken from a tree with three prominent limbs coming out at the same level at the top. A low brush arbor fence surrounds the pole about ten or fifteen feet away, with an entry to the east. Three buffalo skulls dedicated to the buffalo spirit and the white buffalo spirit are placed on the east side of the pole. Twelve vertical posts are placed twenty or so feet farther out than the arbor fence and are connected by a ring of cross beams going around the lodge. Further cross beams connect the posts to the center pole and crisscross at the center pole teepee style. Shrubs and small trees are leaned against this ring of outer beams lean-to style, creating something of a shelter next to the outer wall where the dancers sleep at night. The space between the inner ring and the center pole is reserved for the dancers. They space themselves evenly around the center pole and dance in place, bouncing up and down, shaking a rattle and blowing a bone whistle, while channeling their mental and spiritual energy on the center pole. They do this for twelve hours a day during each of the three days of the dance without food or water for the entire three days.

At the top of the pole is the eagle's nest, which is a tangle of brush and cloth offerings woven around the center pole and the cross beams. This nest is dedicated to the thunderbird or eagle spirit which is seen as a messenger spirit that takes the channeled prayers to Manato. Grandfather Sun is also invoked and worshiped at the Sundance. During the six hours of rest the dancers have dreams and visions and receive animal guides. A special medicine man, called in English the "Sundance Maker," groans, chants, drums and performs pipe ceremonies throughout the three days. The Sundance Maker has attendants under him who help the dancers and make sure they follow protocol.

I know less about ceremonies such as the Chicken Dance, the Tea Dance, the Ghost Dance, and the Horse Dance. The Ghost Dance honors ancestors who have passed on and brings a new round to the circle of life. Associated with the invocation of ancestral spirits to fight enemies, the Ghost Dance is not Cree in origin. Some Cree traditionalists associate it with "bad medicine" (witchcraft). There seems to be a relationship between Ghost Dances and violence in the Hobbema community. When I hear about people doing a Ghost Dance, I expect an escalation in the violent crime rate in the community for the next several weeks. In a community in which Native Spirituality is practiced, just about every bad thing that happens gets attributed to bad medicine. Some of the bitterest conflicts in Hobbema are over someone accused of putting bad medicine on another person.[6]

Another component of Cree religion is the ceremonial feast eaten in honor of a deceased person. This feast is connected with a pipe ceremony and the people understand themselves to be eating with a relative or relatives who have died. Somehow the dead person eats through the mouth of the feaster. A plate is filled with food for the spirits and is sent outside and left in a nearby thicket. I ate at several feasts before I realized what they really were. On one occasion "bad medicine" was put on me as a consequence, and I was paralyzed for several hours the next day.

Culture and the Church

Christians engaged in Native ministry rightly share a strong desire to be sensitive to Native cultures and to avoid the insensitive tactics of churches and mission movements in the past. Such a desire is legitimate and important to the success of any ministry project, whatever the context. However, general North American society, which at one point was extremely racist and hostile to all non Anglo-American cultures, has now swung to a relativistic pluralism, which argues that all cultures (and their ceremonial components) are equally good. Our Postmodern culture embraces all cultural and religious traditions as long as they embrace the core Postmodern value of social and religious relativism.

This swing to relativism necessarily influences the church. When general society is xenophobic (fearful of those who are different) we can expect the church to err either on the side of exclusiveness or oppression. When the society is xenophilic (everything different is celebrated) we can expect the church to err on the side of a boundary-blurring inclusiveness that eventually leads to gospel-denying syncretism with other religions.

Given the current cultural tendencies, the church needs to guard against syncretism in deciding cultural sensitivity issues. Those who have drunk deeply at the well of Francis Schaeffer, Abraham Kuyper and others have long taken culture seriously, recognizing that the redemption of culture is a major part of the church's mission. These Christians rightly encourage the celebration of God's creation and the cultural expression of God's image in man. However, they may be especially vulnerable to falling into syncretism with Native religions in the name of redeeming culture. Astute Christians believe that art, science, industry and government are all affected by the Fall, but all can be taken up by Christians and used redemptively for the glory of God. I am in favor of redeeming culture if "culture" is what Francis Schaeffer meant by the term. Schaeffer used the term to include all aspects of human interaction with one another and the social environment. For Schaeffer, redeeming culture meant conforming all aspects of culture to the teaching of Scripture. Such an endeavor meant abandoning non-Christian religions and the unbiblical philosophical, ethical and ceremonial influences of these religions on culture.

When most Native Americans and First Nations Canadians speak about "culture," they do not mean what Francis Schaeffer meant by the word. Natives have in mind the *religious* and *ceremonial* aspects of "culture." When I invite Hobbema people to church, they say, "I pray through my culture," or "I'm cultural." When Native "Christians" speak of redeeming culture, they usually wish to redeem (i.e., keep) the Native religious cultural expressions. They want to bring the sweat, the pipe, the tobacco, the sweet grass and the medicine drum into the church and use these things for Christian worship. They specifically want to redeem the "cult" aspect of culture. These are the very aspects of culture that the Bible teaches us to jettison when we embrace Christ. Hear the words of the Apostle Paul:

> What agreement has the temple of God with idols? For we are the temple of the living God; as God said, "I will make my dwelling among them and walk among them, and I will be their God, and they shall be my people. Therefore go out from their midst and be separate from them, says the Lord, and touch no unclean thing; then I will welcome you...." (2 Cor 6:16–17)

Fathers, brothers, sisters and mothers, beware of Native ministries that talk about "redeeming culture" without defining the word. "Redeeming culture" is a very lovely slogan, but adopting sacred practices such as cleansing rituals and sacrifices derived from animistic religions does not redeem such practices, which are in direct opposition to the truth of the gospel. What components of Native culture are to be "redeemed"? Are we to redeem sweats? The pipe? Mother Earth and the grandfather spirits?

Richard Twiss, who is probably the best known Evangelical advocate for redeeming "Native culture," leads Christian sweats and brings Christians into traditional sweats led by medicine men all in the name of redeeming culture. Is it not an act of idolatry for a Christian to enter a sweat led by a medicine man when the lodge is understood to be the womb of Mother Earth? If not, exactly what *would* it take for a Christian to break the First Commandment? Is this not parallel to a Jew worshipping in pagan temples? Perhaps this is not a sin until temple prostitution occurs? Or maybe child sacrifices? Christians in denominations far more conservative than that of Twiss are enamored with his ideas, and toy with the idea of "Christian sweats." Let us suppose that by some cultural wash, we could eradicate the notion of a sweat lodge as the womb of Mother Earth in the mind of a traditional Native. It would still remain, in the mind of a person brought up in the plains culture, a gift from Mother Earth or some other spirit. The sweat would also remain an ordeal of suffering used to gain favor with God or the spirit world and convince them to hear prayers.

In Colossians, Paul speaks directly to the issue of self-inflicted pain in the context of religious practices prescribed by spirits in visions, dreams and traditions when he says:

> See to it that no one takes you captive by philosophy and empty deceit, according to human tradition, according to the elemental spirits of the world, and not according to Christ...Therefore let no one pass judgment on you in questions of food and drink, or with regard to a festival or a new moon or a Sabbath...Let no one disqualify you, insisting on asceticism and worship of angels, going on in detail about visions, puffed up without reason by his sensuous mind, and not holding fast to the Head...If with Christ you died to the elemental spirits of the world, why, as if you were still alive in the world, do you submit to regulations—"Do not handle, Do not taste, Do not touch"...These have indeed an appearance of wisdom in promoting self-made religion and asceticism and severity to the body, but they are of no value in stopping the indulgence of the flesh. (Col 2:8–23)

Whatever rituals or ascetic practices Paul was addressing, they had the following elements in common with sweats and Sundances:

- they constituted traditions of men;
- they originated from commands from spirits given through dreams and visions;
- they involved the punishment of the body for the purpose of winning favor with God;
- they involved the worship of angels (spirits).

We must consider sweats, cleansing ceremonies, the Sundance and other traditional sacrifices of Native Spirituality from the perspective of the tenth chapter of Hebrews.

> For if we go on sinning deliberately after receiving the knowledge of the truth, there no longer remains a sacrifice for sins, but a fearful expectation of judgment, and a fury of fire that will consume the adversaries. Anyone who has set aside the law of Moses dies without mercy on the evidence of two or three witnesses. How much worse punishment, do you think, will be deserved by the one who has spurned the Son of God, and has profaned the blood of the covenant by which he was sanctified, and has outraged the Spirit of grace? (Heb 10:26–29 ESV)

What sin is referenced by the author of Hebrews for which there is no more sacrifice? I believe it is continuing in Jewish rituals that deny the efficaciousness and the once-for-all nature of Jesus' sacrifice. Continuing in Jewish sacrifices is the practice against which the larger passage of Hebrews chapter ten is arguing (vv 1–17). When Hebrews says "if we go on sinning deliberately" (v 26), it is speaking of an ongoing activity and surely has Jewish sacrifice in mind. If someone continues in the sacrifices, sin is not atoned for because the repeated nature of the sacrifices demonstrates the ceremony's ineffectiveness for removing sin. Deliberately continuing in such sacrifices, after receiving Hebrews' teaching on the once-for-all nature of Christ's atoning death, constitutes a denial of faith in Christ's unique sacrifice. The one continuing in sacrifices is left with no sacrifice at all, until he repents and embraces the sacrifice of Christ.

Before Hebrews speaks of a sin for which there is no sacrifice it says:

> Where there is forgiveness of these, there is no longer any offering for sin. Therefore, brothers, since we have confidence to enter the holy places by the blood of Jesus, by the new and living way that he opened for us through the curtain, that is, through his flesh...let us hold fast the confession of our hope without wavering, for he who promised is faithful....(Heb 10:18–23 ESV)

Really trusting Jesus means forsaking repetitious sacrifices. If continuing in repeated sacrifices and ceremonies dictated by Old Testament Scripture and communicated through God's prophets is forbidden in such strong terms, how much greater would be the condemnation of rituals and sacrifices instituted by demonic spirits like Mother Earth and communicated through traditions of men, dreams and visions!

The sweat, the Sundance and smudging are all rituals that teach some continual need for atonement. In the sweat, one sits and prays while suffering in a boiling hot and humid hut so that prayers get heard. The Sundance always involves pain and the sacrificing of one's physical body in exchange for favors from the spirit world. These rituals are seen as sacrifices through which people put some sort of obligation either on the spirit world or on the Creator. To bring such ceremonies into Christianity not only brings great risk of importing the worship of earth spirits into the church, but teaches works righteousness through the performance of ceremony and the experience of self-inflicted pain. Use of traditional spiritual ceremonies wars against a biblical understanding of the Gospel, which teaches us that our righteousness comes from Christ's work on the cross alone, and is accessed through faith, not through tugging bones through our skin!

The issues here are bigger than Native Spirituality. Christians around the world must make similar decisions about cultural practices in their own countries. One Christian leader told me of Christians who teach that you can be a Christian and continue in the ceremonial life of the mosque. The blessing in our time of a more globally aware church makes these issues crucial as we think about crosscultural missions, whether it is Christians from the East going West, or vice versa. These issues are important whether you are a Korean working in New York City, an Indonesian Christian working in Brazil, a Canadian ministering to Native Americans or an American working with Sudanese immigrants. Even if you have little or no contact with Native ministries, it is crucial to understand syncretism with other religions. You are probably already considering some integration issue in your church or neighborhood.

7

Syncretism in the Jungle

Native South American Spirituality

Davi Charles Gomes

Son of a Brazilian father and an American mother, I bring to the discussion of native South American spirituality a double cultural perspective. With this double vision, I examine a culture which is itself affected by two distinct influences that you would see if I could show you around the sites of Brazil. We would see modern thought and old ways existing in an estranged yet symbiotic relationship. We would see the university culture juxtaposed with the favela subculture in São Paulo or Rio de Janeiro, or the illustrious traditions of science coexisting with the African religious heritage of Salvador, Bahia. We would see its Baianas wearing white turbans, long beads and white gowns, chanting and dancing at Candomblé yards against a backdrop of Portuguese edifices and old Catholic churches. We would see the imported worship of the Virgin Mary, in Aparecida, São Paulo, with its modern cathedral and its patios packed with fancy, imported cars as well as inexpensive Brazilian-made cars, and with multitudes of rich and poor, healthy and sick pilgrims. We would see the messianic figure of Padre Cícero, in Juazeiro, Ceará, along with evidence of scientific research on irrigation in the desert, or desalinization of the oceans. In the bookstores, scholarly and political works from European traditions mingle with publications on anthropological and social theories about native Indian fables. How can we understand these centers of popular religious devotion throughout South America?

As both Jew and Roman, the apostle Paul also had a double perspective on the cultures of his time. Waiting in the city of Athens for Silas and Timothy, he examined the religious ethos of the city, prompting one the most striking apologetic encounters of the early Christian church.

His words in Acts 17:23–24 show his deep compassion and passion for the gospel: "For as I walked around and looked carefully at your objects of worship, I even found an altar with this inscription: "To an Unknown God." Now what you worship as something unknown I am going to proclaim to you" (Acts 17:23 NIV).

Our brief tour of Brazil reveals a kingdom of idolatry. So much idolatry numbs us, but we must earnestly ask God to give us what he gave Paul—revulsion to idolatry, but a compassion for those caught up in it. Many interpret Paul's Athens speech as saying, "I see that you are religious people; I will show you how to complement your religion with the true one." In fact, he was saying, "I see that you are very superstitious, worshiping all sorts of things, but I am going to show you reality." Paul was extremely upset. Wherever we see such idolatry, we Christians understand Paul's sudden, intense desire to break into the darkness with the penetrating truth of the resurrected Jesus.

In the French quarter of New Orleans, I once unwittingly entered a witchcraft store. A shiver immediately went through me and I couldn't breathe. The saleswoman said, "You are not welcome here," and I left. I have occasionally experienced a similar feeling in Brazil. Is your spirit provoked when you face idolatry coated with a Christian veneer so thin that it hardly hides the pagan grain underneath?

Idolatry: Our Theme

Understanding idolatry is crucial in analyzing our modern, Postmodern or ultramodern world. The biblical theme of idolatry is inseparable from the concept of paganism, with which this volume is concerned. The apostle Paul reminded us of the basic binary tension in life: we worship God or idols. There is no other possible motive for human life.[1] Idolatry (paganism) provides an excellent theological axis for reflection and application in apologetics, counseling, sociology, philosophy and other areas of concern.

There is also a personal side to this discussion. We are never safe from making a clear and poignant biblical concept such as idolatry into something abstract. Individuals can create sophisticated, hidden "idols of the heart," and cultures also can cover idolatry with philosophical and traditional layers that stifle an appropriate revulsion.

My grandfather, a missionary in Brazil, began his work faithfully but later wandered in a spiritual desert for twenty years. Near the end of his life, he returned to his Lord and reconciled with his neglected family, only to learn that he had terminal cancer. As he lay very sick in the hospital, he told me how his heart had been filled with idols that led him away from the Lord. Thinking he was immune to influence, and in an attempt to reach a young man for Christ, he had agreed to go with him to meetings sponsored by a popular French spiritist group. "That's when something began to change inside of me," he told me on his deathbed. "I didn't feel that I needed to be close to God anymore."

Some spiritual oppression occurs without magic or spectacular evidence of demonic possession. I first read Umberto Ecco's *Foucault's Pendulum* in two days, at a moment when I felt far from God. I went to the Pocono Mountains and spent two more days walking, praying and seeking God. I had been playing with the idols of my heart and losing sensitivity to Paul's wise words: "the sacrifices of pagans are offered to demons not to God, and I do not want you to be participants with demons." (1 Cor 8:4; 10:20 NIV). Whether paganism takes an obvious or disguised form in our culture, our spirit should be "stirred and provoked," because paganism exchanges the Truth of God for the Lie of the devil! We must understand its diabolical "twist," in order to expose it and to shine on it the clear, purifying light of the gospel.

Our numbed cultural acceptance of idolatry sometimes occurs not in slow increments but in leaps and quick turns. Is it some kind of emergence inherent in the culture of fallen humanity? Whether it has just appeared unexpectedly or is the result of some spiritual conspiracy, a sudden revival of idolatry and paganism has occurred in the last few decades, not only in native South American spirituality but all over the globe.

PERVASIVE IDOLATRY: HOW DID WE GET HERE?

The revival of idolatry and paganism in South America, though unique in its cultural expression, is no different in principle from that occurring elsewhere. Dick Keyes suggests that idols come in pairs that mimic the transcendence and the immanence of God. Cultures have a "far away" idol that gives direction and meaning, but they also need a "touchable" idol. In the Old Testament, people had idols of the "high places" and "household" idols. The idols of the high places were named and publicly acknowledged, whereas household idols were served in secret, since anyone who could name them had power over them. Public idols seemed dominant, but their worship was determined by the power of the household idols.[2]

People still put their "transcendent" idol at the service of their secret heart idols. Pastors know how easily people Baalize Jehovah. Claiming to serve Jehovah, we make him a distant idol, perverting his true transcendence while also stripping away his true immanence. Even ministry leaders can put this "God" at the service of secret idols—human appreciation, a huge church, or success in ministry that will, for example, prove wrong those seminary professors who said they would never succeed. We keep secret our heart idols, while allowing them to dictate our service to a falsified Jehovah. Finally, we Baalize Jehovah. We no longer serve Jehovah, but an idol substitute.[3]

Such idolatry is not only personal but cultural. Our society makes its exalted "gods" mere servants of more private idols. Such idolatry then affects social, political, economical and historical trends, as well as psychology and the arts. Godly wisdom will uncover the idolatry in a culture, no matter how philosophical or symbolic it is. Though idolatry tries to camouflage its identity and our guilt, it is pathetic from a biblical perspective; God laughs in mockery at mute, powerless idols, made from created things. But by God's grace, we can also laugh when we discover the empty nature of our most sophisticated idols.[4]

Western Christians rightly think of idolatry in its spiritual form, as a heart issue. Today's paganism, however, has suddenly emerged from the shadows. Blatant, open, unapologetic, physical idolatry is growing in influence worldwide and affects many areas of modern life. How did this happen so suddenly? Societal changes usually take a long time to develop. European democracy took nearly one hundred fifty years to develop. Marxism took time to become a respectable intellectual force. But paganism and open idolatry, which used to be the object of jokes, have blossomed nearly overnight. Serious intellectuals, both pagan and Christian, are researching and writing about the subject. This compendium itself is the product of a conference dealing with the abrupt return of open pagan spirituality in the West. Though aspects of the new paganism are to be expected in a sinful world, other phenomena suggest that something new is occurring. Has the current fascination with pagan idolatry taken a step beyond any taken in the past?

Christians know that history has purpose and direction. Though not cyclical, it can travel in loops, vacillating between the Truth and the Lie. The loops were once large, taking a long time to turn. But they are now tightening and reaching a point of tension that makes us wonder how much tighter they can become. History is under God's control as he separates recipients of his special grace from those who have hitherto only experienced his common grace, yet this tightening of the dialectic also happens through the will of men. In his providence, God uses people—positively or negatively, but always for his glory.

To hypothesize that this new fascination with the pagan and the idolatrous might be an emerging characteristic of Postmodernity is inadequate, since the "emergence" presupposes that something new can appear from within a given system. We have argued that this situation is actually part of God's purpose, as he decreases the restraining activity of his Holy Spirit in the world. People are not mere subjects in this process, however; they are also actors. In this sense, the idea of conspiracy may carry some weight. As sin runs its course and idolatry and paganism reach new levels of pervasiveness and acceptability (perhaps greater than in pre-Christian times), we must be reminded that there is indeed, an evil, devilish conspiracy to distort the truth, to falsify religion, and to make remarkably more acceptable the worship of the creature in place of the Creator.

SOUTH OF THE EQUATOR: FACT AND FICTION

In recent decades North Americans and Europeans have come to the mountains and jungles of South America in search of a different spirituality. Portrayed as a spirituality amenable to the new ecological awareness, the animism and shamanism of Native South Americans have been romanticized by artists and the media.

Consider the movie *Dragonfly*,[5] in which a medical doctor travels to the Amazon to do relief work with his wife, who dies. When a child he treats has visions about his wife, he suspects that she may still be alive. This film endorses mystical communication with the spirit world and emphasizes the peaceful role of the Indians, whose spirituality enriches the empty lives of Westerners enslaved in cold naturalism. The pagan propaganda is so blatant that the film's website still offers visitors a "free spiritual reading."

In another movie, *The Serpent and the Rainbow*,[6] a scientist travels to the Amazon, where a witch doctor helps him discover his spirit guide (a jaguar) and a deep spirituality, understood by the native Indians. In Haiti, the hero dabbles in voodoo, using plants that create a magical state. The movie's idealization of the Amazon Indians made me remember a different reality. I once spent forty days with the Apurinã people in the Amazon, where two women Bible translators had spent twenty-five years. In the village, almost all the natives had come to Christ, though they were only a few decades from their cannibalistic past. Some had been believers for nearly twenty years. No ordained minister had yet visited, so they had neither been baptized nor offered the Lord's Supper. I was a young seminary graduate who had come with a team to build an airstrip. Imagine my delight at baptizing believers who had first confessed Christ when I was a baby!

We celebrated their first Lord's Supper. One elderly gentleman, whose sharpened teeth gave him a fierce appearance in spite of his small stature, testified that day. "I was already a young man when we stopped eating human flesh," he told us. "I was feared because people knew that if I came across an enemy I would not stop until I could eat his liver." He continued: "we stopped doing that and later I met Christ; now I am happy because for the first time ever in many, many moons, I am eating a person again—I'm eating the flesh and blood of Jesus Christ, my Savior, the only one I will ever eat again."

That brother was not nostalgic about his old native spirituality. He did not see it as a deeper, more natural fulfilment of an eco-friendly spiritual wisdom. This man and his friends told me that their "native" ways included physical and sexual abuse of young children, incest, violence to the point of cannibalism and terrifying spiritual (demonic) encounters in the middle of the jungle. They delighted in the liberty from such practices that Christ had given them.

The pure, innocent, naked jungle dweller is also a myth. One of the translators in the village told me about being arrested because an anthropologist had accused her of perverting the pristine lifestyle of the natives. As evidence, they brought two tribesmen eight hundred kilometers from their jungle home to the courthouse in Manaus, hoping they would testify to losing their native ways. An officer began to interrogate the natives:

"You are wearing shorts and sandals. This is an influence of this missionary, for that's not how you usually dress."

Judy could see immediately where the questions were leading. The officer continued:

"Was there a time before this missionary came when you walked around in the jungle without any clothes?"

To Judy's dismay they answered: "Yes, of course!" By this time, Judy was quietly begging God for deliverance. It is not a good thing to be jailed in Brazil.The officer turned to another tribesman and asked,

"When did you begin to wear clothes?" The tribesman said nothing. Now angry, the officer commanded:

"Tell me! Was it this missionary who made you wear clothes?"

"No, sir!" answered the two frightened Apurinã together.

"Then, who made you wear clothes?"

"Our mothers," they replied, "when we grew up!"

That men would rather walk around in the jungle naked would only occur to someone who has never lived in a jungle. Without clothes, you would tear yourself to pieces on thorns, or be devoured by mosquitoes.

SOURCES OF BRAZILIAN PAGAN SPIRITUALITY

Ancient, Native Spirituality

The spiritualities of South and Central American Indians, such as the Incas and the Mayas, are also romanticized, but here we focus on the spirituality of the Amazon Indians by examining one mainstream native

South American spirituality. There is a genuine native religion, a form of animism or nature worship, to which a semblance of ancestral worship was added. Both animals and ancestors are spirit guides for those who are brave and who pay them homage. Such a follower experiences unity and harmony (Xai). Upon death, he may return as something more evolved, like a jaguar, and then become a spirit guide to others.

It is this primitive religion that supposedly expresses the best of traditional "earth" culture and ecological harmony. As evidence of its value, researchers point to the low ecological impact of such a lifestyle. They argue that the forests and rivers of South America were relatively untouched until the Europeans arrived. But was Indian religion and culture really ecofriendly? The Indians collected from nature and cultivated small scale crops such as peanuts and manioc. Yet, their agricultural methods were, and still are, versions of slash and burn. Is it not more sensible to think that their low environmental impact was due rather to their limited population? Five million Indians, even using slash and burn techniques, had little impact on a country as large as a continent.

In Indian spirituality, mankind does not look after nature. The relationship between men and nature is determined by a rudimentary form of animism that imagines a spiritual world within and inseparable from nature. Sun, moon, stars, rivers, trees and animals are all mysterious simply because they are beyond human control. This spiritual world is not expressed in terms of deeper wisdom, but by an anthropomorphic worldview in which all the spiritual beings and powers act according to human attributes and vicissitudes.

It is believed that the spirituality of native Brazilians is one of peace and harmony because it assumes the continuity of all that exists, with no clear distinctions between humans and animals, between divine and created or between visible and unseen. Everything is part of Xai (peace, harmony). Yet, this connectedness actually inverts the value structure of life. Since all things are united in one whole, animal spirits are valued more highly than human spirits, because they follow their instincts better and more consistently than humans. The claim that such harmony is a deeper wisdom and a truer spirituality because it recognizes connectedness only occurs to post-Christians who have not thought through the implications: Nature is divinized and humanity is debased! Such thinking is by no means a nobler approach. It is actually antihuman, a worldview that stands against human values and dignity and, ultimately, against life—could we call it anti-existence?[7] How else do we take the pervasiveness of cannibalism among original native South Americans?

Not many people know that in 1557 John Calvin and the Geneva city council decided to colonize a newly discovered land—Brazil, hoping to create Antarctic France as a haven for persecuted Huguenots. Ten thousand Huguenots were to establish a colony where Rio de Janeiro and Guanabara Bay now stand. A scouting party arrived to prepare a fort. Can you imagine Brazil as a haven for Huguenots? It never happened, because Catholics quickly made the first South American Protestant martyrs. The Huguenots of Guanabara Bay were slaughtered, but not before producing a beautiful confession of faith in the period of four days, while in jail. The confession became known as the Brazilian Confession of Faith of 1557, one of the oldest reformed confessions and the first written in the New World. A few Huguenot colonists survived and hastily found return passage to Europe. Those who stayed were executed. It would be two hundred and fifty years before Protestantism made a significant return to Brazil.

Among the select few that Calvin sent in the scouting group, was a shoemaker who had been trained in theology at the Geneva Academy. His name was Jean de Léry. Persecuted by Nicholas Durand de Villegaignon, de Léry fled and spent two months with the Indians, preaching the gospel. We know about the native Brazilian cannibals, in part, because of his book, *Voyage through the Lands of Brazil*, a classic of anthropology, which even the unbelieving Claude Levy-Strauss considered the "grandfather of modern anthropology."[8] De Léry studied and described the cannibalism among native Brazilians more thoroughly than any European before him.

He recorded how the Indians prepared a body, noting what many misunderstood: the Indians did not eat human flesh primarily for dietary purposes, but for spiritual and religious reasons. A cannibal eats his enemy to absorb his spirit—to take in the man's courage or another quality, to internalize it, not as a wild animal eats, but with purpose and consciousness. Jean de Léry wisely observed that these natives never ate a coward.[9] To avoid becoming the next meal for a cannibal, advises de Léry, one should beg and cry. This won't avoid death, but one's flesh would either rot or be thrown to the animals and children. Real men would never eat a coward. The anecdotes of Jean de Léry show clearly that effacing distinctions between wild life and human beings is not prolife, but reflects the blurring of a deeper distinction—that between the Creator and the creation.

Roman Catholicism

The original religion of Brazil was highly influenced by the arrival of Portuguese colonizers. These were a particular sort of European. After the Reformation, missions and religious thinking in Europe were polarized. Protestants declared: "In the name of truth, I no longer need to submit myself to human authority," and Roman Catholics (whose philosophy was defined by the Counter Reformation and was reflected in the Spanish mentality of the Jesuits) claim: "Nothing can supersede the authority given by God to the mother church."

Even liberal North American missionaries still cling to shreds of confidence in truth as an absolute, relying on such an instinct in determining behavior and cultural standards. But any analysis of transcultural anthropology in Brazil needs to understand that post-Catholic, post-Jesuit countries instinctively believe that authority stands above truth. Which is the final court of appeal—truth or authority? In America, despite recent changes, we can challenge authority in the name of truth. This is still true, at least for now, even in legal terms with regard to the government: a clear reading of the constitution says that one can bear arms so that if the government becomes tyrannical and overthrows the constitution, it can itself be overthrown. North American culture still appeals to *lex rex*—the law is king. Law will always be associated with some concept of truth. The Jesuit mentality, on the other hand, was *rex lex*—those in authority dictate the truth (the law).

The question is one of authority and power. Built into the foundation of the Brazilian mindset is the ungodly view of men, "who hold the truth in unrighteousness" (Rom 1:18 KJV). That is why Brazil became easy pray for Positivism. The motto on the Brazilian flag reads "Order and Progress," not "Truth and Justice." The Portuguese did not come to colonize but to subdue and take spoils from the new land. Roman Catholic missionaries wanted to submit the natives to authority, not to truth. Though French and Dutch Protestants had a minor influence on the brewing mindset, the Roman idea of conquest by assimilation took over. This approach has already been used in the spread of the Roman Catholic Church to the farthest reaches of early Europe. For example, when Christian catholicity reached the British Isles, missionaries encouraged the natives to reinterpret their Lady of the Lake by renaming her the Virgin Mary. Christianity thus absorbed the pagan worship of personified femininity. This allowed them to continue their devotion by redefining it and adapting it to a new system.

Assimilation enforces an outward conformity while leaving the deeper commitments and beliefs untouched. It is a syncretism that forces the exchange of names and appearances, yet absorbs and perpetuates the idols beneath those new Christian names. This was how the Church of Rome proceeded, through consecutive waves of missionaries who catechized the natives of Brazil, baptizing them and their culture, while allowing their old pagan ways to persist.

This sanctioned syncretism has become so normal in Brazilian lands that it seldom surprises people. One example is the influence of an originally French spiritism, codified by one Alain Kardec. This occult religion mixes good works and suffering (as the path to spiritual evolution) with séances and spirit communications. It claims to be Christian and draws people who consider themselves good Catholics, presenting itself as a scientific religion. People practice science and séance, calling down spirits to reveal the occult, as was the practice of Pierre and Marie Curie. The Catholic Church has not been vehement in rejecting this popular cultic practice in Brazil.

One Roman Catholic priest told me, "It's horrible that I preach to a parish on Sunday and I know that sixty per cent of them went to the spiritist séance on Friday." Partly in jest, I suggested that he become a Protestant. "After all," I reasoned, "you teach your parishioners to talk to some dead people. Why not all dead people?"

African Religions

The catechetical education imposed on the original natives, containing inherent syncretism, is only part of Brazil's special spiritual brew. As the number of Portuguese and the Catholic priests increased, slaves from Africa also arrived—chiefly the Yorubás (Nagô, Ketu, Egbá), and the Jejes (Ewê, Fon). They brought African animistic religions more elaborate than the Brazilian variety. The *orixá* religion, in particular, which became known as Candomblé, had a somewhat organized theology. There are no distinctions between good and evil, but only qualities and defects relative to the purpose of each person. The universe consists of a hierarchy of beings, at the top of which is a being that never incarnates, has no contact with the world, cannot receive offerings and remains unspoken. From him, everything emanates. He sent his oldest son, Oxalá, to create the universe, but a younger brother,[10] Exu (the equivalent of the devil), got Oxalá so drunk that he forgot to create anything. So Exu created a visible world himself. To remedy the situation, the high and mighty told his beloved son, "I will allow you to create human beings, so that people can live in between the spiritual realm of *orixás* and the created world. Thus, by worshiping gradations of deities, humans manipulate their fate and the forces of nature." Candomblé speaks of the existence of two hundred *orixás*. These are higher demigods, similar to those in the Gnostic structure, though only twelve can be worshiped by men.

This African religion adapted to and blended with the native Brazilian religion and survived within the increasingly syncretistic, popular Catholicism. A modified form of the African religion emerged, forming what is now called Umbanda. An enormous number of Umbanda called *pais-de-santo* (those who receive spirits and lead the *terreiros*) identify themselves as Roman Catholics. Umbanda mixed popular Catholic piety, native religion and the religion of the *orixás*, and began to speak of *babalorixás*—spirit guides, slightly lower than the *orixás*. *Babalorixás* usually take the form of an older black man, a native Brazilian or a beautiful female. They are wise spirit guides who appear to those who call on them and who bring sacrifices and gifts. Some Catholic prayers and general Christian symbols are incorporated in the liturgy of Umbanda. A similar crossover occurs between Umbanda and Kardecism: from the latter, Umbanda borrowed a model of ethical-religious conduct that has succeeded in guaranteeing its public image on the face of accusations of "primitivism." Umbanda maintains a dubious, tense relation with its rival, Candomblé, which has grown steadily in the last decades. Protestants have always been guarded with regard to Afro-Brazilian religions. Lately, conservative Catholics and Evangelical Pentecostals have waged an intense campaign against Afro-Brazilian religion.

Syncretism as a Modus Operandi

Roman Catholic catechizers brought their theology to Brazil, where a simple animism believed in the unity of everything and in the power of magic. One might expect that a huge worldview clash would have ensued. However, Jesuit Roman Catholic philosophy was highly influenced by the Plotinian concept of the great chain of being. That Neoplatonist tradition, clearly monistic, proposes a gradation of beings, ranging from nonbeing and rising in steps (including things, animals, man, angelic beings, archangels and God himself at the top, as pure being). In such a scheme, the Creator/creature distinction is destroyed, becoming a matter of degrees. Since Catholic missionary practice absorbed new cultures, and since the Catholic Jesuit theology already favored a "scale of beings," it readily absorbed such aspects as they were found in primitive Brazilian or African animistic religions. All three streams—Catholic, Brazilian and African—divorced religion from its final source of truth: God the Creator, entirely distinct from his creation, a God who reveals truth from the outside in his Word.

This syncretistic process developed in a setting where a dominant, organized church (mainly Roman Catholic) controlled religion and authority. The Roman Catholic Church still dominates most Latin American cultures but has not challenged their pagan roots. Though many laboring within the Catholic Church would reject syncretism, the church's modus operandi is still amazingly amenable to it. The African religion brought by slaves, outwardly bowed to the authority of the established white church. They adapted, attended Mass and kissed the crucifix. But they also went to the terreiros and continued practicing their Candomblé worship sessions. This represented no problem, since they were taught that Santa Barbara, for example, was nothing but a white man's name for Yemanjá, the deity representing fertility and the power of the feminine. She is similar to the Lady of the Lake, the Asian Mother of Waters or the ancient Ishtar (Inanna or Semiramis).

Today's Landscape

Until a few decades ago Brazil was considered a Roman Catholic country, containing a small Protestant presence, some primitive religions among the lower classes, a few Pentecostals and several other oddities. The landscape has changed radically in the last thirty tears. The last Brazilian census found that Roman Catholic presence has dropped to sixty percent (about a quarter of whom now identify themselves as Catholic/spiritists). About ten percent claim involvement in one of the two old African religions (Candomblé has become theologically organized, but Umbanda remains more popular). Over a quarter of the population claims to be Evangelical or Protestant.

There is much talk about the growth of Evangelicalism, but the issue must be carefully weighed. Historic Brazilian Protestants started to realize in the last twenty years that there is an important difference between the emerging Evangelical groups (mainly Neocharismatic or Neopentecostal) and traditional Protestantism. A growing number of Neopentecostal communities mix Christian principles and vocabulary with practices akin to popular paganism, derived from synthesized Umbanda and popular Catholicism. These new churches market a gospel garbed in a popular, mystical, Brazilian style. Much of this Evangelicalism is a Postevangelical version of the old syncretism, with a better instinct for making money.

This current approach poses new challenges for the church. Even as the gospel is preached all over Brazil (and the numbers are amazing), some of the success is actually the growth of a falsified gospel, which, instead of challenging the surrounding culture, adapts to it, absorbs it, cannibalizes it and internalizes its pagan heart. I do not wish to deny the encouraging growth among true evangelicals who steer clear of all syncretism. Yet, a significant part of "evangelical" growth is a recasting of the old pagan idolatry. Many self-proclaimed pastors, bishops, apostles and "fatherpostles" ("*paipóstolo*" in Portuguese—this peculiar office trumps the office of apostle) are only a new breed of evangelical-sounding pagan priests and prophets, gurus of "health and wealth," and "signs and wonders." They are now armed with spells, incantations and other portentous tools to manipulate circumstances and produce blessings. People who come to these leaders quickly reabsorb old pagan habits, associating the new prophets with their former *babalorixás*. Their "Christian" life differs little from their life of idol worship, in which they tried to control their saints, devils or spirits. They once gave offerings to all kinds of spirits, without knowing who they were, in order to force them to work in their favor, "mediating between the material and spiritual worlds." Now they discover that the Holy Spirit is a more powerful spirit who can be made to give them what they need while he "mediates between the material and spiritual worlds" on their behalf. All they have to do is step out in faith, cough up the money and say: "Good morning, Holy Spirit!"

If this sounds exaggerated, remember the cultural and religious soup described above. Much of Evangelicalism jumps into the mainstream of Brazilian popular spirituality. Consider some of the popular practices of Brazilian Postevangelicalism. Someone with marital problems can break a spell cast on the marriage simply by attending the next "bondage breaking marriage service," where the pastor will bless the wedding rings with consecrated oil or holy water from some unknown Jordan River. If that doesn't work, a *descarrego* can be dispatched to expel deeper evils, spells of envy, evil eyes and other maladies. Financial crisis? There is a "service for entrepreneurs": give enough and you can dictate to God the expected rate of return. Everything must be healed, from cancer to bad breath, through "powerful prayer" (that, of course, traditional Christians do not have). But don't forget—if you don't tithe, it won't work.[11]

These "churches" sell earthly redemption, based on a mishmash of human-faith-as-works, to guarantee the grace of some god. Some teach that the power is in the heart of the worshipper; others say that this power is in the church or in the priest. They all agree about buying and selling some kind of grace. Such a theology might be called a theogony, a god birthing. (Remember Calvin: the heart of man is a "is a veritable idol factory."[12]) Mixed with the idea of continuity in the spiritual world, it is nothing short of pagan and demonic.

Of course, the syncretism of Christianity and paganism has its counterparts in other places and cultures. Santeria, in Mexico and in Central America, also mixes elements from Christianity with old African and Native American paganism, as does voodoo in Haiti. Similar types of religious synthesis are described in this volume. What they all have in common is a belief in the continuity between all that exists, so one must find a bridge between the spiritual and the material realm. Once you find that bridge, you can manipulate the spirit world and find happiness and success, which, in turn, will assure you a higher reincarnation in the next life.

Most forms of reincarnation theology in eastern and less syncretistic types of pagan idolatry propose that one evolves until one is absorbed into allness, or nothingness, or into the light of God. The syncretistic spiritualities described in this chapter do not propose such an end, but rather an infinite series of reincarnations. Life at any given point is always a reflection of how one handled the previous life.[13]

What Is it Really About?

What do Westerners seek in turning to these religions? Is it a quest to find themselves through drumbeating, chanting and communing with spirit guides? If that were the case, they could seek peyote-stimulated visions in the deserts of Nevada. Perhaps they think South American paganism more powerful or exotic. Whatever they are seeking, when they receive the South American version, they get a package deal. With their trip to the Amazon, they get *orixás*, syncretism and contact with demonic forces. Their desire to control the forces of nature in order to worship the secret idols of their heart commits them to communing with devils. They must erase the distinctions between humans and animals, the Creator and the creature, and cannibalize everything spiritual in order to be empowered by what is absorbed. Ultimately, they are on a quest for better idols of the high places, who will better serve the selfish, petty household idols that lurk in the depths of the sinful heart.

To Christians eager to help such seekers, the questions are different. How do we preach to a world south of the equator that practices theological cannibalism, devouring religions served on earthly dishes, seasoned with demonic condiments and intent on satiating carnal appetites? Certainly we have received the Gospel that illumines hearts and exposes the folly of such quests—a Gospel that addresses life and death, while giving hope of eternal life. In the words of the apostle Paul:

> Since, then, you have been raised with Christ, set your hearts on things above, where Christ is seated at the right hand of God. Set your minds on things above, not on earthly things. For you died, and your life is now hidden with Christ in God. When Christ, who is your life, appears, then you also will appear with him in glory. Put to death, therefore, whatever belongs to your earthly nature: sexual immorality, impurity, lust, evil desires and greed, which is idolatry. Because of these, the wrath of God is coming. (Col 3:1–6 NIV)

8

TECHNIQUES OF AFRICAN PAGAN SPIRITUALITY

YUSUFU TURAKI

Because techniques of African Pagan Spirituality vary across the continent, this chapter serves only as a basic guide for those unfamiliar with African Traditional Religion.[1] The principles of the African pagan worldview affect religious, psychological, philosophical, moral, social and anthropological thinking. Here, we limit our discussion to the techniques of enhancing pagan spirituality that so fascinate Westerners today.

An African pagan believes that he can, by a variety of methods:

1. communicate with, and receive communication from, the spirit world;
2. acquire powers from the natural and the spirit world;
3. exercise those powers in and through human beings, other creatures, nature and the spirit world;
4. experience spirituality through festivals, rituals and ceremonies;
5. consult professional communicators who contact the spirit world and help the practitioner exercise spiritual power.

Traditional African spirituality is rooted in two related categories: *spiritual phenomena* and *power phenomena*, which combine to form what I call spirit-power. Traditional religions are religions of powers and mysteries. Reality lies not in the material world, but in the spirit world, which is densely populated with

1. spirit beings, spirits, and the living-dead or the spirits of the ancestors[2] and
2. impersonal, mystical, mysterious, unseen powers and forces.

COMMUNICATION WITH THE SPIRIT WORLD

Initiated by the Devotee

Traditional Africans have a strong desire to communicate with the spirit world about world harmony, as well as their own specific needs. Communication with the spirit world is reciprocal: humans both initiate and receive communication. A law of cosmic harmony works to maintain a spiritual equilibrium between the human and spirit world. Without this harmony, one cannot achieve one's goals. But the human world is unstable, chaotic, vulnerable, fragile, and subject to the invasion and caprices of the more powerful gods and spirits. The desired harmony is constantly under attack. Continual effort is required to restore it, to repair breached relationships and to achieve reconciliation. Traditional religions must answer questions of communion and relationship. Are we in good standing before the gods? If things have gone wrong, how can they be put right? Answers to these and other questions are sought by observing taboos and prescribed ceremonies and rituals.

Taboos

Taboos operate on various levels to govern numerous aspects of African social, cultural and religious life. Some reflect common sense prohibitions; others sanction authority and institutions; while still others relate to levels of hierarchy or social status, or to mystical and spiritual powers. Taboos govern sacred places, land use, the celebration of festivals and special days, what animals may be eaten, marriage and procreation, relationships with the ancestors, and the roles of males, females, fathers, mothers and children. They function as sacred moral codes that prescribe the social, customary and religious behavior required to maintain cosmic harmony. Taboos maintain sociocultural and religious conditioning, the social order, harmony, the structure of meaning, and worldviews.

Religious Festivals, Rituals and Ceremonies

Religious festivals, rituals and ceremonies also regulate African religious and social life. Some are communal and cyclical, dictated by the calendar. Thus, new yams and new moons are celebrated, as are the beginning of the hunting, planting, harvest and rainy seasons. Some rituals are performed as the need arises: rites of passage, birth, initiation, marriage, death, rainmaking and purification. Ceremonies may include meals, dance, music (using a variety of instruments such as drums, animal horns, trumpets, vocal and choral groups), chants, incantations, storytelling, recitation, drama, sacrifices and offerings, and parades in honor of deities, ancestors or heroes/heroines.[3] Philip Steyne emphasizes the profound influence of such ceremonies:

> Ritual sustains and generates the myth underlying the belief system, while it also binds people together socially, psychologically, and physically as they participate. Shared activities such as dancing, clapping hands, singing, reciting liturgies, praying, carrying burdens, sacrificing and performing ceremonies of various sorts all serve to reinforce collective sentiments . . . They are cathartic and therapeutic experiences, producing a sense of well-being.[4]

Sacrifices and Offerings

In Traditional African culture, offerings are voluntary, while sacrifices are obligatory to atone for wrong. Specific offerings and sacrifices are prescribed for certain occasions. The gift must be valuable to the presenter, since it signifies giving up one thing for another. The gift may include cereals or other vegetable life, prepared food and/or drink, and animal (or human) victims. The object for sacrifice may be determined by custom or by divination, but the shedding of blood is an essential element.[5]

Tradition demands offerings or sacrifices in marriage ceremonies, land transactions, migration issues and other areas. Some pay homage to the gods or ancestors. These gifts open the door to ask the spirit world to: bless or protect; help in time of need; heal diseases that have been sent as a judgment; send off the dead or welcome them into important communal ceremonies; restore relationships among opposing individuals, families and tribes; mend broken relationships with the spirit world; purify or cleanse, through acts of consecration.

Initiated by the Spirits

Taboos and sacrifices are initiated by the practitioner. However, communication may also be initiated in the opposite direction—from the spirit world. A direct communication from the spirits may be necessary during adverse circumstances, and only the spirits can show how to acquire power and to discern personal or communal destiny. Though the practitioner hopes that the spirit world will initiate communication, he or she still seeks such communication through dreams, visions, vision quests and divination.

Dreams

Africans seek the meaning of dreams, which are the chief source of revelation from, and the means of communication with, the spirit world. Through dreams, the living communicate with the gods, spirits and the dead. Dreams are sources of guidance, commands, good messages of blessing or bad omens and warnings. In sleep, it is believed, the human soul can leave the body and travel to other places, especially in the spiritual realms.

Visions

The Eerdmans Bible Dictionary describes a vision as follows:

> A supernatural visual manifestation, which may also involve the aural, that serves as a divine revelation of something otherwise secret. Visions are closely related to such other revelatory phenomena as dreams and journeys through heaven and hell.[6]

In visions, unlike dreams, people "perceive an event as external to their own senses, something which imposes itself upon the mind." In traditional African religions, visions have great significance and "bring guidance, warnings and promises of blessings."[7]

Vision Quests (Spirit Possession)

African traditional believers undertake vision quests when they use rituals and ascetic practices as a means of inducing a spirit to take possession of them. Such means include "meditative and contemplative exercises, self-inflicted tortures ([including] jumping from heights, walking on burning coals, thrusting skewers into cheeks and tongue), using drugs, dancing, drumming, chanting [and] singing oneself into a frenzy."[8]

The bori dance was common among the Hausa of Northern Nigeria.

Commonly associated with folk Islam, it was often used to heal sickness, which is thought to be due to spirit possession. These spirits can be exorcised through the bori dance, in which the traditional priest, male or female, uses music through drums, harps, lyre or goge to bring about possession. The possessed person dances to the rhythm of music, according to the nature of the possessing spirit. The type of dance or noise made is determined by the type of spirit that either possessed a person or caused the sickness. In the bori dance, or similar practices, a possessed person has contact with the spirit world and may receive ecstatic experiences, glossolalia, or unusual visions and dreams. "The indwelling spirit is also thought to be the personal guardian of the possessed."[9] This practice is also associated with keeping totem animals, whose spirits are said to possess persons.

Divination

Steyne defines divination as "a technique with which to interpret phenomena of nature and occult spirits," while the *Eerdmans Bible Dictionary* defines it as "the art of determining the future or ascertaining the divine will."[10] Because in traditional belief anything that happens has a spiritual cause, the use of divination is widespread in Africa. People use divination:

- to learn their own or their family's future;
- to contact spiritual powers to meet their needs;
- to protect themselves from witches, sorcerers or unpredictable spirit powers;
- to gain power and boldness to triumph over adversity through esoteric powers;
- to overcome human limitations, impotence and dependence;
- to receive and interpret messages from the spirit world for personal and communal well-being;
- to maintain harmony between humans and the spirits or gods.

Ordeals

One means of communication with the spirit world that is used in exceptional circumstances is trial by ordeal. An ordeal:

> is a test used to determine the guilt or innocence of someone who is suspected of some violation of custom or taboo. Even if the test is not dangerous or painful in itself, if the suspect is guilty, supernatural power will supposedly bring the required judgment to bear. ....Therefore the innocent have nothing to fear, but the guilty will not escape the punishment due them.[11]

Common ordeals involve oath taking, boiling oil, drinking poison, divination, the use of hot articles and of fire, and sorcery. The goal of an ordeal is to ascertain innocence or guilt in regard to moral behavior. Since human knowledge is limited, the legitimacy and finality of judgment must be left in the hands of the gods, who speak through oracles (lesser beings who administer some aspects of justice). Certain ordeals can only be administered by particular oracles, and people travel long distances to reach renowned oracles who can administer them.

ACQUIRING POWER

Because life is full of fearful and unpredictable powers, the traditional African believer must attempt to wield some power himself, for protection and peace of mind. The spirit-beings and the impersonal, mystical, mysterious and unseen powers and forces, collectively called by some the *mysterium tremendum,* cause him a great deal of anguish.

Langdon Gilkey describes the human situation in the face of this *mysterium tremendum*:

> Men are also deeply troubled by anxious fears arising from their weakness as creatures. The feeling of dependence and contingency, of being subject to uncontrollable forces, forms the content of one of these anxieties. The experience of temporality and mortality, of an approaching "deadline to one's powers and life," forms the frightening content of the other.[12]

In the face of these anxieties, Africans turn to spiritual and mystical powers. Often drawing on the help of traditional specialists, they seek mystical means of communicating with the spirit world and acquiring power that enables a certain control over the spirit world. Since the life force itself is believed to permeate everything, especially animal life, the more life force a human can acquire, the greater his or her strength, power and success. Those with an abundant supply of life force rise above the ordinary and are able to do extraordinary things. They also receive more protection or guidance than others. This added power gives a sense of security and allays fears and anxieties.

The Senses

A number of physical means heighten awareness of spiritual and mystical powers. These means vary from moderate to extreme, depending on the type of ritual practices. For centuries, in Africa and in other parts of the world, drugs have been used to increase spiritual and mystical potency. Certain religious groups use marijuana, peyote and LSD to heighten their awareness of spiritual powers or to enhance their activities. Severe self-discipline, such as vision quests, night vigils, ritual self-emptying and purification, fasting, meditation, silence, postures and ritual dancing are practiced as means of acquiring life force and spiritual powers. Music is also thought to play such a role.

Ancestors and Associates

The cult of the ancestors plays a significant part in the search for spiritual and mystical powers. Traditional Africans believe that maintaining good relations with the ancestors ensures continuation of the life force and increases the potency of spiritual and mystical powers.

Respect for the ancestors includes continued reverence for them as guardians of the family and community, contact with and use of sacred objects they kept or used, and consultation with their spirits. One can also benefit from being closely associated with people who have acquired spiritual and mystical powers or life force. By touching or keeping in close contact with great men or women (heroes, leaders and warriors), one may absorb a significant measure of life force. Thus, many disciples follow famous people with status and power, including religious leaders, hoping to gain unusual spiritual and mystical powers.

Charms, Sacred Objects, Weapons, etc.

Objects can possess life force, thus charms and sacred objects are used to acquire mystical and spiritual powers. A vast variety of objects are considered to have potency. These include "objects formerly used by ritual and/or religious specialists, objects associated with sacred paraphernalia, parts of animals or human beings, sacred cords, animal claws, precious and semiprecious stones, pieces of leather, special metal objects, religious symbols, sacred Scripture texts, ointment or salve."[13] Objects can be carried about as charms, used as weapons, kept at home, or buried in strategic places. These charms can be used to gain protection but also to harm others or to cause calamity.

Sacrifices

Blood plays a symbolic role in traditional African religions and life. Blood from ritual sacrifices, eaten in the prescribed manner, is believed to empower those who perform the rituals. The potency of the blood depends on what is sacrificed. Some animals have higher life force than others, the life force of a human having the most potency.

Animals may be buried in strategic places to increase spiritual power. In modern Nigeria, certain politicians, military officers and civil servants have apparently buried animals to increase their life force as well as their hopes of political or public power. Rumors abound that humans have been buried under buildings to enhance spiritual power. The type of power sought determines what animal or human should be buried. Wealth, a mark of power, may be acquired through the sacrifice of a whole human being or of certain potent parts of a human being. Drinking human blood or eating human body parts is also associated with witchcraft and sorcery as means of acquiring spiritual and mystical powers.

Religious Rituals and Ceremonies

Mystical powers decrease or disappear if the practitioner loses touch with their source. To maintain contact and enhance life force, one must participate regularly in the elaborate rituals that transfer power to the devotee and enable him to control, conciliate and acquire spiritual powers and life force. Rituals include laying on hands; touching various body parts; anointing the body with sacred oils; painting or tattooing the body; wearing sacred objects; drinking blood or sacred drinks; eating particular foods; burying animals or sacred objects and reciting or singing incantations.

Ray defines ritual as follows:

> Through ritual, man transcends himself and communicates directly with the divine. The coming of the divine to man and of man to divinity happens repeatedly with equal validity on almost every ritual occasion.[14]

Ray's definition interprets ritual exclusively in religious terms. Without denying the religious aspect, Steyne offers a slightly more utilitarian definition:

> A ritual is a formula for eliciting help from the spirit world and mastering nature to serve man's purposes. It is the means whereby the spirits may be manipulated.[15]

Confidence in the ability to tap into a power source through ritual gives those performing the ritual a great sense of security. Their focus is on the end result and their sense of well-being, rather than on issues of morality and ethics. Rituals have more to do with emotions than with reason.

Secret Cult

In African Traditional Religion, "the sense of the sacred and the mysterious is deeply felt." The deep things of life are best understood in secret. The *mysterium tremendum* manifests itself in a law of secrecy about all the methods mentioned in this chapter. Secret knowledge offers a gateway to spiritual and mystical powers, thus we find a proliferation of secret cults and societies into which devotees are initiated.

Onaiyekanhas made a study of these cults. He points out that the law of secrecy means that "there are always some teachings and notions that are reserved to one segment or the other of the society. ... Thus, knowledge of the deeper elements of the traditional religions often requires as a condition an initiation into a secret group...[16]

This same secrecy prevails in worship: "Not everyone has access to every shrine and there are ceremonies which only initiates are allowed to take part in." In almost all cases, "children and women are strictly excluded." Secrecy spills over into areas such as traditional medicine, whose practitioners jealously guard their knowledge and skill.

EXERCISING POWER

Once spirit-power has been obtained, it must be practiced to ensure safety and prosperity and to exercise control. Tools have been developed by specialists who advise devotees on the use of spirit-power. According to Steyne, the most common means of exercising control are incantations, symbolism, magic, charms, fetishes, witchcraft, sorcery or divination.[17]

Incantations (Word Power)

In traditional religion, words have innate power. Steyne stresses that "there is a vital connection between life force, magic and words," whose power can be used for "protection against the contingencies of life brought about by the spirit world."[18] Words can kill and unguarded use is dangerous: for example, a person can be harmed if the secret of his name is known. To avoid this, euphemisms are sometimes substituted for powerful words. Protective or harmful words can be inscribed on objects or made into amulets and charms.

The power of words may be impersonal or associated with spirit powers, if incantations are used to exorcise or summon spirits. The power is in the words and in the way they are said, which may involve "chants, repetitious singing, recitations or other special worship forms." If the words are said correctly, the desired result will automatically follow, especially in the case of the magic formulae used when casting spells and curses, swearing oaths, and attempting to control nature, people and the spirit world. The words have the greatest power when pronounced by a religious specialist in prescribed rituals.

Symbols

Symbols also hold power. Steyne states that "symbols serve to secure and protect places, people and times from the attacks of evil spirits and to invite the benevolent spirits to exercise their good offices on behalf of the supplicants. Under the protection of the symbol, devotees feel secure, endued with power, and confident."[19]

Symbols excite respect and fear and must be handled with caution. They can be used as charms to ward off evil or invite good luck. They are sentries, watching over the welfare of their owner and his goods. Religious symbols include blood, colors, paraphernalia, clothing, objects and shapes. Symbols are closely associated with charms, which are symbolic objects that possess mysterious power through their association with spirits or with someone of high status. Gestures constitute a symbolic language with specific meanings. Religious symbolism is so powerful in traditional religion that even Christian converts sometimes maintain their attitudes toward them. Some independent churches exhibit a marked continuity between their pre- and post-Christian religious heritage.

Magic

The pervasive use of magic, both for good and evil, exerts a profound influence on African Christianity. Magic goes beyond divination because it not only seeks knowledge of, but also power over, the future.

In Steyne's extensive discussion of magic,[20] he identifies the following different kinds of magic:

- Divine magic: "God enters the human context and permits a miracle;"
- Thaumaturgy (conscious and unconscious natural magic): manipulation of impersonal forces to achieve results. Conscious natural magic generates psychic power for the flow of magic energy. The unconscious version uses ritual, instead. Thaumaturgy is used in magical games or to identify criminals. Rituals can involve holy books, prayers, and calling special names;
- Black magic: "Attempts to produce evil results through curses, spells and an alliance with evil spirits."[21] Practitioners are "usually sorcerers, wizards or shamans" who use "magic words or objects to inflict suffering";
- White magic (theurgy): "Tries to undo curses and spells and to use occult powers for the good of oneself or others";[22]
- Homeopathic magic: Based on the law of similarity ("like produces like"), it uses effigies or replicas to effect good or evil on a victim;
- Magic by contagion: "Magic by contagion operates by the law of contact." Steyne states, "once things have been in contact (conjoined), they are forever thereafter conjoined." People seek to avoid magical

contagion in private and public places, such as "houses, villages, towns, fields and other places."

Charms (Amulets and Talismans) and Fetishes

A charm is "an object worn by some people to keep away evil or bring good luck" and is also "an object, act or phrase believed to have supernatural powers."[23] Steyne describes fetishes as objects that "exercise an occult influence according to the possessor's wishes." Belief in and use of charms, amulets and fetishes is pervasive among Africans.

EXPERIENCING SPIRITUALITY

To become spiritual, one seeks unity with this spiritual reality through rituals, ceremonies and practices. At other times, the spiritual reality in itself becomes one with the practitioner—the incarnation of spirit-power in our human and social reality. All that really matters is attaining the states of spirit-power. African pagan religion is man-centered, and possessing spirit-power is a means of acquiring a benefit. Religion is not altruistic or pure. Religious rituals, ceremonies, techniques and methods are always means of obtaining happiness through spirit-power.

Steyne warns that rituals can serve as an outlet for undesirable behaviors. In certain ritual practices, norms of morality and ethics are relaxed and what are "normally considered aberrant behavior forms are exhibited, such as reversal of sex roles, sexual license, drunkenness, drug use, humor, laughter, free speech, glossolalia, etc."[24] He lists some of the effects:

- Renewing, strengthening and in some cases restoring bonds between devotees or worshipers and spirit beings (deities, spirits, ancestors);
- Controlling or gaining favor from the spirit world;
- Providing sociopsychological affirmations for the participants;
- Serving as a social control mechanism in society by establishing patterns of loyalty and prescribing parameters of acceptable conduct.[25]

Consulting Professional Communicators

The complex variety of African traditional beliefs and practices has spawned a class of professionals, to whom people turn for help in communicating with the spirit world. A victim or a person experiencing misfortune may appeal to a shaman, witchdoctor, prophet, priest, medicine man or woman, or a worker of evil (a sorcerer or witch)—all believed to have extraordinary skills and powers both in dealing with human problems and in knowing the secrets and mysteries of the spirit world. The duties of specialists are: 1) to use spiritual and mystical powers and life force to enhance the well-being of individuals and the community; 2) to develop and conduct rituals that ensure harmony, balance and peace for individuals and communities; 3) to develop means of exercising control over the spirit world and human society; 4) to develop effective procedures for communicating with the spirit world.

Both traditional and modern Africans eagerly seek such professionals to protect themselves from the menacing and capricious activities of spirit beings, witches, wizards, and sorcerers, as well as natural disasters, calamities, diseases, human weakness, suffering and death. Each profession has its own beliefs, regulations, practices and rituals. Some use mystical and spirit powers, while others use ordinary human ingenuity and wisdom. Then there are others still, who are cheats and deceivers.

Witches and Sorcerers

Witchcraft and sorcery is deeply embedded in traditional African religions, but there are some differences between witchcraft, sorcery, magic and divination. Leonard Nyirongo, who has written an excellent book on these issues, offers these distinctions:[26]

> Divination is the ability to discover or explain mysterious causes of sickness, death or other misfortune, which cannot be unraveled by the ordinary observer. Magic is the art of using spells to invoke supernatural powers to influence people or events. Sorcerers, witches and "witch doctors" can employ both means in their arts.[27]

Central to the concepts of witchcraft and sorcery is the belief "that certain persons in a community will resort to a means to bring harm to their fellows or to accomplish desired goals by the use of nefarious supernatural means."[28] Witchcraft and sorcery are the two most dreaded social practices. Sorcery, especially, is often motivated by selfish ambition. Such practices create fear, tyranny, panic and death. The deaths of young people, mysterious deaths, accidents and incurable diseases are usually attributed to witchcraft and sorcery. The elderly are sometimes beaten to death, accused of being witches or sorcerers.

Most witches inherit power from parents or grandparents, whether innately or by special gift, though power can be purchased from a commercial sorcerer. The most powerful witches have received their abilities directly from a god. Witches maintain their powers by observing rules and rituals and by staying on good terms with other witches through blood sacrifices and attendance at secret planning meetings. They attend such gatherings as "personality souls," rather than in their usual bodies. Witches adhere to a well-organized hierarchy in which individual witches have specific responsibilities.

Their tools include cultic objects such as a calabash or horn, talismans, beads and rings, small pieces of cloth, a stick, masks and statuettes. Each witch also has a totem, which may be an animal, a bird, a snake or an insect. Witches claim that by applying certain herbs to cultic objects they can transform themselves into their totem. Witches skilled in the use of poison harm or kill their victims, even from a distance, by casting spells or tampering with the victim's hair, nail clippings or clothing.

Both failure and success drive people to consult witches, as Nyirongo points out: "[T]o avoid failure or attain success, one is entitled to use a powerful charm. When one has become successful, one is also expected to shield oneself from one's relatives with a powerful charm. Indeed one is justified to kill those contemplating one's downfall."[29] A poor relationship at home or in public life also leads to consultations with witches, as does the influence of evil spirits, deformity, sickness or insanity, malice or a lack of education. Given this wide range of motives, it is not surprising that almost everyone has made use of witchcraft or a charm.[30]

Nyirongo points out that "witches believe that the ultimate source of all their powers is a great benevolent Being or God." Nevertheless he concludes his study of the African view of witchcraft with the following statement:

> In whatever form, witchcraft is a violation of the first two commandments. Anything I depend on more than God—even if it promises success, riches, good health or protection—is an idol.[31]

Conclusion

Space is lacking to analyze the Christian response to traditional spirituality. In their comparative study of the traditional religions and Christianity, most scholars have ignored the significance of the spiritual powers and forces in traditional religions and cultures. The Bible, in both the Old and the New Testaments, acknowledges the spiritual reality behind the heathen practices of magic, sorcery and witchcraft. It has an "extensive vocabulary for the various aspects of magic, their practitioners and adherents."[32] African Christians contend daily with the impact of rituals, ceremonies and the paraphernalia of the spirit-powers. When Africans become Christians, their human needs remain the same, and their struggles can even increase in intensity. Some Christians incorporate aspects of traditional worship into their lives.

Nyirongo presents several biblical examples to "illustrate the idolatrous nature of witchcraft" (Dt 18:10–13; Acts 8:9–25; 13:6–10). After a thorough analysis of African traditional practices, he states that "witchcraft and whatever "good things" it promises all originate from sinful motives. ...Satan...can project himself as ... a concerned shepherd, but his aim is to destroy. ...African witchdoctors, sorcerers, witches, diviners and magicians can also transform themselves into shepherds...., only to deceive and enslave the community."[33]

Nyirongo stresses God's protection from and victory over witchcraft:

> Christians need not fear witchcraft. Not only are we promised full protection by God when we die (Mt 10:28), but we have more than enough weapons to fight and defeat witchcraft in this life.... These weapons are a) the knowledge of the truth (God's Word) (Acts 8:9–25; 13:6–10); b) the power of the Holy Spirit (Acts 13:9); c) prayer (Col 4:2; 1 Cor 16:13; Eph 6:12; Is 41:10); and d) holy living.[34]

Since its arrival in Africa, Christianity has engaged in spiritual warfare with these spiritual powers (Eph 6). Ignorance of these powers has often produced a shallow Christian theology that does not adequately address the issues of mystical powers in traditional Africa. The analysis of traditional religions and cultures is superficial, ignoring their theological and worldview foundations. I plead with my Christian brothers and sisters to discourage techniques that assimilate into Christian worship or life the pagan practices described in this chapter. I also encourage excellent Bible scholars and theologians to understand the African traditional culture and to reflect with us on biblical principles that will help African Christians develop true spiritual power to confound the wiles of the Evil One.

9

Chinese Spirituality

Toward a Christian Understanding

Samuel Ling

In Romans 3 the Apostle Paul asks if there is any advantage in being Jewish, then answers: Yes, because God's redemptive revelation was entrusted to the Jews. Is there any advantage in being Chinese, we may ask? Yes, for as one of the longest continuous civilizations on earth, the Chinese have enjoyed the most ample opportunity to respond to God's general revelation (Rom 1:18–20). In response to God's revelation in nature and in the human heart, the Chinese built one of the highest forms of humanistic civilization, comprised of four major philosophical/religious traditions. Today, China is home to one of the largest Protestant churches on earth (fifty to eighty million strong), yet Chinese philosophy and religion are very much alive. They remain an enigma to many non-Chinese. Our formidable task in this brief chapter is to highlight some features of Chinese spirituality commonly called Daoism (Taoism).

Religion: Defined System or Diffuse Spirituality?

The Chinese term for "religion" (*jiao*)[1] differs in connotation from its Western counterpart. The word literally means "teachings." In the West, we tend to distinguish between "religion" (the worship of a deity and the meditation on ultimate reality in the universe) and "philosophy" (the academic or speculative study of metaphysics, epistemology and ethics). Chinese "philosophy" and "religion" defy this categorization. Not all Chinese "religions" have a system of belief and practice with a well-defined theology (or pantheon). They lack stated places and times of worship, a system of dogma, and a priesthood or clergy. Chinese religion is diffused and functional. It is diffused rather than institutionalized. Daoism and Chinese folk religion (animism) do not fit into a definition of religion as a faith that demands exclusive loyalty by its followers. Chinese religion is also functional; one uses religion according to pragmatic needs in daily life. These two concepts were formulated by my late uncle, C. K. Yang, in his groundbreaking book, *Religion in Chinese Society.*[2]

Chinese philosophy and religion form a composite cultural tradition, made up of four different but interpenetrating traditions: Confucianism, Daoism, Animism (folk religion) and Buddhism, the latter imported from India and contextualized into several Chinese schools. Philosophical speculation, religious worship, ethical self-cultivation and superstition intermingle, and all four historic traditions have influenced one another.

Integrated Religion: A Biblical Perspective

Because of the composite nature of Chinese philosophy and religion, non-Chinese Christians and thinkers need to exercise extreme caution when approaching the subject or befriending a Chinese religionist. John Calvin and Cornelius Van Til remind us that our knowledge of God, of ourselves and of the world are interrelated, and all must be based on an obedient understanding of God's revelation in nature and Scripture. However, since the Fall of Adam, man has proceeded from a disobedient and idolatrous heart (or presupposition, or worldview) in his understanding of God, self and the universe. Chinese thought is one of the highest forms of humanist (man-centered) culture. It should not surprise us, therefore, that it integrates its understanding of God (religion) with that of the self (art, literature, ethics) and the world (philosophy). Nineteenth century missionaries spent years, even decades, studying the Chinese language, Chinese philosophy and literature, and the major Chinese "religions." The church in the twenty-first century must do no less, rather than rushing into oversimplified formulas and quick-fix methods of evangelism.

Confucianism: Virtue for Men and Rulers

Confucius (Kong zi) was China's first private teacher, traveling among the warring states in the fifth and early fourth centuries BC, urging the warring princes to rule by virtue, in order to bring stability and harmony to society. Virtue is cultivated through understanding the moral law of the universe, the way (*dao*) of heaven (*tian*). The virtuous prince and husband/father practice virtues such as benevolence (*ren*), uprightness (*yi*), filial piety (*xiao*), loyalty (*zhong*), and humility (*lian*). Confucius was agnostic about death and God; he said: "One does not know about life; how can one know about death?" "Revere the spirits (*gui*) and the gods (*shen*), and keep a distance from them." However, part of the practice of filial piety (*xiao*) involves the worship of, and sacrifice to, ancestors. From ancient books, Confucius adopted the concept that death is an extension of life, and that respect for one's parents (*xiao*) should extend into the period after death. Confucius' two major students, Meng zi (Mencius) and Xun zi (the latter not to be confused with Sun zi, who wrote *The Art of War*), disagree about human nature: Meng zi believed that man is by nature good, and should thus be taught and nurtured in moral living; Xun zi believed that man is by nature evil, and thus needs discipline through penalties.

Daoism: Philosophy and Spirituality

Daoism is the "other" tradition which deeply influenced Chinese culture; many argue that its influence is deeper than Confucianism. As a philosophy, Daoism refers to the body of teachings of Lao zi (Lao-tzu), a mythical figure to whom is attributed the short book, *The Way* (*Dao de jing*), and to the writings of Zhuang zi (Chuang-tzu). These teachers believe that the universe (existence) comes from nothing (*wu*), and everything in life is fleeting and relative. There is a strong sense of mysticism in both of these Daoist philosophers. Daoist advice to scholars and officials is to "do nothing" (*wu wei*), because there is very little one can do to change the course of the universe. Daoism encourages escape from society to commune with nature, in contradistinction from Confucian morality, which urges man to live morally and keep his/her station in family, society and government.[3]

A Christian Understanding

The Chinese, lacking God's redemptive revelation in Scripture and responding disobediently to God's general revelation, chose to unite man and the universe by encouraging man's communion with nature (monism), and by teaching that human society can get along without God (humanism). Even Daoist/Animist spirituality is highly pragmatic, serving purposes of the family, material gain and physical health and safety. Traditional Chinese spirituality is:

- *monistic* among intellectuals: communion with nature is the ideal;
- *pagan* among the masses: historical and mythical figures, ancestors, evil spirits and the deceased, make up the world of the spirit;
- *man-centered*: religious rites and practices function for this life;
- *based on fear* (for folk religion, especially): fear of death and the unknown, rather than the fear of the one and living God.

Deities and Energy

Animism originates from ancient records which predate Confucius and Lao-zi, showing a long-standing tradition of nature worship, totem worship, and the belief in immortal spirits (*xian*).[4] Add to this a view of the universe filled with the force of life (*qi*). *Qi* runs through the human body; hence the theories of Chinese herbal medicine, acupuncture and Chinese massage (*tui na*). It also runs through the universe; hence, the practice of "wind" and "water"(*feng shui*). *Qi* may rise to heaven or descend into the earth. The bodies of deceased persons may absorb this *qi* and pass it on to descendants. Mountains, rivers and lakes all have *qi* and personality. Thus, it behooves the living to live in harmony with this force in the universe, or (in Daoist and animist spirituality) to manipulate it for one's own material and this-worldly benefit.[5]

Daoist worship and religious practice is intermingled with animism (folk religion). In this chapter, we treat the two traditions as one. We will call it "Daoist/Animist spirituality," or "Daoism in the broad sense."[6] While this tradition appears polytheistic, it is in fact animist in presupposition. Humans can become spirits and deities; moreover, there is a monistic union between this world and the next (spiritual) world.

Heaven (*Tian*): Four Phases of Meaning

The concept of heaven is basic to the Chinese view of the universe. Heaven (*tian*), the transcendent ultimate in the universe, has gone through several changes in meaning. Originally, *tian* (also *Shangdi*, "the lord above") was a personal deity. This led many Christians to speculate that God revealed himself to the Chinese as *tian* or *Shangdi*.[7] By the time of Confucius (551–479 BC), *tian* had come to mean the moral order or laws of the universe. During the Han (206 BC–AD 220), *tian* stood for the physical sky. In Daoist/animist spirituality, *tian* is the name of a god (*tian gong*) as well as the name for other deities. It is the last two views of heaven that concern us here.

While Daoist philosophy is abstract, relativistic and mystical, Daoist spirituality transformed philosophy. Daoist spirituality took the realm of nothingness (*wu*) in philosophy and turned it into the realm of the immortal spirits (*xian*). Daoist religious masters, to buttress their authority, even claimed that Lao-zi once taught Confucius a few things! The vocabulary of Lao zi's *Dao de jing* is easy to twist and misinterpret. Because it is rhymed, it is easy to teach and memorize. The Daoist masters claimed secret teachings which they passed on to their adherents only. Daoist spirituality believed in the existence of immortal spirits (*xian*), ghosts (*gui*) and deities (*shen*). This belief is the basis for Daoist practices that seek tranquility, prosperity, riches, longevity and immortality after death.

Humans Can Be Deified

In Daoist/Animist practices in contemporary Taiwan, two types of deities exist: gods who are prior heaven (*xian tian*), and gods who are latter heaven (*hou tian*). The highest god is the *san qing dao zu* (the three pure deities/ancestors of the *dao*). These three kinds of deities are the substance and origin of heaven, earth and the universe. They are collectively called the *dao*. Heaven, earth, mankind and the universe emanated (*hua*) from them. The regent ruler for the Jade Emperor (*dao*) is *yu huang shang di*, who has the highest authority; he is the king of ten thousand heavens. The birthday of the Jade Emperor, or heaven-god (*tian gong*), is celebrated on the ninth day of Chinese New Year. These are the "prior heaven" gods.[8]

The latter heaven gods are the immortal spirits. Every human being can become a *xian* through cultivating his spirituality. Individuals who were particularly virtuous, or who made outstanding contributions to the Chinese people, would be promoted to become gods (*shen*). There is supernatural power in the universe, and humans, by becoming gods, can possess such supernatural power.[9] This explains why Daoism/Animism is a mixture of a) polytheism, b) animism, and c) the worship of deceased spirits.

Spirits Everywhere

Daoists and, in general, Chinese folk religionists have numerous objects of worship: heaven, earth, stars, the four points, the five elements (metal, wood, water, fire and earth), mountains and rivers, trees, crops, ancestors, heroes of the Chinese people, legendary figures, figures from fiction, and the deceased, including ancestors. Even man-made objects like beds, boats, city gates, stoves, wells and mills are worshiped. In the Daoist home is a shrine for gods and ancestors (the plaques for the ancestors' spirits are to the right of center). In order not to miss any deity, some Daoist shrines have one plaque named *tian di qin jun shi* (heaven, earth, emperor and family master).[10]

Daoism is at its core animistic. The Daoist/Animist Chinese believes that there are demons and spirits throughout the universe and that anything can be the object of worship. Elements and things in nature can threaten property and life: heaven, the sun, the moon, stars, mountains, rivers, the earth, thunder, lightning, wind, rain, animals, plants, minerals and others. I have seen a number of shrines in Hong Kong and Malaysia to the "tree-god"—there is no idol, no plaque, but simply sticks of incense at the foot of a tree. Likewise in Taiwan, Hong Kong and elsewhere, the "earth god" is worshiped simply with a few sticks of incense. If one cannot get out to the "earth," one can leave the sticks next to the door of an apartment, store or restaurant.

Gods for Life; Patrons for Trades

In order to protect life, family and work, man-made objects are made into objects of worship: beds, boats, needles, doors, stoves, the city gate and moat, animal dwellings, wells, mills, bridges, waterways, roads, granaries, stones and tiles. We can distinguish animism from polytheism this way: the objects of worship in animism are too numerous to count. There are spirits and gods everywhere. Thus shamanism—the practice of supernatural communion with spirits and gods, along with the ability to exorcise and heal, is a form of animism. It is very prevalent among Chinese in Taiwan, Malaysia and elsewhere.[11]

Human beings can also be objects of worship. The Chinese worship deceased ancestors (see below); historical heroes such as the Yellow Emperor (a prehistoric mythical figure) and Yu (another prehistoric, mythical leader who subdued a flood); as well as other generals, virtuous officials or poets. It is believed that these heroes become immortal spirits. An ordinary citizen with unusual virtues, such as filial piety or patriotism, may be worshiped as an immortal spirit. Another group of deities are the "patron deities" of trades, such as: Guang di or Guang gong (the red-faced general with a sword), often regarded as patron for the military and the police; Confucius, patron of teachers; Hua Tuo, patron of the medical arts; Cang jie, patron of the written language; and other patrons for farming, trading and other business endeavors.

A popular deity is the earth god (*Tu di gong*). Though this god is not regarded with high honor, its temples are everywhere. Sometimes a small temple, one or two meters high, can be seen in the fields. His official name is "the upright god of blessing and virtue" (*Fu de zheng shen*). Most people worship him on the second and sixteenth day of the lunar month. It is said that his birthday is on the second day of the second lunar month. Also on the Dragon Boat Festival (*Duan Wu*, the fifth day of the fifth lunar month) the earth god is worshiped.

Sometimes one can find a small mound near a tomb, with a plaque labeled *Hou tu*. They are earth gods who protect cemeteries and tombs. Since land may be expensive, a large earth god shrine would do for all the deceased buried in an entire cemetery. After people worship their ancestors at the tomb, they would go pay homage to the earth god at the common shrine. I have observed row after row of *tu di gong* shrines in front of apartment units in high rise buildings, as well as along a busy street in Hong Kong. A shop or restaurant may have a shrine for *tu di gong*, along with another deity for the stove.

Worship of the Dead

The Bible teaches that man has no control over death; only Jesus Christ overcame death's curse for those who put their trust in him. Sorcery, or communicating with the dead and the spiritual world, is clearly forbidden by God in Deuteronomy 18. Additionally, Paul teaches that when we worship idols, we are in fact communing with demons, messengers of the Devil. Chinese rites constantly commune with the world of spirits and worship the deceased. This tradition is a fusion of Confucian filial piety (*xiao*) and the Daoist/Animist understanding of the underworld.

Traditional/Confucian Understanding

In traditional Chinese thought, the human soul has two parts: the *hun* and the *po*. *Li Ji* (*The Book of Rites*, one of Confucianism's classic texts that predate Confucius) says that, at death, the *hun* returns to heaven, while the *po* returns to earth. Confucius adopts the ancient tradition of sacrificing to the dead, by teaching that filial piety, as a cardinal virtue for family and society, should be practiced when one's parents are alive, and after they have passed on. Thus ancestor worship is both an integral part of the Confucian social ethic, as well as part and parcel of Daoist/Animist spirituality. In Confucian/Daoist homes, there is an ancestral hall where the ancestors' souls are represented by wooden plaques with their honorific names written on them. Incense is offered to them by the descendants. If a person has no son, he/she is said to be "with no one after him/her" (*wu hou*) and is a lone spirit (*gu hun*). Thus, all Confucian/Daoists want a son, who is the proper one to offer them incense after they die. This practice of filial piety is the glue which keeps the family and clan together, the very fabric of human society.

Funeral Practices

Funeral practices vary from region to region. In contemporary Taiwan, before a person dies, he or she is taken from the bedroom to the main hall of the house, where the ancestral tablets are kept. The soul of a person who dies in the bedroom may not transmigrate properly. Money found on the person is given to the descendants before death, so that sons and grandsons may accumulate great wealth. After death, the whole body is covered with white cloth. A bowl with incense and a cooked duck egg is offered, and two white candles and funerary paper are burned, so that the deceased may have money to spend in the underworld. The ancestral tablets and gods in the ancestral hall are now covered with a large white cloth. On the front door of the home, a white piece of paper is hung with the characters *ji zhong* (in the midst of misfortune) written on it.

Death Announcement and Funerary Garments

The family of the deceased will distribute news of the death (in contemporary society, a newspaper advertisement is often placed), and spread a spirit-table, so that relatives and friends may come and pay their last respects by burning incense. The name of the deceased, the date and time of death, and the names of his/her sons are posted. Sons and daughters, daughters-in-law, the eldest paternal grandson, great-grandsons and great-great-grandsons all have their unique garments for the funeral rites. Most of these are in white, except for great-great-grandsons, who wear red. Daoist priests (*Dao shi*) are hired to recite chants before the deceased, in order to guide him to the underworld. The Daoist view of how many parts the soul has, and where the soul goes after death, may differ significantly from the ancient/Confucian understanding.

Corpse and Casket

The corpse is (figuratively speaking) washed with living water. A Daoist priest will lead a male descendant to a river, and throw money into the water to ask the water god to sell the descendant water. Upon return to the house, an older person (who is both advanced in age and with many descendants) will take chopsticks to pick up a white cloth, dip it with the "living water," and make gestures, as if to wash the corpse, while pronouncing lucky sayings. After this, the hair is combed and makeup is put on, in preparation for dressing the dead with "longevity garments" (*shou yi*).

Before the funeral, a male descendant keeps guard over the corpse. A casket is purchased and taken home. En route, if it crosses an intersection or bridge, money is thrown about, in order to appeal to the lone spirits who are said to hold forth in such strategic spots, asking them to allow the casket to pass through. When the casket reaches home, all descendants must wear the proper funerary garments, kneel, and weep to welcome the casket. They may also hold on to a hemp rope tied to the sleeves of the deceased. The Daoist priest recites chants, and takes a knife to cut the rope, symbolizing that the dead and the living are now separated. The rope is then burned.

The Funeral

On the day of the funeral—which is chosen because it is auspicious—the corpse is placed in the casket, along with certain items: funerary money, plaques for driving out evil spirits, a cooked egg (representing eternal unity between husband and wife), stones and other items to deceive evil spirits who may block the way of the deceased to go to the underworld. Gold, silver or jade is placed inside the mouth of the deceased—sometimes even grains of rice, so that the deceased will have enough to eat. The descendants pay their last respects around the casket, which is then secured with five wooden nails. Another set of ceremonies is prescribed for the burial, including family and public worship (*ji*). An ancestral plaque is made for the deceased, which the oldest grandson carries in a sedan, to be placed in the ancestral hall at home. Thereafter, family members must sacrifice to the deceased morning and evening every day for one hundred days. On the seventh day it is believed that the spirit of the deceased will return, so a set of ceremonies is observed. There is another set of ceremonies for the hundred-day anniversary, and yet another set for the one-year anniversary of death.[12]

Lone Spirits and War Victims

It is very important to have descendants who will offer sacrifices to you when you die. The person who has no children, or whose children have died, will arrange for "godsons" so that the incense fires may not go out. If not, they become lone spirits (*gu hun*). Deceased persons whose corpses or body parts are not claimed by any family members are buried in a public place, and incense is offered to them. The deity for this place of worship is called *You ying gong* (the god who answers prayers). Other deceased spirits include those who die in warfare; special places of burial and worship are arranged for them.

The Spirits Return: Ghost Festival

The seventh month of the lunar year is popularly called *gui yue*, the "month of the ghosts," when the ghost festival (*gui jie*,) is observed. The climax is the fifteenth day of the month. Buddhists and Daoists interpret it differently: Buddhists call this festival *Yu lan*, to express filial piety (*xiao*), while Daoists emphasize the worship of lone spirits (*gu hun*). Daoists believe that on the twenty-ninth day of the sixth lunar month, at midnight, the "king" of the underworld (a deity) opens the "gates of hell,"freeing lone spirits to wander about. Living humans must feed and appease them every day, until midnight on the twenty-ninth day of the seventh lunar month (sometime in August), at which time these lone spirits return to hell.[13] In modern practice, concerts and exotic (discotheque) dances are performed for the sake of the spirits, in addition to offering them food and incense. An outdoor canopy is erected, and an auditorium is put in place. I have observed often in Malaysia and Singapore, that almost no one watches these performances, which are put on for the sake of the lone spirits. Numerous restaurants are closed during August in Singapore and Malaysia in observance of the ghost festival.

Conclusion

Three kinds of deceased are worshiped: ancestors, great heroes and lone spirits. Scripture says that there is no fear in love, because perfect love casts out all fear. The Chinese tradition of worshiping the spirits of the deceased is based on fear, as well as self-serving motives. The Chinese heart and mind needs redemption by the light and love of Christ's redemptive work. The worship of ancestors and funeral practices show that Daoist spirituality is humanist: man seeks to be deified and desires to be worshiped by his ancestors. It is monistic: man becomes part of the spirit world. It is based on fear: descendants worship and appease the ancestors' spirits in order to avoid trouble and suffering in this life.

Chinese spirituality involves several other major dimensions which will not be covered in this chapter, due to space limitations. *Feng shui*, the manipulation of *qi*, the energy in the universe, is monistic—man is in union with the forces of nature. Festivals in the traditional Chinese calendar involve the worship of ancestors, deities and spirits. Chinese family, village and society are filled with this monistic, animistic, view of the universe.

The light of the world has come, and darkness will not overcome it. This is the message which Chinese Daoists and folk religions need to hear. But we who are Christians must proceed with caution, sensitivity and wisdom as we present the gospel to the traditional Chinese heart. A grasp of the Confucian and Daoist worldview is essential preparation. May grace be granted that we learn how to listen and understand, as well as to speak and persuade.

10

Jung & the New Spiritualities
Are They Godless?

Randall Verarde

C. G. Jung has been called one of the twentieth century's most influential thinkers. The legacy of professional psychology and self-analysis that he helped create has significantly shaped modern notions of the self. Jung's contribution has several dimensions and can be appreciated from a variety of points of view. Here I wish to focus on the religious aspects and implictions of Jung's psychological theory.

Jung forged his unique system of self-understanding and analysis from a synthesis of religious and psychological insights. Unlike his mentor Sigmund Freud, Jung viewed religious symbols and experience as positive expressions of psychological development. For those uncomfortable with Freud's reductionism, Jung seems to offer an alternative theory of the personality that validates religious experience and includes some notion of a universal "God-image." It would be a mistake to say, however, that Jung accepted religious experience uncritically or affirmed the existence of a transcendent personal God beyond the psyche.

Jung's ideas range far beyond therapy and have influenced a large number of contemporary spiritual movements. Like the therapeutic attitude he helped to establish, these movements reject traditional Judeo-Christian religious claims, identity, and values in favor of highly individualized forms of spiritual realization. Jung and the contemporary spiritualities he has influenced share a radically revisionist—some would say subversive—stance toward classic forms of Judaism and Christianity.

How does Jung manage to embrace religious symbols while rejecting religious assumptions, dogmas and institutions? Does his approach to self-development successfully avoid the oppressive aspects of Judeo-Christian theology and religion? Or, are his sophisticated theories so mystifying that they obscure their profound religious skepticism and reductionism? We cannot adequately appreciate Jung's influence or the impact of his theories upon modern attitudes toward religion, spirituality and the self until we have looked seriously at these questions.

CHILDHOOD EXPERIENCES

As influential as Jung's psychology has been upon modern spirituality, that psychology itself was shaped by his own spiritual leanings and experiences. Understanding his personal history and the influences that shaped him will help us grasp how he inspired renewed interest in many otherwise obscure ancient religious forms and practices. A short list of these influences includes: Kabbalah, Astrology, Taoism, Shamanism, Hinduism, Buddhism, Tantra, Alchemy, Gnosticism and New Age.

Jung's intense interest in religion began very early. His father was a Swiss Reformed minister, as were several of his uncles. However, his mother was involved with spiritualism and bequeathed to him an interest in the occult. From a very early age, Jung sensed conflict in his home and attempted to reconcile it through his fantasies. In his autobiography, *Memories, Dreams, Reflections,* he discloses several childhood fantasies and dreams that led him to discover a dark god lurking behind what he began to identify as Christianity's religious façade.

Jung recounts a childhood dream in which he discovered an underground chamber. Descending the stone stairs, he came upon a dimly lit room where a "subterranean God" sat upon a magnificent throne. Jung later understood it to be a ritual phallus. From a distance he heard his mother's voice saying, "Yes, just look at him. That is the man-eater." Terrified, his four-year-old imagination confused the dream figure with the Lord Jesus who "took" the dead, which to Jung meant that he ate them. This "God not to be named" appeared to Jung "whenever anyone spoke too emphatically about Lord Jesus. Lord Jesus never became quite real for me, never quite acceptable, never quite lovable, for again and again I would think of his underground counterpart, a frightful revelation which had been accorded me without my seeking it."[1]

In another formative fantasy, Jung struggled as a young boy over a period of several days with the intrusion of a forbidden thought. As he contemplated the cathedral in the town square while walking home from school, along with the beautiful sky and God above seated on his throne, he choked on the sensation that something terrible was emerging in his thoughts that he dare not entertain, for to do so would be to commit blasphemy against the Holy Spirit. Despite his struggles, he concluded that God had created him just the way he was, as he had created Adam and Eve the way they were, and in his omniscience arranged everything so that they would have to sin.

Thus, Jung concluded, God was the author of his desperate problem. "Can it be that he wishes to test my obedience by imposing on me the unusual task of doing something against my own moral judgment and against the teachings of my religion, and even against His own commandment, something I am resisting with all my strength because I fear eternal damnation?"[2] Jung's image of God had bifurcated:

> I gathered all my courage, as though I were about to leap forthwith into hell-fire, and let the thought come. I saw before me the cathedral, the blue sky. God sits on His golden throne, high above the world—and from under the throne an enormous turd falls upon the sparkling new roof, shatters it, and breaks the walls of the cathedral asunder.[3]

Following the "release" of this forbidden thought, Jung felt a great sense of relief, and many things became clear to him, including his pastor father's weakness and tragic error. He had taken the Bible's commandments as his guide; he had believed in God as the Bible prescribed and as his forefathers had taught him. But he did not know the immediate living God who stands, omnipotent and free, above his Bible and his church, who calls upon man to partake of his freedom, and can force him to renounce his own views and convictions in order to fulfill the command of God without reserve:

> From that moment on, when I experienced grace, my true responsibility began. Why did God befoul His cathedral? That, for me, was a terrible thought. But then came the dim understanding that God could be something terrible. I had experienced a dark and terrible secret. It overshadowed my whole life.[4]

Jung remained true to his childhood fantasies in his developed psychology by emphasizing what might be called the dark side of God. Reality is best embodied not in the morally consistent personal God of Judeo-Christian orthodoxy but in the Gnostic god *Abraxis*, who is an amalgam of light and darkness. Truth is found not in virtue and moral development but in the inevitability of inner conflict and the "tension of opposites" within the psyche.

EASTERN RELIGION, GNOSTICISM

Jung became instrumental in interpreting Eastern religious texts for Western audiences. Hindu, Buddhist and Taoist ideas permeate his writings and are embedded into the deepest structure of his thought. More importantly, he recast many esoteric Eastern ideas into the more readily accessible language of psychology, making Eastern thought available to a wider audience. Perhaps most significant among them is the idea that consciousness transcends the ego, or individual personality, and includes a superordinate center, which Jung called "the Self." It was this idea more than any other that led to his break from Freud's more prosaic view of the personality.

An ancient Taoist text, *The Secret of the Golden Flower*, played a key role in Jung's development. He had become isolated and depressed following his break with Freud and had begun working with mandalas, which are circular drawings used in various eastern and native traditions. He began to understand his mandala drawings as "cryptograms concerning the state of the self":

> I acquired through them a living conception of the self. The self, I thought, was like the monad which I am, and corresponds to the microcosmic nature of the psyche....I saw that everything, all the paths I had been following, all the steps I had taken, were leading back to a single point—namely, to the mid-point. It became increasingly plain to me that the mandala is the center. It is the exponent of all paths. It is the path to the center, to individuation. ...I began to understand that the goal of psychic development is the self. There is no linear evolution; there is only a circumambulation of the self. ... everything points toward the center.[5]

Still depressed, Jung created two mandalas that seemed Chinese in form and in choice of color.

> It was a strange coincidence that shortly afterward I receive a letter from Richard Wilhelm enclosing the manuscript of a Taoist-alchemical treatise entitled *The Secret of the Golden Flower*, with a request that I write a commentary on it. I devoured the manuscript at once, for the text gave me undreamed-of confirmation of my ideas about the mandala and the circumambulation of the center. That was the first event which broke through my isolation. I became aware of an affinity; I could establish ties with something and someone.[6]

Jung also recognized affinities with ancient Gnosticism. Years later he purchased, and was among the first to publish, a newly discovered ancient Gnostic manuscript from Nag Hammadi, now known as the Jung codex. He openly acknowledged his indebtedness to ancient Gnostic philosophy and its medieval counterpart, alchemy, which became the model for much of his later writing. One of his earliest works, which he called an "indiscretion of my youth" and that his estate later tried to suppress, was an overtly Gnostic poem called *The Seven Sermons to the Dead*. A radically critical stance toward Judeo-Christian theism is apparent throughout, as the opening lines make clear:

> The dead came back from Jerusalem, where they found not what they sought. They prayed me let them in and besought my word, and thus I began my teaching. Harken: I begin with nothingness. Nothingness is the same as fullness. In infinity full is no better than empty.... This nothingness or fullness we name the PLEROMA. Therein both thinking and being cease, since the eternal and infinite possess no qualities.... I speak of [the pleroma] to make a beginning somewhere, and also to free you from the delusion that somewhere, either without or within, there standeth something fixed, or in some way established, from the beginning.[7]

A note of Buddhist-like Gnosticism is apparent here and rings throughout Jung's writings.

ASTROLOGY, OCCULTISM AND ALCHEMY

Jung provided a crucial impetus to the current revival of astrology. Many of today's most notable astrologists utilize Jungian theory to render astrological symbols into accessible psychological language. The affinity between Jung and astrology is due, they claim, to astrology's influence upon him. Richard Tarnas, a leading contemporary astrological theorist and Jungian-oriented scholar, describes Jung's increasing involvement in astrology as well as his ambivalent public stance toward it:

> The interest gradually developed into a major focus of investigation, and in his later years Jung devoted himself with considerable passion to astrological research. "Astrology," he stated, "represents the sum of all the psychological knowledge of antiquity." Though his published writings presented varying and at times ambiguous views of the subject over the course of his life, it is evident that insights from his astrological studies influenced many of his most significant theoretical formulations in the final, extraordinarily fruitful phase of his life's work.... It is also clear from reports from his family and others close to him that in his last decades he came to employ the analysis of birth charts and transits as a regular and integral aspect of his clinical work with patients in analysis.[8]

Tarnas goes on to explain how Jung's archetypal theory in turn influenced his own interest in astrology. "But more important, and more revealing, I found the symbolic principles associated with the planets at the core of the astrological tradition unexpectedly easy to assimilate, since they proved to be surprisingly similar—indeed, essentially identical—to the archetypes of modern depth psychology."[9] What is striking, however, is not astrology's influence upon Jung but Jung's influence upon astrology. Its Jungian character attracts many to contemporary astrology, which has morphed from a metaphysical and fortune-telling system into a complex network of psychological symbols. In the capable hands of Jung and his followers, astrology has become something other than what it was. In a clever bit of terminological alchemy, the Jungians have caused an ancient divination practice to be "born again" as a current-sounding quasi-psychological system of self-analysis.

Who gains from the claim that Jung was influenced by ancient astrology? Astrology gains psychological credibility by inferring that it understood the mysteries of the psyche long before Jung did. Astrology is now seen as a protopsychology with contemporary relevance. Jungian psychology also gains an aura of perennial wisdom dating back to ancient times. It becomes simultaneously a form of ancient spiritual wisdom and contemporary psychological technology and insight.

The real seedbed of Jung's ideas was not ancient astrology but nineteenth century European occultism, which romanticized the pagan gods of old Europe such as Mithras and Aion and had already begun the process of reshaping their mythologies into a contemporary form. Jung was neither an astrologer nor a Gnostic in anything like the ancient sense but, like Wagner, Nietzsche and Goethe before him, he drew upon the mystique of ancient occult systems in order to give the impression that his theories were a form of perennial wisdom. This has contributed significantly to Jung's popularity.

Jung developed a way of translating ancient symbols and statements of religion into a self-reflexive language of the contemporary psyche. But this "translation" comes at a cost. It is a kind of linguistic sleight-of-hand that first obscures the metaphysical, or supernatural, reference of the original symbols through a series of free-associational, often obtuse, metaphorical interpretations. Then it assimilates the reinterpreted content into the Jungian therapeutic worldview. Religious symbols or statements originally understood as transcendent in character have been reduced to their Jungian psychological equivalent. They have been domesticated and assimilated into the psyche's self-reflexive world of fantasy and projection.

A clear example of the Jungian propensity for reading religious language as psychological metaphor is found in the book *Alchemical Psychology* in which Jungian therapist Tom Cavalli, following Jung's lead, translates the medieval practice of Alchemy into a modern therapeutic protocol. Similar to the claims of Tarnas and others with respect to astrology,[10] Cavalli claims that Jung's system is in perfect accord with the symbolism of alchemy. "[Jung's] ideas about the development of personality from an undifferentiated mass to various levels of refinement accord precisely with the alchemist's symbolism of transmuting the gross *prima materia* into the philosopher's stone."[11]

Cavalli lists many parallels between ancient alchemy and Jungian psychology. For example: "The sun (*sol*) represents the eternal archetype of the Self, gold the perfection of the ego personality, and its integration with the Self, or the Individuated Self."[12] It is not clear whether Cavalli thinks Jung uncovered the parallels through "scholarly interpretation" or through a more direct experience of the collective unconscious. Perhaps some combination of scholarship and mystical experience "provided [Jung] with rich images to translate the mysterious words and symbols of the alchemical texts" into psychological language.[13] In any case, Jung has achieved, according to Cavalli, "a complete picture of mind-body consciousness that has the potential to unify the psyche.... Individuation then is an alchemical experiment that takes place inside the laboratory of the psyche."[14] In a series of deft moves, the metaphysical and historical contexts that define medieval alchemy are dispensed with and we are left with the ahistorical "laboratory of the psyche," which is assumed to be the same everywhere and at all times.

THE GREAT REVERSAL—JUNG AND CHRISTIANITY

Jung's genius consisted in his ability to appear at once scientific and sympathetic to spiritual and paranormal experiences of all kinds. Not only did he give quasi-scientific credibility to then popular occult and pagan practices such as séances and communicating with the dead, he even managed to offer bold new interpretations of Christianity itself. While he appeared sympathetic toward Christianity, he consistently interpreted its symbols in heterodox and subversive ways. Jung delighted in exposing the pagan shadow lurking beneath Christianity's outer façade, insisting that the pagan element was older and more psychically authentic than its institutionalized creedal form.

Jung's suspicion that a dark god lurked beneath the surface of the Judeo-Christian God-image developed into his view that "Christ as a religious symbol... lacks the shadow that properly belongs to it."[15] "The Christ-symbol lacks wholeness in the modern psychological sense, since it does not include the dark side of things but specifically excludes it in a Luciferian opponent."[16] The theological Christ, as developed by the church, represents the psyche's desire for perfection, but the pursuit of perfection is secondary and requires the unhealthy sublimation of a more immediate psychological need. Psychological health is defined, claims Jung, not by the pursuit of perfection but by the more immediate desire for wholeness. Wholeness represents a fundamentally different goal than perfection and involves an entirely different ethos and pursuit.

As Jung put it (rather cryptically):

> Is the self a symbol of Christ, or is Christ a symbol of the self? ...If one inclines to regard the archetype of the self as the real agent and hence takes Christ as a symbol of the self, one must bear in mind that there is a considerable difference between perfection and completeness. The Christ-image [as developed by the Church] is as good as perfect (at least it is meant to be so), while the archetype (so far as known) denotes completeness but is far from being perfect.... Accordingly the realization of the self... leads to a fundamental conflict, to a real suspension between opposites (reminiscent of the crucified Christ hanging between two thieves), and to an approximate state of wholeness that lacks perfection.... Where the archetype predominates, completeness is forced upon us against all our conscious strivings.... The individual may strive after perfection ("Be you therefore perfect—teleoi—as also your heavenly Father is perfect") but must suffer from the opposite of his intentions for the sake of his completeness. "I find then a law, that, when I would do good, evil is present with me." The Christ-image fully corresponds to this situation: Christ is the perfect man who is crucified.[17]

This ingenious inversion of biblical values and symbols implies that the pursuit of perfection, or virtue, prompts the unconscious to respond by generating a compensating experience of the dark shadow. It does so in order to maintain the psychic antinomy—the tension of opposites—and to help us on the path to wholeness regardless of our conscious intentions.

Here we see one of the keys to Jung's appeal across the spectrum of spiritual traditions and practices. He strikes at the heart of the moral accent in religion, declaring it to be secondary and inadequate—a perversion of the psyche's innate desire for wholeness rather than perfection.

He elevates the principle of conflict to equal status with moral virtue and the holy within the psyche. In fact, Jung makes a virtue of both conflict and the dark forces that "compensate" those of light. He insists that a dialectic, or tension of opposites, is normative and necessary for psychological health. In the process, he reinterprets Christ as a figure of conflict, beset by warring opposites within himself.

It is clear that Jung understood God to be a reflection or a projection of the psyche rather than a transcendent being. To establish his view he relied heavily upon the philosophy of Immanuel Kant. This took the form of assertions that we are hopelessly trapped within our own psyche. Whatever can be claimed to be known about God is nothing other than a reflection of the psyche itself. "The psyche cannot leap beyond itself. It cannot set up any absolute truths, for its own polarity determines the relativity of its statements."[18] God can be known, said Jung, but only as a psychic image, never as the absolute, transcendent, and holy being of Judeo-Christian tradition. Mystical and religious experiences of the divine "Other" are products of unconscious fantasy and reveal nothing about the extrinsic reality of God as such.

What our numinous inner images do tell us, Jung claims, is that the unconscious contains material that is not merely personal in nature. The inner images of the psyche, or archetypes as Jung called them, have constant, recognizable forms. They are, says Jung, the ordering structures and motifs of the psyche bequeathed to us through our long evolutionary history. "God," or better, the God-image in the psyche, is the psyche's most complete archetype. Thus, it has the greatest capacity to organize and order our experience. Nevertheless, in Jungian theory, the God-image is dialectical in nature and contains the seeds of its own division within the psyche. According to Jung, the dance of the opposites is destined to continue *ad infinitum*.

The tragedy of organized Judeo-Christian tradition, said Jung, was that it distorts the God-image through moral dualism. Christianity removes God's dark side into the Luciferian shadow where it is opposed and resisted instead of embraced. Jung's therapeutic goal regarding Christianity was to "put it on the couch," as it were, in order to open up its one-sided symbolism to alternate interpretation. Jung's preferred

God-image—the one uncontaminated by organized Christianity—is dialectical like the psyche itself. Its function is to bring the opposites within into some kind of interaction and mutual balance. This is the true importance of religious myth and symbol:

Yahweh's decision to become man is a symbol of the development that had to supervene when man becomes conscious of the sort of God-image he is confronted with. God acts out of the unconscious of man and forces him to harmonize and unite the opposing influences to which his mind is exposed from the unconscious. The unconscious wants both: to divide and to unite.... the unconscious wants to flow into consciousness in order to reach the light, but at the same time it continually thwarts itself, because it would rather remain unconscious. That is to say, God wants to become man, but not quite. The conflict in his nature is so great that the incarnation can only be bought by an expiatory self-sacrifice offered up to the wrath of God's dark side.[19]

> In Jungian theory, the God-image functions—or ought to function if it is authentic—to move the personality from one-sided consciousness to a more expansive, empathetic awareness of the opposites within it. It is the conflict engendered by the call to religious faith and duty that most interests Jung:
> The fact that Christian ethics leads to collisions of duty speaks in its favour. By engendering insoluble conflicts and consequently an *afflictio animae*, it brings man nearer to a knowledge of God. All opposites are of God, therefore man must bend to this burden; and in so doing he finds that God in his "oppositeness" has taken possession of him, incarnated himself in him. He becomes a vessel filled with divine conflict.[20]

And again:

> This great symbol [the crucifixion] tells us that the progressive development and differentiation of consciousness leads to an ever more menacing awareness of the conflict and involves nothing less than a crucifixion of the ego, its agonizing suspension between irreconcilable opposites....[21]

Jung saw the psyche as the larger context within which religious symbols should be interpreted. He did not regard religious revelation as a larger context within which to interpret the psyche. In his words, Christ is a symbol of the Self; the Self is not a symbol of Christ. Jung's was an enclosed system of self-experience. The gods are projections of the psyche, which he defined as "a dynamic process which rests on a foundation of antithesis, on a flow of energy between two poles."[22] If, at bottom, the psyche is a process of antithesis, then the deities that it projects onto the landscape of myth and religion must possess the same qualities.

Here we have the basis of his antagonism toward the Judeo-Christian religious tradition as well as his appeal to Neopagan religions of all types. The Judeo-Christian God is too one-sided and full of light to be an adequate representation of the psyche, especially of its dark unconscious. One cannot at the same time have both a God of light only and a psyche of wholeness, which by definition involves a continual interplay of light and dark elements. Given his assumptions regarding the psyche's self-confinement, Jung interpreted all God-images as nothing other than creations of the psyche, just as some ancient Gnostics had claimed.[23] God must therefore be dyadic, amoral, and equally at home as a figure of evil as well as of good.

The Reign of the Subjective

It is a similar tendency to emphasize the metaphorical nature of religious language that led one modern scholar to characterize ancient Gnosticism as peculiarly modern and psychotherapeutic in nature. In her well known book, *The Gnostic Gospels,* Elaine Pagels describes what she sees as a similarity between Jung and ancient Gnosticism as follows:

> Such Gnostic Christians saw actual events as secondary to their perceived meaning. For this reason, this type of Gnosticism shares with psychotherapy a fascination with the nonliteral significance of language, as both attempt to understand the internal quality of experience. The psychoanalyst C. G. Jung has interpreted Valentinus' creation myth as a description of the psychological processes.[24]

In addition to his denial of the plain sense of language, and related to it, Jung also denies the objectivity of truth, especially of religious truth. What we call true is, in Jung's thought, really only true for us. Or, better, it is psychically true. The great religious truths, says Jung, are nothing other than the great truths of the psyche, projected outward and developed into myths, legends, parables, and the like. These "truths" can never be proven as historical or actual facts:

> Physical is not the only criterion of truth: there are also psychic truths which can neither be explained nor proved nor contested in any physical way....Religious statements are of this type....The reality of the spirit or *meaning*... is something that demonstrates itself and is experienced on its own merits....That is why whenever we speak of religious contents we move in a world of images that point to something ineffable.[25]

Once religious language has been reduced to metaphor and truth has been reduced to the psychic, Jung's most significant denial can hardly be resisted. His linguistic sleight-of-hand domesticates the ultimate truth, God, into the service of the Jungian project. He denies the category of transcendence itself. God cannot be what theistic traditions claim because we cannot know God as anything other than an image of our own psyche. Jung repeatedly insists that this is not a metaphysical statement but a psychological one. That claim has not gone unchallenged.

It is no wonder that Jung has been severely criticized as a Gnostic religionist rather than a scientific researcher. One of Jung's most serious critics, the Jewish religious scholar Martin Buber, correctly charges Jung with overstepping the bounds of psychology and making pronouncements upon metaphysics, despite his repeated protests that he has not done so. In substantiating his charge, Buber exposes a fundamental contradiction in Jung's theory and approach.

His argument goes something like this: On one hand, Jung says that all experience and all statements, including statements about God, are psychic. They say nothing about things outside the psyche *per se*, but only about what the psyche experiences. On the other hand, Jung warns that psychologists ought not to go beyond the boundary of making statements about the psyche, which is their proper domain, and claims that he himself does not do so. But, says Buber, here is the rub:

> In contradiction to his assertion that he wishes to avoid every statement about the transcendent, Jung identifies himself with a view "according to which God does not exist 'absolutely,' that is, independent

> of the human subject and beyond all human conditions." This means, in effect, that the possibility is not left open that God... exists independent of as well as related to the human subject. It is made clear that He does *not* exist apart from man. This is indeed a statement about the transcendent. It is a statement about what it is not and just through this about what it is. Jung's statements about the "relativity" of the divine are not psychological but metaphysical assertions....[26]

Jung's core claim that we cannot escape the psyche and that God is therefore nothing but a psychic image, is contradictory, for such a thing cannot be known with certainty unless one has escaped the psyche in order to know it. But how does Jung know this? He has turned psychological confinement into *gnosis* or spiritual knowledge, the very thing he says is not possible. Left unchallenged, he is free to turn it this way or that—into a statement of quasi-scientific skepticism regarding transcendence or a quasi-spiritual statement of the psychic character of the gods or the divine character of the psyche—as he pleases, to suit the situation.

Conclusion

Jung's religious theory is a complex mixture of profound insights, obscurant leaps of logic and theological reductionsim. It was born in a child's wounded spirit, seeking a way to subvert his parents' world, especially the religion that seemed to young Carl to be responsible for their conflicted existence. It destroyed his relationship with his mentor and psychological father, Sigmund Freud. It attacked and subverted the entire Judeo-Christian tradition. And it grew strong by reinterpreting and assimilating many occultic ideas and practices along the way. Jung stayed true to the initial visions of his childhood, offering others an individualized alternative to the seemingly grandiose claims and repressive character of traditional theistic religions. It could be said that Jung fought against the terror of his childhood dream of Christ the "man-eater" by becoming, as it were, C. G. Jung the God-eater, devouring any notion of the transcendent God and denying it to those who follow him.

Those who embark on the Jungian path in any of its current spiritual forms should be aware of how profoundly it differs from classic Christianity.

11

THE SPIRITUALITY OF QUANTUM MECHANICS

FRANK STOOTMAN

In the fifty or so years from the end of nineteenth century to the 1930s, physics made momentous progress in discovering and understanding the properties of the atomic world. Heinrich Hertz discovered Electromagnetic Radiation (1885–1889), Wilhelm Roentgen discovered Xrays (1895), Henri Becquerel discovered radioactivity (1896), J.J. Thompson discovered the electron (1897), Ernst Rutherford discovered the positively charged nucleus (1905), Albert Einstein proposed that light is a particle (1905), and Chadwick discovered the neutron (1932). In that same period, Albert Einstein proposed a new way to think about space and time with his relativity theory (1908 and 1914). Nobel Prize winners Niels Bohr (1913), Werner Heisenberg (1927), Erwin Schrodinger (1926), Max Born (1926) and Paul Dirac (1930) made great strides in describing the strange behavior of the atomic world—sometimes called the quantum world. The difficulties in exploring that world were not created so much by the primitive nature of the experimental apparatus as by the puzzling contradictions such research raised, disappointing our hopes for a simple picture or analogy of how this minute world functions.

Foremost of the dilemmas was that electrons, protons, neutrons and light particles (photons) could behave as a *wave* or as a *particle*. In our everyday world these are mutually exclusive. A wave transfers energy without mass transfer. A particle bobs up and down *in* a wave and is not carried along *with* it. No mass is transferred, only energy is handed on from atom to atom in the material which carries the wave. On the other hand, energy transfer of *particles* can only be done when its mass is actually moved. There is no handing on of energy from atom to atom in the material. A *net* movement of atoms in the material must occur to transfer energy.

The apparent contradictions of the data that arise from atomic experiments do not mean that this world is arbitrary and unknowable. Modern physics has found the world to be mathematically quite reasonable, though everyday pictures are now meaningless as a means of understanding it. Many of us feel that if we can draw a picture, we can understand a concept, which is why student textbooks are full of charts and illustrations. It is nearly impossible, however, to understand the atomic world with pictures, so physicists create mathematical symbols to represent objects, imbue them with properties and then perform logical operations on these symbols. This mathematical understanding is called *Quantum Mechanics* (QM).

Like all great advances, the discovery of the apparent properties of the atomic world has opened the door to metaphysical speculation. The prefix *meta* means beyond. Thus metaphysics is speculation about things beyond physics. Questions such as why the physical laws are the way they are or why the form of our physical universe is the way it is are metaphysical questions. In 1935 Albert Einstein wrote: "[S]cience can only ascertain what *is*, but not what *should be*, and outside of its domain value judgments of all kinds remain necessary. Religion, on the other hand, deals only with evaluations of human thought and action: it cannot justifiably speak of facts and relationships between facts."[1] Questions that cannot be answered directly from physics are metaphysical questions. Nevertheless, physics acts as a foundation to support the conclusions we come to about metaphysics.

Consider some of the things that allow science to be done, but which cannot be explained by science and are thus presupposed metaphysics. Firstly, the universe admits to reproducible measurement. We have laws and principles which can be discovered. Why? Though science cannot answer this "why," the answer is absolutely necessary for science. Secondly, the universe does not have an arbitrary form but is differentiated into distinct describable processes and categories. Once we understand these categories we are able to predict, operate and manipulate the processes which occur in nature. The success of such operations has made science and the subsequent technology the hallmark of the twentieth century. Why the universe is not ephemeral flux allows for real understanding of the universe by science but cannot be explained by science. Lastly, the universe is able to be described in terms of mathematical symbols and logical operations connecting these symbols. This deep truth undergirds the success of much of science and yet as a property is, once again, *discovered*, rather than *explained* by science.

We see that both physics and metaphysics exist and must be thought about together. Traditionally, Western metaphysics is completely consistent with a transcendent God (the God who reveals himself in the Jewish-Christian Scriptures), Creator and Designer of the form in which we can do science. This God has created a universe which has a distinct form, and in which categories and differentiation are real. If this is accepted, as it was by many scientists in the sixteenth and seventeenth centuries, then real progress can be made in understanding our universe. Even if God is rejected and metaphysical questions ignored, believing in the reality of distinct particular categories allows modern science to continue unabated just because the categories exist and are reproducibly stable. In an Eastern, monistic worldview, categories and distinctions are ultimately illusions (in Hindu tradition this is called Maya—reflections of the pure one mind or Brahma) and all is one. In such a worldview, science has no ultimate justification and so it is not surprising that in the East there was clever technology but no interest in fundamental science rooted in experimental measurement. Even the Greek philosophers tended to theorize about nature and its operation rather than perform measurement. The Jewish-Christian God, particularly the post-Reformation God, allowed science to flourish in Europe because nature had value and its form existed as identifiably real and measurable.

The physics of QM has brought forth metaphysical speculation about the nature of what is real at the very *small end* of the universe. The fundamental difficulty has been in the interpretation of the experimental data by using analogies which are consistent in our macroscopic experience. In our dimension, the logic of antithesis states: $A \neq \bar{A}$. For those unfamiliar with mathematics, this simply says that a thing (A) is not equal to its opposite (written as $\bar{A}$). For instance, we cannot say good is equal to evil. Likewise, a wave is not a particle. The trouble is that in order to make sense of QM, we have to mathematically write the outcome of a measurement as the statistical sum of all possible outcomes. This makes QM seem to be all about synthesis and has led many to conclude that the fundamental logic of the universe is one of syntheses. Those with an Eastern metaphysical worldview—Buddhism, Hinduism, and the New Age movement in the West—have embraced such a conclusion, arguing that Science concurs with the monism (all is one) they have always taught. Such thinking began early, with some of the Nobel prize winners who contributed to the development of QM. They saw parallels between the metaphysics of the quantum world and Eastern philosophy, without using one to justify the other, as later writers like Capra[2] and Zukav[3] have done. Two such examples are Werner Heisenberg and Erwin Schrodinger. Heisenberg had developed a matrix or discrete mathematical approach to QM around 1926. He had misgivings about the pragmatism of logical positivism. Logical positivism is a philosophy (now passé), which proposed that the limit of scientific knowledge is set by measurement only. Metaphysical speculation beyond the immediate data is "loose" science and must be regarded with suspicion. Heisenberg recognized that metaphysics had a place. In 1952, he attended a meeting in Copenhagen that brought together the best atomic physics minds to discuss a European particle accelerator. There, in conversations with Wolfgang Pauli (another Nobel prize winner in physics), Heisenberg revealed that whilst he had problems with positivism, he did not believe in a traditional Jewish-Christian worldview, but in a central order, or One, to which all religions pointed.[4] Schrodinger, who developed an alternative approach to QM using mathematically continuous functions, is more specific. In an intensely personal book of essays written as early as 1925, he expresses a belief in the Hindu Vedanta,[5] because it tackled the synthesis of multifaceted truth as a reflection of the one universal mind. The essays were written at the time of the development of the "wave" mechanics approach to QM and are consistent with his deeply held view of unity.

Is the connection between QM and monistic or Eastern thought inevitable? Does monism ultimately describe the fundamental nature of the universe? Has the traditional Jewish-Christian idea of an independent creator been superseded by the results of QM in favor of monism? To answer these questions, one must first recognize that in every generation the physical world has been used to support a metaphysical position. Ptolemaic astronomy, in which the Earth was the centre of the solar system, was adopted by the Scholastic Thomas Aquinas (1225–1274) because it agreed with the emphasis the Bible placed on the centrality of man in creation and on the closeness of God just above the heavens (*coelum empireum*). Galileo (1564–1642), arguing that the Sun is the centre of the solar system, suggests on aesthetic grounds that it is more worthy of God the Creator to have done so. Deism of the late seventeenth and the eighteenth centuries is supported by a mechanistic universe developed from the success of the ideas on gravitation that Isaac Newton (1642–1727) propounded. It should come as no surprise, then, that at the end of the twentieth century the shift away from traditional religion to a new romanticism (with monistic overtones of spirituality) would find support for its Eastern monism in an embrace of the results from QM. A notable example of this is the Dalai Lama who is the spiritual leader of Tibetan Buddhism. At a follow-up meeting of the sixth "Mind and Life" conference (1998), the Dalai Lama discussed with noted physicists like Anton Zeilinger the implications of QM and its relationship to Buddhism.[6] Similarly, the popular 2004 film *What the Bleep Do We Know?* produced by the Ramtha School of Enlightenment, juxtaposes interviews with quantum physicists and others with a story of how QM impacts and changes the life of a fictional character.

There is a great deal in the physical world, however, which speaks against Eastern monism. The categories, the differentiation of the particulars, the consistent laws and theorems, the existence of something created rather than nothing in the universe, all point away from Eastern monism. Reality as we know it, and indeed science, cannot operate as if it is ultimately secondary and an illusion. Our inability to create consistent analogies between the atomic world and our macroscopic world does not affect the reality that the logic of antithesis operates in our world. These difficulties seem to imply a limitation of knowledge and of reductionism as a philosophy rather than offering ultimate support for the veracity of monism.

Let us consider in more detail the main ideas of QM and their interpretation, then critique its appropriation in support of metaphysical monism.

WAVE-PARTICLE DUALITY

An elementary experiment performed in high school shines a narrow laser beam through a small slit. On the screen appears not a simple picture of the slit, but multiple images of the slit, gradually fading out on both sides. This diffraction pattern fits mathematically with the assumption that laser light is made of a wave. A similar elementary experiment is to shine light onto a metal surface contained inside a glass valve.[7] With a little care and a few bits of apparatus, one can easily show that the light shining onto the surface creates electrons that are "boiled off" the metal surface, creating a tiny current. When Einstein did the mathematics for this in 1905, he discovered that by far the best explanation is that light must be thought of as a particle. He called this particle of light a photon.

Only one experiment is needed to generate *both effects simultaneously*. Shine the laser beam onto a small slit, but now use a fluorescent screen, which gives a small pin prick or flash of light every time a photon hits it. The results of this experiment are amazing. First, we reduce the intensity of the laser beam right down, so that we see only occasional pin pricks on our fluorescent screen. Second, we watch where these pin pricks fall on the screen. To our amazement, the pin prick distribution precisely forms the same multiple images of the slit as if the intensity of light was much larger. This indicates very simply that light is both a wave (otherwise it would not form multiple images of the slit on the screen) *and* a particle (otherwise there would be no individual pin pricks of light on our screen). It is as if the photon spreads out like a wave, creating the diffraction pattern, and then, at the point it arrives at the fluorescent screen, dissolves into a pin prick of light, which means it is focused rather than spread out. We know no analogous behavior in our macroscopic physical world of something which is both spatially spread out and yet focused at the same time. In 1952, David Bohm, a famous physicist, showed mathematically that perhaps we could imagine an invisible pilot wave (also called a quantum potential) connecting the slit and screen. The photons of light follow this wave pattern and so only *appear* to have both wave and particle properties, because we think about them incorrectly.[8] One trouble in verifying Bohm's theory is that such waves are invisible—an interesting mathematical construct. Invisible quantities like pilot waves in *aether* (a theoretical substance which carries light waves and which cannot be directly and experimentally measured) have always been rejected by physicists. Bohm's work does highlight an important tension, however, that arises in QM interpretation. It seems that we have to let go of either *realism* or *locality* in interpreting the atomic world. *Realism* is the idea that we measure something that is actually there. Most science in our world operates this way. *Locality* means that an event can be localized in space and time and distant events are separated in space and time. Communication between space-time events cannot happen faster than the speed of light. Again most science in our world operates as if this is fundamentally true. Bohm's interpretation shuns locality, positing an interconnection which is everywhere and instantaneous (the pilot wave) and retains *realism* in the sense that a particle moves along this wave in a deterministic way. Most QM interpretation shuns *realism* but retains the notion of *locality*.

Hence, whilst the results of QM experiments are reproducible, their explanation defies us drawing a simple analogous picture of what light "really" is. In fact, it behaves as both a wave and a particle, and both properties can be brought out by specific experiments. The truly remarkable discovery is that not only do photons of light behave this way, so do electrons, protons and neutrons. Initially they were considered particles, but their wavelike property has been amply demonstrated. The most common position taken by physicists is that we can *describe* what we measure in terms of mathematics but that this is really only a convenient means to operate with the atomic world. This is called the Copenhagen interpretation of QM and is attributed to Niels Bohr and Werner Heisenberg who were important architects of QM. It is as if the limitation of analogy of the atomic world with our experience of the physical world is a fact, but a mathematical workaround is possible. Some might say that such pragmatism hides our ignorance of hidden variables which we cannot measure but are actually there. Surely some noncontradictory and consistent base-level picture analogue is possible. Unfortunately, the experimental QM world has proven beyond a shadow of a doubt to have no hidden variables. We have hit the rock bottom of the stuff of reality and its properties are that it has both *analogous wave* and *particle* properties.

QM has brought us to the limitation of a reductionist worldview. There is a point beyond which it becomes meaningless to speak in terms of consistent analogy with the macroscopic world in which we live. The reductionist enterprise of showing the universe to be a complex assemblage of elements with specific properties, operating like a mechanistic clock, is doomed. Somewhere, there is a limit to knowledge because of the fundamental nature of the universe. Werner Heisenberg captured this in his now famous Uncertainty Principle, which measures this limitation exactly! The idea is simple and yet profound. We can imagine that a particle thrown between two points ought to have at an instant of time an *exact* position and an *exact* speed with respect to some reference point. By exact we simply mean that the measurement of identical particles thrown in an identical way at an identical position and speed ought always to have an identical position and speed. Of course, in practice it *does* have statistical error but we can *imagine* a perfect experiment in which no error occurs in either the position or speed. Heisenberg's Uncertainty Principle (HUP) says that this assumption is false. Not because of practical limitations, which are real, but because even such a thought is not possible! According to HUP, it is not possible, *even in principle*, to measure both the position and speed without statistical variation. Imagining that one does this for both position and speed is precluded. *If* I could know the exact position and speed of every quantum mechanical object, then I could imagine the universe as a giant mechanistic clock because I could then also, in principle, predict its next moment of history. Unfortunately HUP simply says this is impossible, even in principle, and therefore the universe is not a giant machine.

For a monistic thinker like Capra, the wave-particle duality of the atomic or quantum world means that reality is beyond opposites. The mind is not in a fixed framework as it is in classical logic but is ever moving between opposite manifestations. He quotes the Lama Govinda: "The Eastern way of thinking rather consists of circling round the object of contemplation ... a many-sided, i.e., multidimensional impression formed from the superposition of single impressions from a different point of view..."[9] This appropriation of one aspect of QM to an ultimate monistic metaphysics needs to be considered carefully. The limitation of knowledge at the quantum or atomic level is real, and metaphysical speculation is valid, but it seems careless to argue that such limitation demands synthetic logic in our dimensions. At the macroscopic level, the logic of antithesis, mentioned earlier, works just fine in our world and in the world of science generally.

The Role of the Observer

Let us return to our experiment. Instead of using only one slit through which we pass laser light, let us use two very narrow slits, close enough together so they are both covered by the laser beam. Once again we see multiple images of the slits on our screen, now called an interference pattern. As in the previous case, the explanation of the pattern on the screen (though it differs slightly from the previous pattern) is best given by assuming light to be a wave. And once again, if we use a fluorescent screen and decrease the intensity of the laser beam, we see individual pin pricks or flashes of light, indicating that the photons are *particles*. As before, the flashes of light fall into the distinct interference pattern only explained by assuming light is a *wave*.

The question now is a little different. Through which narrow slit did each photon of light pass on its way to the screen to create the interference pattern? We can set up apparatus near the narrow slits to answer this question. Suppose further that the intensity of the laser light is so low that only individual photons approach the slits at any one time. Our apparatus proves that the photon only goes through one of the slits at a time and *not* through both. Amazingly, we get two possible results on the screen *depending on whether the slit photon detection apparatus is on or off*. Turn the slit photon detection off and the interference pattern on our fluorescent screen is still the same as before, but is built up over time. Turn the slit photon detection on and the interference pattern *disappears* and only a picture of the two slits is built up over time and *not* an interference pattern. "Knowing" the path of the photon at the slits destroys the interference pattern! Commensurately, not knowing the path allows the interference pattern to develop. There is no experiment which can be done to sidestep this result, which implies that photon detection changes the mathematics[10] and hence the detected pattern. It is as if the observer, in detecting which slit the photon goes through, has made the choice of particle or wave using the particle detection device at the slit. From that point on, the photon behaves as a particle or wave depending on that choice.[11]

Much has been made, by those in Eastern mysticism, of the role of the observer apparently being causal in creating reality. Capra writes

> In Eastern mysticism, this universal interwovenness always includes the human observer and his or her consciousness, and this is also true of atomic physics. At the atomic level, "objects" can only be understood in terms of the interaction between the processes of preparation and measurement. The end of the chain of processes always lies in the consciousness of the human observer...[12]

The persuasiveness of this argument is its psychological projection. Capra is not simply saying that our mind creates reality. It is the interaction of quantum systems with the *environment* that creates the universe as we see it with its categories and ultimately its logic of antithesis. This does not necessarily involve the human observer at all and is an important area of study called quantum decoherence. An atomic object like a photon that has not been measured by macroscopic apparatus to ascertain which of the two slits it has gone through, is described, in the language of QM, as the sum of the probability amplitudes[13] of going through both slit options, and is a called a coherent state. This sum, when converted to probabilities, has a mathematical term in it that gives us the interference pattern on the screen. When the coherent state interacts with the environment, such as a macroscopic measuring device, the QM probability amplitude sum is mathematically altered so that it no longer has the interference term when converted to probabilities. The state is said to have de-cohered and so also we no longer get the interference pattern on the screen. It has been shown by Zurek[14] that this occurs when an environment (not necessarily a mind) interacts with our quantum object. Indeed, talk of wave function collapse is also not necessary. Simply put, the environment alters the mathematics in such a way that QM behavior becomes classical behavior that we are used to in our dimensions.

Conclusions

Historically, physics has always been employed in the service of metaphysics. The question is; which does it better serve: monism or traditional theism? Science has recently moved comfortably into monism with the rise of the new romanticism of our age. Intrinsically, the overriding philosophy of science has been naturalism—all physical phenomena need only physical explanations. This is a type of *atheistic* monism and the parallel works comfortably with those who hold to *spiritual* monism, as in the New Age movement in the West. Atheistic monism left its adherents longing to make sense of being human in a paradigm in which the universe is made up ultimately only of collocations of atoms. Owen Flanagan in his recent book, *The Problem of the Soul,*[15] loudly echoes the scientific position that we are animals "evolved according to the principles of natural selection." This is at odds with what he says elsewhere: "most defenders of the scientific image either ignore the dominant humanistic image or deem it silly and misguided, while defenders of the humanistic image simply assert that the scientific image is de-meaning."[16] Flanagan sets himself the task of defending the reality of the scientific image, destroying the perennial philosophy which includes the existence of God, and yet retaining human dignity. Interestingly Flanagan is attracted to Buddhism for its introspection and its path to wisdom, which offers meaning for life without the need to look to an external God. He writes with atheistic warmth which reflects the parallel monism to which I have referred:

> The view I have promoted so far is similar to the one held by most Buddhists ...it is worth pausing to reflect on the apparent accident that Buddhism, almost alone in the great ethical and metaphysical traditions, holds to a picture of persons that is uniquely suited to the way science says we ought to see ourselves and our place in the world.[17]

Serious debate over a meaningful place for the human in a naturalist paradigm is an inevitable development if we examine the flow of culture over the last hundred or so years. The rejection of traditional Jewish-Christian metaphysics by European society at large has been followed by a spiritual vacuum, which Eastern metaphysics has filled in the popular culture. The results of the quantum mechanical interpretation of atomic physics happen in the same period and are thus also appropriated, tentatively at first, by some of its architects, and then later more explicitly. The new romanticism of the culture at large inevitably impacts writers of the science paradigm, who use it to warm up cold science. Whereas Bertrand Russell merely shakes his fist at the reality that we are a collocation of atoms,[18] Flanagan embraces and (with the Eastern paradigm to which he is personally sympathetic) seeks to make philosophic sense out of this collocation by looking for meaning within. For the collocation of atoms to make sense, there must be some spiritual fulfillment in *belonging* to the overarching "oneness" of all that exists.

Science does not exist to prove or disprove the existence of God. It is about understanding the physical world: its categories, its symmetries, its laws and principles, how it functions and operates, and how the physical world is interrelated. However, the very form of the universe allows for meaningful science, and points beyond itself to metaphysics. Discovered mysteries of quantum mechanics contest a simplistic picture of reality which can be endlessly reduced into a set of final elements. A holistic picture of the universe includes both physics and metaphysics as starting points. Believing only in physics for answers leads to atheism. Believing only in metaphysics for answers leads to baseless spirituality or introspection. Both physics and metaphysics are required for a holistic understanding of the physical world, with its ontological categories and the form of those categories. In addition, our human nature (with its self consciousness, hope, fear, creativity, moral agency and search for cosmic significance, along with our deeply felt alienation) is also part of the data that needs explanation. Again, we see the need for both physics and metaphysics as starting points.

The Jewish-Christian metaphysical assumption that there is a God who is personal, and the Creator, Designer, Artist and Engineer of all that exists fits the broad gambit of reality derived from understanding the physical world and our place in it. Can we find this God by looking at the physics? No, but the form and voice of the universe shouts loudly of something (someone) beyond itself. One needs to look seriously at revelation as a source of knowledge if one is to get a complete picture of God. Extrapolation like that done by Paul Davies (also a physicist) in *The Mind of God*[19] is interesting and valuable, but incomplete. To our epistemology of measurement of the world we must add the epistemology of revelation. Only as these inform each other do we get a complete picture.

Quantum Mechanics is an important discovery, but its metaphysical monistic projection to our macroscopic world is dubious because the macroscopic world with its laws, symmetries, categories and conscious thought are more convincingly understood with the traditional Jewish-Christian worldview, which includes the existence of a distinct yet involved God, who is both the Creator and a Person to whom we can relate to understand our cosmic significance and spirituality.

Quantum Mechanics reveals a real limitation of knowledge and limits reductionism. The universe is not finally a giant machine, as imagined by Laplace.[20] This knowledge limitation is meant to open the door, as is all physical reality, to transcendence. The existence of a transcendent God does not stop scientific discovery as many scientists often argue. Rather, knowing that the construction and operation of the world we live in is reasonable (having been designed and engineered by a reasonable God, who is also a Person) invigorates science, because it has a firm *a priori* basis.

Paul the Apostle contested the counterfeit alternatives to the existence of a transcendent God, when he wrote, the best part of two thousand years ago, to the early Roman church:

> The wrath of God is being revealed from heaven against all the godlessness and wickedness of men who suppress the truth by their wickedness, since what may be known about God is plain to them, because God has made it plain to them. For since the creation of the world God's invisible qualities—his eternal power and divine nature—have been clearly seen, being understood from what has been made,

> so that men are without excuse. For although they knew God, they neither glorified him as God nor gave thanks to him, but their thinking became futile and their foolish hearts were darkened. Although they claimed to be wise, they became fools and exchanged the glory of the immortal God for images made to look like mortal man and birds and animals and reptiles. (Rom 1:18–23)

It is a nice summary of my sentiments in this chapter.

12

DEEP ECOLOGY, NEOPAGANISM & GLOBAL WARMING

E. CALVIN BEISNER

In 2007 I was one of about eighty participants—scientists, politicians, economists, religious leaders—in a global conference on climate change sponsored by the Pontifical Council for Justice and Peace at the Vatican. During the shuttle trip from Vatican City to our hotel the first evening, I conversed with a tall, middle-aged woman. She had an impressive resume. Senior Lecturer and Scholar at Yale University, Mary Evelyn Tucker holds influential positions in ecological forums and has organized lectures and a book series on the subject of religion and ecology.

She challenged my right to promote any opinion about global warming, since I was not a climate scientist. Having learned that she was not a climate scientist either (she has degrees in the history of religion and in English), I asked why she offers opinions on ecology. She appealed to overwhelming scientific consensus that manmade warming is real and sure to become catastrophic if not thwarted by drastic actions to cut carbon emissions. I asked her what opinions she had read by climate scientists critical of that view.

"There aren't any!" she retorted.

"None?" I asked.

"No," she replied.

I said I was surprised, since I had read fifteen full-length books by climate scientists critical of the theory, plus scores of refereed and hundreds of nonrefereed articles—as well as several books and hundreds of articles by climate scientists who embraced her view. I averred that I thought it a little irresponsible of her to refuse to read those who disagreed with her. Her face hardened and she looked out the window of the shuttle bus. Our conversation was over.

The next day I delivered my paper. As I neared the end, I spoke of how the ecology debate is carried on. I said that as a logic teacher, I was grieved at the illogical arguments often used by the alarmists (e.g., correlation taken for causation,[1] and consensus rather than data or explanation in science[2]). I mentioned the singular lack of charity and mutual respect in the discussion, and the misuse of arguments from prudence by resting them on a *petitio principii* of the reality, magnitude and negative impacts of manmade warming. My experience on the shuttle prompted me to mention the sad tendency for people to reach conclusions before examining counter-arguments—and then to declare flatly that they do not exist. Tucker left the room shortly afterwards.

No specialist in Neopaganism, I had never encountered Tucker, but a few weeks later Peter Jones sent me the draft of a chapter in which he discussed Tucker's views at length. He described her as "an ardent pagan believer who occupies a very powerful place in the international field of ideological paganism." Peter's quotes of Tucker show an integral relationship between her "deep ecology" and a "this-wordly spirituality remarkable for its holistic and comprehensive qualities," as Tucker herself puts it.

Pagans and modern liberal Protestants share Tucker's attachment to a monistic, ecological redefinition of the Spirit. Neopagan thought redefines more than the Holy Spirit. The concept of spirit as incorporeal mind, "thinking thing," as Descartes called it, is replaced. In historic Christian thought, the distinction between spirit and matter/energy plays a part in the distinction between God and creation, guarding against pantheism. In Neopaganism, both distinctions break down, contributing to its irrationalism, including its understanding of ecology and the environment. Embracing the worldview of Neopaganism and deep ecology leads many thinkers in the global warming debate to adopt irrational tactics.

DEEP ECOLOGY

Most deep ecologists are pantheists, and many explicitly embrace Hinduism, Buddhism or Confucianism.[3] Deep ecologists are spiritual and religious in their attitudes toward environmental issues. Some actively seek to revive Druidism, witchcraft, Native American religions and—among feminists—goddess worship. Drawing from both the Eastern religions and Darwinian science, they place man's identity with the rest of nature in his ascent through the evolutionary chain of being. Thus, "one itinerant environmentalist conducts 'workshops' in which participants are urged to remember their alleged evolutionary history by rolling on the ground and imagining what their lives were like as dead leaves, slugs, and lichens."[4]

Fifteen years ago and more, most deep ecologists (known to be mystical and intuitive) rejected the political approach of the Greens (who depended on science) in favor of direct action groups like Greenpeace, Earth First!, Sea Shepherds, and so forth. Today, deep ecologists collaborate more closely with politically active environmentalists, who tend to share the same basic worldview and communication strategy. Arne Naess, the Norwegian philosopher of ecology who would like to rid our planet of ninety-eight percent of its people, is one of the chief framers of the deep ecology worldview and the coiner of the phrase *deep ecology*.[5] He said his work consists not "of philosophical or logical argumentation" but "intuitions."[6] Naess describes his worldview as "ecosophy." The intuitive nature of his thinking is illustrated in his student and translator's description of a Naess lecture in Oslo:

> After an hour he suddenly stops, glances quickly around the stage, and suddenly leaves the podium and approaches a potted plant to his left. He quickly pulls off a leaf, scurries back to the microphone, and gazes sincerely at the audience as he holds the leaf in the light so all can see. "You can spend a lifetime contemplating this," he comments. "It is enough. Thank you."[7]

The focus on intuition in the deep ecology movement explains, in part, why feminism allies itself with environmentalism, particularly with deep ecology and animal rights. Feminism rejects science outright—or redefines it—because science, a "masculine" discipline, is not sufficiently sensitive to "feminine thought patterns." Says feminist theologian and animal rights theorist Carol Adams, author of *The Sexual Politics of Meat: A Feminist-Vegetarian Critical Theory*: "Science's insistence on being tough, rigorous, rational, impersonal and unemotional is intertwined with men's gender identities."[8]

At the root of deep ecology is the insistence that "all life is fundamentally one." From this principle flows a new vision of self-realization: "a bold attempt to connect the general statement that 'all life is fundamentally one' with our individual needs and desires." Here all distinction between God and the world collapses in the vision of the one Self that encompasses not only all of life but all of everything.[9]

Deep ecology explicitly rejects any distinction between man and nature. Naess complains that although "Shallow Ecology" fights "against pollution and resource depletion," its central objective is "the health and affluence of *people*." In contrast, deep ecology involves "Rejection of the man-in-environment image in favour of *the relational, total-field image*."[10] Man's needs and desires are no more important than those of the rest of nature, for man is nothing more than a part of nature. Nature does not exist *for* man.

Naess embraces the implication of his views: "*Biospherical egalitarianism—in principle*....is an intuitively clear and obvious value axiom. Its restriction to humans is an anthropocentrism with detrimental effects upon the life quality of humans themselves."[11] Or as Earth First! founder David Foreman puts it, "... man is no more important than any other species.... It may well take our extinction to set things straight."[12]

THE WORLD AS BODY OF GOD

To aid this too brief discussion, I have chosen to represent the deep ecology movement by considering the thinking of one representative thinker, Sallie McFague, professor of theology and former dean of Vanderbilt Divinity School.[13] Perhaps her most important book is *The Body of God: An Ecological Theology*. On the book cover, Carol Adams (*The Sexual Politics of Meat*) endorses the message: "McFague weaves a unified vision of theology, joining what have been separated: body and soul, humans and the rest of nature, God and the earth. She invites us to think and act as if bodies matter for, as she shows, they do."

In *The Body of God*, McFague presents a "model" in which the universe is literally the body of God. This model of immanence she opposes to the model of transcendence, in which God as Creator is distinct from his creation, which he made out of nothing. Her aim is to "balance the heavy transcendence of the Christian doctrine of God." "What would it mean," she asks, "to interpret creation as all the myriad forms of matter bodied forth from God and empowered with the breath of life, the spirit of God?" She says forthrightly that her "organic model is . . . a fundamental way to reconceive Christian faith [and] an offering that Christianity can make to the planetary agenda of our time, the agenda that calls for all religions, nations, professions, and people to reconstruct their lives and their work to help our earth survive and prosper."[14]

For McFague and others like her, science and religion are intricately *intertwined* and significantly *redefined*. "The model of the world or universe as God's body is...in keeping with the view of reality coming to us from contemporary science," writes McFague. "[Such a model] is a plausible theological response to that reality, a response that ought to make Christian interpretations of the relations between God and the world more credible than interpretations based on outmoded views of reality," for, she adds, "the credibility of faith depends upon that connection" between theology and "the contemporary scientific picture of reality."[15] McFague employs the logical fallacy of *argumentum ab annis*, appeal to age. She claims that Christianity's view of God's relation to the world is "outmoded." McFague forgets that "scientific" cosmologies are also outmoded. The twentieth century saw two major cosmologies come—the Steady State and Pulsating Universe views, superseded by the Big Bang theory, itself now undermined by cutting edge theoretical physics. It is not only all flesh that is like grass, but also all scientific theories—yet the Word of the Lord endures forever.

McFague suggests that "the primary belief of the Christian community, its doctrine of the incarnation (the belief that God is with us here on earth)[16]. . . be radicalized beyond Jesus of Nazareth to include all matter." "God is the breath or spirit," she says, "that gives life to the billions of different bodies that make up God's body. But God is also the source, power, and goal of everything that is, for the creation depends utterly upon God."[17] McFague does not mean "depend" as a pendulum *depends* on the rod, but as *I* depend on *I*; if I did not exist, I would not exist. So also, the universe depends on God in that God simply *is* the universe; if the universe did not exist, God would not exist.

This model of the world as the body of God then serves an ethical and political agenda: "The liberating, healing, and inclusive ministry of Jesus that overturns hierarchical dualisms, heals sick bodies, and invites the outcast to the table should in our time be extended to a new poor—nature."[18] She explicitly denies the biblical doctrine of human dominion over the Earth:

> We are not lords *over* the planet, but products of its processes; in fact, we are the product of a fifteen-billion-year history of the universe and a four-billion-year history of our earth. . . . The most important ecological knowledge we can have, then, is not how we can change the environment to suit us . . . but rather how we can adjust our desires and needs to what appear to be the house rules.[19]

This leads McFague to assert that "restraint, doing less, pulling back, may be the better part of wisdom....Not to act, but to abstain; not to control, but to 'let be'; not to solve the problem, but to simplify one's life; not to want more but to accept less; all this goes against the grain."[20] (Paradoxically, she also writes that we must "refuse the role of victim, to become active, to participate in the vocation of the planetary agenda."[21])

In the face of the "androcentric, hierarchical, dualistic models of God in the Christian tradition," she, as "a feminist theologian" and now as "ecological theologian," is suggesting "alternatives."[22] Ironically, traditional Christian theology is the least domineering in its method, since it bows to the authority of Scripture and seeks to set forth the model, the world-view and the theology therein revealed. The Christian stands in humility before the Creator. How unlike the domineering picture she gives of the traditional "androcentric, hierarchical" models!

The World as Body or Machine?

McFague contrasts two views of the universe, "an organic and a mechanical one, the world as body or machine." The organic model

> takes the perspective of the world as a whole and sees all parts, from the largest to the smallest, as interrelated and interdependent; the [mechanical model] takes the perspective of the parts and sees them related only in terms of the larger parts being dependent on or influenced by the smallest. The first has been called holistic, with top-

> down and bottom-up causation, while the second is called atomistic or reductionistic, with only bottom-up causation. Atomism, or the machine model, reduces all living things to their most basic chemical compounds.[23]

Christianity, feminism and ecology, she writes, exhibit ambivalence or even abhorrence of the body and must be corrected by the realization that "we do not *have* bodies, as we like to suppose, distancing ourselves from them as one does from an inferior, a servant, who works for us (the "us" being the mind that inhabits the body but does not really belong there). We *are* bodies, 'body and soul.'"[24]

Elsewhere she says,

> One of the most important revelations from Postmodern science is the continuum between matter and energy (or, more precisely, the unified matter/energy field), which overturns traditional hierarchical dualisms such as nonliving/living, flesh/spirit, nature/human being .... Whatever we say about that part of ourselves we call brain, mind, or spirit, it evolved from and is continuous with our bodies.[25]

That is a rather interesting assertion, which rejects the revelation of God in Scripture that to be "at home in the body" is to be "absent from the Lord" and that, between death and the resurrection, "to be absent from the body" is "to be at home with the Lord" (2 Cor 5:6, 8 NAS). Her assertion also substitutes for God's revelation other "revelations from Postmodern science" (although Postmodern science usually deconstructs "revelations"). Finally, McFague's assertion makes a leap from the supposition that matter and energy are aspects of a unified field to the elimination of the immaterial soul from human nature. It is not clear how one can infer from "Matter and energy are a unified field" that "The soul is not distinct from the body," since the two propositions share none of their four logical terms. But perhaps McFague would object that logic is masculine and hierarchical and that she prefers the feminine and egalitarian.

McFague further develops the implications of her "body of God" model of the universe:

> What if we dared to think of our planet and indeed the entire universe as the body of God?....Since we now know that our bodies and spirits

> (or minds, souls)[26] are on a continuum, is it so odd to think of God as embodied, since the Western tradition has always considered God in terms of personal agency (as having a will, mind, and spirit)? ....We are not describing God as having a body or being embodied; we are suggesting that what is bedrock for the universe—*matter, that of which everything that is is made*—might be, in fact perhaps ought to be, applied to God as well.[27]

McFague here asserts that matter is "that of which everything that is, is made," implying that there is nothing *but* matter. That is precisely the view of Secular Humanism, of Marxist dialectical materialism. Whenever McFague writes of "spirit" or "spirituality" or things "spiritual," she does not mean what a biblical Christian would mean. Neopaganism is tricky, even deceitful, presenting itself as a form of spirituality and referring to spirit and spirits. However, it is only metaphysical materialism rechristened—shed of the Enlightenment rationality it borrowed from historic Christianity. For McFague, God is matter and matter is God. What meaning then is left to the words "God, the Creator and Redeemer of the universe"? Nothing.

Do we hear an echo of another voice in McFague's question? "Is it so odd to think of God as embodied?" she asks. "What if we dared to think...?" And she goes on to ask, "Is it an impossible, abhorrent, or obscene thought? ....Or is it an interesting, inviting, provocative thought...?"[28] Do we not hear the ancient voice asking, "Hath God said?" Are we not reminded of Eve's question, "Is it not good for food, a delight to the eyes, and desirable to make one wise?" Like the serpent of old, McFague appeals precisely to the drive for the novel, the titillating, the risky. Such tactics are an important element of Neopaganism's appeal to modern Americans.

But to return to McFague's focus: "what is bedrock for the universe—*matter, that of which everything that is is made*—might be, in fact perhaps ought to be, applied to God as well." For McFague, God, like human beings, is nothing but matter. "As the embodied spirit of all that is, God would be closer to us than we are to ourselves, for God would be the very breath of our breath." Has she reversed herself? Is God, "the embodied spirit," distinct from the material world after all? No. "In this body model,

God would not be transcendent over the universe in the sense of external to or apart from, but would be *the source, power, and goal—the spirit—that enlivens (and loves) the entire process and its material forms* [italics mine]."[29] This is all McFague ever means when she writes of God or spirit. This definition of God is not Christian theism, but simple pantheism.

Immanence and Transcendence

How does McFague reach her views about God? She moves from "Postmodern" science's revelations of the matter/energy continuum to the view of humans as solely material, to the view that God, too, is solely material. What we have meant all along by saying we are embodied spirits is that we are matter in which processes occur. "As we are inspirited bodies—living, loving, thinking bodies—so, imagining God in our image (for how else *can* we model God?), we speak of her as *the* inspirited body of the entire universe, the animating, living spirit that produces, guides, and saves all that is."[30] Of course, if God has not spoken, if Scripture is not his self-revelation, we can do no better than to reason from ourselves to him. But as Francis Schaeffer put it in his famous book *The God Who Is There*, "He is there, and he is not silent."

What temptation drives this great exchange of historic Christian theology and anthropology for the theology and anthropology of Neopagan pantheism? How is it good for food, a delight to the eyes, and desirable to make one wise? "There is one obvious advantage to this model," McFague writes, and that is that "it allows us to think of God as immanent in our world while retaining, indeed, magnifying God's transcendence. The model of the universe as God's body unites immanence and transcendence."[31]

Is that so? Rather, it collapses God's transcendence into his immanence. If matter is all that is, and if God is inspirited body, and if spirit is nothing but "the source, power and goal...that enlivens (and loves) the entire process and its material forms," then God is not in fact transcendent at all, regardless of what McFague claims. Here is the irrationalism, the self-refutation, of Postmodernism and Neopaganism: "Immanental transcendence or transcendent immanence is what the model of the universe as God's body implies, and it is...what Christian incarnationalism implies as well."[32] She might just as well write of "black whiteness" or "positive negativeness" or "false truth." Self-contradiction, the height of irrationality, is inherent in pantheism and, consequently, also in Neopaganism. No wonder, then, that she soon repeats one of the mantras of all pantheistic mysticism: "No human words can describe God,"[33] which of course means "God is something human words cannot describe" (a self-refuting statement).

After so carefully constructing this ambitious (but by no means novel) model, McFague backs off, saying that

> it will invite us to imagine boldly and radically while insisting that *models do not provide descriptions* [italics mine].... Many other models exist, some mutually exclusive of the body model, others complementary to it, and still others that correct its biases and partiality.... Metaphors and models are *not* descriptions, and, to the degree we keep this in mind, we will be open to experience the potential insights they can offer us.[34]

In other words, McFague does not claim any of this to be *true*, only that it is a *model*. Contradictory and complementary models exist, and none of them is true, either—but then neither is any false. In the final analysis, *all* thoughts are only models, and *nothing* is true—one more instance of the self-refutation of non-Christian thought.

Before discussing the implications of McFague's Neopagan, pantheist model of God and the world for the global warming hysteria, I want to point out two things:

1. an instance (among many) of how her relativism can become the platform for vehement judgments of those who disagree with her, and
2. the degree to which she makes theology subservient to contemporary science.

Near the close of the chapter from which most of this discussion is taken, she writes,

> A society that ... refuses in international congresses to join other nations in protecting biodiversity and limiting chemicals that contribute to global warming ... hates the body, human bodies, and all other animal and plant bodies that make up the body of our planet.[35]

The person who dares to disagree with her empirical claims about the environment and what needs to be done about it, is full of hate. So much for the nonhierarchical, cooperative character of Postmodern, Neopagan environmentalism!

Near the start of the next chapter, on cosmology, in which she compares the organic, "world as the body of God" model with the mechanistic model of the universe (which she calls the "classic" model, namely, the Big Bang followed by cosmic and biotic evolution), McFague writes, "Theologians always have paid and always should pay serious attention to the picture of reality operative in their culture. If they do not, theology becomes anachronistic and irrelevant."[36] She cites Wolfhart Pannenberg, who bemoaned Karl Barth's "decision 'in principle' that a theological doctrine of creation should not concern itself with scientific descriptions of the world." Pannenberg, correcting Barth, says "If theologians want to conceive of God as the creator of the real world, they cannot possibly bypass the scientific description of that real world."[37] We may embrace Pannenberg's rejection of Barth's upper storey/lower storey dualism that put the *Geschichte* of faith in the upper storey and the *Historie* of reality in the lower storey, but we must equally reject Pannenberg's—and McFague's—enslavement of theology to the fleeting claims of science. Science cannot tell a consistent story through even a few decades, so theology need make no apologies for standing firmly on the axioms of Scripture: "To the law and to the testimony! If they do not speak according to this word, it is because they have no dawn" (Is 8:20 NAS).

Consensus or Coercion?

I have come nearly full circle. We began with a Neopagan, ecofeminist Yale theologian who took offense at my point that people ignore evidence that disagrees with their models. Such tactics are not surprising. The irrationalism of pantheism, of Neopaganism, of Postmodernism, and indeed of modernist materialism itself has raised its head repeatedly in the debate, which has become a verbal conflagration over catastrophic, manmade global warming and other environmental crises. These systems cannot support truth claims, because they have no axioms, unlike the epistemology of biblical revelationism. Critics of global warming alarmism are now routinely called "deniers" (the comparison with Holocaust deniers is intentional). Some have called for Nuremberg-style trials, since the "deniers" have committed a crime against humanity—nay, against the whole Earth. Critics of global warming alarmism routinely face charges that they and their opinions are bought and paid for by industry. The first response to those who dare challenge the global warming dogma is, "But an overwhelming scientific consensus affirms this claim"—as if consensus were relevant to science. As the great sociologist of science Robert K. Merton put it in 1938, "Most institutions demand unqualified faith; but the institution of science makes skepticism a virtue."[38]

However, the wheels are coming off the consensus bandwagon. Study after study reduces the magnitude of estimated human contribution to global warming. Study after study enlarges the magnitude of the estimated contribution of other factors—cycles of solar energy and solar wind output, longterm cycles of ocean/atmosphere circulations, cycles in Earth's tilt and rotation around the sun, even changes in Earth's position relative to the arms of the Milky Way and consequently, cycles in the intensity of cosmic rays entering Earth's atmosphere. Study after study reduces human influence and enhances natural influence on global climate change.[39]

Though the consensus has never been successfully documented, it is widely accepted. In part, this is because Al Gore gets sycophantic media coverage. Allow me to address the consensus idea. A study published in *Science* in 2004 claimed to have found that no papers in a large database of refereed publications from 1993 through 2003 rejected the consensus that "[m]ost of the observed warming over the last fifty years is likely to have been due to the increase in greenhouse gas concentrations."[40] But another scholar, attempting to replicate the results, discovered serious flaws in the study's method and concluded that no such consensus existed in the refereed literature. A new study of the same database, this time covering the period 2004 through early 2007, found that the proportion of scientific papers endorsing the "consensus" had fallen relative to the corrected earlier proportion, while the proportion rejecting it had risen. This result suggested "a significant movement of scientific opinion *away from* the apparently unanimous consensus which [the author of the 2004 study] had found...from 1993 to 2003."[41]

A 2003 survey of climate scientists asked, "To what extent do you agree or disagree that climate change is mostly the result of anthropogenic [manmade] causes?" Of the 530 valid responses, 9.4 percent strongly agreed, while 9.7 percent strongly disagreed. A much more extensive survey reported in 2007 found little support for the claim of consensus and concluded, "the matter is far from being settled in the scientific arena." Climatologists *do not share a strong consensus* that climate change is mostly caused by human activities.[42] In late 2007 one hundred prominent scientists, most working in fields dealing with climate change, signed an open letter to United Nations Secretary General Ban Ki-Moon saying that climate change is largely natural, cannot be stopped by human action, and that adaptation is a better response than attempted prevention. A week later, a report of the US Senate Committee on Environment and Public Works listed over four hundred prominent scientists who disputed man-made global warming, many of them involved in the United Nations' Intergovernmental Panel on Climate Change.[43]

Models Cannot Describe

Let me conclude by referring to Sallie McFague's concession *that models do not describe*. Those who promote the "conventional wisdom" about global warming—that it is largely manmade and will soon become catastrophic—are mostly computer modelers. Those who reject the conventional view are mostly data gatherers. The modelers know that models do not *describe*, cannot *predict*[44] and even fail to retrodict past climate changes without multiple, enormous, *ad hoc* adjustments. Yet they insist that governments the world over commit trillions of dollars to policies predicated on their unreliable models. The data gatherers, meanwhile, point out instance after instance in which the data contradict the models. For example, it has become obvious that the fit between rising atmospheric carbon dioxide concentration and rising global temperature is very poor. In fact, over long periods carbon dioxide *follows* temperature rather than vice versa, and in the past century and a half temperature has *risen and fallen* erratically while carbon dioxide has *risen on a fairly smooth hyperbolic curve*. On the other hand, the fit between temperature and sunspot cycles (closely related to cycles in solar energy and solar wind output) is tight.[45] In the summer of 2006 Danish physicist Henrik Svensmark and his colleagues published research not only showing that there is an extremely tight correlation between changes in solar wind output and global temperature but also explaining how the solar wind changes affect temperature—namely, by changing the rate of cosmic ray influx into the atmosphere and thus changing the rate of cloud formation, which is heavily determined by cosmic ray concentration.[46] The Danish researchers, along with others in Israel and America who have cooperated in or duplicated their work, estimate that this influence alone could explain between seventy-five to one hundred percent of the climate change recorded in the past century and a half. In August of 2007 University of Alabama senior research climatologist and Cornwall Alliance contributing scientist Roy Spencer and colleagues published the results of a six-year study of data from NASA satellites showing that tropical cirrus clouds (which trap low-level heat) *diminish* rather than *increase* with higher surface temperature, making them a negative rather than a positive feedback on surface warming—precisely the opposite of the assumption of *every* general circulation model used by the climate modelers.[47] "To give an idea of how strong this enhanced cooling mechanism is," Spencer explains, "if it was operating on global warming, it would reduce estimates of future warming by over seventy-five percent.[48]

In December 2007, another University of Alabama senior climatologist, John Christy, and coauthors published the results of additional research from NASA satellites showing that, although every global climate model predicts that warming generated by rising carbon dioxide would be greatest in the tropical troposphere, that signal of anthropogenic warming is simply nonexistent in the hard data—which makes it extremely unlikely that rising carbon dioxide is causing global warming.[49] In the same month, University of Guelph economist and Cornwall contributing scholar, Ross McKitrick, and colleagues demonstrated that the formulae used by climate modelers to adjust surface temperature readings to filter out the urban heat island effect were wrong by so much that the apparent post-1980 increase in global temperature must be cut in half, with the result that the warming rate over the period no longer differs from the wholly natural rates of previous periods, and its evidentiary role in the argument for manmade warming disappears.[50] These are just a handful of many findings reported in peer-reviewed articles over the past three years that thoroughly undermine the catastrophic manmade warming scenario.[51]

The Postmodernist epistemology of much of the environmentalist movement (including its evangelical subset) fails to recognize what Sallie McFague knows: *models do not describe*. The movement refuses to recognize the enormous failures of the General Circulation Models that underlie the catastrophist claims.[52] The same people who embrace Postmodern science fail to embrace the view of many physicists that by the very nature of the types of differential equations involved, many elements of the incredibly complex land/ocean/atmosphere circulation system (a fluid dynamic system every bit as chaotic as that of subatomic physics) are outside the realm of possible human knowledge. It is in principle, therefore, impossible to support the kinds of predictions warming alarmists routinely make.[53] The delight many evangelicals have shown in chaos theory and quantum physics at the micro level (some even extrapolating improperly from it to Postmodern physics and relativism), they fail to find at the macro level of global climate.

The findings of science are shifting and temporary. The Word of the Lord endures forever. And he is the One who swore to himself, "I will never again curse the ground on account of man, for the intent of man's heart is evil from his youth; and I will never again destroy every living thing, as I have done. While the earth remains, seedtime and harvest, and cold and heat, and summer and winter, and day and night shall not cease" (Gn 8:20–21 NAS). "Cursed is the one who trusts in man. Blessed is the one who trusts in the Lord" (Jer 17:5; Ps 40:4 NAS).

13

Pagan Contemplative Techniques

Pamela Frost

A group called "Global Spirit" tells us we are in an existential, dimensional, deep, global shift in consciousness.[1] One spiritual technology facilitating this shift is the contemplative mind (mysticism), which affects not only society, but the Christian church.[2] Decades of Seeker pragmatism have shoved theology and doctrine off church property in many cases. In the remaining void, Christians are turning to the spiritual disciplines of medieval monasticism and to mystics, some not even Christian. Terms like Spiritual Formation, Soul Care, Spiritual Director, and Contemplative Prayer are now common in evangelical circles.

Integral philosopher[3] Ken Wilber views Ultimate Reality as the non-dual integration of matter, consciousness and spirit into an undifferentiated One.[4] Wilber's mystical evolution of consciousness finds devotees in emerging church leaders like Brian McLaren,[5] Leonard Sweet[6] and Rob Bell.[7] While the first Reformation returned to the Bible, a new reformation returns to medieval monasticism on which it hitches a ride to New Spiritual futures on the spiral galaxy of evolving consciousness. The world's religions are converging in the sacred space of contemplative mysticism to sing in harmony for the god of the New Spirituality.

Is this a New Age daydream? Perennial philosopher[8] Frithjof Schuon doesn't think so. In *The Transcendent Unity of Religions*, he marginalizes *exoteric* (theological/doctrinal) differences and elevates the unifying power of *esoteric* (contemplative/mystical) practices. Experience trumps belief, as mysticism synthesizes religions on the mount of contemplative experience.[9] Neat trick! But it isn't new.

The seeds of religious synthesis were originally sown in the Garden of Eden when the serpent promised Eve self-realization through the "godlike" knowledge of good and evil. In the development of Western monasticism, they were sown by Neoplatonism's[10] promise of direct mystical union with the divine through contemplative practice. Thomas Merton argues that "Oriental" religions also affected Hellenistic philosophy and thus shaped the Christian monastic movement as it made the "eschatological" shift from the hope of the literal return of Christ to the metaphysically "intuited" "reestablishment of all things in Christ."[11]

Neoplatonism

Pseudo-Dionysius: Fifth to Sixth Centuries

By the fifth century, pseudo-Dionysius[12] had escorted Neoplatonism, disguised in Christian terminology, into the medieval church. In Neoplatonism, the One, an unknowable, unintelligible ground of Being, emanated into Intelligence through nine angelic orders arranged into three triads of celestial hierarchies.[13] From Intelligence, a unified Cosmic Soul emanated. Individuation into human beings occurred as souls incarnated bodies. Everyone is thus infused with essential divinity, but a false self arising from the development of the individuated egoic-self[14] obscures remembering original union in the One.[15] Contemplative techniques eliminate this self-aware ego-state through bypassing the mind to awaken the *true self*, eternally existent within the undifferentiated One.

Pseudo-Dionysius taught inward, mystical experience as the Reality that transcends intellectual knowledge of God. His students were instructed to "leave behind the senses and the operations of the intellect, and all things sensible and intellectual...that thou mayest arise by unknowing towards the union...into the superessential Radiance of the Divine Darkness."[16] Of Jesus, he said, "the superessential Jesus enters an essential state in which the truths of human nature meet."[17] This "Jesus" emanated from the superessential One into a human body—the essential state—as a herald of the way to integration within the One. This Jesus is also "the superessential Head of the supercelestial Beings above Nature."[18]

The influence of pseudo-Dionysius was not marginal, but formed the spirituality of medieval monasticism. Jesuit Harvey Egan says, "The word 'mystical' entered definitively into Christian vocabulary...through the important writings of pseudo-Dionysius."[19] Thomas Merton credited pseudo-Dionysius with "set[ting] the Middle Ages on its ear."[20] And, Evelyn Underhill wrote: "Mediæval mysticism is soaked in Dionysian conceptions. ...[T]he phrase 'Dionysius saith'...has for those who use it much the same weight as quotations from the Bible."[21]

The Contemplative Path

Contemplative mysticism still treads pseudo-Dionysius' classic three-fold path of "purgation," "illumination," and "union," which are taken directly from his work *The Celestial Hierarchies.*[22] In the early twentieth century, Evelyn Underhill increased the stages to five, insisting that "awakening" and "the dark night of the soul" are essential, historical stages on the mystical path. The five steps are:

1. Awakening (spiritual birth): The mystic is called to "consciousness of Divine Reality."
2. Purgation (self-crucifixion): By severe discipline, the false self or self-conscious egoseparating from the One is eliminated.
3. Illumination: "Apprehension of the Absolute...but not true union with it."
4. The Dark Night of the Soul: A "mystic death" purges the sense of "I-hood" through "spiritual crucifixion," rendering the mystic "utterly passive, and...thus prepared for...Union."
5. Union (ultimate rebirth into God): The "true self" hidden within the One, awakens, producing absolute certitude of spiritual equilibrium in the Divine.[23]

As they progress, advanced mystics experience phenomena such as "[e]cstasies, raptures, visions, locutions, revelations...levitations," reduced breathing, heart rate, and temperature, suppression of the senses, paralysis of the intellect, apparitions, automatic writings (like those of Teresa of Avila), the stigmata (experienced by St. Francis and Teresa) and ecstatic flight.[24] Not surprisingly, trained Spiritual Directors must guide contemplatives through the perilous interior journey of the soul. Richard Foster states that the "final step into Contemplative Prayer is spiritual ecstasy"[25] and warns that those seeking this "*unmediated* communion with God [emphasis added]" are "entering deeply into the spiritual realm, and there is such a thing as supernatural guidance that is not divine guidance." He cautions that some of the spirit beings one might encounter "are definitely not in cooperation with God."[26]

Some Contemplative Techniques

In order to attain the contemplative state of ecstatic union, mystics throughout the centuries have continued to use the techniques developed in medieval monasticism under the influence of pseudo-Dionysius.

The *apophatic*[27] technique of pseudo-Dionysius enters the contemplative path by repeating a "holy word" as a mantra to bypass the mind, suppressing all knowledge of God under a "cloud of forgetting." Pure consciousness arises toward direct union with the Divine Mystery where "infused contemplation"[28] flows through the passive mystic.

The *kataphatic*[29] technique focuses mental faculties with intentionality[30] on symbols, Bible stories, or icons moving beyond them into mystical experience as the soul enters a deeper state of *interiorization*[31] awakening *infused contemplation*.

Lectio divina is a kataphatic technique for "spiritual reading of a sacred text," leading first to "*meditatio*," or "reflection," then to "*Oratio*... movement of the heart," and finally into infused "contemplation." *Lectio divina* is not about understanding the text but awakening contemplation beyond the text.[32]

Contemplative silence eliminates thought. Thomas Keating says, "By interior silence we refer primarily to a state in which we do not become *attached* to the thoughts as they go by."[33]

The discipline of *solitude* found extreme expression in the Anchorites who were occasionally bricked into cells within churches for contemplative devotion.

Contemplative transformation is the goal of Christian mysticism. As Jesuit Harvey Egan describes it:

> Mystical transformation shifts the mystic's personal center of gravity from the ego's tiny sphere[34] to the true self. ...The fully developed mystical life renders the mystic *integral: wholly one with God, self, and all creation* [italics added].[35]

Spiritual formation is the mystical formation of the soul on its inward journey to God. Jesuit William Johnston describes the process:

> growth in contemplation… is a development toward *cosmic consciousness* so that *the contemplative puts on the mind of the cosmic Christ and offers himself to the Father for the salvation of the human race* [italics added].[36]

John Scotus Eriugena: c. 815–877

In the ninth century, Irishman John Scotus Eriugena translated pseudo-Dionysius into Latin. Eriugena blended Neoplatonism, Druidic nature mysticism and Pelagianism into a mystical creation spirituality[37] that would influence Flemish mystic John Ruysbroeck in the thirteenth century and Rhineland mystics Meister Eckhart and Johannes Tauler in the fourteenth. In the twentieth century, Matthew Fox reinterpreted Eckhart's creation spirituality in a New Age gospel of salvation through Mother Earth and deep ecumenism—uniting the wisdom of the world religions[38] through mysticism.[39]

Chartres Cathedral

In the tenth century, Fulbertus built Chartres Cathedral on the site where Celtic Druid priests had worshiped the Black Madonna following the winter and summer solstices, representing the "polarity of darkness and light," the cycles of death and rebirth of the goddess Natura.[40] Fulbertus dedicated Chartres to Mary as the "Eternal Feminine" and established the Chartres School of Wisdom, which synthesized Celtic and Greek mystery religions with pseudo-Dionysius' Christianized Neoplatonism.[41] In this pagan gospel, Christ, the Sun Spirit, descended on Jesus of Nazareth in baptism, incarnating into humanity. The portal between heaven and earth opened through the "birth of the inner man, the higher self,"[42] for direct experience of "Christ and the spiritual hierarchies."[43] The design of the cathedral[44] is said to be a "path of initiation"[45] into the spiritual world, facilitating conversation with the dead.[46] Thomas Merton said, "…the School of Chartres had … something permanent, that cannot be taken away."[47]

The Labyrinth

In the thirteenth century, a labyrinth forty feet in diameter was installed in Chartres[48] as a path of pilgrimage to Jerusalem or to communion with Mary, the divine feminine. It fell into disuse and lay forgotten until Pierre Teilhard de Chardin introduced it to Jean Houston in 1955.[49] Houston incorporated it into her Mystery School as a pathway into the mind of God, a journey to the "center of one's very being."[50] Lauren Artress of Grace Cathedral in San Francisco experienced the labyrinth in Houston's Mystery School[51] and popularized it as "an ancient symbol for the Divine Mother, the God within."[52] Artress' labyrinth inspired the Alternative Worship movement, which packaged it as a prayer journey, following the contemplative path of purgation, illumination and union. The labyrinth is invited annually to the National Pastors Convention, offered by the United Kingdom Youth for Christ website,[53] and promoted in a variety of evangelical churches.

The New Chartres Mystery School

Says Anthroposophist, René Querido: "The veil of mystery that hangs over Chartres can be lifted. ...The new mysteries are no longer celebrated in secrecy within the temples of yore. They have come out into the marketplace and are available to all."[54] In 2006 the new Chartres Mystery School opened on the original site55 and teaches "the Erotic Sciences of Sacred Art, Alchemy and Astrology"[56] Courses initiate students into seven mystery traditions over seven years in the seventh month of each year:

2006: "The Mystery of the Birth of the Divine Human," emphasizing Sufism "in the spirit of the Moon."

2007: "The State of the World: Wisdom and the Apocalypse," emphasizing Kabbalah "in the spirit of Mercury."

2008: "Re-imagining the World: The Perennial Wisdom and the Poetry of Beauty," emphasizing Medieval Christian mysticism "in the spirit of Venus."

2009: "Awakening Divine Creativity: The Arts of Healing and Ecstasy," emphasizing Hindu mysticism "in the spirit of the Sun."

2010: "The Indigenous Mind and the New Cosmology," emphasizing Shamanic mysticism "in the spirit of Mars."

2011: "The Mysteries of the Divine Feminine," emphasizing Tibetan Buddhist mysticism, "in the spirit of Jupiter."

2012: "Sacred Activism: Birthing the New World," emphasizing Integral mysticism "in the spirit of Saturn."[57]

The project will be "...Finished When Seven Are One."[58] This occult Law of Seven synthesizes everything into One under the reign of Saturn. "Core Faculty" at the new Chartres Mystery School include Jean Houston, Barbara Marx Hubbard, Rupert Sheldrake, Lauren Artress, Alex Grey, Matthew Fox, and Marianne Williamson.[59] Naturally, the labyrinth is a featured symbol of the school.[60]

The Cloud of Unknowing

In the fourteenth century, an anonymous English mystic wrote *The Cloud of Unknowing* based on the *apophatic* path of pseudo-Dionysius.[61] *The Cloud* uses a mantra like "God" or "love" to "beat upon the cloud of darkness above...to subdue all distractions [rational knowledge of God], consigning them to the *cloud of forgetting* beneath."[62] *The Cloud* says this "contemplative work of love by itself will eventually heal you of all the roots of sin."[63]

In his forward to *The Cloud,* Huston Smith describes how Western thought has left the emptiness of modern scientific rationalism (with its denial of spirit and emphasis on matter) and moved comfortably into the "new winds of the spirit." According to Smith, quantum mechanics proves that "*the* transcendental object is Spirit [italics added]," not God, so that the "new spirituality" is a place where even atheists find comfort in the cosmic sea of evolving consciousness.[64] The *Cloud* awakens this consciousness. Centering prayer, developed in the 1970s, was derived directly from *The Cloud of Unknowing* by Thomas Keating, Basil Pennington, and William Menninger. Many leaders within the emerging/Emergent paradigm, like Tony Jones,[65] Leonard Sweet,[66] and Spencer Burke[67] have been deeply influenced by *The Cloud of Unknowing* and the practice of centering prayer.

Evelyn Underhill: 1875–1941

Evelyn Underhill blended Neoplatonism, medieval mysticism, and strands of hermeticism "turn[ing] the raw stuff of human nature into alchemic gold."[68] Underhill is praised by New Age mystics like Ken Wilber who compares her to pseudo-Dionysius,[69] and Jean Houston, who calls her "the great student of mysticism."[70] Richard Foster says of Underhill, "I realize that I am in the presence of someone who truly knows God and I must yield to her greater authority."[71] Underhill's mystical interpretations view Jesus as the "spirit of Christ [that] sweeps through the world on its journey to the Father...catch[ing] to itself every lesser spirit on its path."[72] She bows before Mary Magdalene, whom she portrays as Sophia[73] and Mother Earth.[74] For Underhill, "Mary completes the spiral way which links Divine and human," having transcended all separations and becoming "one with the life of the All."[75]

Pierre Teilhard de Chardin: 1881–1955

French Jesuit priest, Pierre Teilhard de Chardin, synthesized Christianity with evolutionary theory. The historical Creation, Fall, Incarnation, and Redemption he called "a grossly immature view which is a perpetual offence to our reason."[76] He proposed a substitute: spirit-infused matter spiraling upward in progressive "complexification."

For Teilhard, *geogenesis* formed the geological earth; *biogenesis* produced plant and animal life and began the process of *hominization* toward *cerebralization*, the development of thinking man. The process of *noogenesis* is developing the cosmic soul of the earth in the *noosphere*. *Christification* evolves the *noosphere* toward the Omega Point of cosmic Christ consciousness, which will sweep everything, including the world religions, into the Universal Christ.[77]

Julian Huxley saw in the *noosphere* the development of a "new level of cooperative interthinking, into the equivalent of a person." Individual personhood disappears behind the new "person" of the community mind of cooperative interthinkers.[78]

Marilyn Ferguson concurs. In *Aquarius Now: Radical Common Sense and Reclaiming our Personal Sovereignty*, she speaks of our "misconception about the nature of the self": "[t]he idea of a single self may be little more than a useful convention."[79] She tells of children raised by "enlightened adults" who "discover that by putting their heads together they can listen to each other's thoughts. Over time they...function as a single mind."[80]

Such theories have chilling implications. Groups like Awakening Mind,[81] Global Mind Shift,[82] and the Center for Contemplative Mind in Society[83] are working aggressively toward a global contemplative consciousness that will, they believe, synthesize everything into the One.

Thomas Merton: 1915–1968

In 1966 the Second Vatican Council opened the door for Catholics to engage in interreligious dialogue. Father Thomas Merton, whose influence was popularizing contemplative prayer across denominational lines, pursued interreligious dialogue with Zen Buddhists, D. T. Suzuki and Thich Nhat Hahn, as well as with Tibetan Buddhists and Hindus finding common ground in contemplative consciousness.[84]

Drawn to the East, Thomas Merton went on pilgrimage to India in 1968 where he spoke to an audience of Hindus, Buddhists, Sufis, Jains and Catholics at the Temple of Understanding's conference on religious unity.[85] Merton called the interreligious group to brotherhood saying, "My dear brothers, we are already one. But we imagine that we are not. And what we have to recover is our original unity."[86] While in India, he formed a spiritual bond with the Dalai Lama[87] and planned to undergo initiation into Tibetan Buddhism, though he understood it to have magical and sinister undertones.[88] But Merton never tasted the Tibetan secrets, dying by accidental electrocution on a trip to Thailand in 1968.[89]

Thomas Keating: 1923–

In the 1970s, Abbot Thomas Keating's centering prayer technique for contemplation issued the call to follow the stream of consciousness toward the "*undifferentiated*, general, and loving presence of God beyond any thought [italics added]." Keating describes centering prayer as a process of "interiorization," moving one beyond words into "pure awareness," a state in which "your whole psyche gathers itself together and melts into God."[90]

Recognizing the universal nature of contemplative practice within all the religions, Keating invited Zen *roshis* to lead intensive Buddhist meditation retreats called *sesshins* at St. Joseph's Abbey in Spencer, Massachusetts in the early 1970s.[91] He also collaborated in exploring interreligious mysticism with Chögyam Trungpa Rinpoche,[92] founder of the Naropa Institute for Tibetan Buddhism,[93] who recognized that the "way to join the Christian tradition and the Buddhist tradition together is by means of bringing together Christian contemplative practice with Buddhist meditative practice."[94]

In 1982 Keating established the Snowmass Conference for interreligious dialogue among fifteen leaders from different religions. They met annually for twenty years working to "produce a holistic model of inter-mystical wisdom."[95] The first guideline issued by the conference said, "The world religions bear witness to the experience of the Ultimate Reality to which they give various names: Brahman, the Absolute, God, Allah, Great Spirit, the Transcendent."[96] Such religious synthesis is based on the mutuality of contemplative experience.

Keating has served as president of the interreligious Temple of Understanding[97] and partners with Naqshbandi Sufism in presenting the seminar "Oneness and the Heart of the World" hosted by The Golden Sufi Center.[98] He is currently on the Advisory Council for the Center for Contemplative Mind in Society,[99] founded by Thich Nhat Hahn and Ram Dass[100] to baptize the West into contemplative consciousness.[101] Working in the fields of education, social justice, law, youth programs, philanthropy and business,[102] they use the contemplative techniques of contemplative silence, contemplative prayer, centering prayer, *lectio divina*, labyrinths, the Jesus Prayer,[103] sacred space, *qi gong*,[104] sufi dancing,[105] mindfulness,[106] yoga, sweat lodges[107] and sand mandalas[108] to develop the global, contemplative mind.

Thomas Keating is also a founding member of Ken Wilber's Integral Institute,[109] and a collaborator with Wilber in the Integral Contemplative Christianity project,[110] which reinterprets Philippians 2:5 through the lens of evolving consciousness:

> Integral Contemplative Christianity...[is] the leading-edge map of human consciousness and development. ... [T]he seminar will explore St. Paul's statement, "Let the same consciousness that was in Christ Jesus be within you as well."[111]

This "Integral" vision of consciousness is the nondual experience of everything united in the One—monism. Contemplative mysticism continues to facilitate religious convergence.

Jean Houston: 1937–

Inspired by Pierre Teilhard de Chardin, New Spirituality leader Jean Houston is training "Social Artists" to facilitate the shift from the once rational mind of the Judeo-Christian West to the indigenous (pagan) "world mind" through contemplative awakening of "a new myth."[112] She says:

> Embracing the work of Re-patterning Human Nature, the Social Artist learns to think like a planetary citizen; to appreciate cultures and cultural stories and myths, while searching for the emergence of a new story, a new myth...so that contemplation and meditation informs each action, and so that inward life and outward expression are complementary.[113]

According to Houston's web site, "she has been working with the United Nations Development Program, training leaders in developing countries throughout the world in the new field of social artistry" since 2003. Through mass indoctrination of the contemplative mind, Houston intends to facilitate a global shift in consciousness toward establishing the raw paganism of revived indigenous spirituality as the mandated utopian spirituality. Evangelicals are not immune.

THE EVANGELICAL CHURCH CONNECTION

In 1978 Richard Foster introduced contemplative prayer to the evangelical church through his landmark book *Celebration of Discipline,* which is based on the contemplative practices of Ignatius of Loyola, Thomas Merton, Evelyn Underhill and creation spiritualist Meister Eckhart. The first printing taught an exercise of awakened imagination strongly resembling astral projection.[114] Foster says, "In your imagination allow your spiritual body, shining with light, to rise out of your physical body. ...Go deeper and deeper into outer space until there is nothing except the warm presence of the eternal Creator." In his more recent work, *Spiritual Classics,* Foster presents weekly meditations on mystics like Thomas Merton,[115] *The Cloud of Unknowing,*[116] Meister Eckhart,[117] Evelyn Underhill,[118] Pierre Teilhard de Chardin[119] and Karl Rahner,[120] "one of the chief architects of the Second Vatican Council,"[121] who said, "...the Christian of tomorrow will be a mystic, or not a Christian at all."[122] In this book, Foster recommends Teilhard's *Hymn of the Universe* as a resource for "Going Deeper"[123] in the contemplative life. *Hymn of the Universe* presents the world as the divinity-infused, body of God, the "one world-womb" from which a "new humanity" arises through evolution of consciousness toward the "plunge into the all-inclusive One."[124] This is the heart of the New Spirituality's vision of the emergence of a new utopian world realized by a new, integral humanity.

Evangelical churches are often influenced toward contemplative spirituality through their youth programs as many embrace the perceived "authenticity" of contemplative experience. Youth Specialties is an influential parachurch organization providing training, materials and retreats for youth workers. In 1996 San Francisco Theological Seminary joined Youth Specialties in founding the Youth Ministry & Spirituality Project, headed by Mark Yaconelli in order to "form...young people in contemplative understanding through silence, solitude, and a variety of contemplative practices."[125] A week-long retreat called "Sabbath: A Youth Ministers' Retreat" was their first project. Thomas Keating's *Open Heart, Open Mind* was recommended reading in preparation for training in centering prayer, chanting, silence, *lectio divina* and *Ignatian examen.*[126]

The contemplative mind has been being formed in earnest in the evangelical church since the 1970s when Richard Foster further broke down the doctrinal division between Roman Catholicism and the Reformation upon the heals of Vatican II. Now evangelical writers like Adele Ahlberg Calhoun comfortably blend contemplative spirituality with professions of evangelical faith. Calhoun's book *Spiritual Disciplines Handbook: Practices That Transform Us* is a comprehensive manual training evangelicals in such contemplative disciplines as centering prayer, walking labyrinths, silence and solitude. Calhoun commends her readers into the spiritual care of mystics like Richard Foster, the anonymous author of *The Cloud of Unknowing,* Thomas Keating, Tilden Edwards and Richard Rohr.

Willow Creek has also embraced the contemplative mystique. In the 1990s Ruth Haley Barton and John Ortberg developed the course "An Ordinary Day with Jesus,"[127] which inspired Willow Creek's Spiritual Formation Program.[128] Haley Barton was trained as a spiritual director at the interreligious Shalem Institute for Spiritual Formation, founded by Tilden Edwards, who says of contemplation, "This mystical stream is the Western bridge to Far Eastern spirituality."[129] In a talk given at the National Pastors Convention, Haley Barton also spoke of the pre-existence of the soul, a concept Christian mystics borrowed from Neoplatonism:

> there is something in us that is very true. There is an essence of us... which I believe is the soul of us. *It's the part of us that existed before we were bodies on this earth.* It's the part of us that will exist after these bodies go into the ground. And it is a part of us that knows how to commune with God [emphasis added].[130]

A recent Willow Magazine article titled "Rediscovering Spiritual Formation" further reveals the deep influence of contemplative spirituality on Willow Creek as they draw from contemplative leaders like Alice Fryling and Father Richard Rohr.[131] Alice Fryling is the wife of Robert A. (Bob) Fryling, publisher of InterVarsity Press and Vice President of InterVarsity Christian Fellowship. He also teaches the contemplative path of spiritual formation and has co-authored three books with his wife who is published by InterVarsity Press (IVP). Alice Fryling is also a certified Enneagram presenter[132] who joins Father Rohr in using the Enneagram of personality types as a tool for contemplative transformation. Fryling recently taught a course on the Enneagram at the National Pastors Convention,[133] which is sponsored by IVP, Zondervan and Youth Specialties. Ruth Haley Barton recently hosted a pastor's retreat called "The Enneagram: A Window to Self-Knowledge" led by Alice Fryling.[134] In the Emergent sector, Doug Pagitt of Solomon's Porch identifies himself as an eight on the Enneagram,[135] represented by the animal totem of the rhinoceros. Leonard Sweet draws spiritual insight from Gurdjieff, the man who brought the Enneagram west,[136] and Tony Jones, national director of Emergent Village, was introduced to the labyrinth by Jill Kimberly Hartwell Geffrion,[137] who overlays the Enneagram and the labyrinth as a contemplative "mirror of [the] interior life" and "road map to the soul."[138] With the subtle yet growing influence of the Enneagram, it is worth examining its history, meaning and use.

THE ENNEAGRAM

The Enneagram is a nine-pointed star formed by overlaying a triangle on a hexad (an unusual six-sided figure) within a circle. The name is derived from the Greek words *Ennea* (nine) and *Gramma* (point).[139] Some trace its origins to the Egyptian mysteries and Pythagoras,[140] others to the Desert Fathers[141] and Sufi mystics.[142] Its symbolism is rooted in divination,[143] "universal wisdom"[144] and "perennial philosophy."[145] According to Enneagram teachers, Don Riso and Russ Hudson, the Enneagram is a "Sacred Psychology...a tool for transformation that uses...psychology as a *point of entry into a profound and universal spirituality* [emphasis added]."[146]

Georges Ivanovich Gurdjieff: 1877–1949

The Enneagram was introduced to the West in 1922 by Greek-Armenian occultist George Gurdjieff, through his Institute for the Harmonious Development of Man. From the institute, Gurdjieff disseminated his "Fourth Way" teachings, which synthesize the three esoteric wisdom centers of body (hatha yoga), heart (contemplative monk) and mind (jnana yoga) into one "harmonious" center of enlightened consciousness, called the "work."[147]

As a young man, Gurdjieff learned of a "perpetual hierarchy"[148] of highly evolved holy men possessing the universal keys of perennial wisdom.[149] His quest for this esoteric knowledge eventually led him to Central Asia where he was initiated into the secrets of a "Universal Brotherhood"[150] of Naqshbandi dervishes[151] known as the "Masters of Wisdom,"[152] who claim direct transmission of knowledge from the spirit *Kutb-i-Zaman*, or Green Qu-Tub, head of the celestial hierarchy.[153]

The Sufis used the Enneagram for "numerological divination."[154] The circle represents a "universal mandala" symbolizing One and is often depicted as the Ouroboros serpent biting its own tail,[155] which represents the unification of the human psyche with the cosmic forces.[156] The triangle stands for the internal dynamism of the Law of Three that removes all distinctions, such as Creator and creation, good and evil, male and female.[157] The points of the triangle correspond with the numbers 3, 6 and 9 representing what Gurdjieff called "demiurgic essences," or spiritual hierarchies, charged with harmonization on earth.[158] The hexad corresponds with 1, 4, 2, 8, 5, and 7 (1÷7=.142857),[159] which represents the Law of Seven's evolutive power of "becoming"[160] and aligns vibrations of consciousness with the One. This is the occult principle of "as above, so below" that views humanity as a microcosm of the universe through which the spiritual realm is manifesting itself on earth.

Alice Bailey

Theosophist Alice Bailey used the Enneagram as "the symbol of self-sustaining evolution or transformation." Bailey's biographer, Sir John R. Sinclair, says the human body itself is "a symbolic city of nine gates or orifices, with the tenth opening as the 'brahmarandra' centre on the crown," the chakra through which yoga consciousness ascends to higher levels. Sinclair says, "The Grand Ennead [Enneagram]," represents "original Unity...the return to the source."[161]

Oscar Ichazo: The Enneagram of Fixations

In the early 1970s Oscar Ichazo, founder of the occult Arica Institute, developed the "Enneagram of Fixations"[162] around nine "ego-types"[163] defining the separated *false self*. He added arrows to the internal lines of the Enneagram designating the downward pull of the ego-types. Progress is made by moving back against the arrows[164] toward "remembering"[165] the soul's essential union with the Divine so that the undifferentiated true self, the essential personality, can be regained. Notice the similarity with the contemplative process. Ichazo also synthesized the Enneagram with astrology and assigned animal "totems" to the types suggestive of the familiar spirits of shamanism.[166]

Fr. Bob Ochs

Chilean psychiatrist, Claudio Naranjo, studied the Enneagram with Ichazo in 1970 and began teaching it in Berkeley in 1971.[167] His student, Jesuit Bob Ochs, combined the Enneagram with yoga and Sufi meditation in his program of "spiritual, psychological, and physical exercises [designed] to awaken higher states of consciousness and enlightenment."[168] Ochs spread the Enneagram's secrets throughout Jesuit retreat houses where they took off like dandelion seeds blown by the wind.

Jerome Wagner

One of Ochs' seeds took root in the consciousness of Jerome Wagner,[169] clinical psychologist and psychotherapist at Loyola University in Chicago.[170] Wagner uses the Enneagram to achieve "self-realization" and "self-transcendence."[171] Wagner synthesizes perennial wisdom and Sufi mysticism with evolution's theory of brain development from reptilian to human and uses Gurdjieff's "Fourth Way" to integrate these systems into the emerging consciousness.[172]

Alice Fryling

Alice Fryling (wife of IVP publisher Bob Fryling) is an evangelical spiritual director who received her certification in the Enneagram through Jerome Wagner's program at Loyola.[173] She now presents the Enneagram to evangelicals as a tool for spiritual transformation through its "nine windows into reality" and as "a tool to read the soul."[174]

Fryling includes Bible verses with her presentation of the Enneagram, yet during a course she taught at the National Pastors Convention, she recommended the work of Helen Palmer, Don Riso and Russ Hudson, and Richard Rohr for further insight into using the Enneagram for personal transformation.[175] Helen Palmer links Buddhist "Mindfulness" with the Enneagram.[176] Riso and Hudson say the Enneagram "is a condensation of universal wisdom and the perennial philosophy," releasing "the light of Divinity [that] shines in every individual."[177] Franciscan Richard Rohr says the Enneagram has "almost clairvoyant" powers that help move people away from "Bible Quotations," "dogmas," and "moralistic value judgments" to learn from "creation spirituality [and] from native American Indian Spirituality."[178] Rohr also says that "[t]he entire Enneagram typology leads to the tenth quality of God in the kabbalah, the feminine SOPHIA, or WISDOM OF GOD [Capitals in original]."[179]

Fryling closed her Enneagram course at the National Pastors Convention[180] with centering prayer to help the pastors "let go" so they could listen in silence for the voice of God.[181] But whose voice is really speaking through the Enneagram?

Concluding Thoughts

Contemplative spirituality is an ancient path combining the externalism of religious symbolism with the interior journey towards mystical experience of the divine. It is rooted in the ancient spiral of perennial wisdom that began to uncoil in the Garden of Eden when Satan said to Eve: "[Y]ou will be like God, knowing good and evil" (Gen 3:5). Eve left the protective boundary of God's revealed Word and, in her sin, sent fallen mankind on the quest for self-deification through the forbidden fruit of esoteric knowledge. The ancient mystery religions, the esoteric wisdom traditions, and the mystics of the world's religions have been swept along the spiral way through history, moving toward culmination in the Omega Point of global, religious synthesis into the One. Through contemplative mysticism, the church is being baptized into the interreligious, global mind as evidenced by Christian contemplatives like Thomas Merton, Thomas Keating and Richard Foster. To use the parallel of Dr. Peter Jones,[182] the pagan Lie tells us that mysticism opens the spiritual portals to union with God through transcendence of consciousness. The Gospel Truth is that only through the blood of Jesus Christ do we find "confidence to enter the holy place" (Heb 10:19).

14 HOLLYWOOD, ENTERTAINMENT & NEOPAGANISM

JOEL PELSUE

From the *Matrix* to Madonna, and from the *Lion King* to the *Secret*, pop culture provides a steady diet of Neopaganism from which the populace can choose, according to its tastes. Even my three- and six-year-old children are bombarded with pagan content in films, music and video games designed to catch their attention. Christians must gain tools for discerning the philosophy and religious views present in the media they and their children consume. This study is not exhaustive, but it will show a broad sampling of Neopaganism within the entertainment world.

FILM

Many popular films today are produced, written or directed by film-makers whose Neopagan notions are inherent in their artwork. *The Golden Compass*, which appeals to children and young people, is the first of three films based on novels by Phillip Pullman, who admires Richard Dawkins, an apologist for the anti-God movement. Conclusive evidence of Pullman's worldview emerges blatantly and honestly in the final novel, in which the characters kill God. His conclusions are the natural implication of a worldview absolutely at odds with Christianity.

On the film's website, you will find a clickable icon inviting you to "meet your daemon." After answering a twenty question quiz, you will discover which is "fitting" for you. Pullman's work uses the word "daemon" to mean a disembodied spirit, rather than the biblical notion of a fallen angel. In Pullman's imaginary world, your spirit is *outside* your body in the form of an animal that resembles your personal characteristics. If you are brave, your daemon might take the form of a wolf; if you're scared, a mouse; and if you're curious, a ferret. This search for a "daemon" may seem harmless, but it can open a door to the occult, animism and familiar spirits.

Other fantasy literature and film use sorcery, mythical characters and magic to bring depth and complexity to their storytelling. The *Harry Potter* book and film series is doubtless the most popular in this genre. J. K. Rowling has written engaging storylines and develops interesting characters, both of which have been enjoyed by millions of Christians and non-Christians.

In the Harry Potter movies we find pictures of redemption, illustrations of biblical principles such as sacrifice, and godly character traits such as honesty. However, we must not stop there. We must look at the film as a whole. How do the unbiblical elements affect the storyline as a whole, and how does the film affect the audience? Christians differ in their opinion of the books, but both the books and the films depict sorcery, divination and the occult as attractive and morally neutral. Christians know that these acts are not presented as morally neutral in the Bible. God said to Moses, "*There shall not be found among you...anyone who practices divination or tells fortunes or interprets omens, or a sorcerer*" (Dt 18:10).

The reader or moviegoer who identifies with Harry Potter, enters into a story that makes sorcery and magic attractive, normal and exciting. Harry's friends all practice magic and are the misunderstood and downtrodden minority, whom the reader is meant to admire. Attitudes to witchcraft are thus subtly affected. Such attitudes are dangerous for children and adults alike, if they are left unchecked, unfiltered, and unnoticed.

I am not saying Christians should never *watch* these movies. We *read* about divination in the Bible even though we are told never to *explore* it. If we do watch movies like this, we must watch them with discernment and parents must realize that children do not have adult cognitive filters when watching these movies. Adults can (and should!) say to themselves, "this is not a biblical worldview; I don't want to pursue this." They can separate the story from the medium through which it's communicated. Children don't usually have the ability to break apart these movies, discarding inappropriate content while remaining engrossed in the powerful storytelling.

According to George Barna, teenagers thirteen to nineteen years of age who have read or seen the Harry Potter books or movies are more likely to experiment with psychic or occult activities. A friend I know once asked a twelve-year old girl, who was gripping her newly acquired Harry Potter book, whether she was more inclined to think favorably of witchcraft after reading the stories. The girl said wistfully, "Yes, I think so. But what I really wish is that I could get my letter for Hogwart's school." Wiccan leaders have noted that the Harry Potter series has created a growing interest in witchcraft. Harry Potter has hit its target market of teens (and a gold mine along with it). However, media for even the youngest children is steeped in Neopaganism.

Disney poignantly presents the Neopagan worldview in two of its highly acclaimed animated features, *The Lion King* and *Pocahontas*. *The Lion King* is one of the most explicitly pagan movies made by Disney. The anthem, "The Circle of Life" by Elton John, denies the existence of God as Creator and sees creation in all its beauty as a self-sustaining cycle. We have only to live our lot in life. If you're the future Lion King (Simba), then you have a great destiny, but if that is not your lot, there is no hope to find the greater meaning or redemption that Christianity provides. The destiny of thousands of hedgehogs, mice or other animals is to be crushed by elephants or to starve in a drought. Disney doesn't emphasize the fatalism inherent in this worldview; the film shows only the positive, because we all want to identify with the king.

Components of this film seem to mirror biblical elements such as sacrifice, forgiveness, and the victory of good over evil, but we must remember that the framework is clearly pagan. Some Christians might see the love of God the Father in Mufasa's statement to his son Simba: "You have forgotten who you are, and so have forgotten me. Look inside yourself, Simba. You are more than what you have become. You must take your place in the Circle of Life."

This powerful scene of a Father's benediction upon his son encourages *looking inside ourselves* for hope, which is a pagan method. Biblical hope comes from looking to God—our only source of strength, joy and courage. Furthermore, we are not simply "taking our place." Rather, we are being transformed and empowered through the work of the Holy Spirit.

The "wise man" is the pagan shaman, or "medicine man," Rafiki. It is he who speaks wisdom into Simba's life, and it is he to whom other animals bow as he prepares to anoint Simba. This scene is a pagan parallel to Christian baptism. Simba's "baptism" has nothing to do with a Creator God who redeems us from the guilt and shame of sin. Instead, it symbolizes Simba's birth into royalty and his natural right to the kingship. The vulture is born to eat carcasses. Simba finds his identity as he relates to the great Lion Father in the sky, an indirect appeal to ancestor worship. The "spiritual" feel of the movie is created by an entirely earth-based philosophy.

Though the *Lion King* is an original story with a strong pagan thrust, Disney goes against the grain with *Pocahontas*, radically changing the story to put forth a deliberately pagan philosophy. In the historical account, Pocahontas converts to Christianity and is attracted to the character and spiritual life of Captain John Smith. In the Disney version, John Smith "converts" to paganism. The settlers are depicted as imperialistic men and women who commit the worst evil—having no care for nature. Disney makes Pocahontas the evangelist for environmentalism which is infused with her pagan perspective on the environment. The lyrics of the theme song exemplify this pagan belief of spirits inhabiting all parts of creation:

> You think you own whatever land you land on.
>
> The Earth is just a dead thing you can claim,
>
> But I know every rock and tree and creature
>
> Has a life, has a spirit, has a name.

Notice the pantheistic view that everything has a spirit. The wise pantheist opens the poor Christian's eyes to the value of the earth.

Adult Christians may be able to detect and discard these pagan notions as they watch the film. However, films have an exponential effect on young children. Adults typically see a movie once and move on. Children watch a movie they love thirty or forty times. The inherent theology or worldview of that movie will thus have a greater influence as the child hears and sees anti-Christian beliefs depicted over and over.

Martin Luther saw the power of this type of repetition. He believed the theology in the music sung during worship has *more impact* than the preaching on a Sunday morning. Two or three weeks after you've heard a sermon you may not remember it. However, people continue to sing worship songs for weeks or months as they go about their daily lives. The theology inherent in the lyrics continues to have a voice long after the worship service. As people sang Luther's lyrics, "A mighty fortress is our God, a bulwark never failing," they were reminded to hold onto God's sovereignty and strength. In the same manner, children who watch and sing along to pagan music, singing, "every rock and tree and creature has a spirit..." will begin to believe that rocks and trees and creatures share the same life that humans possess. The subtle indoctrination achieved through movies and television can far surpass that of any classroom.

Thirty years of *Star Wars* shows the staying power of such pagan ideas in what was once considered a Christian nation. This epic film inspired the entire nation, but *Star Wars* cut a hole in the cultural fence, and Neopaganism crept in. Producer George Lucas said, "I put the Force into the movie in order to try to awaken a certain kind of spirituality in young people—more a belief in God than a belief in any particular religious system." He goes on to make this claim: "all the religions are true."[1] Such a statement seems tolerant, but is actually intolerant. To say all religions are true is to say that any religion that claims to know the truth is automatically wrong. So Christians, Muslims and Jews are all wrong. Lucas is actually saying that everyone is wrong, except those who agree with his statement. Saying "all religions are true" is a pantheistic and Neopagan way to say that only pagans have the whole truth. Christians are not the only ones to make truth claims!

Lucas was highly influenced by Joseph Campbell, who followed the perspectives of Carl Jung. In fact, Joseph Campbell's interview with Bill Moyers was filmed at Lucas' Skywalker Ranch. Campbell has been a tremendous inspiration for many artists and creative professionals. His books, *The Power of Myth* and *Hero with a Thousand Faces,* are regularly used as textbooks in university classes to explore the stories of religions and mythology. Joseph Campbell explored the history of myths and many religions and concluded that: "all myths are the creative products of the human psyche, that artists are a culture's mythmakers, and that mythologies are creative manifestations of humankind's universal need to explain psychological, social, cosmological, and spiritual realities."[2]

Campbell believes *all* myths (including stories in the Bible) are nothing more than a product of the human psyche. For him, there is nothing beyond the story. Stories are like dreams striving to explain the parts of reality that confound us. The Bible's story is, for him, a grand story of sacrifice and redemption that fills the need of our psyche to be loved and valued. He would not pause to consider any historical veracity of the claims or the possibility that a real God would truly become man and do everything Christ did.

Campbell understands something Christians have often failed to recognize; namely, the power of storytelling, and the universality of the major archetypes. In these particulars, C. S. Lewis would no doubt have agreed with Joseph Campbell—artists are the myth creators. Tolkien and C. S. Lewis utilized the term *mythopoeia* (myth makers). Artists *are* the cultural myth makers, and stories like *Star Wars* have great power for inspiring and forming our view of the world. However, the goal of myth makers such as Tolkien, C. S. Lewis and the Inklings was to point people beyond these stories to a transcendent God. For them, the great stories awaken in the heart what we know underneath to be true (Romans 1) and point us to the reality of a sovereign and gracious God.

Christians who understand Tolkien and Lewis will realize this. After all, most of the Bible is written in narrative form. The unique difference of the Bible is its historical nature. While studying in Israel, I was surprised to hear my agnostic archeology professor say it would be foolish not to use the Bible as a textbook. This is because it is a major source of historical data. In great contrast, Homer's *Iliad* and *Odyssey* were never meant to convey historical facts. This is the key distinction missed by Jung, Campbell, and George Lucas. The Bible is not one of many myths. It is the true story of which all other myths and archetypes are imperfect reflections. This is why the archetypes are so "moving" to the human heart—because God *placed those desires within us* for unconditional love, forgiveness, redemption and other universally true themes.

C. S. Lewis says in the preface to his book *Pilgrim's Regress* that he was a pantheist before becoming a Christian. After he came to be a

Christian, he saw his pagan yearnings in a different light:

> The books and music in which we thought the beauty was located will betray us if we trust them. It was not in them, it only came through them and what came through them was a longing, for they are not the thing itself. They are only the scent of a flower we have not found, the echo of a tune we have not heard, news from a country we have never yet visited.[3]

For C. S. Lewis, the point of this myth making, this *mythopoeia*, is to point beyond. Narnia beckons us to understand the Christ figure and to believe in a God who redeems. Tolkien's *Lord of the Rings* shows us beauty, and that good conquers evil. He also shows us how the temptation for power can ruin a man. These stories beg us to see our need for something outside of ourselves to redeem us. Myths reflect worldview. The Lewis/Tolkein myths point to the true reality of the gospel, but the myth of *Star Wars* and other such films communicates another worldview entirely.

An extremely popular set of films for gen-ex and younger generations was *The Matrix Trilogy*. These films contained stunning and revolutionary visual effects, and were written and produced by the Wachowski brothers. The brothers, and particularly Larry, are even more focused on Neopaganism than was George Lucas. The first *Matrix* film had many Christian symbols, but by the end of the third movie, it was apparent the film was far from a Christian trilogy. The Wachowski brothers were expected to record a commentary on the DVDs when the trilogy was released as a set. However, they declined, asking the Neopagan guru Ken Wilber to give the commentary instead. His analysis shows that a purposeful mixing of philosophies and religions supported the thesis that the only true religion is the pagan philosophy of Ken Wilber and his Integral Institute.

Wilber suggests that it's not until the last twenty minutes of part 3, *Revolutions*, that the key to the trilogy is revealed. Listen to this:

> although Neo [the protagonist] is physically blind, he sees the machines as luminous, golden light—not quite how the "bad guys" are seen in most movies. And yet Neo is unmistakable in what he says to Trinity: "If you could see them as I see them, they are all made of Light...." Indeed, the machines represent Spirit, but Spirit as alienated

> and therefore attacking.[4]

Wilber summarizes, "Zion represents body (filmed in blue tint), the *Matrix* represents mind (green tint), and the machines [this is the kicker revealed in part 3] represent spirit (golden tint)." Then Wilber adds:

> For those of you keeping track, this is indeed quite similar to the Great Nest of Being as taught by the world's wisdom traditions, a spectrum of being and consciousness reaching from body to mind to spirit.[5]

The worldview and philosophy behind the Matrix becomes clear. Christianity is nowhere to be found—unless as an aspect of an inspiring myth. The trilogy preaches a Neopagan, pantheistic worldview that believes salvation to be a higher level of consciousness. Sin does not exist; there is no need for forgiveness. There is only a lack of remembering. We need to remember what we knew before we were born so we can raise our consciousness.

Another Neopagan film with tremendous box office success is *Gladiator*. This Ridley Scott epic begins and ends with pagan prayers and afterlife scenes specifically designed to bring out the pagan worldview which was so dominant in that era. One of the most famous lines from the film is uttered by Maximus when he says, "Father of a murdered son, husband to a murdered wife and I shall have my vengeance in this life or the next." Here we see the reincarnation doctrine specifically cited, and with a strong sense of his ability to impact the world. However, the pagan worldview does not authenticate such desires. The nihilistic result of pagan notions is stated elsewhere by Maximus, "Death smiles at us all. All that a man can do is smile back."

Most reviews focused on the violence, missing the subtle message of the Roman pagan worldview with its determinism and fatalism. You don't really have a choice; you just have to live what lot in life you're given. This stands in great contrast with a Christian worldview, of a sovereign God who reaches down, and who is willing to die for us, to save us, and offer us redemption, hope, forgiveness and joy. Neopaganism offers no such hope. The yearning for redemption and forgiveness within each man and woman's heart simply cannot find satisfying answers in the pagan world of the *Gladiator*.

Another interesting, though violent, film embodying a pagan worldview is *Pan's Labryinth*. The director transitions between the two worlds of fantasy and reality almost effortlessly. This is not merely an artistic choice, but something driven by his worldview. In fact, he does this because he doesn't think there should be a distinction between the two. The writer and director, Guillermo del Toro says,

> Organized politics and religion are much more fairy tales than fairy tales. . . . I don't believe in religion making us different. . . immortality is simply a mind trip. It has nothing to do with God, or redemption, or forgiveness.[6]

He goes on to say,

> In my mind, this fable is just another variation on the same old platonic theme that in our soul-state we know everything, but the trauma of being born causes us to forget everything we knew. That's why the Socratic method was invented and is so effective because the process of asking questions causes us to "remember" the things we knew before.[7]

This epitomizes the pagan worldview—all is one. There are no boundaries, religions or geography. The only way for us to evolve is to "remember" or come to a higher state of consciousness in order to let go of distinctions, hierarchies and rules.

Music

In such a short chapter, we can only examine three icons of the music world. I have chosen these older musicians since they continue to inspire young artists today. We can see their personal transitions into Neopaganism as a religious trend that young artists are following in a myriad of ways.

British artist *Sting* became famous with his band *The Police* before pursuing his successful solo career. That he grew up in the church is evident in his music. However, later in life he abandoned his Christian beliefs to pursue Neopaganism. His biography, *Broken Music*, provides us with an illustration of his journey into Neopaganism.

Before releasing the *Soul Cages* CD, both of his parents had died within a few months of each other. He initially took the modern-day approach of pushing through the pain of his loss without taking time to mourn—he did not even attend the funerals. After a couple of years, however, his creative juices were absolutely stifled. To rejuvenate his creativity, he flew to Brazil and took part in an ancient pagan ritual to mourn the death of his parents.[8] This ritual included drugs in the form of a liquid substance called ayahuasca which induced "altered states" in the context of indigenous pagan ceremonies. Sting refers to himself as an agnostic, but yearns for an experience that points beyond this life. Neopaganism can be very attractive to people of this mindset.

He says specifically in his music that he gave up on the holy church. He sings, "I lost my belief in the holy church…but if I ever lose my faith in you…." The "you" in this case refers to his wife. He replaced his belief in church with his belief in his wife and his marital relationship. In some pagan circles the elevation of sex, and the female in particular, is an integral part of pagan thinking. In the press, Sting also spoke of his studies and his utilization of the pagan-infused intimacy known as tantric sex.

In his CD *Sacred Love* he sings, "You're my religion, you're my truth; you're the Holy Grail at the end of my search." This sounds reminiscent of *The DaVinci Code*, because the center of his religion and religious experience is his wife. He also has spoken in interviews of his use of tantric sex, a practice that comes out of the Buddhist tradition. The sexual union is worshiped, rather than enjoyed as a gift from God. Sexual union in the Song of Solomon shows us a foretaste of heaven, a glorious picture of our union with Christ. Sexual union gives us a picture of what it's like to be fully united with God. To be fully vulnerable with our defenses down, to be fully naked emotionally and spiritually, and be loved—this is what we desire from God. Sex should be a picture of that, not a substitute for it.

The second artist, Santana, has had great success in collaboration with younger artists and continues to express his spirituality in these collaborations. Santana's journey into Neopaganism began in 1972 when he became a fan of the fusion band *Mahavishnu Orchestra* and its guitarist John McLaughlin. McLaughlin introduced Santana and his wife to a guru, who accepted them as disciples and gave Carlos Santana the

Buddhist name, "Devadip." The titles of Santana's work show the pagan influence: *Shaman, Sacred Fire, Moonflower* and *Supernatural*. In recent years Santana has had amazing success collaborating with young new artists, such as Wyclef Jean, Lauryn Hill, Rob Thomas, Dave Matthews and others. In an age where so many young artists are interested in spirituality and disinterested in institutions, Santana is an inspiration. The admiration young artists have for Santana's phenomenal musical skills opens them to exploring his pagan spirituality. Santana's influence is magnified by his stunning success. The first CD of collaborations sold over fifteen million copies and garnered nine Grammy Awards. Pagan ideas inspired many of these exceedingly popular songs, which were produced by one of the all time greatest music producers, Clive Davis.

The last musician I want to examine is Madonna, originally known as the "material girl." She pushed the cultural boundaries of sexuality with songs such as "Like a Virgin," and was very vocal against the church. But Madonna has come full circle and now embraces Kabbalah, a mystic strain of Judaism. Traditional Judaism sees Kabbalah as heretical, but its popularity and impact are growing. Speaking with Shimon Perez in Israel, Madonna said, "I'm an ambassador for Israel." Her interest in Israel has come out of her passion for the Kabbalah's pantheistic understanding of the Torah. She has influenced many young women in the industry. During the VH1 and MTV awards, she emerged as the one revered by the other artists and from whom they sought advice. Madonna sees herself in a maternal role for some of the young women in the music business, like Britney Spears.

The Neopaganism of these three and other older artists has opened the door for younger artists to adopt pagan beliefs and to express them through their music.

Literature

Literature has been a tremendous hotbed for Neopaganism in recent years. The more popular books are often made into films, and thus impact the culture through two media outlets. The *Da Vinci Code* made a big splash, proposing the thesis that the Holy Grail is really a woman's body, and more specifically, Mary's womb. The suggestion that salvation came through a woman's body, and not through Christ, is a radical departure from the gospel. Many valuable books and websites have exposed the ancient Gnostic heresies and historical inaccuracies in Dan Brown's work, so we need not go into a lengthy discussion here. The immense popularity of the book reveals the American culture's insatiable curiosity about the sex life of celebrities. Who could be a bigger celebrity than Jesus Christ? No wonder the *Da Vinci Code* was such a big seller. It also rode the wave of curiosity about the pagan worldview—a curiosity heightened by years of subtle messages found in film and music. The *Da Vinci Code* pushes a pagan worldview that sees Christ not as the Creator who steps into his creation and becomes incarnate for man's salvation, but as a spiritual figure who inseminates the "feminine," bringing salvation through Mary Magdalene's womb, in a mystic, mysterious connection through a woman's body.

Another book/movie combination is the *Golden Compass*. The antagonist is an organization called "the Magisterium," which symbolically portrays the Roman Catholic Church. The writer/director of the film, Chris Weitz, tried to water down the book's antireligious component in order to gain religious viewers. At a screening of the film here in Hollywood, I heard Weitz describe how he changed the character of the *Magisterium*. In the book it is easy to see how the *Magisterium* resembled the Catholic Church, but in the film it became a mere social and political organization. The Christian response to Mel Gibson's *Passion* and Dan Brown's *DaVinci Code* had made people in the industry much more aware of potential ticket sales to Christians.

The Secret is the third book I want to consider. It is a self-help book that has sold at an astounding rate. Already selling 10,000 copies a week *before* Oprah plugged it, *The Secret* moved to 100,000 a week afterwards. Consider these quotes from the book: "Everything that's coming into your life you are attracting into your life." The author Rhonda Byrne writes: "You are the most powerful magnet in the universe...so as you think a thought, you are also attracting like thoughts to you." The assumption in such a statement is that your personal desires govern your future. Such a precept is in direct contrast to the Bible, which teaches us that the architect and finisher of our faith is God. Who created everything? God.

Who is the Alpha and the Omega? God. Who rules and directs all that takes place? God alone. Of course, God does work through us. He uses us to feed the poor, to seek justice, to pursue the good of the city, and to speak the truth to our neighbors. But (fortunately!) our desires do not drive the future. God determines the future.

Like many expressions of false spirituality, *The Secret* quotes the Bible in an attempt to persuade Christians of its legitimacy. The author quotes Matthew 21:22 ("Whatsoever ye shall ask in prayer, believing, ye shall receive") in order to justify the so-called "law of attraction," which means that God will give you whatever you ask for. This is a bastardized and heretical interpretation, because God never promises to give us whatever we want as if he were a vending machine. God promises to do great things through us as we put our faith in him, obey him and seek his will—not our own comfort and pleasure.

The "law of attraction" in the *Secret* breaks down into three steps:

1. Know what you want and ask the universe for it.
2. Feel and behave as if the object of your desire is on its way.
3. Be open to receiving it.

There are aspects of this law that are clearly attractive to the human heart. Who doesn't want to think they are in ultimate control over their lives? Who wouldn't want everything their heart desires? We would all like to control our destinies and feel that the universe is at our beck and call. As book reviewer, Tim Challies succinctly points out:

> There is a problematic component: if you follow this through logically it implies that the Jews brought the holocaust on themselves. Equally as tragic, it implies that the sexually abused child invited the abuse. These are horrific problems you cannot discard. Not to mention the question of what happens when two people desire the same thing.[9]

The *Secret* tells us that if we sacrifice for others, we show a "belief in lack." Instead, we should always look out for ourselves. By sacrificing himself, Jesus failed to be all he could be. According to *The Secret's* philosophy, the choice Jesus made to become human and to die on the cross was a foolish choice. He should have pursued selfish desires. This could not be farther from the gospel.

True to Neopaganism, the author ascribes divinity to humanity:

> The earth turns on its orbit for You. The oceans ebb and flow for You. The birds sing for You. The sun rises and it sets for You. The stars come out for You. Every beautiful thing you see, every wondrous thing you experience, is all there, for You. Take a look around. None of it can exist, without You. No matter who you thought you were, now you know the Truth of Who You Really Are. You are the master of the Universe. You are the heir to the kingdom. You are the perfection of Life. And now you know *The Secret.*[10]

Note the crazy claim, "none of it can exist without you." Really? If all the universe exists for me, then my death would cause everything to stop. I think if I died today the world would go on just fine. My wife would mourn, my children would mourn, my friends would mourn, but the earth would not stop on its axis. The earth does not exist for me. I am not so delusional as to think so.

The *Secret* makes the same mistake all pagan ideologies make—it takes a good and right respect for the dignity of humanity and raises this respect to the level of worship. Instead of giving honor to the Creator for the fact we humans are made in the image of God—"fearfully and wonderfully made," as King David put it in the Psalms, pagans start worshiping themselves. The naïve self-help principle of the *Secret* fails as a philosophy because it only describes positive wishes. What about the man who wishes his boss were dead or a jealous lover who desires to beat her boyfriend to a pulp? The desires of our heart are not always good for society or even for us. As the old Chinese curse supposedly goes: "May you get what you wish for." In this case, *The Rolling Stones* have better theology than Oprah: "You can't always get what you want." More to the point here: we shouldn't.

A Biblical Response

With so many films, songs and books filled with pagan worldviews, how should we respond? Christians have typically committed one of two great errors when responding to art, films and pop culture in general. On the one extreme we retreat from the culture into our own little Christian ghetto of Christian music, films and art that is sentimental and safe. On the other extreme, we embrace the mainstream culture without discernment, which leaves our minds and hearts vulnerable to unhealthy compromises and moral corruption. In both cases we fail to be salt and light to a world desperately in need of God's grace and truth.

Some Christians have been astute critics of their culture and have taken solace in this inflated sense of accomplishment. Christians must not only critique but *create* art that fits a Christian worldview, and then contribute that art to mainstream culture. As Destouches wrote so poignantly in his famous play, "Criticism is easy, art is difficult."[11]

Christians must also realize the role of discernment for themselves and their children. It is foolish to think that telling our children which art to see and which to avoid is sufficient to educate and equip them. It is essential to preview questionable content for our children and to act as guardians of their spiritual development. We need to think hard about what content is age appropriate. However, protecting our children in their early years is not sufficient. As they grow in wisdom and understanding it is critical that we hand them the *tools of discernment,* rather than laying down dictates. Even young children are able to exercise a surprising amount of wisdom, if they are well-instructed. At the early ages of two or three children are capable of understanding right from wrong. We must not underestimate the value of pausing movies or music at home in order to dialogue with your children about how plots and lyrics compare to biblical truths and stories. It is also helpful to discuss the manner in which films depict (or fail to depict) the consequences of sin.

The adults must first acquire these tools of discernment. They should know what content may lead them down a sinful path, and what content will encourage them to pursue godliness. On a more complex level, they must know how to watch content which requires sifting in order to recognize which components are consistent with a Christian worldview and which are contrary to it.

For the sake of future generations, and for the glory of our King, we must take media, and popular culture seriously. If we are passive in this endeavor and simply ignore these issues, we will be like the frog in the kettle–boiled alive without the awareness or strength to leap to safety. If, on the other hand, we are simply religious and retreat from the culture, we will be like salt which never leaves the salt shaker and will be of little use to those around us. May we resist both the temptation to retreat and the temptation to compromise. May we not be conformed to this world, but transformed in our thinking and life, so that we can be agents of cultural transformation wherever God places us.

15

Christian Spirituality

Andrew Young

The explosion of interest in spirituality in recent decades compels us to think clearly about the distinctive character of Christian spirituality. This is particularly so because much of what passes as spirituality is decidedly anti-Christian. As such, it needs to be exposed and guarded against, but this can only be done if we first understand the precise nature of biblical spirituality. Spiritualities are invariably connected to belief systems or to the story that underlies such systems. What people think about themselves and the larger realities of life affects the way they attempt to relate to existence beyond themselves. And that, in essence, is what spirituality is about.

While every aspect of Christian belief impacts the spirituality it generates, three central events in the Christian story are particularly influential. These are the creation of the heavens and the earth, the incarnation of the Son of God, and the sending of the Holy Spirit at Pentecost. Rightly understood, these three events provide the defining structures for Christian spirituality and distinguish it from all others.

Spirituality and the Creation

The Christian understanding of reality is shaped by the opening chapters of the Bible. There we learn that the universe in which we live is the creation of a pre-existent God. We and all that exists around us, including the unseen realm of spirits in the heavens, came into being through the mere Word of that God. It was not formed out of pre-existing matter, nor did it come into being through a tortuous process of conflict among rival deities. One God, who eternally existed as three persons, freely called it into being out of nothing for his own glory (Gn 1:1–31).

As such, the world and all else that exists can be said to be both from God and yet essentially distinct from him. Unlike pantheistic worldviews, Christian cosmology insists that God is transcendent or separate from the things he has made. Consequently, our human quest to connect with larger reality never involves finding ourselves in what exists about us. We are not all parts of one universal essence, but distinct, yet related, creatures. Discovering ultimate reality means looking beyond ourselves and our creaturely existence to a transcendent Creator.

In seeking him, Christians find a God who delights to reveal himself. He is not a deity who, having created and imbued the cosmos with self-regulating laws, then withdraws as a silent spectator to some remote sphere. On the contrary, he is a God who, having created, continues to uphold everything he has made by the word of his power, governing and directing all things toward a predetermined and certain goal. Furthermore, they discover him to be a personal God—not an impersonal substance but a living, personal being capable of relationship. Indeed, as the Scriptures unfold, the Creator God appears with increasing clarity to be a tripersonal being who relates in love firstly within himself in the fellowship of Father, Son and Holy Spirit, and then toward all that he has made.

It is this feature—the Triune existence of God as a community of perfect love—that impacts the Christian understanding of reality perhaps more than anything else. For it is from this that our understanding of ourselves flows. The Scriptures tell us that in the beginning the Triune God made us in his own image and likeness (Gn 1:26–27). This suggests that we were made to be, like him, personal, relational beings intended for community. It also implies that this community embraces fellowship both with the Godhead and with our fellow humans, and that this fellowship is in essence a fellowship of love. Awareness of this fellowship is a defining feature of Christian spirituality.

But there is more. The creation account not only reveals the existence of God, explains the origin of the cosmos, and defines our nature as human image bearers, but it also explains our relationship to the world in which we live. In a very real sense we were made for the earth and the earth for us. Created a little lower than the angels, human beings were to rule over the birds, the fish, the animals and every other living creature (Gn 1:28; Ps 8:5–8). They were to act as stewards of God's good world, bringing all its latent potentialities to fulfillment, and in doing so, also bringing honor and glory to the Creator. In the beginning, there was no sense that material existence was somehow temporary or inferior to a state of disembodied union with God. Our first parents were at home in the wonderful world God had fashioned.

As happy as they were in their surroundings, it is clear from the opening scenes of history that Adam and Eve were never meant to fulfill their calling alone. Having made them, God intended to live in communion with them. To that end, he planted a garden in Eden and met there with the first man and woman (Gn 2:8; 3:8). It was evidently meant to serve as an earthly sanctuary for God, a place to which humans might return again and again to commune with him as they fulfilled their mandate in the world. The first man and woman were made "open to God," capable of intimate fellowship with him, and intended for cooperative labor for him.

One more detail of the creation story bears mention. The intimacy and functional partnership established by God, though imbued with blessing, freedom and delight, was nevertheless bounded by responsibility. As lavishly as Adam and Eve might enjoy the world in which they had been placed and the access its Garden provided to God, they were not autonomous creatures. Their relationship with their Creator was neither accidental nor casual; still less was it one of equals. It carried the obligations of love—complete devotion, self-giving and obedience. On the part of the Triune God it was a relationship which involved the promise of presence, blessing and faithfulness. On the part of his creatures it required total loyalty and unfailing obedience (Gn 2:15–17). Later this relationship is called a "covenant" (Gn 6:18)—a structured, accountable agreement in which faithfulness and failure both carry consequences. The one ensures a continuing and ever-enlarging experience of life, and the other, the severe judgment of death.

Creation Structures for Spirituality

Together, these elements of the creation account establish broad structures for Christian spirituality. First, they determine that it is a theistic spirituality. As Christians seek to understand themselves and their world, and to relate to that which transcends themselves, they do so knowing that the ultimate source of all being is a personal God, not an impersonal force or ubiquitous essence. They understand that they are like him, were made for him, and find meaning in him.

Second, the creation account establishes Christian spirituality as relational. The God who creates is himself full of communal life and extends that life to his human creatures. He communicates in ways that can be understood and regulates human life through his law. He meets with humans in his garden-sanctuary to provide loving support, encouragement and direction. God and those made in his image are intended for friendship and partnership. Biblical spirituality is thus necessarily communal and relational. It bears no trace of sublimation into the divine essence through altered states of consciousness or ritualistic techniques. It is based on intelligent, communicative, interpersonal relationships.

Third, the opening chapters of the Bible lay the foundation for what might be called a holistic spirituality. The first man and woman are physical and spiritual beings living in a world that has been progressively fashioned out of an undifferentiated mass. They are related both to the material dust of the earth from which they were made and to the God who breathed life into them (Gn 2:7). There is no tension for them between the material and spiritual aspects of their being. There is no suggestion that the body—as later Greek philosophy advocated—is somehow a prison for the spirit, to be tolerated until freed from it. The body is the good vehicle through which human identity expresses itself in the realm of creation. That realm is what we have been made for. Christian spirituality finds fulfillment in engaging in earthly, bodily activities to the glory of God.

Fourth, creation-based spirituality is purposeful spirituality. In creating us, God gave us a purpose in the world. Thus, we only find true rest in labor and achievement. Christian spirituality does not consist uniquely of private ecstatic experiences of union with God, but also in accomplishing tasks in fellowship with God. It is ultimately practical and enters into all the affairs of daily life. Any spirituality that draws people away from or belittles the value of work, family, art and science is not creational spirituality.

Finally, the biblical account of creation lays the foundations for a covenantal spirituality. The relationship between God and humans is not only personal, intelligent and conversational, but also responsible. It involves obligations and calls for loyalty; it promises blessing for faithfulness but also threatens curses for disobedience. And it does so without reducing the relationship to a cold legal arrangement. The loyalty, obedience, blessing and judgment entailed are all expressions of the perfect, holy love that binds God and his image bearers together.

Spirituality and the Incarnation

Beyond its account of the creation, the Bible tells of the rupture of divine-human relations early in the history of the world. Enticed by a fallen angel, our first parents rebelled against their loving Creator, seeking to become like God themselves (Gn 3:1ff). The consequences were devastating. They incurred guilt, experienced shame and suffered pain and the weariness of work. They were barred from eating from the tree of life, and excluded from the garden-sanctuary of God. Worst of all, they were condemned to die—not only physically but spiritually. Prior to their rebellion, they were alive to God and were recipients of his life through the Spirit. But after turning from him (the Fall), they were not only alienated from his presence but cut off from his life (Eph 4:18). God's wonderful creation seemed ruined.

The story does not end there, however. Human rebellion could not surprise God; on the contrary, it had been ordained in his all-encompassing decree from eternity. So, too, had his redemptive pursuit of mankind. Rather than abandoning his work or starting it over again, he purposed to display the riches of his grace and the strength of his love by redeeming his rebellious image bearers from their ruin. His determination to have people in intimate fellowship with himself ruling with him over the earth would not be thwarted. A child would come from the line of the first woman to undo the effects of the curse and restore the fellowship between God and man enjoyed in the garden in the beginning (Gn 3:15).

The centuries that lapsed before the coming of the promised Redeemer were not without grace, reconciliation, and relationship. In anticipation of his coming, and on the basis on his certain accomplishments, God revealed his covenant to men and their families (see Gn 6:18; 17:7, etc.). Generation after generation he preserved a faithful line to serve as the bearer of the coming child. Rudiments of the Edenic relationship were recaptured—God continued to speak, revealed his will, protected and delivered, and even took up residence again with his people (Ex 25:8). However, everything was in a sense tentative and anticipatory, pointing toward a greater reality to come. The laws, ceremonies, covenants and covenant mediators all demonstrated that the way into the most holy place had not yet been revealed (Heb 9:8–10). Something better was in store.

That "something better" appeared "in the fullness of time" with the birth of the Redeemer, the eternal Son of God incarnate in human form (Gal 4:4). So great was God's love for the world, and so intent was he upon its redemption, that he himself came to redeem it in the person of the Son. As the Son of God, Jesus of Nazareth was able to show men and women what God was like (Jn 1:18; 14:9), and as perfect man, he was able to demonstrate how God intended humankind to live. More than that, in the grace of God, Jesus was able to act not only as the ideal man but serve as the representative man—a second Adam (Rom 5:14; 1 Cor 15:22). He was able to fulfill the requirements of God's law, bear the curse of a broken covenant, and rise again to life—all on behalf of humankind. In this way, he opened the way back to the presence of God and to restoration of true intimacy with him. The paradisiacal relationship lost through human rebellion is restored again in Jesus Christ.

With his coming into the world, the eternal Son of God becomes the focal point of Christian spirituality. In essence, that spirituality is of the same kind as that established at creation. The basic structures remain the same. It is still a spirituality that is intelligent, personal, embodied and responsible, which embraces the whole of life and assumes responsibility to serve. Divine-human partnership in the life of the kingdom is once again re-established.

Now, however, that fellowship and partnership is experienced in union with Jesus. Believing trust in him as the Redeemer unites us to him and to his work. In him, we are accepted by the Father, forgiven our sins, adopted into his family, accounted righteous, restored to life and secured for eternity. The way into the holiest, the heavenly sanctuary is open and we have boldness through him to enter and bring our prayers and praises to the Father (Heb 4:14–16; 10:19–22). Apart from him there is no other way. Spiritualities advocating intimacy with God apart from Christ have forfeited the right to be called Christian. Jesus Christ alone is the way, the truth and the life. No one comes to the Father but by him (Jn 14:6).

Our New Life in Christ

The new life that we have in Jesus Christ is a life of faith. It is faith not in the sense of believing in that which is not real, but in being assured of things we cannot see (Heb 11:1; 1 Pt 1:8). Faith embraces the record of Jesus' life preserved in the Gospels. Furthermore, it affirms his resurrection life at the right hand of his Father in heaven, his rule over all things to the church, and his certain return at the end of the age. To the eye of faith, the Jesus of history still lives. He is ready to save all who come to him and rest in his vicarious suffering; he is ready to commune with those who open their hearts to his Word; he is ready to comfort and protect all who look to him for help; and he is ready to direct those who look to him for wisdom. Spiritual life for the Christian is faith-based and Christ-focused spirituality.

Specifically, it is faith that rests upon his death and righteousness for eternal life. Christians recognize that their identity with Adam in the Fall not only alienates them from God but disables them from doing good. They know that they cannot be justified in God's sight by their own works, nor can they effect reconciliation by themselves (Rom 3:20). Aware of this, and deeply convinced of their guilt and corruption, they look to God to receive them entirely on the basis of his Son. Emptied of self-merit and sorrowful for their sin, they rely on Jesus' perfect life and sacrificial death on their behalf. And in doing so, they receive the assurance of forgiveness and acceptance with God. They are progressively transformed into the image of Christ and, through his power, are able to perform works which, though imperfect, are accepted by God for his sake.

The faith that relies upon Christ for reconciliation does more than embrace him as an objective figure of history. It also receives him as near, as actually personally present in an intimate spiritual union. The apostle Paul could speak of being "baptized into Christ," of being personally united with him in his death and resurrection, and of daily living by faith in him (Rom 6:1ff; Gal 2:20). By faith, he personally appropriated his union with Jesus, and through faith, Christ actually lived out his life within the apostle. Hence, he prayed that the Ephesian Christians might be strengthened through the Spirit inwardly, that "Christ may dwell in your hearts through faith" (Eph 3:17 NIV).

Through this faith-union with Jesus, we are able to receive from his fullness "grace upon grace" (Jn 1:16). All that Jesus is and has is for the enrichment of his people. Faith draws from the riches of Christ all the spiritual blessings God has given us in him (Eph 1:3). Just as Jesus lived his earthly days in total dependence upon his Father, so Christians now live in total dependence upon him (Jn 6:57). Our lives are hidden with Christ in God (Col 3:3), and for us, "to live is Christ" (Phl 1:21). We look to the Lord for wisdom rather than trusting in our own understanding, and we look to him for power to change—to put off the old manner of life dominated by the sinful nature, and to put on the new man in the image of Jesus (Eph 4:24; Col 3:10). We simply cannot think of anything without reference to Christ. We follow him in a life marked by death (a complete renunciation of self-directed existence) and resurrection (participation in his new life "unto God"). We are thoroughly "in Christ" people.

Integral to being "in Christ" is conformity to Christ. As those who believe and follow him, we are bound to obey him. We imitate his example and keep his commands. We do so, however, with a holy willingness born of love. While the "flesh"—our sin-affected human nature with its ingrained habits and inclinations—wars against our desire to follow Christ (Gal 5:17), we, nevertheless, through the Spirit are able to keep the commands of the Lord. What is more, we find them "good, pleasing and perfect" (Rom 12:2; 1 Jn 5:3 NIV). Just as love enabled Jesus to delight in his Father's will, even to the point of dying on a cross, so we too discover the joy of obeying in love (Jn 15:11).

Added to that, the new life in Christ is marked by a radical devotion to him, a readiness to be used in whatever way he determines. As Christians, we consider ourselves no longer our own, but those who have been purchased by Christ for his purposes (2 Cor 5:15). He makes us both kingdom citizens and kingdom servants. As members of his body, we, both individually but especially corporately, constitute his continuing presence in the world and are the vehicle of his redemptive activity. The Christian life is consequently one of total availability, total dependence and total devotion.

There is, then, an inevitable exclusiveness about Christian spirituality. The holy, personal, Creator God can only be approached through a mediator, the man Christ Jesus (1 Tm 2:5). Apart from him we are without life, without God, and without hope. Every attempt to encounter a higher spiritual reality apart from him is deluded. What is more, the only way to know Christ and experience the life he gives is by faith. Faith looks beyond ourselves to the once crucified, now risen Son of God and rests in who he is and what he has done. Mystical techniques and the inward journey have no place in true biblical spirituality. If there is reality experienced in such things, it is a reality other than that promised in the gospel.

Spirituality and the Coming of the Spirit

The third event in the Christian story that shapes its expression of spirituality is the sending of the Holy Spirit. Before leaving his disciples, Jesus renewed the promise of the earlier prophets of the coming of the Spirit, a promise realized on the day of Pentecost (Jn 14:16ff; Acts 1:4–5; 2:1–4). Though active in the redeemed community throughout the centuries prior to Jesus' coming, the Spirit would assume, Jesus assures his followers, a new and fuller ministry after his return to the Father. He would serve as a second Helper, or Paraclete, who would be with and in them forever and would manifest his ascended presence among them (Jn 14:18–21). Sent by the Father and the Son, the Spirit would give himself to glorifying them by bringing the work of the Triune God to its completion.

In doing so, the Spirit acts with all the authority and ardency of the Father and the Son. His role within the Trinity, so easily overlooked, is as significant as the other persons of the Godhead. All things are from the Father and through the Son. But they are also by the Holy Spirit. He has been called the executive of the Godhead, the One through whom God touches his creation. In the beginning, it was the Spirit who breathed life into Adam (Gn 2:7). In the restoration, he empowers and anoints the man Jesus, inspires holy men to write the Scriptures, calls men and women to God through the gospel, renews the sinful human heart, transforms sinners into Christ-like saints, and empowers them for their continuing mission in the world. His work is no less glorious than that of the Son, though it is always subordinate to it and bears witness to it (Jn 16:12–15).

He accomplishes his redemptive role by indwelling those who have believed in Christ. Prior to the coming of Jesus, the Spirit descended upon people for specific functions. At Pentecost, however, he took up residence in the hearts of men. The temple or dwelling place of God is now the human heart and the corporate church (1 Cor 3:17; 6:19; Eph 2:22). His presence unites believers to the Father and the Son, and also to each other. Through the one Spirit they are baptized into one body (1 Cor 12:13), the spiritual body of Christ, and become truly "members one of another" as well as one with their Lord (Rom 12:5 ESV).

Precisely how the Spirit dwells and works within us is beyond our understanding (Jn 3:8). Nevertheless, it is plain that he comes not to destroy our humanity but to restore it. He does not despise and bypass the human mind and heart, but works within to correct that which is amiss and so enable us to live as we are meant to.

In this he particularly uses his Word, the Scriptures. God's way of relating to people has not changed. In the beginning, he communicated with Adam and Eve through speech, and he still does so today. Only now he uses the written word which is in fact the Spirit's own Word, the Word he inspired holy men to write (1 Pt 1:11; 2 Pt 1:21). He now uses that word as it is read, preached and taught, to accomplish his work in the minds and hearts of people. He uses it to draw them to faith in Jesus, to renew their minds so they have the mind of Jesus, and to change their lives so they become like Jesus. In other words, he enables us to return to God through Christ and so re-establishes the fellowship we were intended for. Furthermore, he employs our faculties as instruments in conveying life to others in the body and in bringing the Gospel to the world. Just as God made Adam and Eve to serve him as stewards of the earth, so now the Spirit empowers, equips and enables God's children in Christ to participate in his kingdom purposes in the ways he has prepared (1 Cor 12:7–11; Eph 2:10; Phl 2:12–13). He is truly the Spirit of life, the one who makes our union with Christ effective and our communion with and service for God possible.

Living in the Spirit

Through the gift of the Holy Spirit we experience an even greater intimacy with God than was possible in the Old Testament dispensation, and even in the incarnation of Christ. The Triune God actually takes up residence within us. His love is shed abroad in our hearts by the Spirit and his presence with us consciously manifested through the "fruit of the Spirit" (Rom 5:5; Gal 5:22–23). Through faith in Christ it becomes possible for us to be "filled with all the fullness of God" (Eph 3:19).

Yet there is no confusion of substance induced by his indwelling, as if our nature somehow is infused with or mixed up in the divine. The Holy Spirit and our spirit remain distinct though mysteriously interrelated. Christian spirituality, consequently, does not journey inward in search of an immediate experience of oneness with God. Instead, through the indwelling Holy Spirit it looks toward Christ and through him to the Father. Contemplative mysticism is not the path of biblical spirituality; faith-based relationship with the Triune God is.

The Christian life is one of being "led by the Spirit" (Rom 8:14). Dwelling in us, enlightening our minds, stimulating our affections, and moving our wills, the Holy Spirit enables us to have the mind of Christ (1 Cor 2:16). He never reduces us to robots but works in us and with us, helping us to think and act and choose. His influence, although capable of coming to our consciousness, is usually so closely intertwined with our own activity that we fail to recognize it. Nevertheless, he is ceaselessly at work within us bringing the purposes of the Father and Son for us to perfection. He is grieved through disobedience and neglect, and can at times be "quenched" (Eph 4:30; 1 Thes 5:19). But he, no less than the Son, delights to do the will of God and to finish his work, pursuing all he does with the same love for the Father displayed by the Son (Rom 15:30).

Consequently, those who are "filled with the Spirit" (Eph 5:18) experience lives marked by holy love, peace and joy. The degree to which these qualities are displayed and enjoyed varies, both within and between individuals. Nevertheless, they are real and ought to radiate from the people of God as they shine as lights in a world of hatred, bitterness, fear and strife (Phl 2:15). Even as they live in this way, Christians are filled with hope for what lies ahead. The Spirit within them is in effect a "deposit" guaranteeing the full inheritance to be enjoyed at the return of Christ (Eph 1:14). Christian spirituality is thus also eschatological. It instinctively looks toward the fulfillment of all things and eagerly anticipates the full experience of dwelling with God in a renewed heavens and earth (Rev 21:3).

In these various ways, Christian spirituality manifests itself in character and experience. Engagement with God is real, and participation in his life registers (in some measure at least) in our human consciousness. It invariably does so, however, through the Spirit acting upon and within us. Christian experience is never to be equated with sublimation into the being of God, or into some universal higher essence or state of consciousness. Christian spirituality is invariably personal. It preserves (and perfects) our human personality, and brings us into an intelligent, interactive communion with the tripersonal God. And in doing so, it differentiates itself from every other expression of spirituality.

CONCLUSION

Current concepts of spirituality are fuzzy and amorphous, while Christian spirituality has a specific character, defined in clear, propositional terms. It entails a life of intimate, interactive communion with God through Christ by the Holy Spirit—a communion that embraces a life of loving obedience and devoted kingdom service. Although hidden in many respects, it involves definite spiritual influences producing distinct states of being and action. Christian spirituality is real.

It is also exclusive and cannot be confused with other forms of spirituality, nor does it have elements in common with them. It is not a localized or cultural expression of a universal reality or higher consciousness, in which "many roads lead to God." It is the one true and unique spirituality, which fulfils the purpose of our existence and the longing of our hearts.

Christian spirituality is supremely desirable. It inducts us into a personal, intelligent, loving friendship and partnership with the Creator of the universe. We can know him and experience his life. We can be indwelt, controlled, and comforted by him. Our lives, engrossed in the affairs of his kingdom, have eternal significance. There can be nothing more desirable or imaginable than this. For in his presence is "fullness of joy" and at his right hand there are "pleasures forevermore" (Ps 16:11 ESV).

16

OLD TESTAMENT PAGAN DIVINATION

DEUTERONOMY 18:9–14

MICHAEL HEISER

Much of the Old Testament's recounting of the salvation history of the people of God concerns the disastrous effects of Israelite adoption of the beliefs and practices of the surrounding nations. The people of Israel were to avoid the gods of other nations and any practice that involved the worship of those other gods. The Gentile nations had been put under the jurisdiction of these other gods by God himself as a punishment in response to the rebellion of the nations at the tower of Babel.[1] After disowning the nations at Babel, God called Abram and created his own people anew, confirming his abiding love for the patriarch's descendants by means of a covenant relationship. As a result, any use of divination to contact one of the foreign gods was viewed as a covenant violation and disloyalty to the true God.

THE PRINCIPLE OF REALM DISTINCTION

In reality, the notion of "covenant separateness" was a familiar and frequently reiterated idea to an Israelite. The barrier between God's people and the disinherited pagans was communicated in various ways in the Law of Moses. Some laws were clearly aimed at prohibiting a mingling of the populations due to fear of idolatry, such as laws forbidding intermarriage between Israelites and the peoples that were to be driven from the land promised to Israel.[2] Such laws taught the Israelites in concrete terms that their loyalty and worship was to be directed only to the God of their fathers. Other laws provided more abstract reminders that there were "two realms" of reality—that which was holy and that which was "profane." For example, there were laws aimed at preventing people with disabilities or lack of bodily "wholeness" from entering sacred space[3] The "uncleanness" in these cases was not moral, but reinforced God's "otherness"—that he was without flaw or blemish. The same can be said for laws prohibiting mixing types of cloth or cooking techniques.[4] Maintaining distinctiveness and unmixed wholeness was a reflection of the perfection of God. The lesson for the Israelite was simple: God has set up boundaries that need to be obeyed for spiritual wholeness and holiness before the God who loves us and redeemed us.

"Realm distinction" also lay behind laws forbidding humans from transgressing the boundary between the terrestrial, human realm and the nonterrestrial, spiritual realm. More properly, there was a realm of embodied living beings (humans, animals) and disembodied beings (God, angels, demons).[5] While it is true that Scripture contains examples where members of each group were permitted entrance into the other realm, human efforts to tap into the "other side" apart from God's sovereign permission and initiation were forbidden. In some respects, this prohibition kept humans safe. The disembodied spiritual realm was a place that could not be accurately understood, controlled and processed by humans, who were therefore vulnerable to malevolent forces they could not trust or understand. In another respect, violating the barrier between these realms was an affront to God in that it echoed another yielding to the seduction of the temptation in Eden. Willfully contacting the other side through means of divination without God's approval telegraphed one's desire to "be like a god," to have the knowledge and attributes of God and the other entities that inhabited the disembodied spiritual world.

Abominable Practices: Deuteronomy 18:9–14

The foundational passage in the Old Testament that articulates God's demand that Israel reject pagan divination is Deuteronomy 18:9–14:

> When you come into the land that the Lord your God is giving you, you shall not learn to follow the abominable practices of those nations. There shall not be found among you anyone who passes his son or his daughter through the fire, *anyone* who practices divination or tells fortunes or interprets omens, or makes potions from herbs or a spell binder, or one who consults a non-human spirit that has knowledge,

> or who inquires of the human dead, for whoever does these things is an abomination to the Lord. And because of these abominations the Lord your God is driving them out before you. You shall be blameless before the Lord your God, for these nations, which you are about to dispossess, listen to fortune-tellers and to those who practice divination. But as for you, the Lord your God has not allowed you to do this.[6]

There are a number of terms in this passage that require explanation.

- One "who passes his son or his daughter through the fire" (*maʿăbîr bĕnô ūbittô bāʾēš*)

It is likely, though not certain, that this wording refers to child sacrifice.[7] Either the practice spoken of here involved burning the child in the fire as an offering,[8] or the child was "passed through" the fire but not burned alive. The question depends in part on whether the practice in Deuteronomy 18:10 is identical to that of 12:31, which is a clear reference to child sacrifice, and other texts that speak of child sacrifice for Molech.[9] It is striking that Deuteronomy 18:10 does not call for the death penalty, whereas other clear references to child sacrifice in the Law do (Lv 20:2, child sacrifice to Molech). This may imply that Deuteronomy 18:10 refers to a practice that did not involve killing the child. Additionally, since all the other practices mentioned in Deuteronomy 18:9–12 have something to do with seeking or using knowledge from nonhuman sources, "passing through the fire" may refer to an act of divination that did not involve the death of the child.

- One "who practices divination" (*qōsēm qĕsāmîm*)

This wording casts a broad net of prohibition. The terms refer to the attempt to elicit information from a deity or "supernatural" source through "reading" or "interpreting" natural resources or events. Divination can thus be broken down into more precise practices by the means employed. For example, the use of water for such a purpose is called *hydromancy* (cf. Joseph, Gn 44:5,15). Interpreting the appearance and constitution of a sacrificial animal is called hepatoscopy. One of the more common practices included within this term is casting lots to discern divine information.[10] The description here thus condemns a wide range of practices.

• One "who tells fortunes" (*mĕʿonēn*)

This is another broad portrayal, indicating the practice of telling the future. The great Jewish interpreter Ibn Ezra thought that the term was derived from *ʿanan*, "cloud," thereby indicating the practice of telling the future on the basis of the shape and movements of clouds.[11]

• One "who interprets omens" (*mĕnaḥeš*)

The meaning of this term depends on the Hebrew root from which it derives.[12] If the term comes from *nḥš*, a root which is the basis for the noun "snake," the term may refer to snake charming or some other practice related to snakes.[13] If the term derives from *lḥš*, it likely refers to other types of enchantments.[14]

• One "who makes potions out of herbs" (*mĕkaššēp*)

This term is most frequently translated "sorcery," but comparative terminology in other Semitic language points us in the direction of one who concocts potions from plants or an herbalist.[15]

• One "who is a spellbinder" (*ḥōbēr ḥāber*)

Scholars generally agree that the root *ḥbr* refers to the use of charms and spells since the root conveys the idea of "uniting, joining and weaving," which may by extension speak of the practice of "tying or wrapping magical knots or threads around people or objects . . . to bind the gods to do one's will or to bind (disable) the object or person to be affected."[16]

• One "who consults a nonhuman spirit; that is, a knowing one" (*šōʾēl ʾôb yiddĕʿōnî*)

My translation here is somewhat interpretive. The Hebrew phrase in Deuteronomy 18 literally means "one who asks a disembodied spirit (*ʾôb*)." This Hebrew word is often translated "medium," a misleading term, since Leviticus 20:27 uses the word to refer to an entity that enters or controls or is channeled by a man or woman, not the man or woman themselves. The *ʾôb* being contacted is often accompanied by the word *yiddĕʿōnî* ("knowing one"; an entity who has knowledge). The coupling of the terms conveys the idea of someone who channels a spirit or who is possessed by a spirit for the purpose of communicating with the disembodied spiritual realm. Several passages in Leviticus illustrate the connection [my translations]:

> Leviticus 19:31: Do not turn to the spirits (ʾ*ôbôt*), to the ones who have knowledge (*yiddĕʿōnî*); do not seek them out, and so make yourselves unclean by them: I am Yahweh your God.
>
> Leviticus 20:6: If a person turns to the spirits (ʾ*ôbôt*), to those who have knowledge (*yiddĕʿōnî*), whoring after them, I will set my face against that person and will cut him off from among his people.
>
> Leviticus 20:27: A man or a woman who is with a spirit (ʾ*ôb*) or one who has knowledge (*yiddĕʿōnî*) shall surely be put to death. They shall be stoned with stones; their blood shall be upon them.

The entity (ʾ*ôb*) of Deuteronomy 18:10 is to be distinguished from the descriptive category below, where someone who inquires of "the dead" is condemned for that practice.[17] Since none of the more precise terms for malevolent underworld entities is used here (e.g., *šedîm*, "demons") the warning includes both good and evil nonhuman beings. Contacting *any* nonhuman entity, even an angel, is forbidden. God might send an angel to communicate with a human being—something that happens with a fair amount of frequency in the Bible—but soliciting contact with such a being is something for which permission is never granted in Scripture. For the Israelite, the true God is the only source of information from the disembodied spiritual realm.

- One "who inquires of the human dead" (*dōrēš el-hammētîm*)

This phrase refers to necromancy, contacting the human dead. The fact that this wording diverges from the phrasing considered above, where nonhuman entities are contacted, illustrates that, as in the wider ancient Near Eastern world, the Old Testament distinguishes ghosts (spirits of human dead) from demonic spirits.

The above practices were serious offenses. Deuteronomy 18:9–12 calls them "abominable" and those who do them "abominations." Other texts describe those who practice these things as having "sold themselves to do evil" (2 Kgs 17:17). Specifically, those who made contact with a *nonhuman* spirit were to be put to death (Lv 20:27). However, hiring the medium was not a death penalty offense (read Lv 20:27 carefully), nor does the Bible make contacting the *human* dead or any of the other practices in Deuteronomy 18 a capital crime. Nevertheless, they were all "abominations" to the Lord.

Other Practices and Terms[18]

The Old Testament utilizes other descriptive terms for divination. Space constrains us to consider only those practices that could be construed negatively in some way.[19]

Astrologer

Several Old Testament terms cover astrological divinatory practices, among them "one who gazes at the heavens" (*hōbĕrēw šāmayim*); "one who gazes at the stars" (*haḥōzîm bakkôkabîm*); and an "astrologer" (*gāzĕrîn*). The former two terms occur in Isaiah 47:13, where the prophet mocks the effectiveness of such practices and describes them in terms of apostasy (not trusting the true God). However, no harsh penalty is imposed in the Old Testament for these practices. The last term is Aramaic and is used in connection with the Babylonian magicians, wise men and enchanters described in the book of Daniel (2:27; 4:7; 5:7,11). The job description conveyed by these terms is to "read the signs in the heavens in order to determine and make known that which has been decreed."[20] Daniel is included in this fraternity by virtue of his training in Babylon and his ability to interpret dreams, a task normally performed by "wise men" in Babylon.

13. Dream Interpretation

The interpretation of dreams (*ḥălôm*) or "night visions" (*ḥezyôn laylâ, marĕʾôṯ hallaylâ*) was a widely recognized form of divination, and there are frequent accounts of the practice within the Old Testament and in texts of other ancient cultures.[21] It was Daniel's ability in this area that led to his elevation as "chief of the magicians" (Dn 5:11). Joseph's elevation to high office came by the same route (Gn 40–41). There is no penalty in the Mosaic Law for interpreting dreams per se. God's use of dreams is presumed as a viable method of communicating information. However, false dream interpretation was a capital crime. Deuteronomy 13:1–5 is explicit:

> If a prophet or a dreamer of dreams arises among you and gives you a sign or a wonder, and the sign or wonder that he tells you comes

> to pass, and if he says, "Let us go after other gods," which you have not known, "and let us serve them," you shall not listen to the words of that prophet or that dreamer of dreams. For the Lord your God is testing you, to know whether you love the Lord your God with all your heart and with all your soul. You shall walk after the Lord your God and fear him and keep his commandments and obey his voice, and you shall serve him and hold fast to him. But that prophet or that dreamer of dreams shall be put to death, because he has taught rebellion against the Lord your God, who brought you out of the land of Egypt and redeemed you out of the house of slavery, to make you leave the way in which the Lord your God commanded you to walk. So you shall purge the evil from your midst.

GETTING AWAY WITH DIVINATION?

There is no doubt that the Old Testament condemns the practices sketched above. What is not so clear is why God would allow some of these very same divination techniques to be practiced by Israelites who were his faithful servants, or by people whom God chose to contact. God dispensed information to certain biblical characters by means of these practices.

Before answering the question of how this is theologically consistent, we need to be precise in our inquiry. First, godly Israelites did not engage in *all* these practices. I hinted above that godly Israelites were involved in these practices. People like Joseph and Daniel were blessed, not cursed, by God, and through these practices God gave them revelation, saving their lives. But a close look reveals that no godly biblical character is ever found to be engaging in a practice that was a capital offense (e.g., contacting the nonhuman spirits, giving false dream interpretations, passing children through the fire). Second, in those passages that describe the "procedural use" of the practice in question, it was God who initiated the means of information, often as an answer to prayer, or the person very obviously assumed God was going to speak to him in response to some crisis. We are familiar with how this worked with Joseph and Daniel,[22] but there are other fascinating, less familiar cases.

Jacob and Laban

Readers will recall that the relationship between Jacob and Laban was, to say the least, strained. God had providentially blessed Jacob despite Laban's treachery. During the years that Jacob worked to earn the woman he loved (Rachel, instead of her sister Leah, whom Laban had tricked Jacob into marrying), Laban had also become wealthy through God's blessing of Jacob (Gn 29:1–30). We are never told, though, that Jacob knew this until Genesis 30:27, where Laban says: "But Laban said to [Jacob], 'If I have found favor in your sight, I have learned by divination (*niḥašti*) that [Yahweh] has blessed me because of you.'" The root of the word "divination" here is the same as that practice condemned in Deuteronomy 18:9–14. Apparently Laban had inquired of the God of Israel by some divinatory means, and God had complied, for only God had this information.

The "Fortune-Teller's Oak" / "Oak of Divination"

Judges 6–8 records the story of Gideon's deliverance of Israel from the Midianites under the power of God. Chapter 8 ends with Gideon's death, and chapter 9 picks up with Gideon's son, Abimelech, who decided to rule as king, an office his father had declined. Abimelech ruthlessly murdered all but one of his seventy brothers. Jotham alone escaped (Jgs 9:3–6). The place where Abimelech was declared king is our point of interest:

> And [Abimelech] went to his father's house at Ophrah and killed his brothers the sons of Jerubbaal, seventy men, on one stone. But Jotham the youngest son of Jerubbaal was left, for he hid himself. And all the leaders of Shechem came together, and all Beth-millo, and they went and made Abimelech king, by the oak of the pillar at Shechem. (Jgs 9:5–6)

The passage mentions an oak tree that marked the spot of a "pillar" at the town of Shechem. We read about this same location later in Judges 9, when Abimelech returned to Shechem to ambush the city:

> So Abimelech and all the men who were with him rose up by night and set an ambush against Shechem in four companies. And Gaal the son of Ebed went out and stood in the entrance of the gate of

> the city, and Abimelech and the people who were with him rose from the ambush. And when Gaal saw the people, he said to Zebul, "Look, people are coming down from the mountaintops!" And Zebul said to him, "You mistake the shadow of the mountains for men." Gaal spoke again and said, "Look, people are coming down from the center of the land, and one company is coming from the direction of the [Fortune-Teller's] Oak (*mĕʿônĕnîm ʾēlôn*)." (Jgs 9:34–37)

Readers will recognize that the first Hebrew term in the description of the oak tree is one of the condemned divinatory practices in Deuteronomy 18:9. What was this oak tree? Was it an unholy place used by spiritual rebels during the chaotic time of the Judges? The clear answer to this question is "no," based upon other references to the oak at Shechem (note my italics, added for emphasis):

> Abram passed through the land to the place *at Shechem*, to *the oak of Moreh* [the Teacher/instruction]. At that time the Canaanites were in the land. Then the Lord appeared to Abram and said, "To your offspring I will give this land." So he built there an altar to the Lord, who had appeared to him. (Gn 12:6–7 ESV)

> So they gave Jacob all the foreign gods they had and the rings in their ears, and Jacob buried them under the oak at Shechem. (Gn 35:4 NIV)

> So Joshua made a covenant with the people that day, and put in place statutes and rules for them *at Shechem*. And Joshua wrote these words in *the Book of the Law of God*. And he took a large stone and set it up there *under the terebinth that was by the sanctuary (miqdaš) of the Lord*. And Joshua said to all the people, "Behold, this stone shall be a witness against us, for it has heard all the words of the Lord that he spoke to us. Therefore it shall be a witness against you, lest you deal falsely with your God." (Jo 24:25–27 ESV)

The oak at Shechem marked the place: 1. Where God had appeared to Abram with the promises of the Abrahamic covenant; 2. Where Jacob had buried his family's idols after getting right with God; and 3. Where Joshua had erected a stone that contained some portion of the Word of God—specifically because this was a holy place (*miqdaš*) for the God of

Israel. The biblical text connects a place of divination with holy ground and the God of Israel.

Standing in the Council

How are such passages to be understood? Can God condemn something, then use it or allow it? Once we understand these passages, we can formulate a coherent answer to how faithful Israelites would respond to divination practices of the surrounding pagan culture.

The first concern of a godly Israelite, on hearing of revelation from God, would be the source of the information. The person claiming to have received revelation from an entity other than God was an abomination. The proof of whether Yahweh was indeed the source was whether the prophet in question "had stood in the council of God." Had this person had a direct encounter with the God of Israel, *initiated at first* by the God of Israel to mark out the prophet as his chosen mouthpiece to other believers?[23]

"Standing in the council"—the direct divine encounter—is actually a frequent pattern in the Bible for those who are receiving revelation from God. The tradition goes back to Adam. In the book of Job, we hear Eliphaz, one of Job's friends, ask Job, "Are you the first man who was born? Or were you brought forth before the hills? *Have you listened in the council of God?* And do you limit wisdom to yourself?" (Jb 15:7–8 ESV, italics mine). The questions are obviously rhetorical. They each anticipate "no" for an answer by using contrast. Of course Job was not the first man—Adam was. Job had not listened in the council of God (Hebrew, *sōd 'elôah*)—but the rhetorical contrast implies that Adam *had* listened in the council of God. He had a direct encounter with God in his council throne room—at the time, Eden.

Scripture follows this seed-form idea with the motif of "walking with God" in describing others in the prophetic line (Enoch, Noah).[24] The patriarchs also had direct meetings with God, and this is where we begin to see an explicit pattern of God initiating the contact for the purpose of commissioning human mediators of divine revelation.[25] Moses and Joshua each met the God of Israel and were approved by him as prophetic figures.[26] Samuel and other judges experienced a dramatic divine encounter.[27] Isaiah, Jeremiah and Ezekiel saw God when they were chosen as prophets.[28] The case of Jeremiah is worthy of special attention:

> The words of Jeremiah, the son of Hilkiah, one of the priests who were in Anathoth in the land of Benjamin, *to whom the word of the Lord came* in the days of Josiah the son of Amon, king of Judah, in the thirteenth year of his reign. It came also in the days of Jehoiakim the son of Josiah, king of Judah, and until the end of the eleventh year of Zedekiah, the son of Josiah, king of Judah, until the captivity of Jerusalem in the fifth month. Now *the word of the Lord came to me,* saying, "Before I formed you in the womb I knew you, and before you were born I consecrated you; I appointed you a prophet to the nations." Then I said, "*Ah, Lord God!* Behold, I do not know how to speak, for I am only a youth." But *the Lord said to me,* "Do not say, 'I am only a youth'; for to all to whom I send you, you shall go, and whatever I command you, you shall speak. Do not be afraid of them, for I am with you to deliver you, declares the Lord." *Then the LORD put out his hand and touched my mouth.* And the Lord said to me, "Behold, *I have put my words in your mouth.* See, I have set you this day over nations and over kingdoms, to pluck up and to break down, to destroy and to overthrow, to build and to plant." (Jer 1:1–10; note the italics)

Jeremiah's dramatic call came via the presence and touch of the embodied God of Israel. It was so dramatic that later in his life it served as the touchpoint for his inspired evaluation of any other so-called prophets:

> Thus says the Lord of hosts: "Do not listen to the words of the prophets who prophesy to you, filling you with vain hopes. They speak visions of their own minds, not from the mouth of the Lord. They say continually to those who despise the word of the Lord, 'It shall be well with you'; and to everyone who stubbornly follows his own heart, they say, 'No disaster shall come upon you.'" *For who among them has stood in the council of the Lord* to see and to hear his word, or *who has paid attention to his word and listened?* Behold, the storm of the Lord! Wrath has gone forth, a whirling tempest; it will burst upon the head of the wicked. The anger of the Lord will not turn back until he has executed and accomplished the intents of his heart. In the latter days you will understand it clearly. "I did not send the prophets, yet they

> ran; I did not speak to them, yet they prophesied. But *if they had stood in my council, then they would have proclaimed my words to my people,* and they would have turned them from their evil way, and from the evil of their deeds." (Jer 23:16–22)

The implications are clear: true prophets have stood and listened in the council; false prophets have not. True prophets were first contacted by the God of Israel; they did not solicit that contact as though God were some sort of revelatory vending machine.

This test of prophetic status never went away in Israel. It was alive and well in the days of Jesus and the apostles, as seen with Paul on the road to Damascus and the disciples gathered on the Day of Pentecost.[29] The pattern was so embedded as a necessity in the Jewish mind that even the record of Jesus' early life has the same sort of divine commissioning incident, where God publicly and verbally sent Jesus into public ministry at his baptism.[30]

All of these figures became recognized representatives of the God of Israel. They spoke his words, were uniquely blessed by him, and were empowered to do amazing things in his name. Any rival prophet or newcomer had to be able to prove the same pedigree, and could not contradict the words of the person or persons whom everyone in the believing community already knew was a prophet.

The issue with divination, then, was not the means that were used. After a person was chosen to be the conduit of blessing and divine revelation, God would be open to contact from that person through prayer or other means that would be classified as divinatory. God allowed those people whom he had commissioned to attempt to discern the will of God via the casting of lots or other means well known in the ancient world, and that was God's choice. God even provided such means through the ephod, used by the priests to show God's will to his people: the Urim and the Thummim. The concern was using such means to solicit contact with any other god or spirit. Moreover, methods that involved direct contact with other entities were especially heinous, since their use showed, at best, a lack of faith in the true God and, at worst, disloyalty to God in favor of some other deity.

FINAL APPLICATION

The notion of "standing in the council" provided two answers to the question of how an Old Testament Israelite would react to pagan divination:

1. what is the source of the information, and
2. does the information conflict with revelation previously given by people we know are true prophets of God?

This model compels us to ask the same questions of someone who claims to speak for God through supernormal means, or who claims to be using occult techniques to get in touch with God or Jesus. Are they in contact with other beings from the disembodied spiritual world other than the true God? What proof is there that such people were first tapped by God himself for the role, as opposed to seeking contact on their own? What proof is there that what the person says is binding on the believing community? Is there consistency or contradiction between what the person says and the content of the Scriptures—that body of prophetic truth dispensed over the ages by prophets, embraced by the believing community, and assembled under providence? In today's increasingly pagan spiritual climate, we would do well to go back to the biblical motifs laid out for us in the Scriptures to demand a coherent accounting of those who seek to convince us they have truth "from the other side."

17

The Prototokos Paradigm

Colossians 2

TED HAMILTON

In his book *Rumors of Another World,* Philip Yancey recalled seeing a copy of a New Testament from which all the verses about the "invisible world" had been snipped out. The pages hardly held together, because cutting out references to the unseen spirit world removes nearly one third of the New Testament's seven thousand verses.[1] The unseen spiritual dimensions were an important component of the worldview of the New Testament writers and of Jesus himself. Much of Western Christianity, embarrassed by Postenlightenment scientific and technological advances, gradually but inexorably drifted from the Bible's emphasis on the invisible world to a preoccupation with the visible. One might say that the gospel of Jesus Christ, at least in North America, has become one more coping mechanism to help us survive and thrive in the challenges of the visible world.

The recent rise of interest in alternative spiritualities and Neopaganism rebukes any embarrassment we might have and acts as a wake-up call to the church. It is a potent reminder that we have mostly forgotten what the New Testament writers knew: powerful, invisible spiritual realities oppose the gospel, shaping and operating behind what we see and experience. How should the church of Jesus Christ address the reality of the invisible spirit world today? We fix our eyes on what is seen, whether positive realities (like strong marriages and families, healthy self-esteem, moral civil government, and impeccable personal morality) or negative realities (like abortion, Christian persecution and the decay of social morals). Without discounting the importance of such things, how does the church sharpen its focus on Paul's priority to "fix our eyes not on what is seen, but on what is unseen" (2 Cor 4:18 NIV)?

The Scriptures do not leave us without an answer. In Paul's letter to the church in Colossae, he confronts a powerful form of spiritual paganism energized by contact with the occultic elemental spirits. The paganism Paul stared down in Colossae shares many characteristics with the Neopaganism we confront. Paul's response to the unseen spiritual forces converging on Colossae presents a powerful paradigm for a contemporary confrontation with those same forces. We have a story to tell—a *logos* (word) that is more than a match for the *muthos* (myth) of paganism. This *logos*, though antithetical to paganism, still speaks powerfully to those whose legitimate heart yearnings have led them to paganism for satisfaction. Paul's methodology is more than a "how to" guide. It is also a devotional display of the cosmic power and love of the Lord Jesus Christ, a love that is relevant in any age and in any circumstance.

THE UNSEEN WORLD IN COLOSSAE

The so-called "Colossian heresy" has been a subject of vigorous academic debate ever since the 1875 publication of J. B. Lightfoot's landmark Colossians commentary.[2] Two scholars independently identified over forty distinct (and not completely reconcilable) views of the error Paul addresses in Colossians.[3] The book is problematic because the reader hears only one side of a conversation. We must infer what Paul's opponents proposed by reading Paul's answers to them. Such inference leaves the details sketchy.

Scholars may disagree on the precise contours of the Colossian heresy, but they do not disagree on what elements of Paul's letter illuminate it. First, the emphasis on the "fullness" of the deity that dwells in Jesus, suggests that the Colossian philosophy challenged that fullness, locating some of it outside of Jesus (1:19; 2:9). Second, the Colossian philosophy depended upon the "basic principles of the world" (NIV), better translated as "the elemental spirits of the universe" (2:8,20).[4] Third, the suspect philosophy included restrictions on what could be consumed and handled, as well as requirements regarding participation in various religious celebrations and festivals, including New Moon celebrations and Sabbath days (2:16,21). Fourth, there is a direct reference to self-abasement and the worship of angels (2:18,23). Fifth, and finally, the Colossian philosophy seemingly included various ecstatic visionary experiences of the divine.[5]

This final point underscores both the appeal and the power of alternative spirituality in Colossae. As Christians, we know that "faith comes from *hearing* the message, and the message is heard through *the word of Christ* [italics mine]" (Rom 10:17 NIV). But the preacher of propositional truth will often be trumped by someone proposing an exciting personal experience, even if that experience does not square with the propositional truth of the gospel. The Colossian brand of spirituality offered convincing but misguided personal experience.

David DeSilva provides a good summary of what Paul was facing in Colossae:

> The Colossian philosophy truly "remains an unsolved puzzle," but its major contours are fairly well defined. Human life below and access to the realms above lie under the authority of intermediate spiritual beings (variously called angels, elemental spirits, principalities and the like). Ascetic practices and rigorous self-discipline were required either in obedience to these beings or as the means to enter into visionary experiences of them. Positive interaction with these beings was probably regarded as, in some sense, necessary for human beings to move into the fullness of the divine realm or experience the fullness of God.[6]

That this experiential pagan spirituality had a kind of magnetic attraction to the Christians in Colossae is confirmed by Paul's use of the word *sulagōgeo* in Colossians 2:8 (its only occurrence in the New Testament): "See to it that no one takes you captive (*sulagōgōn*)..." It is a bold word, emphasizing the power of the philosophy to capture its adherents and carry them off, away from the historical and propositional truths of the gospel into the history-rejecting and enslaving error of paganism. The Neopaganism of our day exerts that same enslaving power.

The Cosmic Perspective for Christians in Colossae

So how does the church respond to today's Neopagan challenges? How does it counteract the magnetic attraction of pagan spiritualities that offer ecstatic personal experiences and altered states of consciousness? The church today must see and understand Paul's gospel in all its fullness, and then, wisely and with love, train that gospel on contemporary paganism wherever it rears its ugly head.

At first, Paul's method seems negative, since he goes on the attack against Colossian paganism. He characterizes the philosophy and its practices as:

- "hollow and deceptive," dependent only on "human tradition" (2:8);
- a "shadow of things" rather than "the reality" (2:17);
- involving a "false humility" (2:18);
- an "unspiritual mind" puffed up with "idle notions" (2:18);
- "destined to perish with use" (2:22);
- having "an appearance of wisdom" but "lack[ing] any value" (2:23).

Though undoubtedly accurate, these negative judgments are incidental to Paul's primary—and positive—way of confronting paganism. Paul's primary method is to overwhelm paganism, burying it under a positive presentation of the full-orbed gospel of Jesus Christ. As is always the case, the answer to a problem is the good news of Jesus Christ.

This positive gospel-centered approach is not unique to Colossians. You see the same strategy repeated throughout Paul's writings. It is like killing a fly with a sledgehammer. Whatever the issue, trivial or significant, Paul brings the full weight of the gospel down on it. Peter's refusal to eat with Gentile Christians, mentioned by Paul in Galatians, was a result of Peter's failure to act "in line with the truth of the gospel" (Gal 2:14ff). Christians in Corinth were suing each other in the civil courts because they forgot "that the saints will judge the world" and that they were "washed...sanctified...[and] justified in the name of the Lord Jesus Christ and by the Spirit of our God" (1 Cor 6:2,11). Paul grounds his imperatives against sexual immorality in Corinth in the gospel realities of redemption: "You are not your own; you were bought at a price" (1 Cor 6:19–20) and resurrection: "By his power God raised the Lord from the dead, and he will raise us also" (1 Cor 6:14).

The fact that North American Christians may have some difficulty understanding how and why the gospel can be (and is) the correct and total response to contemporary paganism indicates the extent to which we have bought into a *Reader's Digest* version of the gospel. For many of us, the gospel is about Jesus dying for one's sin and about accepting Jesus as personal Savior and Lord. That is not *incorrect*—but it is *incomplete*. Such gospel reductionism eventually leads Christ-followers to conceive of the gospel as merely the entry gate into Christianity which is then left behind as one matures in the faith. We must not forget that Jesus is not just "the truth"; he is also "the way" and "the life." The gospel is not just about personal salvation. It is the overarching true story of God, through Jesus, reclaiming and redeeming the life of all of creation—the cosmos! So Jesus (who he is, what he did, and what he continues to do on a cosmic scale) is relevant to all of life, whether animate or inanimate, whether past, present or future. Accordingly, the wise application of the gospel story in all its implications is the answer to every alternative truth claim.

The Creed of Christ's Preeminence: The Form

The cosmic scope of the gospel is brilliantly displayed in Colossians. The centerpiece of Paul's gospel response to the Colossian heresy has appropriately been called "the Creed of Christ's Preeminence"[7] (Col 1:15–20). It is an elevated, worshipful passage that poetically communicates deep and ancient truths about the person and work of Jesus Christ.

There may be as many theories about the form and substance of these six verses as there are about the Colossian heresy itself. Was it a pre-existing hymn? Was it Paul's own poetry? Is it modeled after Greek or Hebrew poetic forms? Beyond these academic debates, however, virtually every interpreter has observed a Hebrew-like parallelism in the passage. Other interpreters have persuasively demonstrated that this parallelism additionally reflects a Hebraic chiastic structure that highlights the Jesus-focused truths of the passage.[8]

Here is a schematic structure of the creed:

The Creed of Christ's Preeminence[9]
Colossians 1:15–20 (NIV)

Stanza #1

15a He is (*os estin*) the image of the invisible God,

15b the firstborn over all creation.

16 For by him (*oti en autō*) all things were created:
things in heaven and on earth,
visible and invisible,
whether thrones [visible] or powers [visible]
or rulers [invisible] or authorities [invisible];
all things were created by him and for him.

Center Summation

17a [And] He is (*kai autos estin*) before all things,
[looks back]

17b and in him all things hold together.

18a And he is (*kai autos estin*) the head of the body, the church;
[looks forward]

Stanza #2

18b He is (*os estin*) the beginning
18b and the firstborn from among the dead,
so that in everything he might have the supremacy.
19 For God was pleased to have all his
fulness dwell in him (*oti en autō*),
20 and through him to reconcile to himself all things,
whether things on earth or things in heaven,
by making peace through his blood, shed on the cross.

Paul's poetic creed contains two main stanzas, recognizable by the repetition of certain introductory words. The parallelism is veiled by the translation and versification in our English Bibles. The first stanza

(1:15–16) is marked out by the words "He is..." (*os estin*) in verse 15 and "For in him..." (*oti en autō*) in verse 16. The second stanza is marked out by a repetition of the same words. In verse 18b, we see "He is..." (*os estin*), and in verse 19 we see "For in him..." (*oti en autō*).

These two main stanzas are further highlighted by the reversed repetition of the words "heaven" and "earth." Thus, the first stanza uses "in heaven and on earth" (1:16), while the second stanza reverses the expressions: "on earth or in heaven" (1:19).

Between the two main stanzas (1:15–16 and 1:18b–20) lies a connecting passage comprised of verses 17–18a. This segment is "bookended" by two parallel passages which are identified by their matching introductory words. Verse 17a begins with "And He is..." (*kai autos estin*) and verse 18a also begins with "And He is..." (*kai autos estin*). Verse 17a *looks back* to the first stanza and summarizes what it has told us about Jesus: "He is before all things..." Verse 18a *looks forward* to the second stanza and summarizes what it will tell us about Jesus: "And He is the head of the body, the church..." That leaves verse 17b standing alone at the very center of the creed and so functioning as the powerful summary of the overall point of the passage: "and in Him all things hold together."[10] It is, in the end, all about Jesus. Jesus, in himself, is the total response to all competing pagan ideologies.

The Creed of Christ's Preeminence: The Substance

Moving from the form of the creed to its substance, we see that the two main stanzas present distinct but complementary perspectives on the person and work of Jesus. The first stanza (1:15–16) presents Jesus as the Lord of Creation. The second stanza (1:18b–20) presents Jesus as the Lord of Redemption.[11] The Lord of both spheres—creation and redemption—is celebrated in the poetic climax of verse 17b as the one in whom "all things hold together," including the realities of creation and redemption.

The gospel message with which Paul confronts paganism does not begin with salvation, but with creation. Creation precedes the cross, which cannot be rightly understood apart from an understanding that the One who died on it is the transcendent Lord of Creation.

The Prototokos Paradigm

To illuminate the truths in each stanza, Paul gives Jesus a title: in the first stanza, it is "the firstborn (*prōtotokos*) over all creation" (1:15), while in the second it is "the firstborn (*prōtotokos*) from among the dead" (1:18). Of the numerous threads in Paul's creed, the *prōtotokos* thread is the one we will follow. Paul uses *prōtotokos* only three times (twice here and once in Romans 8). This word unveils a Jesus who is both radically transcendent and radically immanent—a God who is unimaginably far above us, yet a God who has come close and entered our lives, our stories. As we trace this *prōtotokos* thread, theology begins to intersect worship, for Paul's presentation of Jesus as the cosmic *prōtotokos* is no cold, analytical presentation of truth. It is, rather, deep and ancient truth conveyed with passion, awe, wonder and gratitude. "Our creed is never to be a mere code of propositions in the abstract. It is to breathe and glow, even where it is most systematic, with the Christian's own experience of worship, rest and joy, in full sight of the glory of Him who has loved him and has died for him."[12] Paul is certainly speaking in Colossians out of his own experience of worship, rest and joy in Jesus, and what he has to say not only deepens our knowledge of Jesus and strengthens our faith in him, but it also exposes the pathetic smallness of paganism.

The Firstborn over All Creation

In giving Jesus the title "firstborn," Paul is mining a rich Old Testament vein. Used in the Septuagint 130 times, *prōtotokos* often "denote[d] one who had a special place in the father's love."[13] So in Exodus 4:22 God calls Israel, his chosen people, "my firstborn son" (*uios prōtotokos mou*). But more concretely, primogeniture operated in the Old Testament to make the firstborn son of the family the heir of the lion's share of the father's property (see, e.g., Dt 21:17) and ruler of the family itself. When Jacob deceived his blind father Isaac into giving him the blessing of the firstborn (Esau's by right), Isaac pronounced the blessing with these words: "May nations serve you and peoples bow down to you. Be lord over your brothers, and may the sons of your mother bow down to you" (Gn 27:29). The ruling rights of the "firstborn" are further seen in Psalm 89:27, where God gives such authority to the lastborn son of

Jesse, David: "I will also appoint him my firstborn (*prōtotokon*), the most exalted of the kings of the earth."

So when Paul, steeped as he was in the Old Testament, identifies David's greater son, Jesus, as the "firstborn over all creation" he is effectively saying that Jesus is the *ruler* of all creation and the *heir* of all creation. Jesus is the exalted king and the one who, as exalted heir, shall come to possess and own *everything that exists*.

Paul unpacks what he means by "all" and "all creation" in verse 16: "all things…things in heaven and on earth, visible and invisible, whether thrones or powers or rulers or authorities." An unlimited rule over an unlimited dominion! Jesus' supremacy is not only over the visible world, but also over the invisible world, specifically over the spirits operating behind the Colossian paganism and behind the Neopaganism that still lures victims today. Jesus is superior to all lesser spiritual entities, good or bad, because he created them. Accordingly, the right Christian response to Neopaganism is not to question, deny or ignore the reality of the pagan spirits, but to appeal to the greater and deeper reality that is Jesus, the very ground of being for those spirits.

Paul grounds Jesus' status as ruler and inheritor of all things in the breathtaking cosmic truth that Jesus was God's agent in the very process of creating those things. Twice in verse 16 Paul says that all things were made "through him," that is, through Jesus. At the end of verse 16, Paul goes further to say that all things were not only made "through him" but "for him." Jesus is not just the beginning of creation; he is the end of it, the goal of it. The stars, the sun, the moon, the mountains, the oceans, the trees, the animals, the rocks, the people, even the invisible rulers and authorities worshiped by the pagans—all exist *for Jesus*! They will, in the end, all glorify him. Doxology to the Father and the Son overlaps here: "For from him and through him and to him are all things. To him be the glory forever"(Rom 11:36)! At this point we are, like Moses before the burning bush, standing on holy ground. The implications of *everything* being for Jesus extend beyond our finite powers to imagine. No adherent to paganism, in Paul's day or ours, would dare claim that all of creation exists *for* his particular deity.[14] This is a transcendent claim, unique to Jesus.

The Firstborn from among the Dead

Jesus is not only "the firstborn over all creation" and, therefore, the Lord of Creation. He is also celebrated in the second stanza of Paul's creed as "the firstborn from among the dead" (1:18b), and, therefore, the Lord of Redemption. The title "firstborn from among the dead" clearly refers to Jesus' resurrection. This resurrection reference, following as it does the introductory statement that Jesus is "the head of the body, the church" (1:18a), and coupled with the statement that Jesus is "the beginning" (1:18b), describes the risen Jesus as the first and founder of a new humanity, a new race of redeemed people.[15] In the power unleashed in his resurrection, Jesus, Lord of the Old Creation, becomes Lord of New Creation—the head of the church. Paul developed this same truth in 2 Corinthians where he said: "Therefore, if anyone is in Christ, he is a new creation; the old has gone, the new has come! All this is from God, who reconciled us to himself through Christ..." (2 Cor 5:17–18).

Both in his identity as firstborn over all creation and in his unparalleled resurrection, Jesus, the firstborn from among the dead, now has God-ordained supremacy *in everything* (1:18b). Paul reinforces this supremacy of Jesus by asserting that "God was pleased to have all his fullness dwell in him" (1:19). The one who creates, on the one hand, and the one who walks out of a grave, on the other hand, does so because he is fully divine. Only one who is truly God could do these things.

Paul's exalted portrayal of Jesus shows us that there is no need to fear spirits and supernatural forces, and there is no sense in worshiping them—"God in all his divine essence and power had taken up residence in Christ."[16] Since there is no divinity outside of Jesus, it follows that Jesus must be the one and only mediator between God and human beings. No other supernatural power or spirit being stands between God and humans that has any claim to deity. Deity is all wrapped up in Jesus, and he has come to his own.

The gospel remarkably reverses the whole trajectory of paganism. A person does not have to bow and scrape before spirits, angels or other forces in an attempt to reach the divine. The gospel is that God, on his own initiative, has reached into humanity in all his fullness and become accessible to us in the person of Jesus.

Paul's creed does not stop here, though we sometimes do, thus truncating the gospel. New creation is not just about new people. God, through Jesus, as Lord of the New Creation, reconciles to himself not just human beings but "all things, whether things on earth or things in heaven" (1:20). Just as the scope of Jesus' creative work was cosmic, so the scope of his redemptive work is cosmic. Paul wants to convey to those tempted to worship pagan spirits the truth that even those spirits, created through Jesus, are reconciled to God through Jesus.

The reconciliation of the spiritual forces opposed to Jesus is a very different reconciliation from the one we enjoy as believers in Jesus. For pagan spirits, reconciliation is better understood as pacification.[17] This is clear from what Paul says a little later in Colossians at 2:15: "And having disarmed the powers and authorities, he made a public spectacle of them, triumphing over them by the cross." The reconciliation of all things, including us and the spiritual rulers and authorities, comes as a result of the cross. Jesus' death both gives us life and defangs the demons "by making peace through his blood, shed on the cross" (1:20). The intrusion of the cross, in all its bloodiness and shame, shocks us, coming as it does at the end of a creed that has fixed our gaze exclusively on the exalted and cosmic Jesus. Paul almost certainly *wanted* to shock us. By putting the cross in our faces, he is showing us at least two realities. First, at the cross, the radical transcendence (distance) of God becomes radical immanence (closeness) as the Lord of Creation and Redemption is pinned to a Roman cross to die the tortured death of a common criminal—for our benefit. And second, the inheritance of Jesus as the firstborn over all creation included, from all eternity, the tree from which he would hang. And yet Jesus willingly and knowingly accepted the cost of his inheritance "for the joy set before him" (Heb 12:2).

The Firstborn among Many Brothers

Finally, the *prōtotokos* thread takes us out of Colossians 1 and into Romans chapter 8—where Paul speaks of the cosmic effects of Jesus' life, death and resurrection. Here Paul describes the sovereignty of God over creation, even over the pain and suffering and frustration in creation. In verse twenty, Paul says: "For the creation was subjected to frustration, not by its own choice, but by the will on the one who subjected it, in hope."

Only God could have subjected creation to frustration *in hope*. Biblical hope is not wishful thinking, but a settled certainty in a future outcome. The frustration, groaning and suffering that the creation experiences and that you experience within creation are not just natural or random phenomena. Were such groaning natural, there would be no answer to it. Like the pagans, we would have to resort to hope in some vague disembodied future. But, in fact, Paul shows us in Romans 8 that the pain and suffering within creation is a *judicial* phenomenon. It is a result of God's decree against sin in Genesis 3, where God himself, in response to human rebellion, specifically subjected the creation to frustration. The suffering that makes us groan is designed by God to show us just how horrible and repulsive and hideous sin against an infinitely holy God really is. The suffering is intended to drive us back to God, in whom the only hope of rescue exists. The hope, Paul tells us, is that "the creation itself will be liberated from its bondage to decay and brought into the glorious freedom of the children of God" (Rom 8:21).

Paul's Romans reference to the liberation of creation from its bondage to decay is another perspective on his Colossians truth that God is reconciling all things to himself through Jesus' peacemaking crucifixion. The Christian rock group *Rush of Fools* sings of this truth when they sing about Jesus: "You're the only one who can undo what I've become."[18] C.S. Lewis poignantly communicates this Jesus-centered truth in fairy tale form. The resurrected lion, Aslan, explains that the witch who killed him did not know the "deeper magic," or she would have known "that when a willing victim who had committed no treachery was killed in a traitor's stead...Death itself would start working backwards."[19] This is the gospel truth that J. R. R. Tolkien puts into the little hobbit Sam's mouth when he sees a resurrected friend and asks: "Is everything sad going to come untrue?"[20]

Because of the life, death and resurrection of Jesus, Lord of Creation and Lord of Redemption, the answer to Sam's question is, Yes! Undoing what we have become, death working backwards, things sad becoming untrue—these are all expressions of the cosmic effectiveness of Jesus' work.

This happy outcome is a certainty. Paul describes the pain and suffering we know now in creation as "the pains of childbirth" (Rom 8:22). If you are in a hospital, and you hear groaning, it makes a big difference whether you are in the burn unit or in the labor and delivery unit. The groaning in the labor and delivery room signals a good outcome. There will be a birth. It will happen, one way or another. So it is with God's creation. It groans now—in labor, but because of the power unleashed by the death and resurrection of Jesus, the creation that is now groaning (all of it) will be liberated and brought into glory. This has nothing to do with the evolutionary hope of Neopaganism, but it does speak to the utopian hope that Neopagans are vainly trying to find in the myth of evolution. It is the answer to evolutionary hope and the true story they must hear.

Finally, the one who will be the liberator of all of creation is described by Paul in Romans 8:29 as "the firstborn (*prōtotokos*) among many brothers." There is that title again! Here, the cosmic Lord of Creation and Lord of Redemption, who has supremacy in all things, becomes the Elder Brother of the new race of people that he rules. We are elevated by the gospel to a new place of dignity and responsibility. Jesus makes us his brothers and sisters, sharers by grace of his inheritance as the "Firstborn over All Creation" and the "Firstborn From among the Dead."

Neopaganism attracts people today, because it promises a new dignity as individuals and caters to their legitimate concerns for the earth and its ecological well-being. They fail to understand, however, that the gospel of Jesus Christ makes the human dignity and ecological agenda promised by Neopaganism pale in comparison. The gospel says we will rule over a redeemed cosmos with our elder brother, the All-Ruling Firstborn, Jesus Christ. And even now, in the "not quite yet" of our faith journey with Jesus, we are his agents in bringing his cosmic re-creative power to our world, as we pray "thy kingdom come" and serve him to achieve that goal. Therein lie real dignity and responsibility.

The way for Christians to confront Neopagans today is, like Paul, to overwhelm them with the wonder, the beauty and the power of the gospel in all of its implications. Kill the fly with the sledgehammer of glory and love. We have a compelling story to tell. We have *The Story*. It speaks to the spiritual hunger and the deepest yearnings of the pagan heart, even as it speaks to ours. "It is the power of God for the salvation of *everyone* who believes" (Rom 1:16).

18

The Antithesis
Ephesians 4:17–20

Peter Jones

The Need for Antithesis Hermeneutics

This compendium has examined common practices of paganism, both ancient and modern, in order to cast light on the current debate regarding spirituality. What emerges is a clear antithesis between such practices and the Christian faith. In Ephesians 4:17–20 Paul evokes two theological matrices out of which flow two incompatible spiritualities. These verses serve as an entrance into Paul's "antithesis hermeneutic."

- verse 17: "you must no longer walk as the Gentiles"
- verse 20: "[you must walk] the way you learned Christ"

"Hermeneutics" means the theory of interpretation. For centuries, Christian scholars have been writing about the Christian faith in the relative cocoon of Christendom. In such a context, *pagans* are those who play golf on Sunday morning, and *idolaters* are those who "worship" their luxury homes. If this is our definition of pagan, we miss Paul's pedagogical point when he says: "Do not walk like the pagans." For Ephesian Christians it was obvious. The temple of Artemis sat on a hill dominating the city of Ephesus, serving as its commercial and social center. One day this might happen in cities across America and the West.

Modern paganism, whether in its "Christian" or non-Christian form, provides an unobstructed view of the antithesis between two opposing thought systems, and establishes objective lines of demarcation for biblical orthodoxy. The lie cannot help but disclose the truth.

Some feel we do not need to examine the culture too closely, as I discovered while reading a blog of theologically conservative Christian pastors. One clearly stated: "Doctrine...should not be read against 'cultural realities,' to be discerned, judged, and made more or less pressing, but read as self-sufficient, transcendent, reality-generating, life-producing, beauty-consumed Truth. To heck with the culture wars. God's truth can take care of itself."[1]

The very opposite approach to culture is taken by Emergent thinkers, such as theologian John Franke, who says with great optimism: "The conversation between gospel and culture should be one of mutual enrichment" in which the gospel is "informed by" culture.[2] Optimistic openness to culture lessens the Scripture's authority over the church and elevates the authority of "cutting edge" human thinking. Emergent writer Kester Brewin is more explicit: "'Listen,' God says, 'I'm doing a new thing. We need to completely rebirth the church into a host culture...The church is going to have to learn about its own survival from so-called secular institutions.'"[3]

Certainly, the Bible does give culture a place, because it has a place for common grace and for the image of God in human endeavor. It does so, however, without any naïveté, inviting us to establish truth via an antithetical confrontation of fallen pagan belief systems with divine revelation.

Antithesis: Paul's Gospel and Ancient Paganism

At a time when the Greco-Roman pagan empire was a daily reality over against which the Christian faith was defined, Paul unapologetically declares the antithesis—in one place, five times in a row:

> What partnership has righteousness with lawlessness?
>
> Or what fellowship has light with darkness?
>
> What accord has Christ with Belial?
>
> Or what portion does a believer share with an unbeliever?
>
> What agreement has the temple of God with idols? (2 Cor 6:14–16)[4]

A superb Old Testament scholar, Paul draws his exhortation from the Old Testament description of Israel's birth in the midst of the monist/theist conflict. From the beginning, she was to define herself in contrast to the pagan nations. The Five Books of Moses were given when Israel sojourned in Isis-dominated pagan Egypt and settled in Baal-dominated Canaan. "You shall not do as they do in the land of Egypt, where you lived, and you shall not do as they do in the land of Canaan, to which I am bringing you. You *shall not walk* in their statutes" (Lv 18:3). Omnipresent paganism defined the boundaries of Israel's belief and practice. The Scriptures, both old and new, were birthed in a context of radical religious paganism and articulated by a "hermeneutic of antithesis."

Paul seeks a worldview *change of thinking* in these ex-pagans that will show up in *changed ways of living:* you must no longer walk as the Gentiles do:

- in the futility of their *minds* (4:17);[5]
- given over to *practice* every kind of impurity (4:19).

The change of thinking and of living is reflected in the very shape of the epistle, which is in two parts: 1. doctrine (1:1–3:20) and 2. practical exhortation (4:1–6:24). Paul expected the ex-pagans in the church to arrange their lives in a way that would honor Jesus and conform to the understanding of the nature of the world from God's perspective.

TWO ANTITHETICAL WAYS OF THINKING

Pagan Knowledge: "The Futility of their Minds"

> You must no longer walk as the Gentiles do, in the futility of their minds darkened in their understanding... due to their hardness of heart.

Paul does not engage in simplistic rhetoric. He has a healthy respect for what sinners, made in the image of God, do with their minds, and he has thought deeply about pagan thinking, since this text is an obvious reprise of Romans 1:21 ("*they became futile* in their *thinking* and their foolish *hearts* were *darkened*"). Paul is not naïve. Pagan knowing is neither innocent nor neutral; they "suppress the truth" (Rom 1:18). Pagan minds *do* work. The mechanism is God-created and good, an expression of common grace. However, the essential presupposition, before any logical thinking is done, is "futile."[6] "The wicked are estranged from the womb; they go astray from birth, speaking lies" (Ps 58:3). At one level, things in the world can be truly observed, but their *significance* is established by prior, faith-based presuppositions. A false starting point produces skewed conclusions regarding ultimate meaning.

The ancient Jewish world associated paganism with vanity. Qumran calls the pagan world "the nations of vanity."[7] "Vanity" has a specific connotation in the Old Testament. μάταιος is the term for idols: they have been led astray by *false gods* (τὰ μάταια, Am 2:4); they followed *worthless idols* (ἐπορεύθησαν ὀπίσω τῶν ματαίων, 2 Kgs 17:15).The Old Testament text (Ez 14:5) explains what Paul means: "the hearts [or minds] of the house of Israel...are all estranged from me *through their idols*." Human thinking is idolatrous or autonomous because it raises itself to the level of ultimate divine truth, a place only the mind of God can occupy. As creatures, we see a miniscule piece of the cosmos. Of God, we see nothing, except what God chooses to reveal.

In the strictest sense of the term, such pretentious thinking is demonic, an expression of "the doctrine of demons," as Paul says in 1 Timothy 4:1 (NAS) and as Isaiah 14:12–13 shows: "How you are fallen from heaven, O Day Star, son of Dawn!...You said in your heart ("mind," διανοία) 'I will ascend to heaven.'" Intellectual idolatry is the monistic belief that one can explain the world naturally, by the world. Such thinking can be pantheistic or atheistic, spiritual or material, but it is still monistic.

Clinton Arnold believes the "philosophy" referred to in Colossians was founded upon an "act of ritual initiation" into some form of pagan mystery religion, through which there came a visionary experience of gnosis.[8] Arnold explains that such a practitioner "based his knowledge and authority on visionary experiences he received during the final stage of his mystery initiation."[9] Thinking always follows a prior sense or experience of the meaning of existence.

Thomas Berry calls for the recovery of such ancient wisdom, carried by sacred personalities: the elders...the shamans, who are in touch with the "powers in back of all natural phenomena... as personal [presence]."[10] Ultimately pagan *gnosis* comes from within the self. Alex Grey, a popular pagan artist in New York City, describes the source of his painting as: "the profound meditation experience... There is no 'out there.' It's an experience of a consciousness that we create with our brains and minds."[11] Christian insight ("intelligence," σύνεσις) is quite different.

Biblical Knowledge: "The Mystery of Christ Revealed"

The context of biblical knowledge is that of a revealed religion. Ephesians 2:12–13 says: "remember that you were at that time alienated" while Colossians 1:21 uses the term "hostile in mind" (NAS). But now in Christ Jesus you who once were far off have been brought near by the blood of Christ." If alienation from God brings the invention of "natural knowing," reconciliation with God involves the redemption of the mind, which presupposes "hearing" and "being taught" (4:21). These two ways of knowing, a darkened mind and an enlightened mind, also express the antithesis.

Paul evokes two valid kinds of knowing. Natural revelation places the human being before the theistic character of the created cosmos (Rom 1:18, 20). Special revelation, that is, biblical prophecy, both reaffirms the truth about creation and reveals God's project of cosmic redemption. In this Ephesian reprise of Romans 1:21, Paul assumes the place of natural revelation and introduces special revelation (4:17–19) with the phrase: Now this I *say and testify* in the Lord, that you must no longer walk as the Gentiles do, in the futility of their minds (4:17).

Such advice is not optional or off-the-cuff. It is solemn, incontrovertible "apostolic" speech, sanctioned by Paul's knowledge of the Lord's will.[12] The Bible is not "Israel's faith" or the "faith of the early church." It is God's revelation of himself through chosen human vessels. In Ephesians 3:1–7, Paul writes to the church so that they can "perceive my insight into *the mystery of Christ*" (3:4). His insight is based on a special revelatory act of God...*who created all things*. It is knowledge *from the Creator*, a *mystery known only to God* that can only come *through revelation* (3:8–9). The antithesis with pagan knowing could not be sharper. The two antithetical ways of thinking lead to two antithetical types of God, what Paul calls in this epistle, either "the god of this world," or the "God who made the world."

Two Antithetical Views of God

The God of this World

Who is the god of this world? The pagan walk follows the prince of the power of the air (Eph 2:1–2), living under the thrall of spiritual forces of evil, rulers, authorities and the cosmic powers of this present darkness (6:12). This is the experience that precedes thinking. Artemis/Diana[13] reigned in Ephesus, and her temple was one of the wonders of the world.[14] She was known as the "goddess of a thousand names," thus Paul in Ephesians 1:21 says that Christ has been raised above "every name that is named." As "the Queen of the Cosmos," Artemis/Isis is a perfect expression of "the god of this world" (2 Cor 4:4). She was also a gender bender, so that her priests were eunuchs—androgynes who castrated themselves and wore women's clothes.[15]

The God Who Made the World

Though the Emergent "Christian" writer, Kester Brewin, describes the Old Testament God as both rigid and adolescent, modern pagans understand the real issues.[16] The pagan "theologian," Michael York, states that "the Christian God is transcendent, the pagan godhead is immanent...the paganism of indigenous tribal religions is detectable in the absence of doctrines of monotheistic worship, a creation *ex nihilo*, a morally-determined godhead, and salvific redemptionism."[17]

Paul's worldview is fundamentally theistic. The verses of chapter three that bring the teaching section of the epistle to a close contain teaching on God as both Creator and Savior, wrapped up in the term, Father. Radical pagans, both "Christian" and non-Christian, with the emotive force associated with the Spanish Inquisition, have vilified patriarchy as the greatest of evils, thereby expunging from the Gospel one of its essential components.

Father as Creator

The mystery comes from outside the created order. Paul, like Jesus, prays to the Father who is in heaven "of whom the whole family in heaven and earth [the created reality] is named" (3:15 KJV). By the term *Father* he evokes the notion of creator and progenitor, separate from the things created.[18] Paul confesses "one God and Father of all, who is over all and through all and in all" (4:6). According to Jeremiah, the pagans of his day understood the need of a transcendent Father/Creator, but sadly they would "say to a tree, 'You are my father,' and to a stone, 'You gave me birth'" (Jer 2:27). As Father/Creator, God lends his name to the human family. Indeed, naming is an authoritative act of the great Patriarch and Creator who "called the light Day, and the darkness he called Night (Gn 1:5)...[and] called the expanse Heaven" (Gn 1:8). The world does not name itself; God names it. The author of creation and God of structure creates and names a world that bears his name and character, a cosmos of order and of paternal care, as Jesus taught.[19]

Father/Creator as Redeemer

The Christmas carol says with simplicity to the angels: "You who sang Creation's story now proclaim Messiah's birth."[20] The eternal God, who is Father of creation, is present in a unique, personal, caring way as the Father of our Lord Jesus Christ, "the Son of God" (4:13). God's kindness comes to us in Christ Jesus (2:7) because God has uniquely worked in Christ—"God in Christ forgave you" (4:32). What is the power of the Gospel? It is the reconciliation between God and man and between Jew and Pagan, the power of God unto salvation, to the Jew first but also to the Greek (Rom 1:16). The Gospel as God's power is his profoundly personal love for those who believe—1:4; 2:4; 3:17,19; 5:2,25; 6:23. In paganism God is only an impersonal force of Nature.

TWO ANTITHETICAL VIEWS OF HUMANITY

The Pagan, Utopian View of Man

In the ancient world of Paul's day, Alexander was still held in high honor as the great pagan model of human empire. Caligula (AD 37–41) visited his tomb in Alexandria, just as Augustus (27 BC–AD 14) had done. When he became king of Macedonia at age twenty, Alexander set off with high utopian dreams on an expedition to establish an empire governed by tolerance. Thirteen years later he became ruler of the known world, which stretched from Europe to India.

Modern utopianism, now taking in Europe, India and the entire planet, is just as visionary and grandiose, but just as this-worldly. Contemporary visionaries believe that with enough goodwill and planning, the global community will solve all the planet's problems. Indeed, pagan philosophers like Ken Wilber believe that, thanks to evolution, we are on a journey through nine stages for the development of human

Consciousness.[21] A few have reached stage six. This is the stage of "the Sensitive Self (Green egalitarianism)." A small elite, including himself, has reached stage seven, "Integrative Consciousness," but the radically spiritual states of "universal Holistic" and "Integral Holonic" still beckon. In stage nine, Man becomes God.

Paul would not be impressed, knowing that such utopian dreams inevitably derive from "a darkened understanding," and are built on "sensuality, greed and impurity" (4:17,19). He knew that for Alexander, the beginning of the end of global empire came when his best friend and male lover, Hephaestion, died of a fever. Alexander followed to the letter the example of his hero, Achilles, who, deeply grieved over the death of his best friend and lover, Patroklos, killed hundreds of Trojans and beheaded children. To assuage his own grief, Alexander crucified Hephaestion's doctor and put the whole Cossaean nation to the sword. In AD 323, though his mother had assured him he was fathered by Zeus, and thus divine, he caught a fever and died at age thirty-three. After his death, his generals fell to quarreling, and the Empire was divided into four parts.

We have no reason to believe that the planetary era of world peace will be any more successful. First, we are creatures, not gods. Second, all these projects of empire are dashed by a failure to understand that we are all dead in trespasses and sins (2:1) and that all our human projects inevitably end in injustice and death, as the Scriptures predict.[22]

The Biblical View of Man

Soteriology—salvation by grace alone (2:8)—is a wonderful theme in our epistle, but Ephesians also reveals a divinely-created, cosmic empire in which humanity discovers its original and future dignity. The book is all about a biblical, optimistic view of man because it is all about Christ, the Last Man, in whom the plan of God for humanity is realized in a four-dimensional reign over created reality (3:18–19).[23]

What is true of Christ is true for us. Since he is already reigning (1:21), so are we, seated with Christ in heaven (2:6). This is not "me and Jesus and the Rapture" theology. We are seated with Christ, in order to walk with a full-orbed worldview, comprehending all the dimensions of human existence. This is how we should think—cosmically and futuristically. Such a perspective will determine how we behave.

ANTITHESIS BEHAVIOR

This is no time for merely defensive action; no time to judge paganism for not playing the democratic game fairly. Accusing pagans of not being good Americans is not a Christian strategy. Theism does not need the aid of the Founding Fathers. The church does not need the world, however moral and apparently Christian that world may seem. The church stands on the merits of Christ and lives according to the laws of Christ's kingdom.

Just as there are two kinds of thinking, so there are two kinds of behaving. Again, the notion comes from the Old Testament's understanding of the antithesis with paganism.

- Leviticus 20:23 "And you shall not walk in the customs of the nation that I am driving out before you..."
- Deuteronomy 5:33: "You shall walk in all the way that the Lord your God has commanded you..."

A consistent logic runs through Ephesians—putting off and putting on. Paul does not simply exhort Christians not to steal but exhorts them to work, not simply to stop lying but to speak the truth. It is the same with the basic worldview—putting off the pagan worldview and putting on the truth of God, not walking as the Gentiles do but walking in a manner worthy of the calling to which they were called.

Pagan Behavior

Pagan behavior, like pagan thinking, comes from what is sinfully "natural." Ephesians 4:19 says: "they have given themselves up to sensuality" (ἀσελγείᾳ; vulgarity), "greedy to practice every kind of impurity" (ἀκαθαρσίᾳ). These words appear together in other Pauline texts and express a this-worldly lifestyle, ruled by passion and immediate gratification, that pagans naturally adopt.[24]

The Old Testament language of impurity and "abomination" evokes, in particular, what the Bible often considers the ultimate rejection of the Creator's design, the practice of homosexuality.[25] Paul is doubtless referring to sexual perversion and in particular to homosexuality, as he clearly does in Romans 1. For instance, Paul's expression, "they have given themselves up" (παρέδωκαν) recalls Romans 1:26. Also, 2 Peter 2:7 uses the same term as Paul ("vulgarity," ἀσελγεία) to describe the wickedness of Sodom. So does Jude.[26] Pagan behavior symbolized by homosexuality, embraces the eradication of divinely-created distinctions. Biblical holiness, on the contrary, joyfully embraces them.

Christian Behavior

Ephesians 4:17: "You must no longer walk as the Gentiles do." Here, pagan behavior functions negatively as a yardstick for Christian living,[27] just as it does in the Old Testament.[28] The church, the New Israel, must respect the same principles of living as did the Israelites—avoiding the pagan practices of the nations.

Antithesis thinking produces antithesis behavior, as 2 Corinthians 6:17–18 affirms in five antithetical statements that serve as the basis for Paul's exhortation to holy antithetical living. Note the logic. The antithesis between "the temple of God and idols" (2 Cor 6:16), is immediately followed by the exhortation: "Therefore go out from their midst, and be separate from them,...and I will be a father to you, and you shall be sons and daughters to me" (2 Cor 6:17–18). Ephesians 5:7 calls for the same kind of "separation": "Therefore do not associate with them" (the sons of disobedience).

But note! This is not a call to ghetto living.[29] It is a call to antithesis thinking and holy living (4:24), which makes possible both personal reconciliation and communion with the Father/Creator and gives clear meaning to the definition of "holiness." This is the essence of Christian witness in and to the world. "Since we have these promises, beloved, let us cleanse ourselves from every defilement of body and spirit" (cp. 2:3: "desires of the body and the mind") "bringing holiness to completion in the fear of God" (2 Cor 7:1).

As the church militant, we are separate, antithetically different and holy by *standing* against evil (both cognitive and behavioral) in the evil day (Eph 6:10ff), and by *sub–mitting*. This kind of thinking (especially in regards to women, though it is required of everyone) is considered by our contemporaries as "unnerving" and "out-of-touch with society."[30] When you see such principles antithetically backlit by the deliberate anti-Christian, pagan deconstruction of creation's structures, they make enormous sense. In this epistle, a synonym for "standing" is "placing oneself under" (ὑποτάσσω), in the sense of *sub–mitting* or *sub–ordering* oneself to the Creator's designs. "Mitt" is from *missio* or mission, thus we are sent under orders on a mission, joyfully to stand in the divinely created distinctions and to celebrate creational (not politically correct) diversity, as a witness to our Maker and Redeemer. We are to be submissional to God the Creator and missional with God the Redeemer.

This submission to structure will be true of the future cosmos.

- There will always be the Creator/creature distinction. We will always be creatures and God will always be celebrated as the Creator, as the twenty-four elders sing for eternity: "Worthy are you, our Lord and God, to receive glory and honor and power, for you created all things, and by your will they existed and were created" (Rev 4:11).
- There will always be the Redeemer/redeemed distinction. We will never be the author of our redemption. It will always be of God. That structure will *never* change and will be the cause of our celebration, as Paul says in Ephesians 2:7: "in the coming ages he might show the immeasurable riches of his grace in kindness toward us in Christ Jesus." That final marriage with the Lamb will never become a relationship in which the head and the body are mutually interchangeable. Christ will be forever head over all things (1:22).

Erasing the divinely ordained creational and new-creational structures for some form of deconstructed egalitarianism is, to say the least, theologically shortsighted and, in the light of the antithesis, finally pagan, as the domain of sexuality sharply illustrates.

By associating heterosexual marriage as instituted by the Creator (Gn 2:24 cited in Eph 5:31) with the revelational term "mystery," Paul shows that marriage is an element of natural *revelation*. Gods has something to tell us through this structure, particularly about the union of Christ and his bride, the church (5:32). For marriage to function this way, as a picture of union in difference, there must be the creational male and female distinction. In addition, only heterosexual marriage can evoke the eschatological finale, "the marriage supper of the Lamb" (Rv 19:9), where Christ and his bride are finally united but forever distinct. Just how pagan certain "Christians" have become is indicated by the theological judgment of two women in charge of the "judicial" affairs of the Presbyterian Church (USA). Rev. Linda Lee, moderator of the Permanent Judicial Commission, and Rev. Susan Barnes, clerk of Permanent Judicial Commissions of the Synod of the Pacific (PCUSA), state, in defense of a lesbian minister: "The requirement [for ordination] that marriage is for a man and a woman is not an essential. It's a guideline but not an essential."[31]

Here Paul shows how the *essential* realities of creation and redemption, of ecclesiology and eschatology, harmoniously combine to give witness in the area of sexuality to the general truth of biblical theism. By encouraging the church to be aware of the antithesis with paganism which declares homosexual androgyny, in its elimination of difference and celebration of sameness, to be "the sacrament of monism,"[32] Paul reveals the crucial revelational function of monogamous heterosexuality.

Antithetical Spirituality

Pagan Spirituality

In Ephesians, Paul does not describe specific pagan spiritual *techniques*. However, his definition of pagan *thinking* as "vain" (4:18) takes up the Old Testament term, translated "idol." Romans 1:22–23 develops explicitly how "foolish thinking" leads to "foolish" worship. Such spirituality is foolish because it gives ultimate worship not to the eternal, immortal Creator, but to created things like human beings, birds, animals and reptiles, which are marked by death. This is worship and service of the creature rather than the eternal Creator. Isaiah agrees. It is foolish to use one half of a piece of wood to cook a meal or warm yourself, and to worship the other half.[33] Nature, as a created thing, is made to worship, not to be worshiped. The focus of pagan spirituality is on the self as the source of spiritual gnosis.

Christian Spirituality

The many pagan techniques for the worship of Nature are absent in Christianity. This is certainly true of Ephesians. God has blessed us "in Christ with every spiritual blessing in the heavenly places" (1:3), but not one of those blessings comes to us through "spiritual technologies."

Christian spirituality includes the mind, which is renewed (4:23) to understand what God's will is (5:17), for which task we deploy the sword of the Spirit which is the Word of God (6:17). Certainly, our spiritual lives are maintained by the communion of the saints (2:2, 4:3, 5:19); by "being kind to one another, tenderhearted, forgiving one another, as God in Christ forgave you" (4:32), and praying for one another "at all times in the Spirit, with all prayer and supplication." (6:18). In *prayer* one needs faith to understand God's will: "we have access through our faith" (3:12). In *meditation* one seeks *gnosis*. Thus the great antithesis in spirituality is between manipulative gnosis and obedient faith.

Conclusion: Pagans in Biblical Eschatology

There are two significantly different but complimentary pictures of pagans in this epistle to be held in tension:

- Ephesians 5:7: "Therefore do not partake (συμμέτοχοι) with them [pagans]"[34]
- Ephesians 3:6: "the pagans are fellow partakers (συμμέτοχα) of the promise."[35]

Facing paganism, we do not erect a massive wall of partition and live in a ghetto. The die is not yet cast; the drama of life is in full swing, and the devil has not won. Antithesis should never be a principle inhibiting evangelism and cultural transformation, but it should guard us from naïvely baptizing fallen culture as an expression of God's will for the church.[36] Antithesis means separation but also clarity, a true word of hope and salvation for seeking pagans.

The promise to Abraham to bless the nations is what drives Paul. "[God] revealed his Son to me, in order that I might preach him among the Gentiles" (Gal 1:16), but not simply as a missionary. He is "a prophet to the nations" as was Jeremiah,[37] declaring the divine revelation/insight that "the Gentiles are fellow heirs, members of the same body" (3:6). This was *new revelation*, not given to the other apostles. Thus he presents himself as "the apostle of the Gentiles" (Rom 11:13) and speaks of "my gospel"—the final version of the Gospel granted to him.[38] This final revelation gives Paul a radical understanding of the Gospel, a clear understanding of the Antithesis, and boldness. The same Gospel is radically rearticulated to take into account the redemptive-historical endtime event of the inclusion of the pagans.

May I make a plea for antithesis thinking, antithesis hermeneutics, antithesis evangelism, antithesis preaching, antithesis education, antithesis ethical living—over against the great pagan, all-inclusive synthesis that seeks to choke out the truth? To such a calling Paul gives his life. Chained to pagan Roman soldiers, he chooses one prayer to close the epistle: "[Pray] also for me, that words may be given to me in opening my mouth boldly to proclaim the mystery of the gospel" (6:19).

It is a prayer for the mission of the church that he exemplifies: that this truth be heard in the world with unmistakable clarity. It is a prayer for antithesis evangelism in the power of Holy Spirit boldness. The following doxology explains the boldness and the deep motivation:

> Now to him who is able to do far more abundantly than all that we ask or think, according to the power at work within us, to him be glory in the church and in Christ Jesus throughout all generations, forever and ever. Amen. (Eph 3:20–21)

ENDNOTES

PREFACE – JONES

1. Dwight Friesen, "Orthoparadoxy: Emerging Hope for Embracing Difference," *An Emergent Manifesto of Hope*, ed. Doug Pagitt and Tony Jones (Grand Rapids: Baker, 2007), 208.
2. Francis Schaeffer, *Escape from Reason* (Downers Grove, IL: InterVarsity, 1968), 50.
3. See *The Chaplaincy Institute for Arts and Interfaith Ministries* website.
4 Ibid.
5. See "Neo-Paganism: Stepchild of Secular Humanism," John J. Hughes, ed., *Speaking the Truth in Love: The Theology of John M. Frame* (Phillipsburg, NJ: P&R, 2009).

CHAPTER 1: MODERN SHAMANISM – HERRICK

1. Shirley MacLaine, *Dancing in the Light* (New York: Bantam, 1985), 350.
2. Jeremy Narby and Francis Huxley, ed. *Shamans through Time: 500 Years on the Path to Knowledge* (New York: Jeremy Tarcher, 2001), 305.
3. Ibid., 1.
4. Philip Jenkins, *Mystics and Messiahs: Cults and New Religions in American History* (Oxford Univ. Press, 2000), 170.
5. Narby and Huxley, *Shamans through Time*, 5.
6. Ibid.
7. Ibid., 6.
8. First published in 1757, this book appeared in an English translation in 1787.
9. Emanuel Swedenborg, *The Worlds in Space* (1758; rep. Swedenborg Society, 1998), 1.
10. Ibid., 113.
11. Ibid., 14.
12. Ibid., 50.
13. Ibid., 73.
14. Ibid., 65.
15. Ibid., 46.
16. Ibid., 89.
17. Ibid., 93.
18. Bradford Verter, *Dark Star Rising: The Emergence of Modern Occultism, 1880–1950* (unpublished PhD dissertation: Princeton Univ., 1998), 135n.
19. Ibid., 134.
20. Jenkins, *Mystics and Messiahs*, 73.
21. Lawrence Sutin has recently published an extensive biography of Crowley: *Do What*

Thou Wilt: A Life of Aleister Crowley (New York: St. Martins, 2000).

22. Ibid., 2–3.
23. Ibid., 4.
24. See Verter, 129–130, n. "During the early and mid-nineteenth century, sensational yarns, ghost stories and Oriental tales were everywhere: newspapers, magazines, chapbooks, serial pamphlets, and books."
25. Jenkins, *Do What Thou Wilt*, 76–77.
26. Carl Jung, "The Spiritual Problem of Modern Man," *Modern Man in Search of a Soul* (New York: Harcourt Brace, 1933), 210–11.
27. Richard Noll, *The Jung Cult: Origins of a Charismatic Movement* (New York: Princeton Univ. Press, 1994), 64.
28. Jenkins, *Do What Thou Wilt*, 4.
29. Noll, *The Jung Cult*, 83.
30. Helena Blavatsky, *Isis Unveiled*, no. 1 (1877; repr. Pasadena, CA: The Theosophical Society, 1998), 296, italics mine.
31. Ibid.
32. John E. Mack, *Abduction: Human Encounters with Aliens* (New York: Charles Scribner's Sons, 1995). See also Mack's *Secret Life: Firsthand Accounts of UFO Abductions* (with David M. Jacobs, New York: Simon & Schuster, 1992), and *Passport to the Cosmos: Human Transformation and Alien Encounters* (New York: Crown, 1999). Other books in the abduction genre include Dana Redfield, *Summoned: Encounters with Alien Intelligence* (Charlottesville, VA: Hampton Roads, 1999); Dolores Cannon, *The Custodians: Beyond Abduction* (Huntsville, AR: Ozark Mountain, 1999); and Constance Clear, *Reaching for Reality: Seven Incredible True Stories of Alien Abduction* (San Antonio, TX: Consciousness Now, 1999).
33. Mack, *Abduction*, preface.
34. Ibid., 3.
35. Ibid., 3–4.
36. Ibid., 4.
37. Ibid.
38. Ibid., 4–5.
39. Ibid., 6–7.
40. Ibid., 8.
41. Ibid.
42. Ibid.
43. Ibid., 9.
44. Ibid., 32.
45. Joseph Campbell, "Myths from West to East" in *The Universal Myths: Heroes, Gods, Tricksters and Others* (New York: Penguin Books, 1990), 59.
46. Mack, *Abduction*, 18.
47. Ibid., 17.

48. Jenkins, *Do What Thou Wilt*, 172.
49. Mack, *Abduction*, 32.
50. Whitley Streiber, *Communion* (New York: Beech Tree, 1987).
51. Whitley Streiber, *Transformation: The Breakthrough* (New York: Beech Tree, 1988).
52. Whitley Streiber, *Confirmation: The Hard Evidence for Aliens among Us* (New York: St. Martins, 1998).
53. Streiber, *Transformation*, 237.
54. Gary Zukav, *The Seat of the Soul* (New York: Simon & Schuster, 1989), 180.
55. Ibid., 181.
56. Ibid.
57. Ibid., 182.
58. Walsch, *Conversations with God* (New York: Putnam's Sons, 1996), 208.
59. Narby and Huxley, *Shamans through Time*, 305.

CHAPTER 2: ASTROLOGY – MONTENEGRO

1. Despite the controversy over Pluto's status, most astrologers continue to use it as a planet, since Pluto "works" meaningfully in the chart.
2. Jane Evans, *Twelve Doors to the Soul: Astrology of the Inner Self* (Wheaton, IL: Theosophical Publishing, 1979), 5, quoted in Geoffrey Dean and Ivan W. Kelly, "Is Astrology Relevant to Consciousness and Psi?" at tinyurl.com/3boebe.
3. See Dt 17:3; 2 Kgs 21:3; 2 Chr 33:3; Jer 8:1–2, 10:2; and Acts 7:42.
4. We know that God is the master of the universe he created, and that the sun and the moon move at his command. God apparently intervened in the natural course of the heavenly bodies when he caused the sun to "stand still" for Joshua. If he chose to make a star stand still for Jesus, should it surprise us?
5. Some useful tools: John Ankerberg and John Weldon, *Astrology: Do the Heavens Rule Our Destiny?* (Eugene, OR: Harvest House, 1989); Website for Marcia Montenegro: www.ChristianAnswersForTheNewAge.org; Marcia Montenegro, *SpellBound: The Paranormal Seduction of Today's Kids* (Colorado Springs: Cook, 2006).

CHAPTER 3: WITCHCRAFT – HARVEY

1. Their use of the name "Jesus" does not refer to the Jesus Christ of Scripture.
2. Isaac Bonewits, *Essential Guide to Witchcraft and Wicca* (New York: Citadel, 2006), 152.
3. See Raymond Buckland, *Complete Book of Witchcraft* (St. Paul, MN: Llewellyn, 2000), 6.
4. Gerald Gardner, *The Meaning of Witchcraft* (Boston: Weiser, 2004), 1.
5. Marija Gimbutas, *The Living Goddesses* (Berkeley: Univ. of CA Press, posthumous, 2001).
6. Philip G. Davis, *Goddess Unmasked: The Rise of Neopagan Feminist Spirituality* (Dallas:

Spence, 1998), 54.
7. Ibid., 53–83.
8. Ibid., 83–84.
9. Margot Adler, *Drawing Down the Moon: Witches, Druids, Goddess-Worshippers and other Pagans in America Today* (New York: Penguin, 1986), 434.
10. www.hds.harvard.edu/wsrp/scholarship/rfmc/index.htm.
11. Silver Ravenwolf, *Teen Witch: Wicca for a New Generation* (Woodbury, MN: Llewellyn, 1998), 42–46; and Patricia Monaghan, *Wild Girls: The Path of the Young Goddess* (Cottage Grove, WI: Creatrix, 2005), 45–47.
12. Bonewits, *Guide to Witchcraft*, 118–127.
13. Laurie Cabot and Jean Mills, *Celebrate the Earth: A Year of Holidays in the Pagan Tradition* (New York: Dell), 32.
14. Ravenwolf, *Teen Witch*, 8.
15. John Newport, *The New Age Movement and the Biblical Worldview* (Grand Rapids: Eerdmans, 1998), 225–26.
16. Lauren Artress, *Walking a Sacred Path: Rediscovering the Labyrinth as a Sacred Practice* (New York: Riverhead Books, 2006), 15.
17. Bonewits, *Guide to Witchcraft*, 106.
18. Jung as discussed in James A. Herrick, *The Making of the New Spirituality* (Downers Grove, IL: InterVarsity, 2003), 192.
19. Donna Steichen, *Ungodly Rage: The Hidden Face of Catholic Feminism* (San Francisco: Ignatius Press, 1991), 74.
20. Starhawk, *Truth or Dare: Encounters with Power, Authority and Mystery* (San Francisco: Harper & Row, 1987).
21. [See similar practices described in chapter 9].
22. Charlotte Allen, "The Scholars and the Goddess," *Atlantic Monthly* (January 2001) www.theatlantic.com/issues/2001/01/allen.htm.
23. Cynthia Eller, *Living in the Lap of the Goddess: The Feminist Spirituality Movement in America* (Boston: Beacon, 1995), 124.
24. Adler, *Drawing Down the Moon*, 311.
25. Nancy J. Berneking and Pamela Carter Joern, ed., *Re-Membering and Re-Imagining* (Cleveland, OH: Pilgrim, 1995), 59–60.
26. Davis, *Goddess Unmasked*, 28.
27. Elizabeth Johnson, *She Who Is: The Mystery of God in Theological Feminist Discourse* (New York: Crossroad, 1991), 26. Eller, *Lap of the Goddess*, 12–17.
28. Miriam Therese Winter, *The Chronicles of Noah: Genesis and Exodus according to Women* (New York: Crossroad, 1995), 11.
29. Ibid., 20.
30. Ibid., 21.
31. Ibid., 35–37.
32. Adair Lummis, Allison Stokes, and Miriam Therese Winter, *Defecting in Place:*

Women Claiming Responsibility for Their Own Spiritual Lives (New York: Crossroad, 1995), 124–25.

33. Eller, *Lap of the Goddess*, 12–17.
34. Ibid., 18.
35. Starhawk, *Truth or Dare*, 40–47.
36. Ibid., 44.
37. Riane Eisler, *The Chalice and the Blade* (Harper San Francisco, 1987), 88–89.
38. Starhawk, *The Spiral Dance* (Harper San Francisco, 1979), 37.
39. Christopher Penczak, *Gay Witchcraft* (Boston: Weiser Books, 2003), 111.
40. www.adherents.com/rel_USA.html#religion. This estimate includes Neopagans, Native American faith, New Age faith and Unitarian Universalists.
41. www.youthspecialties.com/freeresources/articles/spirituality/ym.php.
42. www.parliamentofreligions.org/_includes/FCKcontent/File/2004report-rev.pdf, 4.
43. www.parliamentofreligions2009.org/whatisparliament.php.
44. Marian Singer, *Dancing the Fire* (New York: Citadel, 2005), ix–x.
45. Penczak, *Gay Witchcraft*, 53: "Yemaya is the *orisha* [goddess] of oceans, rivers and waters....Yemaya is a great sorceress, a powerful patron of magick, and is known to shape-shift into a man at times. As a warrior woman, Yemaya is linked to transgendered and lesbian women."

CHAPTER 4: KABBALAH – KLETT

1. Wearing a red string bracelet that has first been wrapped around Rachel's tomb in Jerusalem is a traditional folk practice to ward off the "evil eye." The Kabbalah Centre has made good profit selling red string! The red color and the woolen material supposedly have special properties that repel negative forces, especially when combined with the spiritual energy accrued through contact with Rachel's tomb. Serious Kabbalists do not endorse this.
2. Brian L. Lancaster, *The Essence of Kabbalah* (London & Edison, NJ: Chartwell Books, 2005), 14.
3. See Gershom Scholem, R. J. Zwi Werblowsky, and Allan Arkush, *Origins of the Kabbalah*, 1st pb ed. (New York: Princeton Univ. Press, 1990), 24–25 and Joseph Dan, *Kabbalah: A Very Short Introduction* (New York: Oxford Univ. Press, 2006), 15–16.
4. Dan, *Kabbalah*, 21.
5. Ibid., 30.
6. The Jewish Renewal movement is a loose network of synagogues and *havurot* (home fellowships) influenced by the ideas of Neohasidic rabbi Zalman Schachter-Shalomi. It seeks a new approach to Judaism, emphasizing mysticism, meditation, contemporary social issues and lively worship. It also incorporates spiritual elements from various mystical traditions into a Jewish framework. One might describe it as a New Age, liberal, unorthodox Hasidic Judaism.

7. Dan, *Kabbalah*, 110.
8. In Hebrew these are the four worlds of Atzilut, Beriah, Yetsirah and Assiah, remembered by the acronym Abiyah.
9. Aryeh Kaplan, *Jewish Meditation: A Practical Guide* (New York: Schocken, 1985), 88–90.
10. Charles Hodge, *Systematic Theology*, vol. 1 (London: James Clarke, 1960 ed.), 323.
11. Neopythagoreanism holds to the transmigration of souls, as does Kabbalah. Kabbalah speaks of thirty-two spiritual paths, from the ten Sephirot and the twenty-two letters of the Hebrew alphabet.
12. Jacob Immanuel Schochet, *Mystical Concepts in Chassidism* (Brooklyn, NY: Kehot Publication Society, 1979), 62–65.
13. Isaac Luria, *The Tree of Life*, see http://www.kabbalah.info/engkab/ez_eng.htm.
14. John Frame, *The Doctrine of the Knowledge of God* (Phillipsburg, NJ: P&R, 1987), 13–15.
15. Avram Davis, *Meditation from the Heart of Judaism* (Woodstock, VT: Jewish Lights, 1997), 18.
16. Mark Elber, *The Everything Kabbalah Book* (Avon, MA: F&W, 2006), 70.
17. See Frame, *Knowledge of God*, 13–15.
18. Bob and Abraham Waxman, *Kabbalah Simply Stated: A Conversation with the Rabbi* (St. Paul, MN: Paragon House Azriel, 2004), 59.
19. Chaim Dalfin, *Demystifying the Mystical* (London: Jason Aronson, 1995), 77.
20. Adin Steinsaltz, *The Thirteen Petalled Rose: A Discourse on the Essence of Jewish Existence and Belief* (New York: Harper Collins, 1980), 51.
21. The Sh'ma is Dt 6:4 which is chanted in the synagogue: "Hear, O Israel: The Lord our God, the Lord is one."
22. Nan Fink Gefen, *Discovering Jewish Meditation: Instruction & Guidance for Learning an Ancient Spiritual Practice* (Woodstock VT: Jewish Lights, 1999), 101.
23. Gabriella Samuel, *The Kabbalah Handbook* (London: Penguin, 2007), 192.
24. David A Cooper, *Invoking Angels* (Boulder, CO: Sounds True, 2006).
25. 2 Cor 11:14.
26. Occultists spell it "Magick" to differentiate it from "magic," meaning sleight of hand entertainment.
27. Stewart Farrar, *What Witches Do*, 3rd ed. (Custer, WA: Phoenix, 1999), 181, 121.
28. From "Morals and Dogma of the Ancient and Accepted Scottish Rite Freemasonry," online at Project Gutenberg. www.gutenberg.org/files/19447/19447-0.txt.
29. Lancaster, *Essence of Kabbalah*, 192.

Chapter 5: Gnosticism – Doveton

1. www.virtueonline.org/portal/modules/news/article.php?storyid=7500.
2. www3.telus.net/gerry_hunter/PastView/Xmas%20What%20Sense.htm.
3. Quoted by Matthew Fox in his introduction to *One River, Many Wells: Wisdom*

Springing from World Faiths (New York: Tarcher/Penguin, 2004).

4. Ibid.
5. Thomas Molnar, *The Pagan Temptation* (Grand Rapids: Eerdmans, 1987), 56–58.
6. See John Shelby Spong, "A Call for a New Reformation," www.dioceseofnewark.org/jsspong/reform.html. Ingham and Spong have much in common with modern Gnostic groups like the International Order of Gnostic Templars who have as their goal the creation of a "one-world" spirituality. This they aim to achieve by a) revealing the common threads that unite all religions, b) revealing that all religions have a common core of "pure spirituality" that doctrine and dogma obstruct, and c) revealing that there are many paths to the truth.
7. From a prayer by Miriam Therese Winter, Professor of liturgy worship and spirituality, author of *WomanWord* and other books of prayers and resources for worship.
8. Fox, *One River, Many Wells.*
9. Marvin W. Meyer, ed., *The Ancient Mysteries* (San Francisco: Harper & Row, 1987), 6.
10. Pagan goddesses are not as remote from modern consciousness as we may think. Jungian analyst Ginette Paris of Pacifica Graduate Institute dedicates her recent book *The Sacrament of Abortion*, to the goddess Artemis. She explores how the Artemis myth can help mothers to cut the connection between themselves and their unborn children, and calls for new rituals and laws to restore the dimension of the sacred to the act of abortion.
11. Tucker Carlson, "The Episcopal Church in Crisis," *The Week Standard* (October 13, 1997).
12. See Elaine Pagels, *The Gnostic Gospels* (New York: Random House, 1979).
13. This practice is spreading—for example at the Episcopal Church of the Redeemer the Lord's Prayer begins with the words, *Our Mother, Our Father in heaven...* The Presiding Bishop of the Episcopal Church in the USA commonly speaks in these terms. See also this example: "God/dess of struggle and blessing, we thank you that you are so willing to meet us in love here and now, as you meet our mothers and fathers, partners and lovers, siblings and children, friends and strangers on their faith journeys, as you entered our human life in Jesus Christ-Sophia..." (From the Sunday Morning Liturgy of Welcome, Ebenezer Lutheran Church, San Francisco).
14. Irenaeus, *Ad Her* 3.16.6.
15. Pagels, *Gnostic Gospels*, 32.
16. Rosemary Radford Ruether says that, "all language for God is analogical or metaphorical, not literal"; she calls orthodox terminology for the Godhead, "idolatry."
17. On June 19, 2006, the PCUSA denomination received a paper suggesting the use of the imagination in naming the Trinity. Among other names suggested were "Rainbow, Ark and Dove," "Speaker, Word and Breath," "Sun, Light and Burning Ray," "Giver, Gift and Giving," "Lover, Beloved and Love," "Rock, Cornerstone and Temple," "Fire that Consumes, Sword that Divides and Storm that Melts Mountains."

18. Tertullian, *Against the Valentinians*, ch. 3.
19. Tertullian, *Adv Her*, ch 1–3.
20. Molnar, *Pagan Temptation*, 166–67.
21. Report by Terry Mattingly, *Liturgical Dances with Wolves*, tmatt.gospelcom.net/tmatt/freelance/wolves.htm.
22. 1 Cor 1:18.
23. See the official website of Grace Cathedral www.gracecathedral.org/church/cathedralTour.shtml.
24. Irenaeus, *Against Carpocrates, Ad Her* 1.25.6.
25. Ebenezer Lutheran Church, San Francisco. See website herchurch.org.hosting.domaindirect.com/index.html.
26. www.brigidsplace.org.
27. www.gracecathedral.org/church/cathedralTour.shtml.
28. Norman D. Livergood, in online article on Perennialist Art www.hermes-press.com/Perennial_Tradition/PTch8.htm. According to Hermetic teachings, perennialist art is a "portal to a higher state of consciousness."
29. "It's not a maze, it's a Labyrinth" excerpt from *The Sand Labyrinth, Meditation at Your Fingertips*, by Lauren Artress, 2001, Journey Editions; available at www.gracecathedral.org/enrichment/excerpts/exc_20010328.shtml.
30. "Interview with Lauren Artress," www.gracecathedral.org/enrichment/interviews/int_19961206.shtml.
31. General information on website : www.gracecathedral.org/labyrinth.
32. "Interview with Lauren Artress," www.gracecathedral.org/enrichment/interviews/int_19961206.shtml.
33. Anne Baring and Jules Cashford, *The Myth of the Goddess* (London: Viking, 1991), 106–120; 135–137.
34. Marcus J Borg, *Me and Jesus—The Journey Home: An Odyssey*, www.westarinstitute.org/Periodicals/4R_Articles/Borg_bio/borg_bio.html.
35. Tertullian, *Against Marcion*, vol 3, ch 2.
36. Irenaeus, *Against Carpocrates, Ad Her* 1.24.4.
37. Fox, *One River, Many Wells*.
38. Borg, *Me and Jesus*.
39. *Seattle Times* (June 17, 2007).
40. Blogger News Network : www.bloggernews.net/112455.
41. Horseman has a qualification from the California-based College of Sacred Mists, headed by Lady Raven Moonshadow and conducts funerals using Christian, Jewish, Buddhist or Pagan elements. See online report at www.thisisbristol.co.uk/displayNode.jsp?nodeId=144913&command=displayContent&sourceNode=221381&contentPK=19515693&folderPk=103586&pNodeId=221386.
42. Gospel of Philip II, 83, *The Nag Hammadi Library in English*, ed. James Robinson, (Leiden: Brill, 1988).

43. "The Church in Hiawathaland," *Episcopal Diocese of Northern Michigan Newsletter*, vol. 18 (September 9, 2007), 2B.
44. Spong, "New Reformation," www.dioceseofnewark.org/jsspong/reform.html.
45. All Saints Church, Hoboken. see www.allsaintshoboken.com.
46. Interview with Katherine Jefferts Schori on National Public Radio www.npr.org.
47. Centre for Progressive Christianity website: www.tcpc.org/about/8points.cfm.
48. *Dialogue of the Savior*, III, 131, 27–30. *NHL*, 249.
49. *Gospel of Philip*, II, 61,30. *NHL*, 147.
50. *Gospel of Thomas*, II, 46 (77), *NHL*, 135.
51. "They Followed a Star: Astrology and Christianity as Allies on the Journey," www.dankeusal.com/page4.html.
52. Veriditas, *Labyrinth Journal* (Fall 2006).
53. *Gospel of Philip*, II, 53, 10–20. *NHL*, 142.
54. Sallie McFague, "Imaging God and 'Another World,'" published online at theotherjournal.com/print.php?id=170.
55. See www.allsaintshoboken.com.
56. McFague, "Imaging God," See also Sallie McFague, "Is God in Charge? Creation and Providence," *Essentials of Christian Theology* ed. William C. Placher (Louisville, KY: Westminster/John Knox, 2003), 93–116.
57. Mircea Eliade, *Myth and Reality* (New York: Harper & Row, 1963), 65.
58. Ibid., 133.
59. magdalenemystique.com/da-vinci-code.
60. Molnar, *Pagan Temptation*, 148.
61. Jeffrey Satinover, "Jungians and Gnostics," *First Things* 46 (October 1994): 41–48.
62. Ibid.

CHAPTER 6: AMERICAN INDIAN ANIMISM – TOOLE

1. Identification with a clan does not necessarily imply animistic beliefs or practices on the part of an individual Tlingit.
2. This belief is one reason I think that the sweat in any form and for any reason, at least in a plains Native context, is off limits to Christians.
3. This understanding of the sweat is common in Native cultures. To find the meaning of sweats from a variety of tribal perspectives, research "sweat lodge" online.
4. For an excellent resource on Plains Native spirituality from a Christian perspective, see Adolphus Kootenay, *Out of Bondage: Finding the Path out of Indian Religion and into the Kingdom of God* (Bloomington, IN: Authorhouse, 2004).
5. Perhaps the apostle Paul affirms this idea in 1 Corinthians 10, where he speaks of having fellowship with demons.
6. [See similar practices in chapter 8.]

Chapter 7: Native South American – Gomes

1. Rom 1:25.
2. See Richard Keyes, "The Idol Factory," in Os Guinness and John Seel, ed. *No God but God: Breaking with the Idols of our Age* (Chicago: Moody Press, 1992).
3. Ibid.
4. See Is 44: 9–20.
5. I have used *anti-existence* as a play on the title of Udo Middelmann's book *Pro-Existence: Man in the Circumference of Reality* (Downer's Grove: InterVarsity, 1974).
6. Claude Levy-Strauss, *Tristes Tropiques* (Paris: Plon, 1955).
7. See Jean de Léry, *History of a Voyage to the Land of Brazil* (Berkeley: Univ. of CA Press, 1992).
8. In the mythology, it is unclear if it is one of the younger brothers or the brother of the unspoken one.
9. The practices cited actual practices, teachings and services offered by the *Igreja Universal do Reino de Deus* (Universal Church of the Kingdom of God), the fastest growing pseudoevangelical group in Brazil. Beware! They have gone international and may be found in a large city near you. See www.uckg.org/cms.
10. See, John Calvin, *Institutes of the Christian Religion*, 1:108.
11. I do not yet understand why the "deification" goal is missing in these systems.

Chapter 8: African Pagan Spirituality – Turaki

1. For a more thorough treatment, readers may consult my two works: *Christianity and African Gods: A Theological Method* (Potchefstroom, South Africa: Potchefstroom Univ., 1999) and *Foundations of African Traditional Religion and Worldview* (Nairobi: WordAlive, 2006).
2. J. S. Mbiti, *African Religions and Philosophy* (London: Heinemann, 1969), 75.
3. Philip M. Steyne, *Gods of Power: A Study of the Beliefs and Practices of Animists* (Houston: Touch, 1989), 98.
4. Ibid., 95.
5. Ibid., 137–40.
6. *Eerdman's Bible Dictionary* (Grand Rapids: Eerdmans, 1987): 1040.
7. Steyne, *Gods of Power*, 126.
8. Ibid., 127–28.
9. Ibid., 127.
10. *Eerdman's Bible Dictionary*, 287.
11. Steyne, *Gods of Power*, 132.
12. Langdon Gilkey, *Maker of Heaven and Earth: The Christian Doctrine of Creation in the Light of Modern Knowledge* (Lanham, MD: Univ. Press of America, 1959), 6.
13. Steyne, *Gods of Power*, 115.
14. B. C. Ray, *African Religions: Symbol, Ritual and Community* (Englewood Cliffs, NJ:

Prentiss-Hall, 1976), 17.
15. Steyne, *Gods of Power*, 93–94.
16. J. Onaiyekan, "Divine Mysteries and Secret Cults in the African Traditional Religions and in Christianity" (Unpublished paper, 1980).
17. Steyne, *Gods of Power*, 100.
18. Ibid., 100–106.
19. Ibid., 106.
20. Ibid., 107–13.
21. *New Concise Bible Dictionary* (InterVarsity, 1997), 328.
22. Ibid.
23. Ibid., 98.
24. Steyne, *Gods of Power*, 95.
25. Ibid., 97.
26. L. Nyirongo, "The Gods of Africa or the God of the Bible? The Snares of African Traditional Religion in Biblical Perspective," *IRS*, series F2, no. 70 (Potchefstroom, South Africa, 1997): 181–194.
27. Ibid., 183.
28. Steyne, *Gods of Power* ,118.
29. Nyirongo, "Gods of Africa," 188.
30. Ibid.
31. Ibid.
32. *Eerdmans Bible Dictionary* (1987): 679.
33. Nyirongo "Gods of Africa," 192–93.
34. Ibid., 193–94.

CHAPTER 9: CHINESE DAOIST/ANIMIST – LING

1. Chinese names and terms are generally transliterated for overseas communities and for academic purposes, using the pin-yin system prevalent in China and overseas Chinese communities such as Singapore and the United States. Famous names are transliterated according to prevailing custom, e.g. Confucius and Chiang Kai-shek's Kuomintang (Nationalist Party). These do not fit any existing system. Sometimes the Wade-Giles transliteration, prevalent among the Nationalists (Kuomintang) in Taiwan, is given in parenthesis, e.g. Taoism and Lao-tzu. Names of persons are not italicized; terms and names for gods and spirits, titles of books and non-English European languages, e.g. *laissez-faire*, are italicized.
2. C. K. Yang, *Religion in Chinese Society* (Berkeley: Univ. of CA Press, 1961).
3. Standard texts in Chinese philosophy include: H. G. Creel, *Chinese Thought from Confucius to Mao Zedong*, (Univ. of Chicago Press, 1971); Yu-lan Fung, *A Short History of Chinese Philosophy* (New York: Macmillan/Free Press, 1997); Wing-tsit Chan, *A Source Book of Chinese Philosophy* (New York: Princeton Univ. Press, 1969); and DeBary, Watson and Chan, *Sources of Chinese Tradition*, 2 volumes (New York:

Columbia Univ. Press, 2001.)

4. Amos Jui-Chen Wang, *Di san zhi yan kan dao jiao* (An Alternative Perspective on Daoism) (Taipei: Campus Evangelical Fellowship, 2000), 25–26, 42, 50.
5. Ibid., 84. See also Laurence Thompson, *Chinese Religions: An Introduction* (Belmont, CA: Dickenson), as well as his other introductory texts on Chinese religion.
6. Wang, *Daoism*, 20.
7. This erroneous hypothesis may have been encouraged by the fact that *Shangdi* sounds like "El Shaddai." Such an interpretation is not supported by Scripture, the good intentions of its authors notwithstanding.
8. Wang, *Daoism*, 49.
9. Ibid., 37.
10. Ibid., 50.
11. Ibid., 50–55.
12. Ibid., 89–99.
13. Ibid., 62–68.

CHAPTER 10: C. J. JUNG – VERARDE

1. C. G. Jung, *Memories, Dreams, Reflections*, rev. ed. (New York: Vintage, 1965), 11–13.
2. Ibid., 37.
3. Ibid., 39.
4. Ibid., 40.
5. Ibid., 196–97.
6. Ibid., 197.
7. Quoted in Robert A. Segal, *The Gnostic Jung* (New York: Princeton Univ. Press, 1992), 181–82.
8. Richard Tarnas, *Psyche and Cosmos* (New York: Penguin, 2007), 62.
9. Ibid., 65.
10. Claims made of affinities between Jung's ideas and this or that ancient system are not without basis but can be misleading. Rick Tarnas, for example, was my professor and graduate advisor, and I know him to be a brilliant and careful scholar. I don't object to his claim of affinity between astrology and Jungian theory. I merely point out that often the degree of affinity is due in large part to the ancient system in question having become Jungianized, that is, reinterpreted along Jungian lines by its modern adherents. Such is not a true affinity but a revisionist interpretation. For example, see Robert Segal's introduction in *The Gnostic Jung*, in which he concludes that Jung is not a Gnostic in the ancient sense.
11. Tom F Cavalli, *Alchemical Psychology: Old Recipes for a New* World (New York: Jeremy Tarcher/Penguin, 2002), 46.
12. Ibid., 47.
13. Ibid.
14. Ibid., 47–48.

15. C. G. Jung, *Aion* (New York: Princeton Univ. Press, 2nd ed., 1969), 45, par. 79.
16. Ibid., 41, par. 74.
17. Ibid., 68–69, par. 123–24.
18. Jung, *Memories, Dreams, Reflections*, 350.
19. C. J. Jung, *Symbols of Transformation* (New York: Princeton Univ. Press, 1912/1956), 633.
20. Ibid., 586.
21. Jung, *Aion*, 44.
22. Jung, *Memories, Dreams, Reflections*, 350.
23. See Elaine Pagels, *The Gnostic Gospels* (New York: Vintage, 1981/1979), 146–169. Pagels quotes the *Gospel of Phillip* as saying, "human beings make gods, and worship their creation. It would be appropriate for the gods to worship human beings."
24. Pagels, *Gnostic Gospels*, 160.
25. C. G. Jung, *Answer to Job, Collected Works* (New York: Princeton Univ. Press, 1958/1969), 11, par. 554. (Jung's italics).
26. Martin Buber, *Eclipse of God* (New York: Harper, 1952), 80–81.

CHAPTER 11: QUANTUM MECHANICS – STOOTMAN

1. Albert Einstein, *Out of My Later Years* (Prineville, OR: Bonanza, 1990), 25 (emphasis in original).
2. Fritjof Capra, *The Tao of Physics* (Boston: Shambhala, 1975). Capra, a physicist, explores the parallels between modern physics and Eastern Mysticism.
3. Gary Zukav, *Dancing Wu Li Masters* (New York: William Morrow, 1979). Zukav is a journalist by profession.
4. Werner Heisenberg, *Physics & Beyond* (New York: Harper and Row, 1972).
5. Erwin Schrodinger, *My View of the World* (Woodbridge, CT: Ox Bow Press, 1983). This book contains two sets of essays: the first written around 1925 and the second around 1960. See also an excellent biography: Walter Moore, *Schrodinger Life and Thought* (Cambridge Univ. Press, 1989).
6. See the journal *Nature*, 434 (2005): 1066.
7. This experiment demonstrates the photo-electric effect, which was first discovered by Frank Hertz whilst looking for evidence of electromagnetic waves.
8. David Bohm, *Physical Review*, 85, no. 166 (1952): 180. Interestingly, Bohm (1917–1992) was also a proponent of Eastern mysticism. See his book *Wholeness and the Implicate Order* (London: Routledge & Kegan Paul, 1980).
9. Ibid, 168.
10. Detection of the photon causes the mathematical distributive law to be enabled. Prior to detection, the logic of the distributive law does not apply. This indeed is a remarkable facet of our atomic world.
11. Quantum mechanically, as stated previously, the photon is a mathematical object called a wave function. The action of the observer to ascertain which slit the photon

has gone through, using a measuring instrument, is sometimes called the "collapse" of the wave function. Nothing actually collapses but the mathematics is changed.

12. Ibid., 152.
13. The probability amplitude is the square root of the probability.
14. Wojciech H. Zurek, "Decoherence, Einselection, and the Quantum origins of the Classical" in the journal *Rev. Mod. Physics* 75 (2003): 715.
15. Owen Flanagan, *The Problem of the Soul: Two Visions of Mind and How to Reconcile Them* (New York: Basic Books, 2002).
16. Ibid., preface.
17. Ibid., 208.
18. *The Free Man's Worship* published in 1903 and available on the web.
19. Paul Davies, *Mind of God: the Scientific Basis for a Rational World* (New York: Simon & Schuster, 1993).
20. Marquis de Laplace (1749–1827) in his writing *Mécanique Céleste.*

CHAPTER 12: DEEP ECOLOGY – BEISNER

1. *non causa pro causa*
2. *argumentum ad verecundiam, and argumentum ad hominem,* etc.
3. See, for example, Steven Rosen, "Ahimsa: Animals and the East," *The Animals' Agenda* (October 1990): 21–25.
4. Robert James Bidinotto, "Environmentalism: Freedom's Foe for the '90s," *The Freeman* vol. 40, no. 11 (1990): 409–420, at 410; citing Lindsey Van Gelder, "It's Not Nice to Mess with Mother Nature," *Ms.* (January/February 1989): 60.
5. Arne Naess, "The Shallow and the Deep, Long-range Ecology Movements: A Summary," *Inquiry* 16:95–100.
6. David Rothenberg, "Introduction: Ecosophy T: From Intuition to System," in Arne Naess, *Ecology, Community and Lifestyle: Outline of an Ecosophy,* trans. and rev. David Rothenberg (Cambridge Univ. Press, 1989), 2.
7. Rothenberg, "Introduction," in Naess, 1.
8. Kim Bartlett, "Of Meat and Men: A Conversation with Carol Adams," *The Animals' Agenda* (October 1990):13.
9. Rothenberg, "Introduction," 8, 9.
10. Naess, *Ecology, Community and Lifestyle,* 28.
11. Ibid.
12. Bidinotto, "Environmentalism," 414.
13. McFague has published highly influential books, including *Metaphorical Theology* (1982), *Models of God* (1987, which won the American Academy of Religion's Award for Excellence), and *Super, Natural Christians* (1987).
14. Sallie McFague, *The Body of god: An Ecological Theology* (Philadelphia: Fortress Press, 1993), vii–viii.
15. Ibid., ix–x. One wonders why she bothers to call this model "Christian."

16. Notice how she truncates the doctrine, making Jesus Christ incidental to it.
17. McFague, *The Body of god,* xi.
18. Ibid., xi–xii.
19. Ibid., 6.
20. Ibid, 6–7.
21. Ibid., 8.
22. Ibid., 13–14.
23. Ibid., 15.
24. Just to be sure we don't misunderstand her and think the phrase "body and soul" indicates some kind of distinction between the two (a "dualism" that she rejects), she later asks rhetorically, "what *are* we without our bodies?" (p. 19)—the obvious answer being *nothing.*
25. McFague, *The Body of god,* 16.
26. Note that quick and subtle assertion, not argued but slipped in so quickly and naturally that we hardly notice that it affirms something antithetical to biblical revelation.
27. McFague, *The Body of god,* 18–19, emphasis added.
28. Ibid., 19.
29. Ibid., 20.
30. Ibid.
31. Ibid.
32. Ibid., 21.
33. Ibid., 23.
34. Ibid., 22.
35. Ibid., 24.
36. Ibid., 28–9.
37. Ibid., 221, n. 5.
38. Robert K. Merton, "Science and the Social Order," *Philosophy of Science* 5:3 (July 1938): 321–37, at 334.
39. More studies are referenced in The Cornwall Alliance's "A Call to Truth, Prudence, and Protection of the Poor: An Evangelical Response to Global Warming," at www.cornwallalliance.org/docs/Call_to_Truth.pdf, which has been endorsed by over 170 leaders, including scores of climate scientists and environmental economists (listed at www.cornwallalliance.org/docs/Open_Letter.pdf), and in my "Global Warming: Why Evangelicals Should Not Be Alarmed" (www.cornwallalliance.org/docs/Global-Warming–Why-evangelicals-should-not-be-alarmed.pdf), "Important Developments on Global Warming in 2006" (www.cornwallalliance.org/articles/read/important-developments-on-global-warming-in-2006), and "Scientific Orthodoxies, Politicized Science, and Catastrophic Global Warming: Challenges to Evangelicals Navigating Rough Waters in Science and Policy," presented at the annual meeting of the Evangelical Theological Society, November 2006, Washington, DC (www.cornwallalliance.org/articles/read/scientific-orthoddoxies-politicized-

science-and-catastrophic-global-warming/), and in issues of The Cornwall Alliance for the Stewardship of Creation's newsletter, some back issues of which are available at www.cornwallalliance.org, where one can also subscribe online.

40. Intergovernmental Panel on Climate Change, 2001.
41. Naomi Oreskes, "The scientific consensus on climate change," *Science*, vol. 306, issue 5702 (2004): 1686, online at www.sciencemag.org/cgi/content/full/306/5702/1686; Benny J. Peiser, Letter to *Science*, January 4, 2005, submission ID: 56001, online at www.staff.livjm.ac.uk/spsbpeis/Scienceletter.htm; Klaus-Martin Schulte, "Scientific Consensus on Climate Change?" prepublication draft for *Energy and Environment*, vol. 19, no. 2.
42. Letter from Dennis Bray to *Science* magazine (December 22, 2004), online at www.staff.livjm.ac.uk/spsbpeis/Scienceletter.htm; D. Bray and H. von Storch, *The Perspectives of Climate Scientists on Global Change* (GKSS Forschungszentrum, 2007), online at dvsun3.gkss.de/BERICHTE/GKSS_Berichte_2007/GKSS_2007_11.pdf.
43. Open Letter to the Secretary-General of the United Nations (December 13, 2007), online at scienceandpublicpolicy.org/images/stories/papers/reprint/UN_open_letter.pdf; "U.S. Senate Report: Over 400 Prominent Scientists Disputed Man-Made Global Warming in 2007," online at epw.senate.gov/public/index.cfm?FuseAction=MinoritySenateReport.
44. Myanna Lahsen, "Seductive Simulations? Uncertainty Distribution Around Climate Models," *Social Studies of Science* 35/6 (2005): 895–922, online at http://sciencepolicy.colorado.edu/admin/publication_files/resource-1891-2005.49.pdf#search=%22%22Myanna%20Lahsen%22%20%22Seductive%20Simulations%22%22.
45. Figure, "Causes of Climate Change," from Fris-Christensen & Lassen, 1991, *Science* 254 #5032, adapted by Tim Patterson, online at friendsofscience.org.
46. Henrik Svensmark and Nigel Calder, *The Chilling Stars: A New Theory of Climate Change* (Cambridge: Totem Books, 2006).
47. Roy W. Spencer, William D. Braswell, John R. Christy, and Justin Hnilo, "Cloud and Radiation Budget Changes Associated with Tropical Interseasonal Oscillations," *Geophysical Research Letters* 34 L15707 (August 9, 2007).
48. University of Alabama press release at www.uah.edu/news/newsread.php?nesID=875, and www.blogs.usatoday.com/weather/2007/08/cloudy-forecast.html.
49. David H. Douglass, John R. Christy, Benjamin D. Pearson, and S. Fred Singer, "A comparison of tropical temperature trends with model predictions," *International Journal of Climatology* (2007), online at scienceandpublicpolicy.org/images/stories/papers/other/Singer_model_wrong.pdf.
50. Ross McKitrick and Patrick Michaels, "Quantifying the influence of anthropogenic surface processes and inhomogeneities on gridded global climate data," *Journal of Geophysical Research*, vol. 112, DS24S09, doi:10.1029/2007JD008465, 2007.

online at www.uoguelph.ca/~rmckitri/research/jgr07/M&M.JGRDec07.pdf. For a nontechnical explanation of the research and its implications by coauthor McKitrick, see www.uoguelph.ca/~rmckitri/research/jgr07/M&M.JGR07-background.pdf.

51. I have reported on many others in the newsletter of the Cornwall Alliance for the Stewardship of Creation (to which you can subscribe at www.cornwallalliance.org) and in papers posted at our website.
52. Neopagan, New Age spirituality has influenced even "evangelical" environmentalism. NAE Vice President for Governmental Affairs Rich Cizik, prominent in the evangelical movement for global warming alarmism, and Jim Ball, president of the Evangelical Environmental Network, as well as other signers of the Evangelical Climate Initiative, testify to the influence of British climatologist and professed evangelical Sir John Houghton in converting them to belief in catastrophic manmade warming. In *Global Warming: The Complete Briefing*, Houghton discusses his religious views and purports to give evidence for his evangelicalism. The two most cited sources in that chapter are Al Gore's *Earth in the Balance* (loaded with New Age thought) and New Age scientist/guru James Lovelock's *The Ages of Gaia*. Houghton's use of Scripture is scanty and superficial. There is no evidence in that chapter that he is an evangelical. If he is, his evangelicalism has had little impact on his worldview and how it ought to influence his science.
53. See Christopher Essex and Ross McKitrick, *Taken by Storm: The Troubled Science, Politics and Policy of Global Warming*, rev. ed. (Toronto: Key Porter, 2008). The famed Italian physicist Antonini Zichichi made the same point in his paper presented to the Pontifical Council on Justice and Peace in April 2007.

CHAPTER 13: CONTEMPLATIVE – FROST

1. globalspirit.org/pages/mission.php.
2. I consider this shift to be contrary to biblical Christianity, which I would describe as Bible-centered, belief-based, relational, and life-transforming through faith in the substitutionary, blood atonement of Jesus Christ.
3. An integral philosopher integrates spirit, matter and mind into a synthesized One—a monistic, pagan system that teaches evolution of consciousness toward a final unity with everything in the One.
4. The One of pagan monism allows for no distinction between the Creator God and his creation—an idea they call "dualistic." But Scripture is clear that God is, in fact, distinct from his creation and is not infused within it as a divine essence (panentheism). The Bible recognizes irrevocable distinctions while monism seeks to harmonize everything into an undifferentiated One.
5. On Brian McLaren's web page www.brianmclaren.net/archives/books/brians-recommen, he recommends Ken Wilber's *A Theory of Everything* and *The Marriage of Sense and Soul*, calling them "powerful and important" books. See also Brian McLaren, *A Generous Orthodoxy* (Grand Rapids, MI: Zondervan, 2004), 279–80.

McLaren draws from Wilber in his understanding of "emergent."

6. Leonard I. Sweet, *Quantum Spirituality* (Dayton, OH: Whaleprints, 1991), 254, 305, 341, 345–47.
7. Rob Bell, *Velvet Elvis: Repainting the Christian Faith* (Grand Rapids: Zondervan, 2005), 192.
8. The term "perennial philosophy" was coined in the middle ages to describe the essence of an eternal and universal wisdom tradition underlying all the religions and philosophies.
9. Frithjof Schuon, *The Transcendent Unity of Religions* (Wheaton, IL: The Theosophical Publishing House, 1993 edition), xii.
10. Neoplatonism was the new school of Platonic thought developed by Plotinus in the third century.
11. Thomas Merton, *Zen and the Birds of Appetite* (Boston and London: Shambhala, 1993 edition), 39–40.
12. In the fifth century, a Syrian Neoplatonist wrote several treatises under the pseudonym "Dionysius the Areopagite," the first-century Athenian convert of Paul mentioned in Acts 17:34. Thus "pseudo-Dionysius," as he is more accurately called, introduced mystical Neoplatonism into the medieval church under the weight of Dionysian authorship. Later scrutiny of his writings revealed internal evidence clearly identifying their fifth-century origin.
13. Dionysius the Areopagite, *The Mystical Theology and the Celestial Hierarchies*, translated by the Editors of the Shrine of Wisdom (Surrey, England: The Shrine of Wisdom, 1965 edition), 17.
14. The egoic-self refers to the self-conscious awareness of personhood as distinct from the ground of Being.
15. Don Richard Riso and Russ Hudson, *The Wisdom of the Enneagram* (New York: Bantam Books, 1999), 22.
16. Dionysius, *Mystical Theology*, 9.
17. Ibid., 13.
18. Ibid., 34.
19. Harvey D. Egan S.J., *Christian Mysticism* (Eugene, OR: Wipf & Stock, 1998 ed.), 2.
20. Thomas Merton, *Conjectures of a Guilty Bystander* (Kent, England: Burns & Oates, 1995 ed.), 181.
21. Evelyn Underhill, *Mysticism: The Development of Humankind's Spiritual Consciousness* (London: Bracken, 1995 edition), 457.
22. Dionysius, *Mystical Theology*, 41.
23. Underhill, *Mysticism*, 169–172.
24. Egan, *Christian Mysticism*, 305–316.
25. Richard J. Foster, *Prayer: Finding the Heart's True Home* (HarperSanFrancisco, 1992), 164.
26. Ibid., 157. Contemplative union with the divine is an unmediated, direct experience

of God. Scripture says we come to God by faith in the substitutionary atonement mediated by Jesus Christ (1 Tm 2:5).

27. *Apophatic:* This is the path of negation or, the *via negativa*, which attempts to describe God only by what he is not. It is the way of "unknowing."
28. Egan, *Christian Mysticism*, 11.
29. *Kataphatic:* This is the path of affirmation, or the *via positiva*, which uses metaphor and image to describe God.
30. This is a process very similar to Buddhist mindfulness that alters consciousness.
31. Egan, *Christian Mysticism*, 49.
32. Wayne Teasdale, *The Mystic Heart* (Novato, CA: New World Library, 1999), 269.
33. Thomas Keating, *Open Heart, Open Mind* (New York: Continuum, 1986, 1992), 53.
34. The "false self."
35. Egan, *Christian Mysticism*, 14.
36. Anonymous fourteenth-century English author, *The Cloud of Unknowing* (New York: Doubleday, 1973), 19.
37. J. Phillip Newell, *Listening for the Heartbeat of God* (New York: Paulist Press, 1997), 23–27.
38. Matthew Fox, *The Coming of the Cosmic Christ* (San Francisco: Harper & Row, 1988), 228.
39. Ibid., 239. Fox advocates building Native American sweat lodges at every school, seminary, and church in order to train a generation of mystical shamans.
40. René Querido, *The Golden Age of Chartres* (New York: Floris Books/Anthroposophic Press, 1987), 24–25.
41. Ibid., 14, 15, 32.
42. Ibid., 40.
43. Ibid., 15.
44. Ibid., 39.
45. Ibid., 51.
46. Ibid., 116.
47. Merton, *Conjectures of a Guilty Bystander*, 260.
48. www.gracecathedral.org/enrichment/crypt/cry_19970701.shtml.
49. Helen Curry, *The Way of the Labyrinth* (New York: Penguin Compass, 2000), ix.
50. Ibid., xi.
51. Lauren Artress, *Walking a Sacred Path: Rediscovering the Labyrinth as a Spiritual Tool* (New York: Riverhead Books, 1995), 2.
52. Ibid., 67.
53. www.yfc.co.uk/labyrinth/online.html.
54. Querido, Golden Age of Chartres, 18.
55. https://www.wisdomuniversity.org/Chartres/dates.htm.
56. https://www.wisdomuniversity.org/Chartres/intensives-VII.htm.
57. https://www.wisdomuniversity.org/Chartres/the-seven-intensives.htm.

58. https://www.wisdomuniversity.org/Chartres/intensives-VII.htm.
59. www.cosm.org/chartres.html.
60. https://www.wisdomuniversity.org/Chartres/dates.htm.
61. *The Cloud of Unknowing* (New York: Doubleday, 1973), 139.
62. Ibid., 56.
63. Ibid., 64. 1 Pt 1:18–19 tells us we were redeemed "with the precious blood, as of a lamb unblemished and spotless, the blood of Christ."
64. *The Cloud of Unknowing*, 3.
65. Tony Jones, *Soul Shaper* (El Cajon, CA: Youth Specialties Books, 2003), 71–80.
66. Sweet, *Quantum Spirituality*, xi.
67. Spencer Burke, "From the Third Floor to the Garage," Mike Yaconelli, ed., *Stories of Emergence* (Grand Rapids, MI: Emergent YS, Zondervan, 2003), 36.
68. John Cordelier, *The Spiral Way* (New York: Cosimo Classics, first published in 1922, 2004 edition), 167–68. John Cordelier is the pen name of Evelyn Underhill.
69. Ken Wilber, *Integral Spirituality* (Boston & London: Integral, 2006), 95–98.
70. Jean Houston, *The Hero and the Goddess* (New York: Ballantine, 1992), 22.
71. Richard Foster, *Spiritual Classics* (HarperSanFrancisco, Renovaré, 2000), 256.
72. Underhill, *The Spiral Way*, 8–9.
73. Ibid., 24–25.
74. Ibid., 77.
75. Ibid., 162, 165.
76. Pierre Teilhard de Chardin, *Christianity and Evolution* (New York: A Harvest Book, 2002), 53.
77. Ibid., 130.
78. Pierre Teilhard de Chardin, *The Phenomenon of Man* (New York: Harper Torchbooks, 1961), 21
79. Marilyn Ferguson, *Aquarius Now: Radical Common Sense and Reclaiming Our Personal Sovereignty* (Boston: Weiser, 2005), 47.
80. Ibid., 182.
81. www.awakeningmind.org.
82. www.global-mindshift.org.
83. www.contemplativemind.org.
84. Merton, *Zen and the Birds of Appetite*, 50–51.
85. Thomas Merton, edited from his original notebooks, *The Asian Journals of Thomas Merton* (New York: New Directions, 1975), 34.
86. Ibid., 308.
87. Ibid., 124–25.
88. Ibid., 82.
89. Merton, *Asian Journals*, 258.
90. Keating, *Open Heart, Open Mind*, 46, 49.
91. Teasdale, *Mystic Heart*, 41.

92. The term "Trungpa" designates one who is thought to be a reincarnation of a llama. Rinpoche is a title of honor meaning "Precious One."
93. Teasdale, *Mystic Heart*, 42.
94. Susan Szpakowski, ed., *Speaking of Silence: Christians and Buddhists in Dialogue* (Halifax, Nova Scotia: Vajradhatu Publications, 2005 edition), vii.
95. Teasdale, *Mystic Heart*, 42.
96. Szpakowski, ed., *Speaking of Silence*, 130.
97. www.peacecouncil.org/peacecouncilors.html.
98. www.goldensufi.org/Boulder.html.
99. www.contemplativemind.org/about/council.html.
100. www.contemplativemind.org/about/history.html#ninety2.
101. www.contemplativemind.org/about/council.html.
102. www.contemplativemind.org/programs.
103. www.contemplativemind.org/practices/subnav/jesusprayer.htm.
104. Qi Gong is an ancient Chinese religion based on manipulation of "Qi" the universal energy force believed to be in everything.
105. Sufism is the mystical branch of Islam.
106. Mindfulness is the altered state of consciousness achieved in Buddhist meditation, which gives the illusion of transcendent reality beyond the plane of outward reality and rational thought.
107. www.contemplativemind.org/practices/subnav/prayer.htm.
108. Mandalas are particularly associated with Tibetan Buddhism, but varying forms of mandalas are found in many indigenous religions. The mandala is a cosmic map for evolution of consciousness through which the "yogin" unites with a deity in the center of the mandala and comes to experience his own body as a microcosm of the whole universe. See John Bowker, ed., *The Oxford Dictionary of World Religions* (Oxford Univ. Press, 1999), 610.
109. www.integralinstitute.org/public/static/abthistory.aspx.
110. it.integralinstitute.org/public/static/integralchristianity.aspx. Integral Christianity is a pagan spirituality understanding Christ as the unifying power of cosmic consciousness, the means of attaining the state of non-dual, monistic reality.
111. Ibid. In this context, "consciousness" refers to the state of mystical experience of reality as "integral" or One.
112. www.jeanhouston.org/lectures/un.html.
113. Ibid.
114. Richard Foster, *Celebration of Discipline* (San Francisco: Harper & Row, 1978), 22, 173–79.
115. Richard Foster and Emilie Griffin, ed. *Spiritual Classics* (New York: HarperCollins, 2000), 17–21.
116. Ibid., 43–47.
117. Ibid., 205–209.

118. Ibid., 253–57.
119. Ibid., 320–26.
120. Ibid., 217–24.
121. Ibid., 217.
122. http://it.integralinstitute.org/public/static/integralchristianity.aspx.
123. Foster, *Spiritual Classics*, 326.
124. Pierre Teilhard de Chardin, *Hymn of the Universe* (New York: Harper & Row, 1961), 23–28.
125. www.ymsp.org/about/history.html, Sleepy Hollow Presbyterian Church was also a partner in the project.
126. Mark Yaconelli, *Growing Souls: Experiments in Contemplative Youth Ministry* (Grand Rapids, MI: Zondervan 2007), 25.
127. www.willowcreek.org/news/3_17_04/ordinary.asp.
128. www.randomhouse.com/catalog/display.pperl/9780877888659.html; www.randomhouse.com/catalog/display.pperl?isbn=9780877889434; www.willowcreek.org/news/3_17_04/ordinary.asp.
129. Tilden Edwards, *Spiritual Friend* (New York: Paulist Press, 1980), 18.
130. Ruth Haley Barton, "The Art and Practice of Discernment" (a talk give at the National Pastors Convention, San Diego, CA, 2005). The contemplative understanding of the preexistence of the soul is derived from the Platonic teaching of the soul's deliverance through successive reincarnations into different bodies. It is a thoroughly pagan concept, denying the Scriptural teaching that God creates unique persons, body and soul, when he knits them together in their mother's womb (Ps 139:13-16).
131. www.willowcreek.com/wcanews/story.asp?id=WN02I42007.
132. David G. Benner with Alice Fryling, "The Enneagram: A Tool of Spiritual Transformation," *Conversations: A Forum for Authentic Transformation*, vol 3:2 (2005): 35.
133. Alice Fryling, "Understanding the Enneagram: Insights for Spiritual Transformation" (Critical Concerns Course, National Pastors Convention, San Diego, CA, 2007).
134. From listserve notification (February 13, 2006) of retreat held April 23–25, 2006.
135. Robert Webber, Editor, *Listening to the Beliefs of Emerging Churches* (Grand Rapids, MI: Zondervan, 2007), 120.
136. Sweet, *Quantum Spirituality*, 148, 253.
137. Tony Jones, *The Sacred Way* (Grand Rapids, MI: Zondervan, 2005), 127.
138. Jill Kimberly Hartwell Geoffrion and Elizabeth Catherine Nagel, *The Labyrinth and the Enneagram* (Cleveland, OH: The Pilgrim Press, 2001), 3, 5.
139. Jerome Wagner, *The Enneagram Spectrum of Personality Styles* (Portland, OR: Metamorphosis Press, 1996), 1.
140. Sir John R. Sinclair, *The Alice Bailey Inheritance* (Wellingborough, UK: Turnstone Press, 1984), 118–119.

141. Richard Rohr and Andreas Ebert, *The Enneagram: A Christian Perspective* (New York: Crossroad, 2006), 8.
142. Mitch Pacwa, *Catholics and the New Age* (Cincinnati, OH: Servant Books, 1992), 101.
143. Ibid., 112.
144. Don Richard Riso and Russ Hudson, *The Wisdom of the Enneagram* (New York: Bantam, 1999), 9.
145. Ibid.
146. Ibid., 28.
147. www.gurdjieffstudiesprogram.org/fourthway.htm.
148. Kathleen Riordan Speeth and Ira Friedlander, *Gurdjieff: Seeker of the Truth* (New York: Harper & Row, 1980), 35.
149. G. I. Gurdjieff, *Meetings with Remarkable Men* (New York: Penguin, 2002), viii.
150. Ibid., viii.
151. Sufi mystics.
152. Speeth and Friedlander, *Gurdjieff: Seeker of the Truth*, 36.
153. Ibid., 35–36.
154. Pacwa, *Catholics and the New Age*, 112–13.
155. J. G. Bennett, *Enneagram Studies* (York Beach, Maine: Weiser, 1988), 17.
156. http://en.wikipedia.org/wiki/Ouroboros.
157. Riso and Hudson, *Wisdom of the Enneagram*, 21. The dedication page says "We dedicate this book to the Ground of Being, the One from Whom we have come, and to Whom we shall return." This is the monism of Neoplatonism.
158. Pacwa, *Catholics and the New Age*, 113.
159. Speeth and Friedlander, *Gurdjieff: Seeker of the Truth*, 20.
160. Riso and Hudson, *Wisdom of the Enneagram*, 21.
161. Sinclair, *The Alice Bailey Inheritance*, 116–19.
162. Rohr and Ebert, *The Enneagram: A Christian Perspective*, 7.
163. Pacwa, *Catholics and the New Age*, 101.
164. Fryling, "Understanding the Enneagram."
165. Riso and Hudson, *Wisdom of the Enneagram*, 22.
166. Pacwa, *Catholics and the New Age*, 101,104,114.
167. www.claudionaranjo.net/navbar_english/autobiography_english.html.
168. Pacwa, *Catholics and the New Age*, 96–98.
169. www.enneagramspectrum.com/articles/history.htm.
170. Wagner, *The Enneagram Spectrum of Personality Styles*, 135.
171. Ibid., 17.
172. Ibid., 30–31.
173. Benner and Fryling, "The Enneagram: A Tool for Spiritual Transformation," 35.
174. Fryling, "Understanding the Enneagram."
175. Ibid.

176. www.enneagram.com/downloads.html.
177. Riso and Hudson, *Wisdom of the Enneagram*, 9.
178. Rohr and Ebert, *The Enneagram: A Christian Perspective*, 22, 29.
179. Ibid., 48.
180. National Pastors Convention, San Diego, 2007.
181. Fryling, "Understanding the Enneagram."
182. Peter Jones, *Gospel Truth, Pagan Lies: Can You Tell the Difference?* (Escondido, CA: Main Entry, 1999).

CHAPTER 14: HOLLYWOOD – PELSUE

1. Bill Moyers, "Of Myth and Men" *Time* (April 26, 1999).
2. Ibid.
3. C. S. Lewis, *The Weight of Glory and Other Addresses* (Grand Rapids, MI: Eerdmans, 1965), 98.
4. Ken Wilber, commentary *The Utlimate Matrix Collection*. Produced and written by Larry and Andy Wachowski. 2004. DVD. Warner Home Video.
5. Ibid.
6. Guillermo Del Toro, commentary, *Pan's Labyrinth*, produced, written, and directed by Guillermo Del Toro (DVD 2006, Optimum Home Entertainment).
7. Ibid.
8. Sting, *Broken Music* (New York: Dial Press, 2003), 5–10.
9. Tim Challies, "Book Review–The Secret," www.challies.com (June 11, 2007).
10. Rhonda Byrne, *The Secret*. (New York: Atria Books, 2006), 183.
11. Destouches, Philippe Nericault, *Le Glorieux* (1732), Act II, scene V.

CHAPTER 16: OT RESPONSE – HEISER

1. See Gn 10:1–32 for a list of the nations dispersed at Babel (recorded in Gn 11:1–9). See also Dt 4:19–20; 32:8–9. On the latter, textual scholars have agreed that the best reading is that God divided up the nations according to the number of "the sons of God" (ESV), not the "sons of Israel" (NIV). The reading "sons of God" is supported by the presence of that reading in the Septuagint translation of the Old Testament and the Dead Sea Scrolls, as well as the fact that Israel did not exist as a nation at the time of Babel, a time prior to the call of Abraham. Note the absence of Israel from the nations of the earth in Gn 10:1–32. For a detailed discussion of Dt 32:8–9, see Michael S. Heiser, "Dt 32:8 and the Sons of God," *Bibliotheca Sacra* 158:629 (2001): 52–74.
2. During the patriarchal period, marriage within one's own extended clan was the norm (cf. Gn 11:29; 20:12; 24:15; 28:9). In the Mosaic Law, the specific prohibition against intermarriage given to Israel refers to the Canaanites, so as to avoid idolatry (Ex 34:15–16; Dt 7:3–4). Specific Mosaic legal issues with respect to the Ammo-

nites and the Moabites (Dt 23:3) prohibited marriage between their men and Israelite women but permitted Israelite men to marry their women (Ru 1:4). Outside of Canaan and the regions on the other side of Jordan, intermarriage laws were more lax (Dt 21:10–14), though the worship of only the God of Israel remained constant (Dt 6:4–5).

3. Lv 12:2; 15:16–18; 21:18.
4. Dt 14:21; 22:11.
5. By this description I do not mean to say that a being that was created to live without a body (e.g., an angel) cannot assume corporeal, physical form. There are several such instances in the Bible (Gn 18; 19: 1–11; 32:22–32; cf. Hos 12:3–4).
6. The translation is the author's.
7. J. H. Tigay, "Deuteronomy," *The JPS Torah Commentary* (Philadelphia: Jewish Publication Society, 1996): 465.
8. See Jer 32:35; Ez 20:26, 31 (scholars are certain that these texts refer to human sacrifice in light of the context of Jer 7:31; 19:5; Ez 16:20–21; 23:37, 39).
9. On Molech, see Lv 18:21; 20:2–5; 2 Kgs 23:10; Jer 32:35.
10. Ann Jeffers, *Magic and Divination in Ancient Palestine and Syria* (Leiden: E. J. Brill, 1996), 96–99.
11. Ibid., 78–80 and Tigay, *Deuteronomy*, 173.
12. Jeffers, *Magic and Divination*, 74–77.
13. David Noel Freedman, *The Anchor Bible Dictionary* (New York: Doubleday, 1992), 4: 468.
14. Ibid. See Is 3:3; 20; 26:16; Jer 8:17; Eccl 10:11.
15. Jeffers, *Magic and Divination*, 65–69.
16. Freedman, *Anchor Bible Dictionary*, 4:469.
17. It is impossible to be completely certain whether the *ʾôb* is a non-human spirit or the spirit of a human dead person, but the former is quite likely. For example, Is. 8:19 contrasts "the dead" with "the living." If non-human spirits were meant by "the dead" this contrast would carry less weight, since non-human spirits were conceived of as living beings. This verse suggests "the dead" refer to human dead.
18. For full treatments of divination terminology in the OT and other ancient Near Eastern cultures, see Jeffers, *Magic and Divination*; F. Cryer, "Divination in Ancient Israel and Its Near Eastern Environment: A Socio-Historical Investigation," *Journal for the Study of the Old Testament Supplement* (Sheffield Univ. Press, 1994); J. A. Scurlock, *Magical Means of Dealing with Ghosts in Ancient Mesopotamia* (Dissertation, Univ. of Chicago 1988); J. Lust, "On Wizards and Prophets," *Studies on Prophecy*, VTSup 26 (Leiden 1974): 133–42; B. B. Schmidt, "Israel's Beneficient Dead: Ancestor Cult and Necromacy in Ancient Israelite Religion and Tradition, FAT 11 (Tübingen 1994).
19. As a result, we will not consider practices such as casting lots, consulting the ephod, and use of the Urim and Thummim. Casting lots was also a widely recog-

nized form of divination across the ancient Near Eastern world, but it was never condemned in the Old Testament. See W. H. Hallo, "The First Purim," *Biblical Archaeologist* 46 (1983): 19–29. It was assumed that this was a means by which God would show his will and dispense it (Prv 16:33; Jb 18:6–10).

20. Freedman, 4:469. For a fuller discussion of astrological terms, see Jeffers, *Magic and Divination*, 146–154.
21. See L. Oppenheim, "The Interpretation of Dreams in the Ancient Near East," *Transactions of the American Philosophical Society N.S.* 46 (1956): 178–353; Jeffers, *Magic and Divination*, 125–143.
22. The situation of Joseph with his divine cup is ambiguous. We are not told how he used it, and there is no story that involves its use. We can presume from Joseph's character that his contact with God was not "self-willed" as though manipulating a deity.
23. After a person was chosen to be the conduit of blessing and divine revelation, God would be open to contact from that person through prayer or other means that would be classified as divinatory. See the discussion.
24. Gn 5:22–24; 6:9.
25. Gn 12, 15, 18; 26:1–5; 28:10–13; 31:11–13; 32:22–30.
26. Dt 34:10; Ex.24:12–18; 33:7–11; Dt 31:14–23; Jo 5:13–15.
27. 1 Sm 3; Jgs 6:11–23.
28. Is 6; Ez 1; Jer 1.
29. Acts 2:1–4; 9:1–9. With the disciples, it is fruitful to note the presence of flames at their encounter and Old Testament encounters. In their case, they were encountered by the Spirit, since the new element in God's program was to spread the commissioning to all believers through the Spirit.
30. Mt 3:13–17.

Chapter 17: Protokos – Hamilton

1. Philip Yancey, *Rumors of another World* (Grand Rapids: Zondervan, 2003), 182.
2. J. B. Lightfoot, *St. Paul's Epistles to the Colossians and to Philemon* (London: Macmillan, 1875).
3. See Peter T. O'Brien, "Colossians, Philemon," *Word Biblical Commentary*, vol. 44: (Waco: Word, 1982): xxxi; and David A. DeSilva, *An Introduction to the New Testament: Contexts, Methods & Ministry Formation* (Downers Grove: InterVarsity, 2004), 692.
4. See Clinton E. Arnold's groundbreaking work, *The Colossian Syncretism: The Interface between Christianity and Folk Belief at Colossae* (Grand Rapids: Baker, 1996), 158–194, for a thorough defense for identifying the *stoicheia tou kosmou* in Col 2:8 and 2:20 as evil spiritual powers frequently associated with and standing behind the physical elements and astral bodies.
5. This reasoning is based on Paul's use of the verb *embateuw* in Col 2:18, a technical

term in local mystery initiation rites. See Arnold, *Colossian Syncretism*.

6. DeSilva, *Introduction*, 694.
7. Handley C. G. Moule, *Colossian and Philemon Studies* (London: Pickering & Inglis, 1945), 75.
8. See especially, Steven M. Baugh, "The Poetic Form of Colossians 1:15–20," *Westminster Theological Journal* 47 (1985): 227–244; and Steven M. Baugh, "Firstborn over All Creation," *Kerux* 1 (1986): 28–34. I am indebted to Dr. Baugh's insightful analysis throughout this chapter for both form and substance.
9. The title comes from Moule, *Colossian and Philemon Studies*, 75. The diagram of the passage is simplified and adapted from Steven M. Baugh, "Poetic Form of Colossians 1:15–20," 227–244.
10. Baugh helpfully illustrates the overall poetic structure: "The effect resembles an hourglass with its focus on the narrow part in the middle; or a butterfly turned on its side with its two wings colored by the same markings of spots and lines and joined in the center by its body." Baugh, "Firstborn over All Creation," 29.
11. Other pairings are Creator and Redeemer or Lord of Old Creation and Lord of New Creation.
12. Moule, *Colossian and Philemon Studies*, 75.
13. O'Brien, *Colossians, Philemon*, 44.
14. Baugh, "Poetic Form of Colossians 1:15–20," 31.
15. In the LXX version of Gn 49:3, both "firstborn" (*prototokos*) and "beginning" (*arche*) are employed in the same context to convey the idea of the firstborn being the founder of a people. See O'Brien, *Colossians, Philemon*, 50.
16. Ibid., 53.
17. Ibid., 54.
18. "Undo" by Rush of Fools (www.rushoffools.com/product/880.htm).
19. C. S. Lewis, *The Lion, the Witch and the Wardrobe* (Harmondsworth, England: Penguin, 1973 repr.), 148.
20. J. R. R. Tolkien, *The Return of the King* (New York: Random House, 1986), 246.

CHAPTER 18: ANTITHESIS – JONES

1. Ned O'Gorman, Common grounds online (September 17, 2008).
2. John Franke, "Reforming Theology: Toward a Postmodern Reformed Dogmatics" WTJ 65 (2003): 19.
3. Kester Brewin, *Signs of Emergence: A Vision for Church that Is Organic/Networked/Decentralized/Bottom-up/Communal/Flexible/Always Evolving* (Grand Rapids: Baker, 2007) 85, 92, 96.
4. Bible quotations in this chapter are from the English Standard Version, unless otherwise noted.
5. Ephesians references contain only chapter and verse, unless in a list.
6. μάταιος– הֶבֶל.

7. War Scroll 4:12 (*goe hebel*), cp 6:6; 9:9 ("the seven nations of vanity").
8. Clinton E. Arnold, *The Colossian Syncretism: The Interface between Christianity and Folk Belief at Colossae* (Grand Rapids: Baker Books, 1996), 232.
9. Ibid., 123.
10. Thomas Berry, *The Great Work: Our Way into the Future* (New York: Bell Tower, 1999), 177–78.
11. www.cosm.org.
12. See 1 Thes 2:12 from the opposite perspective: "we…charged (testified to) you to walk in a manner worthy of God." The context is verse 4: "as we have been approved by God to be entrusted with the gospel."
13. Robert Turcan, *The Cults of the Roman Empire* (Oxford: Blackwell, 1996), 256.
14. Clinton Arnold, *Power and Magic: The Concept of Power in Ephesians* (Grand Rapids: Baker, 1989).
15. Turcan, *Cults*, 30, 33.
16. Brewin, *Signs*, 85.
17. Michael York, *Pagan Theology: Paganism as a World Religion* (New York Univ. Press, 2003), 38.
18. See Ps 89:26; Mal 2:10; Is 8:4 ("father in perpetuity") 63:16; 64:8; Jer 3:4.
19. See the teaching of Jesus, who shows that in his creative work and providential care over creation, God is acting as Father: Mt 5:45, 6:26, 6:32, 7:11, 10:29, 11:25, 18:10; Lk 10:21 ("Father, Lord of heaven and earth"); Jn 5:26.
20. James Montgomery, "Angels, from the Realms of Glory" (1816).
21. Ken Wilber, *A Theory of Everything: An Integral Vision for Business, Politics, Science and Spirituality* (Boston: Shambhala, 2001), 80–82.
22. Dn 8:22.
23. Francis Watson, "Writing the Mystery: Christ and Reality in the Letter to the Ephesians," a paper presented to the Later Pauline Epistles Section, *Society of Biblical Literature*, (Denver 2001).
24. Eph 5:3; 5:5; Rom 1:24; 6:19; 2 Cor 12:21; Gal 5:19; Col 3:5.
25. See Ez 9:11: "The land that you are entering, to take possession of it, is a land impure with the impurity of the peoples of the lands, with their abominations (תּוֹעֵבָה βδέλυγμα) that have filled it from end to end with their uncleanness (ἀκαθαρσίαις αὐτῶν). See also Lv 18:27: "for the people of the land, who were before you, did all of these abominations, so that the land became unclean"; Lv 18:22; 20:13, both of which use the term for pagan abomination (βδέλυγμα) in their prohibition against homosexuality.
26. Jude 1:4: "For certain people pervert the grace of our God into sensuality" (ἀσελγεία). In verse seven that sensuality is defined as the homosexuality of Sodom.
27. 1 Thes 4:4: "that each one of you know how to control his own body in holiness and honor," cp.1 Thes 4:5: "not in the passion of lust like the Gentiles who do not know God."

28. Lv 18:3. See 20:23 and 11:45.
29. See 1 Cor 5:9–12.
30. Linda Lowen, *About.com Women's Issues Guide* (December 18, 2007).
31. See Evan Silverstein, "Jane Spahr acquittal on same-sex wedding charges is overturned," *Presbyterian News Service* (Louisville, KY: August 27, 2007). The failure of the Anglican Church to do serious antithesis thinking about homosexual bishops shows in the fact that Archbishop Rowan Williams, head of worldwide Anglicanism, is now proposing to bring the two sides together with the help of "professionally facilitated conversations," that is, professional mediators. See "Archbishop of Canterbury's Advent letter," *Anglican Communion News Service* (December 14, 2007).
32. June Singer, *Androgyny: Towards a New Theory of Sexuality* (London: Routledge and Kegan, 1977), 22.
33. Is 44:15.
34. Translation mine. See 2 Cor 6:15: τίς γὰρ μετοχὴ δικαιοσύνῃ καὶ ἀνομίᾳ, literally, "what partaking is there between righteousness and lawlessness?"
35. Translation mine.
36. See Brewin, *Signs*, 102: "...we must open ourselves to [culture] and adapt to it...to allow free transfer each way...culturally and socially we need to be dependent on [our local communities]."
37. Jer 1:5 cp. Gal 1:15.
38. See Rom 2:16, 16:25; Gal 1:11, 2:2; 2 Tm 2:8 cp. "our Gospel" (2 Cor 4:3; 1 Thes 1:5; 2 Thes 2:14) or the "Gospel entrusted to me" (1 Thes 2:4, and Gal 2:7).

Subject & Name Index

A

Abbott, Tony *56*
Abortion *245, 278*
Abuse *19, 51, 95, 103, 125, 128, 215*
Adams, Betty C. *85*
Adams, Carol *173, 285*
Adler, Margot *52*
Age of Aquarius *31–32, 37–38*
Alchemy *17, 21, 144, 148–49, 191*
Aliens *16, 19, 25–29*
 Abduction *24–27, 273*
 UFOs *18, 24–27, 273*
Allah *195*
Altered States of Consciousness *19, 39, 82, 212*
Alternative Spirituality *156, 245, 247*
 Celtic Spirituality *50, 190*
Ancestors *13, 75, 92, 105, 116–17, 121, 126, 133–38, 141–42, 206*
Angels *18, 20, 28, 40, 47, 63, 67, 95, 203, 220, 223, 233, 236, 247, 254, 264, 296*
Animal Guides *26, 92, 203*
Animism *87–88, 102, 105, 110, 132, 134, 136–37, 280*
Aquinas, Thomas *161*
Archetypes *26, 33, 148, 150–152, 208*
Aristotle *61*
Arnold, Clinton *261*
Artress, Lauren *49–50, 77, 191–92, 275, 279, 290*
Ascended Masters *22–23*
Astrology *10, 31–43, 50, 82, 144, 148–49, 191, 200, 237, 280, 283*
 Astral Projection *196*
 Birth Chart *31, 33–38, 40, 42, 43*
Astronomy *32, 41, 161*
Avatar *36–37*

B

Baha'i *71*
Bailey, Alice *200, 293–94*
Barna, George *205*
Barth, Karl *181*
Barton, Ruth Haley *197–98, 293*
Becquerel, Henri *157*
Bell, Rob *186, 289*
Berry, Thomas *261, 299*
Bhagavad-Gita *23*
Bird, Isobel *56*
Black Elk Speaks *17*
Black Madonna *190*
Blavatsky, Helena *21–24, 29, 273*
Blood Sacrifice *96, 103, 117, 122, 124, 128, 202, 236, 250, 255, 262, 288, 291*
Body of God *83, 174, 176–77, 181, 196*
Bohm, David *162–63, 284*
Bohme, Jacob *23*
Bohr, Niels *157, 163*
Bonewits, Isaac *50, 274*
Book of Shadows *56*
Borg, Marcus *77–79, 279*
Born, Max *157*

Brazilian Confession of Faith *106*
Brewin, Kester *259, 263, 298*
Buddhism *13–14, 23, 72, 76, 79, 132, 144, 146–47, 161, 167, 172, 191, 194, 201, 212–13, 279, 290, 292*
  Naropa Institute for Tibetan Buddhism *194*
Bulwer–Lytton, George Edward *20*
Burke, Spencer *192, 291*

C

Cabot, Laurie *49, 275*
Calhoun, Adele Ahlberg *197*
Calvin, John *106, 112*
Campbell, Joseph *26, 207–8, 273*
Candomblé *98, 109–11*
Cannibalism *103, 106–7*
Canon of Scripture *53, 85*
Capra, Fritzjof *164, 166, 284*
Cavalli, Tom *149–50, 283*
Chain of Being *110, 173*
Chakras *51, 200*
De Chardin, Pierre–Teilhard *191, 193, 195–96, 291, 293*
Chartres Cathedral *76, 190–192, 290–291*
  Erotic Sciences of Sacred Art *191*
Children's Literature *56*
Child Sacrifice *86, 94, 234*
Christian Spirituality *219–222, 224, 227, 229–231, 270*
Christy, John *184, 287*
Churches, Denominations
  Anglican *72, 300*
  Baptist *71*
  Catholic *98, 107–8, 110, 214*
  Emergent *186, 198*
  Episcopal *52, 71–72, 75, 79–82, 84, 278–80, 319*
  Evangelical *281*
  Lutheran *52, 76, 278–79*
  Methodist *52, 57*
  Neocharismatic *111*
  Neopentecostal *111*
  Pentecostals *110–11*
  Presbyterian *7, 52, 269, 293, 300*
  Roman Catholic Church *52, 108, 110, 214*
  United Church of Christ *52*
  Willow Creek *197–98*
Church Fathers *15, 72, 81*
Cizik, Rich *288*
Clairvoyance *50*
Climatology *183, 287*
Colfer, Eoin *56*
Colossian Heresy *246, 249*
Confucius *23, 132–35, 137–38, 172, 282*
Consciousness *9, 24–26, 29, 67, 72, 76–77, 82–83, 88, 107, 146, 150, 153, 166, 168, 186, 188–90, 192–95, 197, 199, 200–202, 210–11, 222, 229, 230, 248, 261, 278–79, 288, 290, 292*
Contemplative Spirituality *57, 85, 118, 186–200, 202*
  Center for Contemplative Mind in Society *195*
  Centering Prayer *192, 194, 197, 201*
  Contemplative Silence *189, 195*
  Prayer Journey *191*
  The Jesus Prayer *195*
Cordovero, Moses *64*
Cosmology *23, 77, 85, 175, 181, 191, 208, 220*
Countries & Continents
  Africa *13, 109, 119, 121, 129, 130, 281, 282, 318, 323*

Asia *199, 321*
Australia *57, 322*
Brazil *44, 97–99, 104, 106–7, 109, 110–12, 281, 319*
Canada *321*
China *131–32, 282, 321*
England *22*
Europe *22, 45–46, 106–8, 149, 159, 264*
France *49, 76, 106, 320*
India *22–23*
Kenya *323*
Mauritius *318*
Mexico *17, 113*
New Zealand *323*
Nigeria *118, 122, 323*
North America *245*
Portugal *107*
South Africa *13, 281–82*
South America *17, 98, 100, 102, 105*
Covenant *89, 96, 221, 224, 232, 240*
Creation *41, 47, 53, 60–66, 69–70, 78–84, 93, 107, 110, 154, 161, 172, 174–75, 190, 193, 196, 199, 201, 205–6, 214, 219, 220–24, 228, 249–57, 262–64, 267, 269, 278–81, 284, 287–88, 298*
Cross, The *75, 80–81, 92, 97, 215, 250–51, 255*
Crowley, Aleister *21*
Curie, Pierre & Marie *108*
Curley, Marianne *56*
Curse(s) *51, 56, 88, 138, 185, 216, 223–24*

D

Dalai Lama *161*
Daoist *72, 131–36, 138–42, 146–47, 282–83*
Dass, Ram *195*
Davies, Paul *169*
Davis, Avram *60, 63*
Davis, Philip G. *46*
Dawkins, Richard *203*
Deism *161*
De Leon, Moses *60*
Demons *16–17, 20–21, 40–41, 90, 100, 118, 136, 138, 233, 236, 255, 261, 280*
Descartes, Rene *172*
Dialectic *102, 152*
Dionysius *81*
Dirac, Paul *157*
Disney *205–6*
Divination *31, 36, 40–41, 48, 50, 56, 117–20, 124–25, 127, 148, 199, 204, 232–34, 237–39, 241, 243–44, 296–97*
Divine Beings *23*
Divine Spark *63, 66, 82*
Dreams *33, 67–68, 88, 92, 95, 97, 118–19, 144, 208, 237–38, 264–65*
Druidism *50, 172, 190*
Dyad *74*

E

Ecclesiology *269*
Ecology *50, 87, 105, 171–74, 177, 185, 285*
Animal rights *173*
Cornwall Alliance *184, 286–88*
Earth First! *173–74*
Evangelical Climate Initiative *288*
Greens *173*
Houghton, Sir John *288*
Lovelock, James *288*
Ecstasy *188*

Eden *15, 51, 53, 186, 201, 221, 233, 241*
Egan, Harvey *187, 189, 289*
Einstein, Albert *157–58, 162, 284*
Eisler, Riane *55, 276*
Eliade, Mircea *84, 280*
Eller, Cynthia *51, 54, 275*
Emanation *63–64*
Emergent, Emerging *12, 186, 192, 198, 259, 263, 291*
Empowerment *56, 122*
Enchantment *58, 235, 237*
Enlightenment *17, 32, 81, 161, 178, 245*
Enneagram *198–201, 289, 293–295*
  Naranjo, Claudio *200*
Epistemology *131, 169, 181, 185*
Eschatology *269–70*
Evangelical *47, 52, 94, 110–12, 186, 196–97, 283, 286, 288*
Evans, Jane *40*
Eve *15, 44, 52–53, 55, 145, 178, 186, 201, 221, 228*

F

Fairies *28*
False Self *187–88, 200, 290*
Familiars *50*
Farrar, Stewart *68, 277*
Feminism *44, 46–47, 51, 54, 84, 173, 177, 274–75*
  Divine Feminine *73–74, 85, 190*
  Divine Mother *191*
Ferguson, Marilyn *193*
Fertility *48, 54, 111*
Festivals *58, 115–16, 246*
Fetishes *124, 126*
Films & TV *203, 210–11*
  Buffy the Vampire Slayer *56*
  Charmed *56*
  Contact *16*
  Dragonfly *103*
  Gladiator *210*
  Golden Compass *203*
  Harry Potter *204*
  Lord of the Rings *209*
  Matrix *203, 209–10*
  Pan's Labyrinth *211*
  Pocahontas *205*
  Serpent and the Rainbow *103*
  Star Wars *207, 209*
  The Lion King *203, 205*
  What the Bleep do We Know? *161*
Firstborn (Christ Jesus) *252, 254–55, 257, 298*
Folk Islam *119*
Food Offerings *141*
Foreman, David *174*
Fortune-telling *50, 148*
Fox, Matthew *72–73, 78, 190, 192, 277, 290*
Frame, John *63, 272, 277*
Franke, John *259, 298*
Freud, Sigmund *143, 146, 156*
Fryling, Alice *198, 201, 293–95*
Funeral Rites, Chinese *140*

G

Gaia *50, 53, 288*
Galileo *161*
Gardner, Gerald *46, 51*
Geffrion, J. K. H. *198*
Gentiles *41, 76, 258, 260, 262, 266–67, 270, 300*
Ghosts *9, 135, 141, 236, 273*
Gilkey, Langdon *120*
Gimbutas, Marija *46*
Global Harmony *105, 116, 127, 175*

Gnosticism *10, 15, 22–23, 56, 61, 63, 68, 71–85, 109, 144, 146–47, 149, 154–55, 214, 277–78, 280, 283–84*
- **Gnostic Christ** *80*
- **Gnostic Gospels**
  - **Acts of Thomas** *74, 263*
  - **Gospel of Mary** *85, 263*
  - **Gospel of Philip** *83, 263*
  - **Gospel of Thomas** *81, 263*
  - **Gospel of Truth** *82*
- **International Order of Gnostic Templars** *278*
- **Valentinian** *81*

God
- **Creator** *14–15, 41, 58, 63, 69, 75, 83–84, 86–90, 97, 102, 107, 110, 113, 159, 161, 168–69, 174, 176, 178, 181, 189, 196, 199, 206, 214, 216, 220–21, 223, 227, 231, 262–69, 288, 298*
- **God Within, The** *77, 82, 191*
- **Holy Spirit** *51, 74, 75, 90, 102, 112, 129, 145, 172, 205, 219, 220, 227, 229, 230, 271*
- **Humans Becoming** *21, 36, 81*
- **Jehovah** *55, 101*
- **Judge** *22, 74, 84*
- **Names of** *74*
- **Trinity** *70, 74, 79, 209, 219, 220, 227–78*

Goethe *149*
Gore, Al *182, 288*
Gospel, The Christian *14, 29, 41, 47, 81–83, 85, 97, 114, 202, 228, 259, 263–64, 270–71, 284, 295, 300*
Govinda, Lama *164*
Grace Cathedral *49, 76, 191, 279*
Green, Arthur *60*
Grey, Alex *192, 261*
Gurdjieff, George Ivanovich *198, 199, 201, 294*

H

Harry Potter *9, 56, 204–5*
Healing *13–14, 16, 44, 50–51, 68, 83, 89, 176*
Heaven *20*
Heisenberg, Werner *157, 160, 163–64, 284*
Hellenistic *187*
Herbalist *235*
Heresy *53, 72, 246, 249*
Hermeneutics *12, 19, 53, 258, 260*
Hermeticism *22*
Hertz, Heinrich *157, 284*
Hinduism *12–13, 23, 26, 37, 51, 71, 76, 79, 144, 146, 159–60, 172, 191*
- **Upanishads** *23*
- **Vedas** *23*

History, Cyclical View of *34, 84, 85*
Holocaust *181*
Holy Grail *212–13*
Horoscope *10, 31–32, 35, 40, 42*
Houghton, Sir John *288*
Household Idols *53, 101, 113*
Houston, Jean *191–92, 195*
Hudson, Russ *199, 201, 289, 294–95*
Huguenots *106*
Humanist *73, 132, 141*
Huxley, Francis *17*
Hypnosis *24, 39*

I

Ichazo, Oscar *200*
Idolatry *11, 53, 86, 94, 99, 100–2, 111, 113–14, 232, 261, 278, 296*
- **High Places** *101*

Ignatius of Loyola *196*
Immanence *50, 63, 100–1, 174, 179, 252, 255, 263*
Immortality *135, 211*
Incantations *112, 117, 122, 124*
Incarnation *19, 37, 52, 81, 126, 153, 175, 193, 219, 223, 229*
Individuation *150, 187*
Ingham, Michael *72–73, 86, 278*
Inner Self *40*
Interfaith *13–15, 36, 72, 76, 79–80, 195, 272*
Intergovernmental Panel on Climate Change *183*
Irenaeus *74, 78*
Islam *47, 71–72, 79, 207*

J

Jesuits *107, 189*
Jewish Renewal *67–68*
Johnson, Elizabeth A. *52*
Johnston, William *189*
Jones, Tony *192, 198, 272*
Judaism *10, 41, 47, 52, 54, 59, 60–61, 65, 66–72, 76, 96, 98, 131, 143, 155, 159–61, 168–69, 207, 213, 215, 235, 243, 261, 277, 279, 296*
Jung, Carl *10, 22, 26, 32–33, 50, 143–56, 207–8, 273, 278, 283–84*

K

Kabbalah *10, 14, 24, 59–69, 144, 191, 213, 276–77*
  Adin Steinsaltz *60*
  Arthur Green *60*
  Aryeh Kaplan *60*
  Bahir *60*
  Daniel Matt *60*
  Gershom Scholem *60*
  Hayim Vital *60*
  Influential Authors *60*
  Isaac Luria *60*
  Isaiah Tishby *60*
  Jacob Immanuel Schochet *60*
  Joseph Dan *60*
  Moses Codovero *60*
  Moses De Leon *60*
  Rabbi Shneur Zalman *60*
  Sefer Yetzirah *60*
  Yehuda Ashlag *60*
  Zalman Schachter–Shalomi *60*
  Zohar *60, 64*
Kant, Immanuel *152*
Kaplan, Aryeh *60–61*
Kardec, Alain *108–9*
Karma *33, 35*
Keating, Thomas *10, 189, 192, 194–95, 197, 202, 290*
Kellogg, Wilfred *27*
Kerr, P. B. *56*
Keyes, Dick *100*
King, Stephen *20*
Kootenay, Adolphus *89*
Kuyper, Abraham *93*
Kyung, Chung Hyun *52*

L

Labyrinth *12, 49–50, 76–77, 83, 190–92, 198, 275, 279–90, 293, 295*
Lady of the Lake *108, 111*
De Laplace, Marquis *169, 285*
Lasky, Kathryn *56*
Lectio Divina *189, 195, 197*
Lerner, Michael *60*
De Lery, Jean *106*
Levy–Strauss, Claude *106*
Lewis, C. S. *208–9, 295, 298*

Logical Positivism *160*
Lone Spirits *139–41*
Lovelock *288*
Lucas, George *207–9*
Luria, Isaac *60, 62*

M

Mack, John *24–27, 29, 273*
Magdalene, Mary *85*
Magdalen Group *76*
Magic, Magick *17, 21–22, 48, 51, 68, 100, 108, 110, 124–25, 127, 129, 204, 237, 256, 277*
Maimonides *61, 64*
Mandala *146–47, 199, 292*
Marriage *36–37, 112, 116–17, 268–69, 295–96*
Masonry *68*
Maternity *55, 91*
Matriarchy *46*
McFague, Sallie *83–84, 174–81, 183, 185, 280, 285*
McLaren, Brian *186, 288*
McLaughlin, John *212*
Mediator *25–26, 112*
Medicine Man *87–89, 92, 94, 127, 206*
Meditatio *189*
Meditation *37, 39–40, 61, 67–68, 121, 131, 194, 196, 200, 261, 270, 292*
Meister Eckhart *23, 190, 196*
Melnyk, Walter *79*
Memory *19, 24*
Menninger, William *192*
Merton, Robert K. *182*
Mesmer *23*
Metaphysics *46, 49, 51, 59, 131, 148–50, 155–62, 165, 167–69, 178*
Mindfulness *201*
Mirandola, Giovanni Pico della *68, 73*
Molnar, Thomas *73, 75, 85, 278*
Monasticism *186–87, 189*
Monism *28, 36, 83, 88, 110, 134, 141–42, 159–61, 164–65, 169, 172, 186, 193, 197, 261, 288, 292*
  Atheistic Monism *167*
  Spiritual Monism *167*
Mormonism *22, 47*
Mosaic *66, 237, 295–96*
Mother Earth *87–89, 91, 94, 97, 190, 193*
Moyers, Bill *207, 295*
Murray, Margaret *45–46*
Music
  Britney Spears *213*
  John McLaughlin *212*
  Mahavishnu Orchestra *212*
  Santana *212–13*
  Sting *211*
  The Police *211*
Mystery *73, 189, 191–92, 262, 275*
Mystery Religions *83*
Mystical Powers *120–23, 127, 130*
Mysticism *22–23, 57, 59, 60, 66, 78, 115, 122, 133, 152, 166, 180, 186, 188–92, 194–95, 200, 202, 227, 229, 277, 284, 289*
Mystics *12, 22, 26, 59, 186, 188–90, 192, 196, 199, 202, 294*
Myth, Mythology *25, 50, 72, 77, 84, 104, 117, 153–54, 196, 207–10, 246, 257, 278, 281*

N

Naess, Arne *173–74, 285*
Nag Hammadi *147, 279*
Naqshbandi *195, 199*

Naranjo *200*
Narby, Jeremy *16,–18, 29, 272*
National Pastors Convention *197, 201, 293, 295*
Native Peoples *52*
- **Aboriginal** *52*
- **Amazon Indians** *16, 30, 103–4, 113*
- **Apurinã** *103*
- **Cherokee** *52, 88*
- **Cree** *87–92*
- **Hausa** *118*
- **Incas** *104*
- **Jejes** *109*
- **Mayas** *104*
- **Native Alaskans** *88*
- **Native Americans** *10, 13, 17, 84, 113, 172, 290*
- **Sioux** *88*
- **Tlingit** *87*
- **Yorubás** *109*

Native Spirituality *92, 95, 97, 104*
Neopaganism *15, 45–46, 49, 154, 171–72, 178–81, 203, 205, 207, 209–13, 245–47, 253, 257*
Neoplatonism *61, 68, 110, 187, 190, 192, 294*
New Age *18, 35, 38, 60–61, 65–69, 144, 160, 167, 186, 190, 192, 275–76, 288, 294*
New Creation *254–55, 298*
New Spirituality *17, 28, 186, 195, 197, 275*
Newton, Isaac *161*
Nietzsche, Friedrich *149*
Nix, Garth *56*
Nyirongo, Leonard *127–128*

O

Occult *17–18, 20–22, 31, 33–34, 36, 38, 41, 44, 47, 51, 56, 68, 69, 75, 85, 108, 119, 125–26, 144, 148–50, 156, 192, 199–200, 204–5, 244, 246*
Occult Books
- **Book of Lies, The** *21*
- **Breakthrough, The** *27*
- **Communion** *27*
- **Confessions of a Drug Fiend** *21*
- **Confessions of Aleister Crowley** *21*
- **Confirmation, the Hard Evidence for Aliens among Us** *27*
- **Drawing Down the Moon:** *52*
- **Magick** *21*
- **Seat of the Soul, The** *28*
- **Secret Doctrine, The** *23*
- **The Theosophist** *22*
- **The Witch Cult in Western Europe** *45*
- **Transformation** *27*
- **Urantia Book, The** *27*
- **Witchcraft Today** *45*

Occult Organizations
- **Cakes for the Queen of Heaven** *53*
- **Council of American Witches** *45*
- **Dianic Moon Worship Group** *53*
- **Earth Cycle Group** *53*
- **Great White Brotherhood** *23*
- **Lilith** *53*
- **Moon Ritual Gathering Group** *53*
- **Moonwomen** *53*
- **Order of the Golden Dawn** *21*
- **Sacred Space** *53*
- **Sophia's Group** *53*
- **Theosophical Society** *22*

Omega Point *193, 202*

Omens *40, 47, 118, 204, 233, 235*
Oratio *189*
Ortberg, John *197*
OT Stories & Characters
  Adam *15, 53, 55, 65, 132, 145, 221, 224–25, 228, 241*
  Babel *232, 295*
  Babylon(ian) *54, 237*
  Balaam *41*
  Canaan *260, 296*
  Israelites *232–33, 236, 238, 241, 244, 267, 296*
  Moses *60, 65, 68, 96, 204, 232, 241, 253, 259*

P

Padre Cícero *98*
Pagan Goddesses *44–48, 50–52, 54–55, 57–58, 72–74, 76–77, 173, 190, 258, 263, 275–76, 278–79, 291*
  Artemis *263*
  Asherah *15, 53*
  Astarte *74*
  Cybele *73*
  Demeter *73*
  Diana *45*
  Gaia *50, 53, 288*
  Hecate *45*
  Ishtar *73, 111*
  Isis *45, 50, 73, 259, 263, 273*
  Kore–Persephone *73*
  Mother of Waters *111*
  Oshun *45*
  Sophia *52–53, 73–74, 278*
  Yemanja *44, 58, 75, 276*
Pagan Gods
  Aion *149, 284*
  Ausar *75*
  Baal *15, 101*
  Exu *109–14*
  Manato *88*
  Mithras *149*
  Molech *234, 296*
  Oxalá *109*
  Pantheon *44, 131*
  RA *75*
  Vishnu *12, 37*
Pagan Organizations *80*
  Arica Institute *200*
  Center for Contemplative Mind in Society *195*
  Chartres School of Wisdom *190*
  International Order of Gnostic Templars *278*
  Snowmass Conference *194*
Pagan Rituals *48–50, 53, 77, 83, 95–97, 115–18, 121–22, 124, 126–29, 212, 278*
  Amulets *50, 68, 124, 126*
  Cannibalism *104*
  Casting a Circle *48–49*
  Channeling *27, 48, 92, 188*
  Chanting *13, 48, 98, 113, 118, 197*
  Charms *49, 121–22, 124, 126, 235*
  Cleansing, Washing *48, 94*
  Dancing *28, 44, 49, 98, 117–18, 121, 195*
  Drumming *13, 44, 48, 113, 118*
  Drums *92, 117, 119*
  Funeral Rites *138*
  Ghost Dance *92*
  Goddess Rosary *76*
  Initiation *48, 117, 123, 190, 194, 233, 261, 298*
  Ordeals *119*
  Pipe *89–92, 94*
  Purification *48, 117, 121*

Sacred pattern *49*
Smudging *90, 97*
Spells *19*
Sundance *91*
Sweat Lodge *95, 195, 290*
Sweet Grass *91*
Vision Quests *118, 121*
Pagan Worldview *7, 10, 17, 35–36, 41, 44, 46, 48–50, 52, 54–58, 63, 68, 71–79, 83–86, 94, 99–103, 108, 110–13, 115, 126, 130, 134, 149–50, 172, 190, 195, 202–3, 205–7, 209–14, 216, 232–33, 241, 244, 246–48, 251–64, 266–71, 288, 292*
Pagels, Elaine *154, 278, 284*
Pagitt, Doug *198, 272*
Palmer, Helen *201*
Pannenberg, Wolfhart *181*
Pantheism *21, 23, 63–64, 85, 88, 172, 179–81, 206–7, 210, 213, 220, 261*
Paranormal *9, 26, 36, 40, 150*
Parliament of the World Religions *57*
Patriarchy *45–46, 263*
Pauli, Wolfgang *160*
Penczak, Christopher *55*
Pennington, Basil *192*
Pentecost *219, 227–28, 243*
Perennial Philosophy *186, 191, 279*
Persecution *45, 90, 245*
Pisces *35–38*
Platonic *65, 289*
Plotinian *110*
Pluralism *29, 93*
Poison *120, 128*
PoKeMon *56*
Polytheism *50, 136*
Pontifical Council for Justice and Peace *171*
Positivism *107*
Postmodernism *12, 37, 93, 102, 185, 298*
Prayer, Christian *49*
Priest *33, 49, 72, 79, 108, 112, 119, 127, 139, 140, 193*
Prophets *21–22, 33, 41, 47, 78, 96, 112, 127, 227, 237–38, 241–44, 270*
Prostitution *54, 86, 94*
Protestantism *106, 111, 172*
Prototokos *252, 255, 257, 298*
Pseudo-Dionysius *187–90, 192, 289*
Pullman, Philip *56, 203*
Purgation *77, 188, 191*

Q

Quantum Mechanics *158–67, 169, 284*

R

Rahner, Karl *196*
Ramtha School of Enlightenment *161*
Ravenwolf, Silver *49, 56*
Redding, Ann Holmes *79*
Redeemer *58, 178, 224, 264, 268–78, 298*
Reformation *12, 107, 159, 186, 278, 280*
Reincarnation *33, 35, 50, 66, 105, 113, 210, 292*
Revelation *15, 27, 56, 72, 81, 85, 118, 131–33, 144, 153, 169, 177, 179, 238, 241, 243–44, 259, 262, 268, 270, 286, 297*
Riso, Don *199, 201, 289, 294–95*

Roentgen, Wilhelm *157*
Rohr, Richard *198, 201, 294–95*
Rojcewicz, Peter *25*
Rosicrucian *20*
Rowling, J. K. *56, 204*
Ruether, Rosemary Radford *278*
Russell, Bertrand *168*
Rutherford, Ernst *157*

S

Sabbat *48*
Sacred Psychology *199*
Sacred Space *48, 50, 76, 186, 195, 232*
Sacrifices *58, 94–97, 100, 109, 117, 122, 128, 140*
Samhain *48*
Satan, Satanism *15, 21, 130, 178, 262*
Schachter–Shalomi, Zalman *60*
Schaeffer, Francis *12, 93*
Scholem, Gershom *60*
Schrodinger, Erwin *157, 160, 284*
Schuon, Frithjof *186, 289*
Scripture *53, 70, 74, 93, 96, 122, 132–33, 141–42, 176–77, 179, 181, 233, 236, 241, 259, 274, 283, 288, 290*
Second Adam *224*
Secret Knowledge *19, 21, 23, 68, 135*
Sefer Yetzirah *60*
Self–punishment *95, 121*
Self–realization *174, 186, 200*
Self–revelation *179*
Sephirot *62–63, 65–68*
Septuagint *252, 295*
Sex as Sacrament *49, 54, 83*
Sexuality, Biblical *114, 212, 268–69*
Sexuality, General *103, 126, 173, 212–215, 268*
Sexuality, Types of
- **Androgyny** *16, 263, 269*
- **Bisexuality** *54*
- **Crossgender** *55*
- **Heterosexuality** *268–69*
- **Homosexuality** *38, 55, 266, 269, 299*
- **Lesbianism** *52, 54, 269*
- **Pansexuality** *37, 54*
- **Pedophilia** *38*
- **Tantric Sexuality** *212*
- **Transgenderism** *55*

Shaman *16–27, 29–30, 56, 87, 102, 109, 125, 137, 144, 200, 261, 290*
Shekinah *41, 63*
Silence *57, 121, 189, 195, 197, 201*
Silver Ravenwolf *49, 56*
Sin *15, 36, 53, 79–80, 82, 94, 96, 102, 145, 192, 201, 206, 217, 225–26, 249, 256*
Singer, Fred *287*
Singer, June *300*
Singer, Marian *276*
Smith, Huston *192*
Solitude *189, 197*
Sorcery *40, 47, 57, 120, 122, 124, 127–29, 204, 235*
Soul Care *186*
Spears, Britney *213*
Spencer, Roy *184*
Spirit Guides *20, 29, 31, 105*
Spiritism *21*
Spirits *17–24, 26, 29, 40, 48, 50, 56–57, 87–92, 94–95, 97, 105, 108–9, 112, 115–16, 118–1]19, 121, 123–26, 128, 133–42, 177–79, 200, 204, 206, 219, 236, 238, 246–47, 253–55, 282, 296*
Spiritual Director *186*
Spiritual Evolution *22, 27, 28, 35,*

108
Spiritual Formation *186, 189, 197, 198, 201*
Spiritualism *22, 144*
Spiritual Masters *23*
Spiritual Power (Pagan) *19, 115–116, 121*
Spiritual Techniques *10, 15, 18, 20, 105, 115, 126, 130, 187, 189, 195, 222, 227, 233, 238, 244, 269*
Spong, John Shelby *73, 278*
Starhawk *51, 54–55, 275*
Steinsaltz, Adin *60, 65*
Stephen King *20*
Steyne, Philip *117*
Streiber, Whitley *27–28, 274*
Stroud, Jonathan *56*
Sufism *13, 76, 191, 194–95, 199–200*
　Naqshbandi *195*
Suzuki *194*
Suzuki, D. T. *194*
Svensmark, Henrik *184, 287*
Swedenborg, Emanuel *18–20, 22, 24, 29, 68, 272*
Sweet Grass *89–90, 94*
Sweet, Leonard *186, 192, 198, 289*
Symbols *33, 40, 46, 49, 50, 75, 76, 83, 85, 109, 122, 124, 143, 148–51, 153, 158–59, 189, 209*

T

Taboos *116–17*
Talismans *126*
Tantra *144, 212*
Tarnas, Richard *148*
Tarot Cards *50*
Tauler, Johannes *190*
Teen Witch *49, 275*
Telepathy *23*
Templars *72, 278*
Temple of Understanding *194*
Teresa of Avila *188*
Tertullian *74, 78*
Thaumaturgy *125*
Theology *12, 21, 23, 72, 79–81, 175–76, 181, 186, 210, 260–61, 278, 286*
Theosophical Society *22, 33, 273*
Theosophy *22*
Thich Nhat Hahn *194–95*
Thummim (Urim and) *243, 297*
Tibetan Buddhism *161, 194, 292*
Tiernan, Cate *56*
Tikkun *60, 66*
Tishby, Isaiah *60*
Tolkien, J. R. R. *208–9, 256, 298*
Torah *67, 213, 296*
Totem *87, 119, 128, 134, 198*
Transcendence *35, 50, 63, 77, 83, 86, 100–1, 134, 143, 149, 152, 155–56, 159, 169, 174–75, 179, 200, 202, 208, 220, 251, 252, 253, 255, 259, 263, 292*
Tree of Life *59, 68*
Tucker, Mary Evelyn *171–72*
Twiss, Richard *94*

U

Ultimate Reality *186, 195*
Umbanda *109*
Underhill, Evelyn *188, 192–93, 196, 289, 291*
United Nations *183, 287*
　United Nations Development Program *196*
Upanishads *23*
Utopianism *25, 37, 86, 197, 257, 264*

V

Van Til, Cornelius *132*
Vatican *171, 194, 196*
Via Negativa *61, 290*
Virgin Mary *98*
Visions *23, 88, 92, 95, 97, 103, 113, 118–19, 156, 188, 237, 242*
Vital, Hayim *60*
Voodoo *49, 103, 113*

W

Wachowski, Andy & Larry *209, 295*
Wagner, Richard *149*
Walsch, Neale Donald *29*
Weitz, Chris *214*
Wicca *44–45, 47, 51, 68, 205*
Wilber, Ken *186, 192, 195, 209, 264, 288, 295, 299*
Winfrey, Oprah *28, 214, 216*
Winter, Miriam Therese *53, 275, 278*
Witchcraft *10, 17, 44–52, 54–58, 79, 92, 99, 103, 119, 122, 124, 127–29, 172, 204–05, 256, 274–77*
- **Cauldron** *50*
- **Coven** *45, 48, 50–51*
- **Drawing Down the Moon** *52*
- **In Christian circles** *52*

Word *15, 31, 40–41, 85, 110, 124, 129, 175, 185, 201, 219, 228, 240, 278, 297*
Word of Power *124*
Worldview *10–11, 26, 35, 40, 56, 68–69, 78, 105–106, 110, 115, 130, 132, 142, 149, 159, 160, 164, 169, 172–73, 176, 203–6, 209–11, 214, 217, 245, 260, 263, 265–66, 288*
- **Antithesis** *258–60, 266–67, 270–71, 298*

Y

Yaconelli, Mike *197, 291, 293*
Yahweh *47, 67, 75, 153, 236, 239, 241*
Yang, C. K. *132*
Yoga *12, 14, 195, 199–200*
York, Michael *263*
YuGiOh! *56*

Z

Zanoni *21*
Zeilinger, Anton *161*
Zeus *265*
Zodiac *32, 34–35, 37–39*
Zohar *60, 64*
Zukav, Gary *28, 274, 284*

Scripture Index

GENESIS

1:1–31 *219*
1:5 *264*
1:8 *264*
1:26–27 *220*
1:28 *221*
2:7 *222, 228*
2:8 *221*
2:15–17 *221*
2:24 *268*
3:1f *223*
3:5 *201*
3:8 *221*
3:15 *223*
6:18 *221, 224*
8:20–21 *185*
12:6–7 *240*
17:7 *224*
27:29 *252*
29:1–30 *239*
30:27 *239*
35:4 *240*
40–41 *237*
44:5 *234*

EXODUS

4:22 *252*
22:18 *47*
25:8 *224*

LEVITICUS

18:3 *260*
19:31 *236*
20:2 *234*
20:6 *236*
20:23 *266*
20:27 *235–36*

DEUTERONOMY

4:19 *40*
4:35 *62*
4:39 *64*
5:33 *266*
13:1–5 *237*
18 *138, 235–36*
18:9 *232, 240*
18:9–12 *234, 236*
18:9–14 *233, 239*
18:10 *204, 234, 236*
18:10–12 *40, 47*
18:10–13 *129*
21:17 *252*

JOSHUA

24:25–27 *240*

JUDGES

9:3–6 *239*
9:5–6 *239*
9:34–37 *240*

1 SAMUEL

15:23 *47*

2 KINGS

17:15 *261*
17:17 *236*

JOB

15:7–8 *241*

PSALMS

8:5–8 *221*
16:8 *67*
16:11 *231*
40:4 *185*
58:3 *260*
89:27 *252*

ISAIAH

8:20 *181*
14:12–13 *261*
29:14 *41*
41:10 *129*
45:5 *64*
47:12–15 *40*
47:13 *237*

JEREMIAH

1:1–10 *242*
2:27 *263*
8:9 *41*
17:5 *185*
23:16–22 *243*

EZEKIEL

14:5 *261*

DANIEL

5:11 *237*

MATTHEW

10:28 *129*
21:22 *215*

JOHN

1:16 *226*
1:18 *224*
3:8 *228*
6:57 *226*
14:6 *225*
14:9 *224*
14:16ff *227*
14:18–21 *227*
15:11 *226*
16:12–15 *228*

ACTS

1:4–5 *227*
2:1–4 *227*
8:9–25 *129*
13:6–10 *129*
13:9 *129*
17:23–24 *99*
19:19 *47*

ROMANS

1:16 *257, 264*
1:18 *107, 260*
1:18–23 *131, 170, 262*
1:19 *41*
1:21 *260, 262*
1:22–23 *269*
1:26 *266*
3:20 *225*
5:5 *229*
5:14 *224*
6:1ff *226*
8:14 *229*
8:21 *256*
8:22 *256*
8:29 *257*
10:17 *247*
11:13 *270*
11:33–34 *41*
11:36 *253*
12:2 *226*
12:5 *228*
15:22 *224*
15:30 *229*

1 CORINTHIANS

2:16 *229*
3:17 *228*
6:2 *248*
6:14 *248*
6:19 *228*
6:19–20 *248*
8:4 *100*
10:20 *100*
12:7–11 *229*
12:13 *228*
16:13 *129*

2 CORINTHIANS

4:4 *263*
4:18 *245*
5:6 *177*
5:8 *177*
5:15 *227*
5:17–18 *254*
6:14–16 *259*
6:16 *267*
6:16–17 *94*
6:17–18 *267*
7:1 *267*
11:13–15 *40*
11:14 *47*

GALATIANS

1:16 *270*
2:14ff *248*
2:20 *226*
4:4 *224*
5:17 *226*
5:20 *47*
5:22–23 *229*

EPHESIANS

1:3 *226*
1:14 *230*
1:21 *263*
2:1–2 *262*
2:2 *270*
2:7 *268*
2:10 *229*
2:12–13 *262*
2:22 *228*
3:1–7 *262*
3:6 *270*
3:17 *226*
3:19 *229*
3:20–21 *271*
4:3 *270*
4:17 *258, 267*
4:17–20 *258*
4:18 *223*
4:19 *266*
4:24 *226*

4:30 *229*
5:7 *267, 270*
5:18 *229*
5:31 *268*
6:10f *267*
6:12 *129*

PHILIPPIANS

1:21 *226*
2:5 *195*
2:12–13 *229*
2:15 *230*

COLOSSIANS

1:15–20 *249–50*
1:21 *262*
2:6–10 *70*
2:8 *247*
2:8–23 *95*
3:1–6 *114*
3:3 *226*
3:10 *226*
4:2 *129*
4:5–6 *43*

1 THESSALONIANS

5:19 *229*

1 TIMOTHY

2:5 *227*
4:1 *261*

HEBREWS

4:14–16 *225*
9:8–10 *224*
10:1-17 *96*
10:18–23 *96*
10:19 *202*
10:19–22 *225*
10:26–29 *96*
11:1 *225*
12:2 *255*

JAMES

1:17 *41*

1 PETER

1:8 *225*
1:11 *228*
3:15–16 *43*
5:8 *52*

2 PETER

1:21 *228*
2:7 *266*

1 JOHN

5:3 *226*

REVELATION

4:11 *268*
19:9 *268*
21:3 *230*

Authors

Beisner, E. Calvin (PhD)

Cal is national spokesman for the Cornwall Alliance for the Stewardship of Creation (www.cornwallalliance.org), a network of theologians, pastors, scientists, economists and policy experts devoted to bringing biblical worldview, theology and ethics together with excellent science and economics to pursue simultaneously economic development for the very poor and environmental stewardship. A frequent guest on radio talk shows, he has testified as an expert witness before Congressional committees and is in demand as a speaker for churches, colleges and other groups. He has written eleven books, including *Prosperity and Poverty: The Compassionate Use of Resources in a World of Scarcity; Where Garden Meets Wilderness: Evangelical Entry into the Environmental Debate;* and *Psalms of Promise: Celebrating the Majesty and Faithfulness of God,* all of which can be ordered at www.ECalvinBeisner.com.

Doveton, David (MDiv)

Canon of St. Paul's Anglican Church, Plaine Verte, Mauritius, Dave has served as Theologian of the Diocese of Zululand, a teaching and advisory position in the wider Church. He is Director of Training for Ordained Ministries, overseeing the selection and training of candidates for ministry. He teaches at the theological seminaries of St Bede's College and the College of the Transfiguration and has helped establish Anglican Mainstream Southern Africa, a network within the Anglican Church committed to teaching and preserving the Scriptural truths on which the Anglican Church was founded.

Frost, Pamela (MA)

Pam is a gifted researcher, and has thoroughly studied the influence of Postmodern culture and Neopagan spirituality on the Evangelical Church. Her particular focus is on Alternative Worship and the Emerging Church. Pam has been an invaluable help to truthXchange, and serves on the local steering committee.

GOMES, DAVI (PHD)

Davi is an American/Brazilian Presbyterian minister, working in Sao Paulo, Brazil. A graduate of Reformed Episcopal Seminary and Westminster Seminary Philadelphia, Davi was originally ordained by the PCA and now works with the Presbyterian Church of Brazil. He is the director/president of the Andrew Jumper Presbyterian Postgraduate Center in Mackenzie, Sao Paulo.

HAMILTON, THEODORE (JD, MDIV)

In the years between college and law school at Stanford, Ted worked for Ford Aerospace and Communications Corporation. After graduating from law school, he practiced tax and corporate law with the international law firm of O'Melveny & Myers. In 1997, he resigned to pursue theological studies at Westminster Seminary California, where he received his Master of Divinity in 2000. He has been senior pastor of New Life Presbyterian Church in Escondido since 2001. His sermons can be downloaded from www.newlifepca.com.

HARVEY, LINDA

Linda Harvey is the founder of Mission:America, a non-profit organization whose objective is to equip Christians with current, accurate information about cultural issues such as feminism, homosexuality, education and New Age influences. A conference speaker and a radio host and guest, Linda has written a book, *Not My Child: Contemporary Paganism & New Spirituality*, as well as many articles, which can be consulted at www.missionamerica.com.

HEISER, MICHAEL

As academic editor at Logos Bible Software, Mike evaluates potential data projects and oversees existing academic projects. Mike earned a PhD in Hebrew Bible and Semitic Languages and taught biblical studies for twelve years. He also ministers to people whose worldview is molded by occult, paranormal, and esoteric beliefs, many of whom are former

Christians, disillusioned when spiritual leaders failed to answer their questions or address their experiences. Publications: "Divine Council," *Dictionary of the Wisdom and Poetical Writings;* "Angels and Angel-Like Beings: Greco-Roman Literature," *Encyclopedia of the Bible and Its Reception;* "Monotheism, Polytheism, Monolatry, or Henotheism? Toward an Assessment of Divine Plurality in the Hebrew Bible," *Bulletin of Biblical Research.*

HERRICK, JAMES (PHD)

James A. Herrick is the Guy Vander Jagt Professor of Communication at Hope College in Holland, Michigan. Dr. Herrick served as chair of the Hope College Department of Communication from 1993-2003. He is the 2007 recipient of the Ruth and John Reed Faculty Achievement Award. His specialty areas are Rhetoric and Argumentation. Publications include *Scientific Mythologies: How Science and Science Fiction Forge New Religious Beliefs; Argumentation: Understanding and Shaping Arguments; The History and Theory of Rhetoric;* and *The Making of the New Spirituality.*

JONES, PETER (PHD)

Peter is Director of truthXchange and Scholar in Residence and Adjunct Professor at Westminster Seminary California. An ordained minister in the PCA, he taught at La Faculté Libre de Théologie Réformée in Aix-en-Provence, France for seventeen years and at Westminster California for over eleven years. He has had experience in church-planting, missions and evangelism. Since returning to the US in 1991, he has been researching, writing about, and speaking on "one-ism" and "two-ism" and the rise of the New Spirituality. For more information, see www.truthxchange.com. Publications include *Stolen Identity, The God of Sex, Spirit Wars, Capturing the Pagan Mind, The Gnostic Empire Strikes Back* and *Cracking DaVinci's Code.*

KLETT, FRED (MAR)

Fred is an ordained PCA evangelist in full-time Jewish ministry. In 1989, he started CHAIM (Christians Announcing Israel's Messiah), a Reformed ministry to Jewish people. He serves as pastor and church planter of Rock of Israel, a PCA congregation of Russian-speaking Jewish and Gentile immigrants and American Jews in Philadelphia. He has taught as a visiting professor at several seminaries, and has presented papers at the Lausanne Consultation for Jewish Evangelism and the International Jewish Evangelical Fellowship. Fred has researched Jewish mysticism, Kabbalah, Gnosticism, and Wicca, and published articles in *New Horizons, The Christian Observer, The Messianic Times,* and other journals.

LING, SAMUEL (PHD)

Sam is Professor of Systematic Theology at International Theological Seminary, director of China Horizon and president of Horizon Ministries Canada. He teaches in East Asia, Malaysia and Hong Kong. He graduated from Westminster Theological Seminary, and is a PCA minister. Sam has published *The Chinese Way of Doing Things.* and is editing the Chinese translations of works by Cornelius VanTil and John Owens.

MONTENEGRO, MARCIA

Before her conversion, Marcia taught and practiced astrology for years, wrote for astrological and New Age publications, hosted a psychic cable TV show and served as president of the curriculum committee of the Atlanta Astrological Society. Her ministry is CANA/Christian Answers for the New Age, and she is a missionary with Fellowship International Mission, an independent mission board based in Allentown, PA. Marcia is working toward a Masters in Religion in a long-distance program at Southern Evangelical Seminary, Charlotte, NC. Marcia has published *SpellBound: The Paranormal Seduction of Today's Kids.*

PELSUE, JOEL (MDIV)

Joel is Director of Arts & Entertainment Ministries in Hollywood, CA. An ordained minister, Joel has worked with artists for thirteen years and teaches "Christianity, Culture & Creativity" at churches and arts ministries in NY, FL and CA. Joel plays improvisational jazz on both Tenor and Soprano Sax. Joel has produced a CD: *Windsome Thirst.*

STOOTMAN, FRANK (PHD)

Frank is the lecturer in the Macquarie Christian Studies Institute unit: Science and Christian Belief: An Open Dialogue, open to university students and the general public in Sydney and Melbourne, Australia. A physicist, Frank is also an Associate Professor of Physics, School of Computing & Information Technology, University of Western Sydney and Director, Adolon Computer Services Pty. Ltd. He also serves as Director of L'Abri Fellowship (Australia) and is chairman of SETI (Search for Extra-Terrestrial Intelligence) Australia. Publications include *Bio-astronomy 2002: Life Among the Stars.*

TOOLE, MARCUS

Marcus is a church planter of the Western Canada Presbytery and a missionary with Mission to the World, the missions arm of the Presbyterian Church in America (PCA). Marcus ministers to the Cree Nation and deals on a daily basis, at close quarters with the animism about which he writes. The church he has worked to plant is called Jesus Church and has been given official status as a mission church of the PCA.

See the interview in Covenant Seminary's Summer Magazine, 2007, as well as blog contributions.

TURAKI, YUSUFU (PHD)

Professor of Theology and Social Ethics, Yusufu has taught at the Jos Theological Seminary (JETS) since 1980. He has been a research scholar with the Research Enablement Program sponsored by the Pew Charitable Trusts and administered by the Overseas Ministry Study

Center, New Haven, Connecticut, and a post-doctoral Research Fellow at Yale Divinity School. He was the General Secretary of the Evangelical Church of West Africa (ECWA), and he has worked with the Bible Society Africa in Nigeria and Kenya. Publications include a contribution in *Confronting Kingdom Challenges: A Call to Global Christians to Carry the Burden Together*, and two books: *Foundations of African Traditional Religion and Worldview*, and *The Unique Christ for Salvation: The Challenge of Non-Christian Religions and Cultures.*

VERARDE, RANDALL (PHD)

Randy began ministry as a campus pastor in Berkeley in 1976 and has held various ministry positions, including his work with students at Stanford University from 1986–90. His doctoral work focused on Jung's interpretation of self and religious experience. Randy has published "Suspicion, the Seed of Awakening: The Truman Show as Gnostic Fairy Tale," in the *San Francisco Jung Institute Library Journal.*

YOUNG, ANDREW (PHD)

Andrew is an ordained minister and Professor of Practical Theology, as well as Associate Principal (South Island) of Grace Theological College, Auckland, New Zealand. Publications: Study guides for Ephesians and for 1 & 2 Thessalonians, and *Let's Study 1& 2 Thessalonians* (Banner of Truth).

About truthXchange

TruthXchange began in 2003 as Christian Witness to a Pagan Planet. It was birthed in culture shock.

Peter Jones was born in Liverpool, England, where he was a deskmate of John Lennon for five years. After graduating from the University of Wales, he moved to Boston, where he began theological studies that would culminate in a doctoral degree. In 1971, he married Rebecca Clowney and in 1974 they moved to Aix-en-Provence, France, where Peter taught New Testament at the Reformed seminary for seventeen years. In 1991, Peter left France to teach at Westminster Seminary California. He and Rebecca brought seven children to what had become to them a foreign culture. The spiritual landscape no longer looked familiar. Though still strongly spiritual, America had changed religion: from "two-ism" (the Creator/creature distinction) to "one-sim" (all-is-one). The "sacred canopy" of Christian worldview was in tatters, blowing away in the winds of Eastern, monistic spirituality. In the minds of many, God had been brought into the "circle of the earth," and was no longer "the God who is there."

Both fascinated and troubled, Peter began to read, research and write on the New Spirituality, while teaching at the seminary. Eventually, in 2002, a group of respected advisors encouraged him to start an independent organization to facilitate his research. Peter is now the Executive Director of truthXchange and adjunct professor and scholar-in-residence at Westminster Seminary California.

TruthXchange provides written and audio materials, training, consultation, conferences and seminars to a wide variety of audiences in the US and abroad. The articles published in this volume were presented in 2008 at a think tank sponsored by truthXchange, which is a 501 (c) (3) non-profit organization. For more information, please visit www.truthXchange.com.